Re-inventing Islam

Re-inventing Islam

Gender and the Protestant Roots of American Islamophobia

DEANNA FERREE WOMACK

OXFORD
UNIVERSITY PRESS

Oxford University Press is a department of the University of Oxford.
It furthers the University's objective of excellence in research, scholarship,
and education by publishing worldwide. Oxford is a registered trade mark of
Oxford University Press in the UK and in certain other countries.

Published in the United States of America by Oxford University Press
198 Madison Avenue, New York, NY 10016, United States of America.

© Oxford University Press 2025

All rights reserved. No part of this publication may be reproduced, stored in a retrieval system, transmitted, used for text and data mining, or used for training artificial intelligence, in any form or by any means, without the prior permission in writing of Oxford University Press, or as expressly permitted by law, by license or under terms agreed with the appropriate reprographics rights organization. Inquiries concerning reproduction outside the scope of the above should be sent to the Rights Department, Oxford University Press, at the address above.

You must not circulate this work in any other form,
and you must impose this same condition on any acquirer.

Library of Congress Cataloging-in-Publication Data
Names: Womack, Deanna Ferree, author.
Title: Re-inventing Islam : gender and the Protestant roots of American
Islamophobia / Deanna Ferree Womack.
Description: New York, NY, United States of America : Oxford University Press, [2025] |
Includes bibliographical references and index.
Identifiers: LCCN 2024060771 (print) | LCCN 2024060772 (ebook) |
ISBN 9780197699164 (hardback) | ISBN 9780197699195 | ISBN 9780197699171 (epub)
Subjects: LCSH: Islam—United States—Public opinion—History. |
Islamophobia—United States—History. | Protestant churches—
Missions—History. | Christianity and other religions—United States—History. |
Christianity and other religions—Islam—History. |
Islam—Relations—Christianity—History. | United States—Religious life and customs.
Classification: LCC BP67.U6 W654 2025 (print) | LCC BP67.U6 (ebook) |
DDC 297.0973—dc23/eng/20250110
LC record available at https://lccn.loc.gov/2024060771
LC ebook record available at https://lccn.loc.gov/2024060772

DOI: 10.1093/9780197699195.001.0001

Printed by Marquis Book Printing, Canada

For Lily and Willa

Contents

List of Figures ix
Preface xi
Acknowledgments xv
List of Abbreviations xvii

1. Protestant Re-inventions of Islam in Historical Context 1
2. Gender in Protestant Re-inventions of Islam from the Reformation to the Enlightenment 34
3. Re-inventing Islam in Missionary Texts: "When Hagar Returns to Christ, Ishmael Shall Live" 67
4. Islam Re-invented for Young Readers: Children's Work for Muslim Children 112
5. Recasting the Protestant Gaze: Missionary Images of Islam as Material Religion 153
6. Performative Re-inventions: Missionary Costumes, Curios, and Comparative Religion 195
7. The Ongoing Effects of Missions: American Islamophobia and Openings for Christian–Muslim Dialogue 239

Bibliography 263
Index 281

Figures

2.1	Ottoman Sultan Suleiman I (1578)	41
2.2	Title page of *Cosmographiae Universalis* (1550)	43
4.1	"Girls of Turkey" (1864)	117
4.2	"Paper Doll—A Little Girl from Persia" (1907)	119
4.3	Habeeb's mother and baby Fatmeh, in *Habeeb: A Boy of Palestine* (1927)	131
4.4	"Someday he will have a gun" (1926)	134
4.5	Cover image of *Cap and Candle* (1961)	139
4.6	Cover image of *Cap and Candle* (1964)	139
5.1	"Canaanite Lad" at Bet Shemesh (1930)	162
5.2	"Modern Canaanite" at Bet Shemesh (1930)	163
5.3	"Evening Meal Among the Fellaheen"	165
5.4	"Bedouins of Moab" (circa 1880–1890)	167
5.5	"Group of Syrian Bedouins" (circa 1880–1890)	167
5.6	"Sons of Shaykh Diab" (circa 1880–1890)	168
5.7	"Bedouin" (1904)	169
5.8	"Blida Woman in Outdoor Dress" (1908)	171
5.9	"Aissha" (1909)	172
5.10	"Hadia" (1907)	172
5.11	"A Specimen Boy" (1912)	173
5.12	"Specimen 'Wild Elephants'" (1912)	174
5.13	"The Hope of India" (circa 1882)	176
5.14	"How a Moslem Boy Prays" (1902)	179
5.15	"Muslims Praying" (1905)	179
5.16	"Greetings from the Orient: Muslim Prayer, Morocco" (circa 1903)	180
5.17	"Syria—Muslim schoolteacher" (circa 1903)	181
5.18	"Moslems at Prayer" (1903)	183
5.19	"Mohammedan Women in Town Costume" (1903)	183
6.1	United Presbyterian Church sanctuary, Newtown, Iowa (1905)	210

6.2 Islamic prayer beads on display (circa 1943–1944) 212
6.3 Dr. Cornelius Van Dyck (1818–1895) 215
6.4 "Rev. S. Schor as Eastern Scribe" 215
6.5 "Rev. F. B. Mellor in Costume of Eastern Scribe" 216
6.6 Congregationalist missionaries in Middle Eastern attire (1927) 217
6.7 Samuel M. Zwemer in Bedouin headdress (circa 1890s) 218
6.8 William and Elizabeth Freidinger in Turkish attire 218
6.9 Dorothy Blatter as "A Turkish Haneem" (1931) 219
6.10 Dorothy Blatter and Gladys Perry, "Almost Lost the View" (1931) 220
6.11 Dorothy Blatter and Gladys Perry, "Submerged" (1931) 220
6.12 Eva Marshall in Bedouin costume (1927) 221
6.13 Eva Marshall in Ramallah costume (1927) 222
6.14 Dr. Eleanor Taylor Calverley and Grace Calverley in Kuwaiti dress (circa 1914–1915) 224
6.15 Dr. Eleanor Taylor Calverley, Rev. Edwin Calverley, and daughters Grace, Elizabeth, and Eleanor (1922) 225

Preface

Since the 1990s, the term *Islamophobia* has commonly been used in the United States to describe anti-Muslim prejudice, hate speech, and violence. Such dispositions and actions reflect Americans' fear of Muslims and disparagement of Islam as a religion, but they are also predicated on racism, xenophobia, and western gender constructs. As imperfect as some commentators believe the term to be, *Islamophobia* has become a necessary addition to our vocabulary because of the virulent political rhetoric and hate crimes against American Muslims that spiked after September 11, 2001, and rose again in response to the activities of ISIS after 2011. These public expressions of Islamophobia exist alongside the less overt but more pervasive anti-Muslim sentiment harbored even by Americans who condemn acts of violence targeting American Muslims and their places of worship.

This book is a historian's response to the overt and covert forms of Islamophobia that permeate US society today and that are often tied to centuries-old tropes about violent Muslim men and oppressed Muslim women. By covering a significant period of history before the term *Islamophobia* came into being, I hope to expand readers' understanding of the formats through which Protestants have cultivated ideas about Muslims, beyond theological treatises and comparative studies of Islam. And I seek to highlight the role of women in this process. My intellectual and personal commitments to move beyond the western and patriarchal approaches of the academy—and of Christian scholarship—also inform this work, to counter the centuries in which such approaches have prioritized sources of research that are textual and that men have authored. Moreover, as a Protestant historian and theological educator I am concerned about the aftereffects of the missionary movement on Muslims and on US society.

I might have endeavored to study nineteenth- and early twentieth-century missionary narratives about Islam in a vacuum, focusing only on the implications for that historical period. But because I teach on contemporary Christian–Muslim relations and American Islam, it has been impossible for me to write this book without noticing the resemblance between historical missionary re-inventions of Islam and patterns of popular American discourse today. Investigating these similarities is a moral imperative because I want my fellow Americans, my students, and the church to become aware of and break with the dangerous patterns of the past and to recover more life-giving approaches to interfaith encounters.

Likewise, I might have endeavored to explore the ways in which Muslims over the centuries have responded to Protestant ideas about Islam. Indeed, initially I hoped to visit archives in the Middle East and South Asia seeking such voices, but faced with the COVID-19 pandemic travel restrictions, I deferred that research for another time. Instead, in select places throughout the book I have highlighted Muslim beliefs and practices, pointed to the diverse realities of life in Islamic societies, and cited Muslim figures who defy prejudicial narratives. Although the book centers around Protestants' gendered ideas about Islam since the sixteenth century, interested readers will find in my bibliography a starting point for further study of Muslim communities whose own narratives and experiences challenge the monolithic pictures of Islam that many American and European Christians have inherited and perpetuated.

By revisiting our history, I hope that American Christians, Muslims, and others can better understand and challenge the anti-Muslim prejudices pervading American Protestant culture and the unconscious bias that hinders the work of Christian–Muslim relations. When I began conceiving of this project in 2017, the FBI had reported that in the previous year hate crimes against Muslims in the United States had risen to their highest levels since 2001. This spike coincided with presidential candidates' discourses about Islam during the 2015–2016 campaign cycle, including Donald Trump's promise to ban Muslims from entering the United States. I noted the ways in which public figures at that time employed both negative and positive rhetoric about Muslims to achieve their own political or religious ends, and I knew from prior research that such rhetoric was not a new phenomenon in American society. I believed that a deeper look into Protestant thought patterns shaping American views of Islam and gender might help readers grapple with the unexamined discourses they had inherited.

Today—three months since Hamas' murder of around 1,200 Israelis and its taking of over 250 hostages on October 7, 2023, and with the Palestinian death toll of the ensuing Israel–Hamas war in Gaza in the tens of thousands—Islamophobic incidents in the United States have skyrocketed again. (So too have anti-Jewish incidents, suggesting the need for a similar study on the roots of American antisemitism.) Why is it that the violent actions of certain

Muslims in one particular Middle Eastern context prompt some Americans to attack their Muslim neighbors as if in retribution? Why is it that other American onlookers who would never condone such actions nevertheless suspect and fear Muslims—especially Muslim men—regardless of their diverse cultural, ethnic, political, and religious identities? I seek answers to such contemporary questions by looking at a period long before American Islamophobia came into being, investigating the ways in which anti-Muslim prejudices built up over centuries and provided a foundation for the reprehensible behavior we see today. This book, therefore, is not about contemporary Islamophobia, a topic that I address only in the closing chapter. It is, rather, about the roots of this recent phenomenon and, specifically, the historical role of Protestant leaders and missionaries in shaping American views of Muslims.

Through more closely examining this history, identifying problematic legacies, and highlighting surprising instances of interfaith appreciation, I hope to offer new pathways toward dialogue and Christian–Muslim understanding.

January 7, 2024

Acknowledgments

This book took shape over the course of six years and involved extensive travel to American and British libraries and archives before and after the COVID-19 pandemic. It would not have come to fruition without the support I received from numerous colleagues and the assistance of multiple archivists and librarians. I am most profoundly grateful for several writing groups at Emory University's Candler School of Theology, whose members—Joel Kemp, Letitia Campbell, Ish Ruiz, Kyle Lambelet, and Susan Reynolds—provided judicious feedback on my chapters. Arun Jones also has been a valued conversation partner who has shared many resources on missionaries in South Asian Islamic contexts. He is among other colleagues at Emory and elsewhere who have read various drafts or offered feedback on my work, including Kwok Pui Lan, Jonathan Strom, Heather Sharkey, Rahimjon Abdugafurov, David Grafton, Devin Stewart, Scott Kugle, Joseph Ho, Devaka Premawardhana, and Dominic Erdozain. This book has benefited immensely from their guidance.

Several grants and fellowships made possible my research travel and leave time. Emory's Center for Faculty Development and Excellence provided a Scholarly Writing and Publishing Grant, Candler School of Theology gave me two sabbaticals, and Candler also supported my travel with grants from the Brewer Fund for Communities Research. For the first of these sabbaticals, in 2018–2019, I received a General Research Grant from the Gerda Henkel Foundation in Düsseldorf, Germany. My second sabbatical, in 2021–2022, was funded by a Sabbatical Grant for Researchers from the Louisville Institute. I also received a Research Scholarship for travel to the Congregational Library & Archives in Boston, along with helpful guidance from Peggy Bendroth and other staff. In 2021–2022, a Gest Fellowship covered my visits to Haverford College Quaker & Special Collections, and I am grateful to Sarah Horowitz and Mary Crauederueff for assisting with my research there. I would like to offer special thanks also to Ida Glaser and John Chesworth at the Centre for Muslim–Christian Studies in Oxford and to the staff of the Presbyterian Historical Society in Philadelphia, both of which I visited several times while completing this book.

I am especially grateful to my editor and writing coach, Ulrike Guthrie; to my research assistants Tala AlRaheb, Mari Shiukashvili, and Hannah Philipp; and to Theo Calderara at Oxford University Press for this opportunity. Finally, words cannot express what the support of my family has meant over these past several years and throughout my academic career. Lily and Willa, to whom this book is dedicated, have kept me grounded in reality even when my mind strayed to centuries past. And Mike has given me the gift that scholars want most—as much time as possible to research and write—while teaching me that our time together is infinitely more valuable than any book project. For this, I give thanks.

Abbreviations

ABCFM	American Board of Commissioners for Foreign Missions
AMB	Algiers Mission Band
BSM	British Syrian Mission
CCUSFM	Central Committee on the United Study of Foreign Missions
CMS	Church Missionary Society
CWC	*Children's Work for Children*
EGM	Egypt General Mission
FCS	Free Church of Scotland
KJV	King James Version
LJS	London Society for Promoting Christianity Amongst the Jews/ London Jews Society
LMS	London Missionary Society
NRSV	New Revised Standard Version
OSL	*Over Sea and Land: A Missionary Magazine for the Young*
PHS	Presbyterian Historical Society
PCUSA	Presbyterian Church in the United States of America
SVM	Student Volunteer Movement
UFCS	United Free Church of Scotland
UPCNA	United Presbyterian Church in North America
WCC	World Council of Churches
YDS	Yale Divinity School
ZBMM	Zenana Bible and Medical Mission

1
Protestant Re-inventions of Islam in Historical Context

From the end of the American Civil War in 1865 to the start of World War II in 1939, the Protestant missionary movement exerted considerable influence upon American conceptions of Islam. Unbeknownst to them, missionaries' activities tilled the soil in which American Islamophobia would eventually take root. What ideas did missionary women and men in nineteenth- and early twentieth-century Islamic contexts pass on to later generations? How were these ideas connected to centuries-old Protestant discourses about Muslims and gender? And what bearing does this history have on the birth of Islamophobia in the late twentieth century and on efforts for Christian–Muslim dialogue in the United States today?

For answers to such questions, this book turns to the vast archive of material that American missionaries from multiple denominations, and their British counterparts, left behind. It became apparent early on in my research in Anglo-Protestant archives that the typical focus of mission histories on textual material neglects many other mediums through which missionaries informed their constituents. Protestant missionaries were avid collectors and curators of images and objects from the region they called the "Mohammedan World."[1] They were also skilled performers who used written discourses, captivating images, animated lectures, theatrical skits, and material objects to cultivate an audience of supporters. Women engaged in these activities just as often as men—and in even higher numbers if we consider the women teachers, Sunday school instructors, prayer circle leaders, and mission auxiliary members who sustained the missionary enterprise. As the missionary archive also makes apparent, Protestant men and women alike continuously assessed the gender norms of Muslim societies and found them lacking. They critiqued the behaviors and characteristics of both Muslim men and Muslim women in order to reinforce theological arguments against Islam and to justify their evangelistic and humanitarian pursuits. These judgments of Muslim social life became embedded in American Protestant (and wider

American) culture far more deeply than did the doctrinal debates (usually between men) that are the focus of many studies on Christian–Muslim relations. This book therefore identifies *gendered* discourses, images, and performances—not simply "women's issues"—as key in Protestant portrayals of Islam.

What perceptions did American Protestants absorb from the network of British and American missionaries who sent texts, photographs, and material objects to constituents on both sides of the Atlantic? By the mid-twentieth century, these audiences were better informed about Muslim societies than they would have been without the missionary movement. They knew that Muslims lived in North and sub-Saharan Africa, in the Middle East, and in South and Southeast Asia; and they were familiar with the basics of Islam as a monotheistic faith founded by the Prophet Muhammad with the Qur'an as its holy book. Based on the photographs and stories printed in missionary magazines, Protestant audiences also knew that some Muslim women veiled their faces in public and that Islamic tradition permitted men to marry up to four wives. Yet American Protestants' impressions of Islam and Muslim life often rested more on the ideas that missionaries had constructed—and even *invented*—for them, typically of threatening, tyrannical Muslim men and helpless Muslim women.[2] Americans encountered these tropes about Islam as part of a larger body of popular missionary discourse on the plight of Asians and Africans. In the thought world of White Protestant audiences, therefore, Muslims were among the many religious and racial others whom the missionary enterprise sought to save. Yet by the early twentieth century, due to an outpouring of literature on missions and Islam, a growing number of mission supporters saw Muslims as uniquely in need of evangelistic and humanitarian outreach.

The dissemination of negative images of Islam was not an exclusively Protestant nor exclusively missionary phenomenon, as shown in studies on Orientalism—a cultural, political, and scholarly discourse based on a presumed distinction between "the Orient" and "the Occident" used to justify western[3] dominance over the Middle East and Asia.[4] Protestants and Catholics alike engaged with and were shaped by Eurocentric, Orientalist representations of Muslim societies; and they interwove these with the theological content of their own traditions.

I identify this activity as a process of *re-inventing Islam* through repetition, appropriation, adaptation, and the use of existing ideas about Muslims for new purposes. Western Christians did not create the concept of Islam as a religion in the way that Tomoko Masuzawa argued European scholars invented the category of "world religions."[5] Neither were Christians the only ones engaged in reconfiguring ideas about Islam for their own purposes; countless Muslim reform movements have done the same.[6] Nor did the Anglo-Protestant missionaries featured in this book completely fabricate the ideas about Muslims that they transmitted to constituents in Europe and North America. Although many missionary discourses were recycled from earlier, and sometimes completely inaccurate, Christian sources, others were based on Islamic texts and missionaries' personal encounters with Muslims. Why categorize such discourses as *re-inventions*? Because throughout their history of engagement with Islam, Protestants have continually reshaped existing ideas about Muslims—inventing them in new contexts, again and again—in order to sway their audiences toward particular Protestant theological and political purposes, including missionary aims.

Protestant theological discourses about Islam began in the early sixteenth century with the Reformation, when European nations had little power or influence over Muslim societies. The first Protestants re-invented notions about Islam taken from medieval Christian texts at a time when the Ottoman Empire was a formidable Islamic power already controlling West Asia, North Africa, and the Balkans and seeking to expand further into Europe. To understand the unique ways in which nineteenth- and twentieth-century American and British missionaries shaped the discourses they inherited from the Reformation, *Re-inventing Islam* begins in the sixteenth century, long before any systematic Protestant attempt to evangelize Muslim societies. In contrast to the face-to-face contact of the imperial era, from the sixteenth to eighteenth centuries most Protestants who encountered Islam did so from a distance through discourses, images, and material culture. This was true of Anglo-Protestant clergy and theologians, although some diplomats and merchants maintained contact with Muslim counterparts in the Ottoman realms, Persia, and India. Only with the rise of the modern missionary movement at the end of the eighteenth century did large numbers of Protestant religious leaders begin finding opportunities for sustained personal contact with Muslims.

Most of the missionaries who appear in this book were part of the same mainline denominations that today are known for welcoming approaches to Islam. The shift for many of those denominations came toward the middle of the twentieth century, after demeaning pictures of Islam were already well established in American imaginations. Yet, as this book highlights, efforts toward interreligious understanding were not entirely absent in nineteenth- and early twentieth-century missions. The conversionary aim of this enterprise supported missionaries' natural inclinations to emphasize the differences they encountered in Islamic societies, but as they came to know the Muslims among whom they lived, some missionaries saw the commonalities too—even if these were not the focus of their fundraising appeals. In covering Anglo-Protestant missions from 1800 through the 1920s and in identifying the way in which missionary views were shifting by the mid-twentieth century, I recognize this ambiguity. *Re-inventing Islam* tells how Presbyterian, Congregationalist, Reformed, Lutheran, Anglican, Methodist, Quaker, and Baptist missionaries paved the way for an openness to Christian–Muslim dialogue in certain circles while adapting their inherited theological views to the post-Enlightenment context in an era of high imperialism. For example, when missionaries sent home stories or images of specific Muslim children and encouraged their constituents' sympathetic support, they humanized Muslims as individuals rather than presenting Islam as a monolithic, evil force. Such perspectives became more explicit in mainline missionary publications in the decades following World War II. At the same time, during the period under investigation missionaries repeatedly called upon their audiences to help save Muslim men from lives of immorality and violence and Muslim women from ignorance and degradation. Such characterizations of Muslim vice in contrast to Protestant virtue planted in American minds the seeds of anti-Muslim sentiment that by the end of the twentieth century became known as *Islamophobia*—a prejudice against Muslims built on religious anxiety about Islam and racial stereotyping, to which I will return in Chapter 7.[7]

The intellectual currents and colonialist impulses of the nineteenth century merged in Orientalist activities of that period, while shaping the social ethos of Protestantism in Europe and North America. When it came to religion, Orientalism meant an increasing drive for systematized, scientific knowledge about non-Christian faiths and a growing conception of "world religions"—a western construct which assigned Islam a place as a distinct and academically scrutable religious tradition.[8] Occurrences of personal contact between Anglo-Protestants and Muslims were also on the rise, facilitated by British imperial expansion into South and central Asia and North Africa and a growing British diplomatic presence in the Ottoman-controlled lands of the Middle East.

To themselves and to Christians back home, missionaries' firsthand access to information about Muslim life and practices made them authorities, leading them to contribute to the burgeoning literature on the "science of religion"—a nineteenth-century field of study comparing Christianity to other religions, also variously called "comparative religion" or "history of religions."[9] While the printing press that fueled the Reformation also disseminated ideas about Islam through texts and images, nineteenth-century missionaries had increasing access to mass media. The global distribution networks they used and developed extended their experiences of personal Christian–Muslim contact into churches, schools, and homes across Britain and the United States. Through these networks that transmitted similar ideas about Islam to both American and British Protestants, missionaries in Muslim societies joined their peers in other mission fields in cultivating a global community of Protestant readers, writers, and publishers linked by their commitments to missions. *Re-inventing Islam* examines the gender discourses, images, and performances that shaped Protestant ideas about Islam; and it considers the shifts within the Anglo-Protestant missionary enterprise that eventually opened up possibilities for formal Christian–Muslim dialogue.

Most studies on Protestant engagements with Islam center on one region, community, religious figure, or historical period.[10] A select number of studies, for instance, have examined Protestant views of Muslims during the Reformation, with the works of Adam Francisco, Charlotte Colding Smith, and Gregory Miller focusing even more particularly on German-speaking contexts.[11] A larger body of literature on missions features the religious activities of British and American Protestants in various Islamic settings, especially Egypt and Ottoman Syria, in the nineteenth and twentieth centuries.

Among the first of such mission histories on the Middle East published in the early twenty-first century were Heather J. Sharkey's *American Evangelicals in Egypt* and Ussama Makdisi's *Artillery of Heaven*, the latter focusing on Ottoman Syria. Beth Baron's study on Protestant missionaries and the Muslim Brotherhood in Egypt, *The Orphan Scandal*, stood out as well for its attention to Protestant–Muslim encounters, while most other scholarship has primarily documented missionaries' interactions with Middle Eastern Christians.[12] A few notable historical studies have dealt with American Protestants' religious views of Islam. David D. Grafton's *Muhammad in the Seminary* did so with a focus on nineteenth-century seminaries, while Thomas Kidd's *American Christians and Islam* traced evangelical discourses about Muslims from the colonial period to the early twenty-first century.[13]

Beyond these studies in theology and religion, a related body of scholarship has featured Protestant nations' political, economic, and cultural interactions with the Ottoman Empire or other Muslim societies.[14]

Among the aforementioned publications on *religious* history, few have addressed gender except studies of modern missions, and even those have given relatively little attention to Protestant theological articulations about Islam, focusing instead on the contributions of missionary women or indigenous women converts.[15] Supplementing the existing literature, in this book I therefore examine the interconnections between religious thought and gender constructs in Protestant re-inventions of Islam from the Reformation to the twentieth-century ecumenical missionary movement. This broad history tracks the impact of theology on Protestant interpretations of Muslim social life. It also analyzes the ways in which British and American Protestants of multiple denominations characterized Islamic cultural norms for men and women. They did so in an attempt to defend theological doctrines that Islam rejected—namely Christian beliefs in Jesus Christ's divinity and the triune nature of God. Before turning to these gendered approaches, however, I consider the basic theological views of Islam that emerged from the Reformation and that influenced modern Protestant missions.

Islam in Sixteenth-Century Sources and Reformation Theology

In 1517, the year remembered for Martin Luther's Ninety-Five Theses and the start of the Reformation, the empire of Ottoman Sultan Selim I (r. 1512–1520) included present-day Türkiye, most of the Balkans, the Levant, Egypt, western Arabia, Iraq, and Crimea.[16] Three years later, under Suleiman I (r. 1520–1566, known as Suleiman the Magnificent), the Ottomans took Belgrade. In 1529, they unsuccessfully laid siege to Vienna, but by 1542 they had gained control of Hungary.[17] In this period when the Habsburg monarch in central Europe held the title of Holy Roman Emperor, Ottoman expansion represented not only a political threat to Europe but also a loss to Christendom.[18] Reformers in western and northern Europe—including Luther (1483–1546), French Reformer John Calvin (1509–1564) in Geneva, and the Swiss Reformers Huldrych Zwingli (1484–1531), Heinrich Bullinger (1504–1575), and Theodor Bibliander (1504–1564) in Zurich—voiced their awareness of the impending political and religious threat from the most formidable empire on earth as they spoke about Turks and Muslims interchangeably. Luther made thousands of references to Islam in his writings, often representing it in apocalyptic terms as God's punishment for the Catholic Church's failures and characterizing the Ottoman army's expansion toward the Habsburg Empire as a sign of the end times.[19] He published "On War Against the Turk" and "Army Sermon Against the Turks" in 1529 during the sieges of Vienna, recognizing that his own Saxon flock might one day face Turkish rule.[20]

Beyond these political concerns and tales from the battlefront, what sources informed the earliest Protestant discourses on Islam? Because most Reformers lacked knowledge of Arabic and had no personal contact with Muslims, and because the same was true for most European scholars in the early sixteenth century, they all relied on the same small body of Latin literature.[21] These medieval texts on Islam included the Toledo Collection (*Collectio Toletanum*, compiled in Spain) that the French abbot of Cluny, Peter the Venerable (d. 1156), commissioned in the 1140s. Among the collection's translations from Arabic was the Qur'an that the English scholar Robert of Ketton (d. 1160) paraphrased and reorganized in Toledo and a Christian apologetic against Islam titled *Apology of al-Kindi* (*Risalat al-Kindi*).[22] Also available to the Reformers were Peter the Venerable's own writings, *On the whole heresy of the Saracens* and *Against the heretic sect of the Saracens*[23]; the works of Dominican missionary Riccoldo of Monte Croce (circa 1243–1320) on the Qur'an and Islamic law[24]; and *Sifting the Qur'an* by the German cardinal Nicolas of Cusa (1401–1464).[25] With the support of Luther, Bibliander included the entire Toledo Collection, his own edition of Ketton's Qur'an translation, and the works of Cusa and Riccoldo in his three-volume compendium on Islam, first printed in 1543.[26]

Although some authors took a more polemical tone than others, with strikingly uniform theological pronouncements these medieval Latin texts refuted the validity of Islam and posited the superiority of Christianity. Why the uniformity and similarity? Historian Gregory Miller argued that it was because the authors "used each other in a chain of sources, simply repeating the information on Islam which had been passed down to them."[27] The repetition solidified a distorted and dehumanizing picture of Islam, and as European Christians recovered from the turmoil of the Middle Ages, they took up such critiques, employing Islam as "a negative image against which [they] could fight . . . a psychological 'shadow side' of European identity."[28] The Reformers in turn re-invented many of these inherited tropes about Muslims, adapting them to their own contexts and theological priorities.

The literature on Islam circulating in the early sixteenth century was not all theological in nature, however. For example, *Treatise on the customs, habits, and perversity of the Turks* (1481), which George of Hungary (1422–1502) wrote after living in Turkish captivity and servitude, described Muslim ways of life, including social norms for men and women. Protestant leaders reprinted and widely circulated this text in German.[29] Another European Christian who escaped Turkish captivity, Bartholomaeus Georgievic (1505–1566), conveyed similar information. His two-part publication titled *On the Rituals and Ceremonies of the Turks* and *On the Afflictions of the Captive Christians Living Under the Tribute of the Turks* was published in 1544.[30] Bibliander included both George's and Georgievic's accounts in his compendium, giving these texts a Protestant imprimatur and expanding discussions on Islam beyond theology to social norms like Muslims' dress styles, eating habits, and home furnishings.[31]

In addition to written texts, sources of popular culture such as legends, poems, and folk songs shaped early sixteenth-century views of Islam, as did medieval images. French and English illuminated manuscripts featured Saracens and Moors in apocalypses during the twelfth- and thirteenth-century Crusades. Some of these depicted the Prophet Muhammad as the antichrist, a characterization that the Reformers also used. Turbans commonly identified Muslim men in these images, with Moors appearing both turbaned and with darker skin. Thus, both clothing and bodily features distinguished Muslims from the Christians portrayed in these same manuscripts. As Charlotte Colding Smith explained in her study on European images of Islam produced between 1453 and 1600, such scenes represented "the enemies of Christendom bringing about the Last Days with the help of the Antichrist himself, thus reminding Christian readers ... that these ethnic groups are allied with evil."[32] Such depictions foreshadowed western Christian patterns of racializing Islam that would become prominent in the imperial era.

Not all sixteenth-century accounts on Islam were negative, however, as most Europeans were awed by Ottoman military might. Texts documenting the Turkish sultans' accomplishments looked on the Ottoman Empire with a mix of fear and admiration. Many of the Reformers' theological polemics in fact treated Turkish Muslims more favorably than European Catholics. Later in the century, as well, British merchants pursued lucrative trade alliances with Moroccans and Ottomans, recognizing the material advantages of cordial relations with Muslim rulers.[33] Yet the polemical arguments of medieval treatises along with the aforementioned captivity narratives formed the basis of the Protestant Reformers' writings on Islam. They in turn re-invented existing western Christian discourses in theological language that shaped the ways in which Protestant clergy and scholars would teach about Islam for generations to come.

Echoing medieval Latin texts, the Reformers critiqued Islam's portrayal of Jesus Christ (the Qur'an calls Jesus the Word and Spirit of God and the Messiah but emphasizes God's oneness and does not identify Jesus as God's son). Luther noted that Islam recognized Jesus as a sinless prophet, but he critiqued the Prophet Muhammad for failing to accept Christ's divinity and redemption.[34] Calvin asserted that Muslims could not truly know God because "by their rejection of Christ, [they] substitute an idol in his place."[35] Similarly, the Scottish Reformer John Knox (d. 1572) claimed that the Turks' prayers were not pleasing to God "because they do not acknowledge Jesus Christ, for whoso honoureth not the Son, honoureth not the Father."[36] Because Muslims did not understand salvation as coming through faith in Christ, these Reformers charged them with supporting justification by works, echoing their critiques against Catholicism.[37]

Later, during the English Reformation, the Protestant clergyman, historian, and polemicist John Foxe (1516–1587) employed Islam in the contest with Catholicism in a highly influential book, *Actes and Monuments* (1563).[38] In a section titled *The historye and tyrannye of the Turkes* (or *The Turkes storye*), Foxe outright fabricated the historical narrative and denied certain Catholic victories against the Ottomans, while also blaming Rome for any Turkish military successes.[39] Although the Reformers frequently put existing ideas about Islam to new Protestant purposes, *The Turkes storye* went much further: it not only re-invented Islamic realities but intentionally falsified facts in order to advocate for Protestant supremacy over both Muslims and Catholics.

Foxe ended his history with a prayer against the Muslims, claiming that "these Turkish Hagarenes have risen up against us" because the church had "walked hitherto, like sons, not of Sarah, but of Hagar"—implying their waywardness and unfaithfulness. Then he petitioned:

> O Lord God of hosts, grant to the church strength and victory against the malicious fury of these Turks, Saracens, Tartarians, Gog and Magog, and all the malignant rabble of [the] Antichrist, enemies to thy Son Jesus, our Lord and Savior.[40]

This prayer dismissed Muslims as illegitimate heirs of Abraham and characterized them instead as descendants of the enslaved Egyptian concubine Hagar, whom both Abraham and Sarah abused. At that time and in many Christian contexts since, as we shall see in Chapter 3, Muslims have been understood to carry negative traits unfortunately associated with Hagar's son, Ishmael, whom Genesis 16:12 describes as "a wild ass of a man, with his hand against everyone," who shall "live at odds with all his kin" (NRSV).[41] In addition to the theological differences between Christianity and Islam, then, Foxe's polemics suggested that Muslims were the natural enemies of Christians.

Due in fact to the *similarities* between Christianity and Islam, Luther, Calvin, Zwingli, Bullinger, and Bibliander all saw Islam as a deviation from true Christianity. They suggested that the first Muslims were Christians who had strayed by revering Jesus only as a human prophet.[42] Yet these early Protestant writers reserved their harshest critiques for European Christians who they thought had strayed.[43] Bibliander, who had studied Arabic and Islamic texts as a Hebrew lecturer, identified traces of belief in the true God within the congruencies between the Qur'an and the Bible.[44] Muhammad's followers simply lacked opportunities to hear the gospel and receive instruction in Christian faith, said Bibliander. Thus, he and Luther both argued that knowledge of Islam gained from reading the Qur'an would aid in Christian missionary work among Muslims. With a similar goal in mind, Bullinger prayed for Muslims' conversion, and Calvin offered methods for exhorting Muslims to turn to Christianity.[45] These Reformers were confident that Turks who had an opportunity to hear the gospel would reject the teachings of Muhammad and convert, yet none of them actually evangelized Muslims. Their contact with Islam occurred through the oral narratives and written texts of other Christians and a select number of Islamic texts that European Christians had translated.[46]

Protestant Missions in Muslim Contexts

In the nineteenth century, Protestants found more opportunities for long-term, personal contact with Muslims than ever before, as a result of European imperialism and advancements in global travel and communication that facilitated the spread of missions to Islamic contexts from North Africa to Southeast Asia. Missions to Muslims were part of a wider enterprise that had its genesis in late seventeenth-century Pietism and gained momentum after the eighteenth-century Great Awakenings. By the early nineteenth century, participants in these religious revivals in Britain and the United States had turned their sights toward Asia and Africa with a sense of urgency to fulfill the Great Commission's call to "teach all nations" (Matthew 28:19, KJV).[47] From an initial few British foreign missionary societies operating in the eighteenth century,[48] by the early 1900s the Anglo-Protestant missionary movement had grown to involve hundreds of societies and thousands of personnel, including Asian and African employees.[49] With their vast support networks, these missionaries, mission board personnel, and local auxiliaries became primary means through which American and British Protestants received both factual information and re-invented ideas about Islam.

Whereas the Reformers had treated Islam as a spiritual and a military threat to their own societies, by the start of the modern missionary movement in the late 1700s the balance of power in southern Europe and the Mediterranean had shifted, giving Protestants a stronger sense of political and cultural superiority. As comparative literature scholar Mohja Kahf argued, building on Edward Said's work, previous western critiques of eastern societies were not made from positions of power. Rather, modern Orientalism came into being only in the eighteenth century, when naval developments gave European nations a growing economic and military advantage and aspirations of political mastery over Islamic and other eastern societies.[50] Orientalist scholarship, literature, and fantasies about the Middle East likewise fed cultural imperialism and imaginings of religious destiny.

Indeed, as the Ottoman Empire lost much of its European and North African territory in the nineteenth century—shrinking to the still considerable regions of Anatolia, the Levant, and parts of Arabia—Protestant missionaries interpreted these geopolitical shifts as providential. They praised God also as Muslim dynasties in Persia, West Africa, Indonesia, and South Asia came to an end with European colonial-imperial expansion.[51] Protestant imperialism paved the way for missionaries of various denominations to arrive in Islamic societies, including the Dutch Reformed; British Anglicans, Baptists, Methodists, and Quakers; German and Danish Lutherans; and American Congregationalists, Presbyterians, and Methodists. Because the United States was not yet a global power and did not develop its spheres of influence in the Middle East until the mid-twentieth century, American missionaries usually traveled to regions with a British diplomatic presence or colonial administration, including Egypt and

India. In the latter region, Britain dissolved the Mughal Empire (established in the sixteenth century) after the anti-colonial uprising of 1857. The missionary network that nineteenth-century Anglo-Protestants built across Asia and North Africa followed the expansion of the British Empire. These mission societies carved out areas of influence in various parts of the world just like the colonial empires had. They began with South Asia and then turned to the Middle East, encountering Muslims in both regions.

One of the first British Protestant clergy to engage with Muslims, the English Anglican priest Henry Martyn (1781–1812), arrived in India in 1806 as chaplain of the British East India Company and several years later moved to Persia. During his six years in the field, he produced New Testament translations for Muslims in Urdu and Persian with assistance from local scholars.[52] Before Martyn's arrival in India, newly founded British mission societies had already begun sending representatives there to work among Hindus, Muslims, and others. The interdenominational London Missionary Society (est. 1795) operated in India, as did the English Baptist Missionary Society that William Carey (1761–1834) founded in 1792. Carey, known as the "father of modern missions," worked with Bengali Muslims, among other groups.[53] The Church Missionary Society (CMS, est. 1799), a low-church Anglican organization and the largest British mission society during the nineteenth and early twentieth centuries, also worked in India and established stations in Muslim contexts in Persia, Palestine, Egypt, the Sudan, and sub-Saharan Africa. Early on the CMS partnered with the Basel Mission (est. 1815) and supported the work of German and Swiss Lutheran missionaries. Among these was Karl Gottlieb Pfander (1803–1865), a Pietist who publicly debated Muslim scholars in India and produced several apologetic tracts in Urdu.[54] Anglicans also partnered with Germans in Palestine, where from 1841 to 1887 the Church of England and the Church of Prussia (a united Lutheran–Reformed body) operated the Anglo-Prussian bishopric of Jerusalem.[55] Scottish missionaries focused on parts of the Middle East as well, with the Church of Scotland aiming to evangelize Jewish communities in Palestine, beginning in 1839 and the Free Church of Scotland (FCS) establishing a mission in Lebanon in the mid-nineteenth century.[56]

The first American foreign mission society, the American Board of Commissioners for Foreign Missions (ABCFM, est. 1810), was a nondenominational society that became a Congregational mission board after 1870. Its missionaries worked in Islamic contexts in Ottoman Syria (Syria and Lebanon), Turkey, Persia, India, the Philippines, and some regions of Africa.[57] The Board of Foreign Missions of the Presbyterian Church in the United States of America took over the ABCFM's Syria Mission and its stations in Persia in 1870 and supported missionaries in India.[58] The Reformed Presbyterian Church of America established a mission in Syria in 1856, and another American Presbyterian society, the Board of Foreign Missions of the United Presbyterian Church in North America (UPCNA), focused on Egypt and South Asia (primarily present-day Pakistan).[59] American and British Quakers together established mission schools in Lebanon and Palestine, and British Quaker missionaries also worked among Muslims in India.[60] British and American Methodists sent missionaries to India in the nineteenth century, but they were not active in the Levant at that time. The American Methodist Episcopal Mission also ventured into Southeast Asia, including parts of present-day Malaysia, Indonesia, and the Philippines.[61] American Lutherans, Episcopalians, and Baptists were minimally involved in missions to Muslims in the nineteenth century, although some supported the efforts of their European counterparts.[62]

None of these denominational societies in the nineteenth century focused primarily on Muslims. In Muslim-ruled Ottoman and Persian contexts, where laws forbade conversion from Islam, missionaries found the existing Christian communities more receptive than Muslims or Jews. In the religiously plural context of South Asia, where British rule made evangelization of Muslims less risky, missionaries wrote about Muslims as one community among others. For example, among the rare women of the nineteenth century to publish books commenting on Islam, the American Methodist missionary Emily Jane Humphrey (1833–1894) informed Protestant readers about both Muslim and Hindu customs and history through two substantial texts: *Six Years in India* (1866) and *Gems of India* (1875).[63] Despite her characterization of Muslim rule in South Asia as oppressive, she noted the similarities between Christianity and Islam rather than dwelling on theological differences. Humphrey told her readers that "Many things indeed meet our eyes daily that remind us that the Bible is an Eastern Book," including the Muslim custom of dropping everything and bowing "humbly to the ground" upon hearing the call to prayer.[64] In addition to these accounts based on her personal encounters with Muslims, Humphrey helped the American Methodist Episcopal Mission highlight the story of its first Indian Muslim convert, Zahur al-Haqq, by translating his Urdu autobiography for English publication.[65]

Throughout these nineteenth-century mission fields, certain individuals—like Martyn, Pfander, Jessie Taylor (d. 1907), Mary Louisa Whatley (1824–1889), and Ion Keith-Falconer (1856–1887)—focused on Muslims because of their own geographic location and personal interest in Islam. The English Whatley founded schools for Muslim girls and boys in Cairo in the early 1860s, Taylor was a Scottish missionary who started an orphanage and school for Muslim and Druze girls in Beirut in 1868, and in 1886 Keith-Falconer, another Scottish missionary, founded the South Arabia Mission in Aden with the aim of establishing a church for Muslim converts.[66] Other missionaries, like Presbyterian Henry Harris Jessup (1832–1910) of the American Syria Mission, gave frequent attention to Islam in their writings even though their missions invested little in the evangelization of Muslims. The Syria Mission's one high-profile Muslim conversion, of Kamil abd al-Masih, came only in the 1890s; and Jessup published an account of the conversion along with translated excerpts from Kamil's travel journal after the young man's death.[67] Like the autobiography of Zahur al-Haqq, missionaries offered Kamil's story as an inspiration and guide for future evangelization of Muslims.

Missionaries often employed male converts like Kamil and Zahur,[68] as well as *Biblewomen* (indigenous women preachers), as evangelists among Muslims. For example, by the 1870s the British Syrian Mission (BSM), a nondenominational female-led mission, began supporting Biblewomen as "harem visitors" for Muslim women in their homes.[69] Biblewomen in South Asia similarly visited zenanas, the women's quarters in upper-class Muslim and Hindu houses. Responding to gender segregation in the mission field and the limitations Anglo-Protestant society itself placed on women's religious leadership, nineteenth-century British and American women adopted the Victorian-era concept of "woman's work for woman" that legitimized—even necessitated—their work as missionaries within a separate female sphere into which missionary men could not enter.[70] Such women became principals and teachers of girls' schools, like the one the BSM opened for Muslims in Damascus, St. Paul's School. Missionary women also became evangelists, nurses, and doctors for Muslim women. Female doctors—like Mary Pierson Eddy (1864–1923) and Elsie Harris (1883–1970) of the America Syria Mission and Clara Swain (1834–1910), an American Methodist in India—were considered especially vital in Muslim (and other) contexts where local women hesitated to visit male doctors.[71] In India, British missionaries of the Zenana Bible and Medical Mission (ZBMM, est.

1880) began providing women missionary doctors for Muslim and Hindu women for the same reason.[72] Just as the "separate spheres" ideology opened new possibilities for western Protestant women's religious leadership, so too did Asian and African women mission employees carve out space for themselves in educational, evangelistic, or medical roles.

It was not until the late nineteenth century, however, that British and American Protestants began founding nondenominational missions aimed specifically at evangelizing Muslims—taking advantage of European colonization of North Africa and the British occupation of the Arabian peninsula.[73] Among the earliest initiatives was the North Africa Mission (originally called Kayble Mission, est. 1881), a British society that began in Algeria and expanded to Morocco, Tunis, Tripoli, and northern Arabia. Charismatic individuals, like Isabella Lilias Trotter (1853-1928), Samuel Zwemer (1867-1952), and Annie Van Sommer (1852-1937), spearheaded other Muslim-focused societies. Lilias Trotter was an English evangelical who arrived in Algeria in 1888 with Blanch Haworth and Lucy Lewis. In 1907, five additional missionary women joined the work, and the group then became known as the Algiers Mission Band (AMB), with Trotter as their leader.[74] In 1889, Zwemer and James Cantine (1861-1940), both American ministers of the Dutch Reformed Church, founded the Arabian Mission. They established stations around the Gulf region in what is present-day Iraq, Kuwait, Bahrain, and Oman.[75] As the mission expanded, it employed medical services as a means for reaching Muslims with the gospel, and in 1911 it recruited Eleanor Calverley (1887-1968), an American Methodist, as a missionary doctor to work among Arab women in Kuwait.

Van Sommer was another notable British woman visionary in North Africa. She worked independently alongside several Protestant mission societies in Egypt and in 1900 inspired a group of seven men in Belfast to form the Egypt Mission Band, which was renamed Egypt General Mission (EGM) in 1903.[76] The new mission focused on evangelization of Muslims and did so more persistently than the established Anglican and Presbyterian missions in Egypt.[77] Van Sommer also founded the Nile Mission Press in Cairo, and she partnered with Zwemer on several publications emphasizing the plight of Muslim women.[78] These activities were part of a mainline Protestant push toward coordinated, ecumenical efforts for missions to Muslims, which British and American Protestants spearheaded together from the start of the twentieth century through the 1920s. Among the newer societies created in this period were the Methodist mission in North Africa that British and American missionaries founded in Algeria (est. 1910)[79] and the American Lutheran Orient Mission to Kurdistan (est. 1910).[80] Due to the efforts of Temple Gairdner (1873–1928) and Constance Padwick (1886–1968) in the early twentieth century, the CMS also increased its work among Egyptian Muslims.[81] Although these leaders of the Anglo-Protestant movement for missions to Muslims voiced concern about the growth of Islam in sub-Saharan Africa,[82] their attention and fundraising campaigns focused most especially on the Middle East and North Africa.

Islam in Missionary Men's Apologetics

Despite the dramatically transformed geopolitical context for Protestant–Muslim relations in the nineteenth century, Protestant *theological* critiques of Islam had changed little since the sixteenth century. The divinity of Christ and the differences between Jesus and Muhammad remained key points of disagreement that most Protestant missionaries addressed. Yet with Orientalist scholarship and missionary study of the languages and customs of various Muslim communities, nineteenth-century Protestants were better informed than their predecessors. More frequent western Christian travel to Muslim societies had also resulted in appreciative views of Islam as well as appropriation of Islamic culture, or "romantic Orientalism," as Said termed it.[83] Protestants in the United States and Great Britain held such views by the start of the nineteenth century, as Christine Leigh Heyrman has shown,[84] although these more open attitudes did not necessarily negate Protestant leaders' critical religious assessments of Islam. Personal contact with Muslims provided missionaries with plentiful examples to reinforce old prejudices and solicit support, while immersion in Islamic contexts also opened new possibilities for deeper learning, sustained Christian–Muslim relationships, and more favorable representations of Muslims. These tensions existed across the Protestant missionary movement, within various mission societies, and between the published and private writings of individual missionaries. Although missionaries' personal views of Islam and Muslims were diverse and nuanced, their publications and lectures for supporters at home tended to use similar Eurocentric cultural critiques of Muslim societies to uphold their theological claims. In a context of western imperial expansion into Islamic societies of Africa and Asia, missionaries re-invented Reformation polemics to construct narratives not just of Protestant supremacy but of western superiority.

Such cultural critiques served missionaries' fundraising needs and were often gendered, as we shall see in the coming chapters. Missionaries cited evil practices within Muslim societies or innate tendencies toward immorality to reinforce their theological claims against Islam. British and American Protestants did not share the Reformers' concern that their own people might be conquered and converted to Islam, but they repackaged the religious discourses of the sixteenth century in their attempt to convert Muslims. Drawing from Orientalist research on the Islamic tradition, missionary tracts (in Turkish, Arabic, and other languages common to Muslim societies) constructed detailed arguments for accepting the Bible, not the Qur'an, as divine revelation. Missionaries' comparisons between Christian and Muslim scriptures and doctrine reflected the nineteenth-century Christian view of Islam as a distinct religious tradition within a hierarchy of world religions, at the pinnacle of which was Christianity.[85] The basic patterns of Protestant theological discourse about Islam during the missionary movement emerge clearly in three evangelistic tracts of the nineteenth century—by Henry Martyn, Karl Pfander, and George Rouse—published in Urdu, Persian, and Bengali and later translated to English for fellow missionaries and mission supporters.[86]

Missionaries and scholars alike remember Martyn for his relatively open, respectful attitude toward Muslims and South Asian culture in comparison to other Britons' hostility and sense of superiority over Indians.[87] Although Avril Powell noted that his engagements with Muslims were short-lived, Martyn took seriously the Protestant emphasis on vernacular preaching by becoming proficient in Urdu, Arabic, and Persian, allowing him to engage in discussion with Muslim scholars. This linguistic facility was apparent in the tracts he wrote in Persian, which were translated into English after his death as *Controversial Tracts on Christianity and Mohammedanism* (1824).[88] Martyn was, however, just as vehement as the Reformers in arguing against Islamic teachings. Referencing Qur'anic verses to make his points, Martyn asserted that the Qur'an was neither divine nor a miracle of Muhammad, as Muslims believed. Rather, he said, the text came from Muhammad, who merely claimed to have received revelation but, unlike Jesus and the biblical prophets, did not perform miracles and was not a true prophet. Martyn concluded that the Arabs of Muhammad's time must have been motivated by fear or material gain to accept the Qur'an as a miracle.[89] Thus, he underscored his theological attack against Islamic doctrine by portraying the early Muslims as greedy and insincere in their beliefs. Like most missionary polemics, this was only conjecture and did not match Muslims' understandings of their faith or the reverence they give to the early generations of Muslims, called *al-salaf al-salih* (the pious forebears).[90]

Echoes of Martyn's arguments would appear in other missionary texts of the nineteenth century. For example, Karl Pfander's apologetic treatise *Mizan ul-Haqq*, translated into English as *The Balance of Truth* in 1866, compared the three holy books which Muslims recognize (the Old and New Testaments and the Qur'an). It argued that contradictions exist between the Christian and Muslim scriptures not because parts of the Bible were "corrupted or changed," as Islamic tradition holds, but actually because the Qur'an had been "tampered with."[91] Pfander then asserted that if his Muslim readers would only accept the doctrines of Christian scripture as they should, they would see that Muhammad was neither a prophet nor a recipient of divine revelation nor a miracle worker. Rather, the treatise claimed, echoing Martyn, the Qur'an was Muhammad's creation and combined religious teachings similar to Christianity with his own personal desires.[92] Also like Martyn, Pfander speculated that the Arabs followed Muhammad because they were possessed with "the hope and thirst for plunder." While describing the prophet of Islam as "a man of winning manners and eloquent speech... who cared for and protected the poor and weak," Pfander also made disparaging remarks about Muhammad, continuing a pattern of refuting Islam by critiquing its prophet that was also common in the Reformation.[93] He therefore reinforced Protestant theological claims with unsubstantiated attacks on the Prophet Muhammad's character and by vilifying the moral status of the first generation of Muslims.

Later in the nineteenth century, another English clergyman in India, George Henry Rouse (1838–1909) of the Baptist Missionary Society, spoke favorably about Islam in his introduction to *Tracts for Muhammedans* (1897), which he published in Bengali and then translated for English readers. Reflecting the prevailing hierarchical view of world religions, he contended that Islam "contains the largest amount of truth" of all non-Christian religions and that early on the Prophet Muhammad was "a sincere inquirer after truth" whom the Christian might view as a brother, "preaching the same God." Yet Rouse believed that Muhammad became corrupt and immoral after gaining political power, which might have been avoided if he had "come into contact with pure Christianity."[94] Thus, the original tract sought to convince its Bengali readers to reject Islam and embrace Christianity.

Rouse referenced the Torah and Psalms—as holy books that Muslims revere—to prove Jesus' identity as savior and son of God, he defended a Christian understanding of Jesus' death by crucifixion and his resurrection,[95] and he criticized Muhammad, arguing against Muslim claims that he was the Paraclete whom Jesus foretold.[96] Although he ultimately affirmed theological and biblical arguments against Islam like those that Martyn and Pfander had produced, Rouse's reference to the truth within Islam reflected some positive shifts in missionary thinking about Christian–Muslim commonalities by the late nineteenth century.

Significantly, these three evangelistic tracts came from missionaries in South and central Asian colonial contexts. While such tracts were translated into Turkish and Arabic, Protestant mission societies in the Ottoman Empire did not produce much of their own evangelistic literature for Muslims until the turn of the century, due to publishing restrictions and prohibitions against proselytism in regions not under European imperial control. As one early twentieth-century American Methodist missionary in India, Bishop Frank W. Warne (1854–1932), put it, although the Methodist Episcopal Church did not have a separate mission focusing on Muslims, his mission had received more converts from Islam than some mission societies giving their time exclusively to work in lands under Islamic rule. The lack of what he called "government persecution" made a difference in British-ruled India, Warne explained, noting that among the Indian Methodist pastors alone were over fifty names of Muslim origin.[97] Nothing comparable existed in the Ottoman Middle East or even in British-occupied Egypt at that time.

Gender Constructs in Protestant Re-inventions of Islam

The nineteenth-century works of Martyn, Pfander, and Rouse, along with the activities of other missionary men like Samuel Zwemer in the early twentieth century, exemplified a masculinist approach to evangelizing elite Muslim men through theological controversy (a strategy of winning converts through debate). This approach largely excluded missionary women from participating in or receiving recognition for such highly valued evangelistic activities. Protestant missionary men did emphasize the importance of women's work among Muslim women and children, but with few exceptions (such as Lilias Trotter) women were not then and still are not now acclaimed as trailblazing missionaries among Muslims.[98] Telling in this regard were the images of "pioneers in Moslem lands" that appeared inside the cover of Zwemer's 1908 book *Islam: A Challenge to Faith*. It showed portraits of European and American men—including Martyn, Pfander, Keith-Falconer, and Peter Zwemer, Samuel's brother—along with one Muslim convert to Protestantism, the Syrian Kamil abd al-Masih.[99]

The works of missionary men dominated the Protestant publishing industry on Islam, with texts either centered on establishing the truth of Christianity in contrast to Islam or aiming to give a scholarly assessment of Islamic societies. Even when more opportunities opened toward the late nineteenth century for missionary women to produce literature informing Protestants about Muslim contexts, their writings were constrained by gender norms. Women missionaries made their voices heard through lectures for women's groups, through articles for women's magazines, and by exploring the uses of fiction for children and young adults. Yet, as Séverine Gabry-Thienpont and Norig Neveu have argued, women missionaries were usually excluded from scholarly societies focusing on the Middle East and from the production of scholarly work generally.[100] The theologically inflected assessments of Islam that Protestant men produced throughout the nineteenth century continued to be *their* purview in the early twentieth, and thus even women who broke the gender boundary to write evangelistic literature—like Trotter did later in her career—have been overlooked in histories of Protestant missions to Muslims that gravitate toward theological themes and male scholarship.

The existing literature on Protestant–Muslim encounters in the Middle East, for example, overlooks missionary women's writings, including their scholarship. Gabry-Thienpont and Neveu described this obstacle as a "masculism that still blots various [scholarly] approaches," pointing to the need to examine mission history from the perspective of gender studies.[101] Women's minimal presence in the earliest scholarship on missions, these authors noted, "means that today there is little understanding of how these women viewed the [Middle] East."[102] This is especially true when it comes to women missionaries' approaches to Islam and how they shaped the understandings of mission supporters. The idea of a separate sphere of "woman's work for woman" that empowered Anglo-Protestant women to present themselves as authorities on the status of Muslim women has shaped scholarship on missions to overlook women's influence within the broader

Protestant movement for missions to Muslims. Scholarship on Protestant–Muslim relations has too often either ignored missionary women's work or treated it as operating in a separate (and lesser) sphere rather than as being a primary component in the missionary enterprise.

We cannot rectify this oversight simply by producing more women's mission histories, although such work remains necessary. For women were not marginal to the Protestant missionary movement but came to outnumber men in most mission fields. They also activated the participation of women supporters at home, who in turn were instrumental in fundraising, in the production and distribution of missionary literature, and in providing educational and devotional programming for men, women, and children centered on the work of missions. *Re-inventing Islam*, therefore, treats the activities of women missionaries as reflections of the Protestant missionary enterprise *as a whole* and not of a particular gendered sphere. Approaching women's mission history therefore as *mission history*, this book gives substantial attention to the texts, images, and performances through which British and American missionary women re-invented and profoundly shaped their constituents' understandings of Islam. When including women in the story of missions to Muslims, I intentionally recognize both their contributions as religious leaders and the roles they played in perpetuating stereotypes about Islam.

This book's central questions, however, revolve around Protestant discourses about *gender*—not just about Protestant or Muslim *women*. I follow feminist historian Joan Scott in treating gender as "a social category imposed upon a sexed body," a cultural construction that has varied across different historical periods and geographical contexts.[103] In examining Protestant re-inventions of Islam, I attend to the "social creation of ideas about appropriate roles for women and men"[104] and trace how these ideas influenced Protestant views of Muslims in relationship to their own theological and cultural presuppositions. Studying gender, then, implies more than studying women's histories. I apply gender as an interpretive lens because assumptions about masculine and feminine behavioral norms guided Protestant approaches to Islam from the Reformation onward. Protestant men and women alike used rhetoric about Muslim men and about Muslim women to uphold their own beliefs, to critique Islam, and to achieve their evangelistic, humanitarian, and imperialist aims in Islamic contexts.

By the nineteenth century, gender constructs were a formative component of British and American Protestants' theological discourses about Islam. Yet few studies on Protestant–Muslim relations give substantive attention to gender. For methodological resources, I therefore look beyond Protestant history and theology to scholarship on gender and Orientalism that explains the Eurocentric notions shaping Protestant re-inventions of Islam. When introducing his seminal critique of Orientalism as a western form of knowledge that "places things Oriental in class, court, prison, or manual for scrutiny, study, judgment, discipline, or governing,"[105] Said suggested that assumptions about gender were often part of Orientalist production. This opened the way for numerous publications on Orientalism from the perspective of feminist and gender studies.[106] Some, like Lila Abu-Lughod's *Do Muslim Women Need Saving?* and Maryam Khalid's *Gender, Orientalism, and the "War on Terror"* have responded to recent American stereotypes of Muslim women and men.[107] Both texts indicated that these stereotypes have deep historical roots in American and larger western cultural norms. Other studies have traced such thought patterns to their modern origins. Kahf, for example, noted the diversity of ways in which Muslim women were represented in medieval western literature—as remarkably similar to Christian women, as heroines who converted to Christianity, or as masculinized, overbearing Muslim noblewomen.[108] However, after the eighteenth century, western writers repeatedly used the image of the Muslim woman imprisoned in the harem (women's space in the home) "as a negative ideal to make the glorified domesticity of the ideal Western woman look benign by contrast."[109]

These shifting ideas about Muslim women merged with the preexisting western conception of Muslim men as monsters who were violent, hypersexual, and "toxically masculine"—the subject of Sophia Arjana's study on *Muslims in the Western Imagination*.[110] Thus, the idea of Islam as a monolithic religion of threatening men and oppressed women came to permeate modern western thought. Yet as Billie Melman argued in an early study on women and Orientalism, even then "Europe's attitude towards the Orient was neither unified nor monolithic." Rather, she demonstrated that diverse images of the Middle East and Islam can be found in the writings of women travelers from the eighteenth to early twentieth centuries.[111] Both the dominant Orientalist discourse and more nuanced perspectives like those that Melman found appear within the Protestant narratives on Islam examined in the following chapters of this book.

Despite their value in delineating the context in which European and American views of gender and Islam shifted in the modern period, the aforementioned cultural and literary histories give little attention to the ways

Orientalist logic influenced Christian theologies and religious practices. I set out in this study, therefore, to address the overlooked role of gender constructs in Protestant religious engagements with Islam, tracing the shifts in Protestant views from the theological polemics of the Reformation to British and American missionary images of Islam in the nineteenth and twentieth centuries.

I take gender as a lens because prejudices against Muslim men and misperceptions about Muslim women remain significant barriers to American Christian–Muslim relations today. My analysis focuses most closely on the late nineteenth- and early twentieth-century period in which missionary messages solidified such gendered ideas, rather than centering around mid-twentieth-century missionaries who offered irenic views of Islam, like Wilfred Cantwell Smith or Kenneth Cragg.[112] As a result, this book grapples with the negative gender prejudices that have stubbornly persisted despite these later efforts to foster Christian–Muslim theological understanding.

Guided by Said's *Orientalism*, I am mindful of the critiques leveled at his book for focusing on European and American discourses and actions to the neglect (according to these critics) of Middle Eastern voices. Said responded, in part, by giving attention in a subsequent book, *Culture and Imperialism* (1993), to local resistance to colonialism in the Middle East and elsewhere.[113] Like *Orientalism*, my research examines European and American knowledge production. This book's focus on historical Protestant discourses about Muslim women might therefore lead readers to ask: If such discourses were skewed, then what was the typical Muslim woman's life actually like in the nineteenth or twentieth century? I do not attempt to answer this question because the rich scholarship already produced on Islamic societies in various regions and historical periods demonstrates that there is no "typical" Muslim and that—like women everywhere—Muslim women have both faced extreme challenges and been active agents in shaping their own communities for the better.[114] In select places throughout the book, I point toward such scholarship to help readers counterbalance the impact of the anti-Muslim critiques quoted in these pages—critiques that have become embedded in many American minds. I repeat some of them here not to reinforce such claims but in an attempt to question them and break this cycle.

Finally, this book does not focus on the effects of Christian missions on Middle Eastern or other Muslim communities.[115] I do not deny the positive educational and humanitarian impacts that Protestant missions had, especially on women, nor do I set out to examine the damage that missionaries may have done to local Muslim–Christian relationships in Islamic contexts. Instead of attempting to weigh the benefits against the harms, I point to the ambiguities and contradictions of mission history. Indeed, if some roots of American Islamophobia are of Protestant missionary origin, so too are some of the contemporary movements for interfaith dialogue.

Overview of *Re-inventing Islam*

Prior to the nineteenth century, Protestant religious leaders participated in the re-invention of Islam in a context in which the Ottoman Islamic state—and not Christian Europe—was the dominant political power. Thus, the book's second chapter considers early Protestant ideas and images of Islam from the sixteenth to early nineteenth centuries. Beginning with the Reformation in continental Europe, it examines representations of Islam and Muslims in theological and polemical texts and in artistic renderings, like theatrical plays and wood block prints, that made their way to Britain and later into colonial North America. It then shows how critiques of Muslim women's veiling, which were not the norm during the Reformation, became part of the standard discourse on Islam during the Enlightenment period.

The book then turns in Chapters 3 to 6 to the modern missionary movement, beginning in the nineteenth century, when European powers gained a foothold in Muslim-majority regions and missionaries experienced close long-term contact with Muslims at a level unprecedented for Anglo-Protestants before this period. This was the case for Americans who—unlike their British and Dutch Protestant counterparts—had only a feeble commercial and diplomatic presence in the Mediterranean and Asia in the first half of the nineteenth century.[116] Why the Anglo-Protestant focus in a study concerned with the roots of *American* Islamophobia? Because British and American missionaries developed a symbiotic relationship, particularly as part of the movement for missions to Muslims. Through collaborating in publications and conferences and through reading and promoting both British and American literature, they streamlined the messaging that Protestants on both sides of the North Atlantic received about Islam.

The third and fourth chapters attend to the ways in which British and American missionary texts extended and re-invented earlier Protestant discourses for American consumers. Since men dominated missionary publishing, I include the writings of a significant number of women and look beyond theological polemics and academic publications to other genres like fiction, through which women missionaries found ways to shape their audiences' conceptions of Islam.[117] Chapter 3 examines the gender discourses in texts published for adult mission supporters in the nineteenth and early twentieth centuries, while Chapter 4 turns to the ways in which the missionary movement repackaged these ideas about Islam for children.

By examining the colossal archive of missionary images and objects collected from Muslim contexts, the fifth and sixth chapters reach beyond text-based approaches to explore overlooked sources of material culture that missionaries used to educate and elicit support from their constituents at home. Chapter 5 centers on images, including photographs and printed postcards, of Muslims and Islamic rituals that missionaries published, sent to their supporters, or displayed in slide shows, scrapbooks, and albums at churches and mission gatherings. Chapter 6 places the movement for missions to Muslims in the broader context of global Protestant missions and western imperialism as it delves further into the material objects and "curiosities" that missionaries collected and the Islamic costumes they used performatively to draw attention to their work.

In reinforcing longstanding Protestant theological discourses and solidifying American views of Muslim men and women as exotic, immoral, or threatening, missionaries re-invented Islam. Based more on Protestant norms than on Islamic sources, missionary texts, images, and material displays contributed to American Protestant understandings of Muslims as part of a monolithic entity that was wholly other to Christianity and to western culture—all to serve the aims of Protestant missions. Yet, this is not the only picture of Islam that Anglo-Protestant missionaries painted for their constituents. The central chapters of this book also hint at the subtle ways in which their writings, photographs, and material performances indicated that missionaries' personal views of Islam were more nuanced than the common discourse suggested.

Because this book traces the most influential and widespread ideas about Islam and gender that the British and American public received from missionaries, Chapters 3 through 6 focus on missionary materials that were intended for broad audiences before the start of World War II. Like all performers, missionaries usually framed their publications in accordance with the norms and expectations of their target audiences. As one might expect, they wrote under pressure to recruit new missionaries and to motivate readers to contribute financially to their work. Editors revised and shaped these texts further, ensuring that most of the material Anglo-Protestants consumed repeated a similar story of oppressed and ignorant Muslim women, brutal Muslim men, and heroic missionary efforts to save what they described as the "Mohammedan World." Divergent views certainly existed among missionaries who recognized the exaggerations, neglected truths, and misinformation. These were present in missionaries' personal writings during the nineteenth and early twentieth centuries and became more prominent in their published writing in the mid-twentieth century.

The seventh chapter therefore concludes the book by considering the shifts in missionary thinking after World War II, identifying a new openness which some mainline Anglo-Protestants showed to Islam and Muslim cultures while also still critiquing gendered practices such as veiling. Moreover, this chapter considers the connections between earlier anti-Muslim sentiment among Protestants and contemporary American Islamophobia, a phenomenon that took full form only in the late twentieth century and that I therefore leave to this final chapter.

As I indicated at the outset, Anglo-Protestant missionaries tilled the soil in which contemporary American Islamophobia would take root. They did so when employing gender critiques and disseminating such views widely to men, women, and children in all forms of textual, visual, and material media. They re-invented Islam for a variety of reasons: to reinforce Protestant theological claims, to justify their evangelistic endeavors in Muslim societies, to express both humanitarian concern and Eurocentric views of the world, and to support British and American cultural, economic, and military expansion. Simultaneously, however, this same missionary movement educated its constituents about diverse Islamic cultures, in part by providing humanizing images of Islam; and missionaries formed personal relationships with Muslims that would open pathways toward formal efforts of Christian–Muslim dialogue. In revisiting this history, Americans may find a new opportunity to choose which of these legacies will guide their future.

Notes

1. This book avoids the terms *Muslim world* and *Islamic world* that essentialize the diversity of Muslim communities and Islamic contexts in a way similar to antiquated missionary language like "Mohammedan World."
2. This act of *re-inventing* was not the introduction of the concept of Islam as a religion, and therefore it differs from the nineteenth-century "invention" of Hinduism. See Brian K. Pennington,

Was Hinduism Invented?: Britons, Indians, and the Colonial Construction of Religion (New York: Oxford University Press, 2005).
3. While unable to avoid dichotomous terms such as *western* and *eastern* entirely, this book keeps both terms lowercase in an attempt to challenge presumptions about European superiority and about insurmountable differences between the "East" and "West."
4. Edward W. Said, *Orientalism* (New York: Vintage Books, 1978), 2. Said's influential and still highly relevant book rested on the premise that Europe invented "the Orient" as its opposite, seeking intellectual, cultural, and political dominance (p. 40).
5. Tomoko Masuzawa, *The Invention of World Religions* (Chicago: University of Chicago Press, 2005), 179–206.
6. For some modern examples, see Albert Hourani, *Arabic Thought in the Liberal Age, 1798–1939* (Cambridge: Cambridge University Press, 1983); Shireen T. Hunter, ed. *Reformist Voices of Islam: Mediating Islam and Modernity* (New York: Routledge, 2009).
7. On contemporary Islamophobia, see Todd H. Green, *The Fear of Islam: An Introduction to Islamophobia in the West* (Minneapolis: Fortress Press, 2015); Stephen Sheehi, *Islamophobia: The Ideological Campaign Against Muslims* (Atlanta: Clarity Press, 2011); Peter Gottschalk and Gabriel Greenberg, *Islamophobia and Anti-Muslim Sentiment: Picturing the Enemy*, 2nd ed. (Lanham, MD: Rowman & Littlefield, 2019).
8. Masuzawa, *Invention of World Religions*, 179–206.
9. Carsten Colpe, "The Science of Religion, the History of Religion, the Phenomenology of Religion," *Historical Reflections* 20, no. 3 (Fall 1994): 403–11.
10. Some scholars have focused on Protestant theological discourses or constructed their own theologies. Notably, Joshua Ralston put Justin Martyr, Thomas Aquinas, Martin Luther, and Karl Barth into conversation with Muslim thinkers like Ibn Taymiyya and Mohammad al-Jabri. Joshua Ralston, *Law and the Rule of God: A Christian Engagement with Shari'a* (Cambridge: Cambridge University Press, 2020).
11. Charlotte Colding Smith, *Images of Islam, 1453–1600* (New York: Routledge, 2018); Gregory J. Miller, *The Turks and Islam in Reformation Germany* (New York: Routledge, 2018); Adam S. Francisco, *Martin Luther and Islam: A Study in Sixteenth-Century Polemics and Apologetics* (Leiden: Brill, 2007). Among the few studies focusing on Islam and the English Reformation, see Christopher Toenjes, *Islam, the Turks and the Making of the English Reformation: The History of the Ottoman Empire in John Foxe's Acts and Monuments* (Frankfurt: Peter Lang, 2016). Several studies exist on British political and cultural engagements with the Ottomans, including Nabil Matar, *Islam in Britain, 1558–1685* (Cambridge: Cambridge University Press, 1998); Daniel Vitkus, *Turning Turk: English Theater and the Multicultural Mediterranean, 1570–1630* (New York: Palgrave Macmillan, 2003).
12. Heather J. Sharkey, *American Evangelicals in Egypt: Missionary Encounters in an Age of Empire* (Princeton, NJ: Princeton University Press, 2008); Ussama Makdisi, *Artillery of Heaven: American Missionaries and the Failed Conversion of the Middle East* (Ithaca, NY: Cornell University Press, 2008); Beth Baron, *The Orphan Scandal: Christian Missionaries and the Rise of the Muslim Brotherhood* (Stanford, CA: Stanford University Press, 2014). For studies published on missions in Muslim contexts of the Middle East before 2012, see the bibliography in Eleanor Tejirian and Reeva Spector Simon, *Conflict, Conquest, and Conversion: Two Thousand Years of Christian Missions in the Middle East* (New York: Columbia University Press, 2012). More recent publications include Deanna Ferree Womack, *Protestants, Gender and the Arab Renaissance in Late Ottoman Syria* (Edinburgh: Edinburgh University Press, 2019); Inger Marie Okkenhaug and Karène Sanchez Summerer, eds., *Christian Missions and Humanitarianism in the Middle East: Ideologies, Rhetoric, and Practices* (Leiden: Brill, 2020); Ramy Nair Marcos, *The Emergence of Evangelical Egyptians: A Historical Study of the Evangelical-Coptic Encounter and Conversion in Late Ottoman Egypt, 1854–1878* (Lanham, MD: Lexington Books, 2024).
13. David D. Grafton, *Muhammad in the Seminary: Protestant Teaching About Islam in the Nineteenth Century* (New York: New York University Press, 2024); Thomas Kidd, *American Christians and Islam: Evangelical Culture and Muslims from the Colonial Period to the Age of Terrorism* (Princeton, NJ: Princeton University Press, 2009). See also David D. Grafton, *An American Biblical Orientalism: The Construction of Jews, Christians, and Muslims in Nineteenth Century American Evangelical Piety* (Lanham, MD: Lexington Books, 2019).
14. Matar, *Islam in Britain*; Vitkus, *Turning Turk*; Matthew Dimmock, *New Turkes: Dramatizing Islam and the Ottomans in Early Modern England* (Aldershot, UK: Ashgate, 2004); Timothy

Marr, *The Cultural Roots of American Islamicism* (Cambridge: Cambridge University Press, 2006); Jacob Rama Berman, *American Arabesque: Arab, Islam, and the 19th Century* (New York: New York University Press, 2012); Malini Johar Schueller, *U.S. Orientalisms: Race, Nation, and Gender in Literature, 1790–1890* (Ann Arbor: University of Michigan Press, 1998).

15. Studies on women and missions in the Middle East include Carolyn McCue Goffman, *Mary Mills Patrick's Cosmopolitan Mission and the Constantinople Women's College* (Lanham, MD: Lexington Books, 2020); Barbara Reeves-Ellington, *Domestic Frontiers: Gender, Reform, and American Interventions in the Ottoman Balkans and the Near East* (Amherst: University of Massachusetts Press, 2013); Inger Marie Okkenhaug, *The Quality of Heroic Living, of High Endeavor and Adventure: Anglican Mission, Women, and Education in Palestine, 1888–1948* (Leiden: Brill, 2002); Christine B. Lindner, "'Long, Long Will She Be Affectionately Remembered': Gender and the Memorialization of an American Female Missionary," *Social Sciences and Missions* 23, no. 1 (2010): 7–31; Ellen L. Fleischmann, "The Impact of American Protestant Missionaries in Lebanon on the Construction of Female Identity, c. 1860–1950," *Islam and Christian–Muslim Relations* 13, no. 4 (2002): 411–26.

16. I have adapted a portion of this section and the next, with permission, from Deanna Ferree Womack, "Protestant Portrayals of Islam: From the Reformation to Modern Missions," *Interpretation: A Journal of Bible and Theology* 76, no. 2 (2022): 140–55.

17. Katya Vehlow, "The Swiss Reformers Zwingli, Bullinger and Bibliander and Their Attitude to Islam (1520–1560)," *Islam and Christian–Muslim Relations* 6, no. 2 (1995): 230. Suleiman gained control of parts of Hungary in 1526. The Ottomans took Constantinople in 1453.

18. In 1452, Frederick III became the first Habsburg ruler to be confirmed as Holy Roman Emperor, a title that the Habsburg monarchs would carry until 1806. On this dynasty, see Benjamin Curtis, *The Habsburgs: The History of a Dynasty* (London: Bloomsbury, 2013).

19. On Luther, see Vehlow, "Swiss Reformers," 245. Bibliander offered a similar portrayal of Islam as a punishment. Gregory J. Miller, "Theodor Bibliander's *Machumetis saracenorum principis eiusque successorum vitae, doctrina ac ipse alcoran* (1543) as the Sixteenth-Century 'Encyclopedia of Islam,'" *Islam and Christian–Muslim Relations* 24, no. 2 (2013): 249.

20. The original German titles were *Vom Kriege wider die Türken* and *Heerpredigt wider den Türken*. Luther relied mainly on the works of Cusa, Riccoldo, and George of Hungary until he acquired the new Latin translation of the Qur'an shortly before his death. David D. Grafton, "Martin Luther's Sources on the Turk and Islam in the Midst of the Fear of Ottoman Imperialism," *The Muslim World* 107 (October 2017): 666–67. Luther made careful use of the available Latin sources and supported the controversial publication of the Qur'an in Latin because he believed Christians ought to be educated about its contents. See also Vehlow, "Swiss Reformers," 245.

21. Faculties of Arabic and Oriental studies were not yet prominent in European universities, and those that existed by the start of the Reformation (1613 in Leiden) had not produced significant literature on Islam.

22. The collection included three other texts translated from Arabic. Vehlow "Swiss Reformers," 236–37, 241–42; Francisco, *Martin Luther and Islam*, 10–12.

23. Francisco, *Martin Luther and Islam*, 11; James Aloysius Kritzeck, *Peter the Venerable and Islam* (Princeton, NJ: Princeton University Press, 2016). The Latin titles were *Summa totius haeresis ac diabolicae sectae Saracenorum siue Hismahelitarum* and *Liber contra sectam sive haeresim Saracenorum*.

24. Riccoldo da Monte Croce wrote *Confutation of the Qur'an* and *Against the Saracen Law*. The full Latin titles were *Confutatio Alcorani seu legis Saracenorum, ex graeco nuper in latinum traducta* and *Contra legem Sarracenorum*. Francisco, *Martin Luther and Islam*, 12–16.

25. The Latin title was *Cribratio Alkorani*. Francisco, *Martin Luther and Islam*, 17–18. See also Il Kim, "Reading Cusanus' Cribratio Alkorani (1461) in the Light of Christian Antiquarianism at the Papal Court in the 1450s," in *Nicolas of Cusa and Times of Transition: Essays in Honor of Gerald Christianson*, ed. Thomas M. Izbicki, Jason Aleksander, and Donald Duclow (Leiden: Brill, 2018), 113–27; David Choi, "Martin Luther's Response to the Turkish Threat: Continuity and Contrast with the Medieval Commentators Riccoldo da Monte Croce and Nicolas of Cusa" (PhD diss., Princeton Theological Seminary, 2003).

26. Luther wrote the preface for Bibliander's edition of Ketton's translation. Luther and Bibliander were not natural allies, but both wanted Islamic texts to be available for Christian readers, an idea that other religious leaders found objectionable. The compendium was titled *Machumetis Saracenorum principis*. Bibliander commissioned the collection to be printed by Johannes Oporinus in Basel. A second, expanded edition came out in 1550. All the texts

of *Collectio Toletanum* appeared in the first volume of the compendium, except for *Apology of al-Kindi*, which Bibliander included in the second volume. Miller, "Bibliander's Machumetis saracenorum," 243, 245, 250. See also Bruce Gordon, "Theodor Bibliander," in *Christian–Muslim Relations: A Biographical History 1500–1900*, ed. David Thomas (Leiden: Brill, 2014), 6:680–85.
27. Miller, *Turks and Islam*, 13.
28. Ibid., 14.
29. Ibid., 2, 152. At least twenty editions of George's tract were published in German, and Luther wrote a preface to one of these. The Latin title was *Tractatus de moribus condictionibus et nequicia Turcorum*.
30. Ibid., 2, 153–55. The original Latin titles were *De Turcarum ritu et caeremonius* and *De affliction tam captivorum quam etiam sub Turcae tribute viventium Christianorum*.
31. Miller, "Bibliander's Machumetis saracenorum," 250–51. George's account appeared in the first edition of 1543, and Georgievic's was added to the 1550 edition.
32. Smith, *Images of Islam*, 15.
33. Vehlow, "Swiss Reformers," 239; Jerry Brotton, *The Sultan and the Queen: The Untold Story of Elizabeth and Islam* (New York: Viking, 2016).
34. Francisco, *Martin Luther and Islam*, 114.
35. John Calvin, *The Institutes of the Christian Religion*, trans. Henry Beveridge (London: James Clarke & Co, 1953), book 2, chapter 6, section 4.
36. John Knox, "A Treatise on Prayer," in *Writings of the Rev. John Knox, Minister of God's Word in Scotland*, ed. The Religious Tract Society (London: William Clowes, 1831), 82.
37. Vehlow, "Swiss Reformers," 240.
38. Toenjes, *Islam*.
39. Ibid., 101.
40. Frederick Quinn quoted Foxe's prayer in *The Sum of All Heresies: The Image of Islam in Western Thought* (Oxford: Oxford University Press, 2008), 46–47.
41. On Christian views of Hagar, see Nyasha Junior, *Reimagining Hagar: Blackness and Bible* (Oxford: Oxford University Press, 2019).
42. Vehlow, "Swiss Reformers," 236–38, 240–43; W. P. Stephens, "Understanding Islam—In the Light of Bullinger and Wesley," *Evangelical Quarterly* 81, no. 1 (2009): 23–37; Bruce Gordon, "Heinrich Bullinger," in *Christian–Muslim Relations: A Biographical History 1500–1900*, ed. David Thomas (Leiden: Brill, 2014), 6:716–19.
43. Calvin declared that those who knew Christianity but rejected true doctrine were idolaters who deserved to be put to death. Michael Servetus, whom Calvin condemned for antitrinitarianism, was burned at the stake in Geneva in 1553. Servetus advocated that Christians focus on Jesus' prophethood and reject his divinity because it was a stumbling block to Muslims and Jews. Stuart Bonnington, "Calvin and Islam," *Reformed Theological Review* 68, no. 2 (August 2009): 81–84; Jan Slomp, "Calvin and the Turks," *Studies in Interreligious Dialogue* 19, no. 1 (2009): 61.
44. Miller, "Bibliander's Machumetis saracenorum," 243, 258.
45. Stephens, "Bullinger and Wesley," 25; Bonnington, "Calvin," 81–82; Francisco, *Martin Luther and Islam*, 91–92; Vehlow, "Swiss Reformers," 252.
46. The first Lutheran Pietist mission to the Middle East in the seventeenth century was short-lived and did not result in the evangelization of Muslims. David D. Grafton, *Piety, Politics, and Power: Lutherans Encountering Islam in the Middle East* (Eugene, OR: Wipf & Stock, 2009), 59–106. Quakers also made attempts to evangelize Muslims in the seventeenth century. Justin J. Meggitt, *Early Quakers and Islam: Slavery, Apocalyptic and Christian–Muslim Encounters in the Seventeenth Century* (Eugene, OR: Wipf & Stock 2013).
47. I cite the King James Version as the text nineteenth-century American and British Protestants used.
48. These included three Anglican missions: Society for Promoting Christian Knowledge (1698), Society for Propagation of the Gospel in Foreign Parts (1701), and Church Missionary Society (1799). The Baptist Missionary Society was founded in 1792.
49. Early twentieth-century statistics are available in James S. Dennis, *World Atlas of Christian Missions: Containing a Directory of Missionary Societies, a Classified Summary of Statistics, an Index of Mission Stations, and Maps Showing the Location of Mission Stations Throughout the World* (New York: Student Volunteer Movement, 1911).
50. Mohja Kahf, *Western Representations of the Muslim Woman: From Termagant to Odalisque* (Austin: University of Texas Press, 1999), 15, 53, 57–58.

51. Henry Jessup in Syria, for example, considered the growing British influence in Muslim lands to be "providential" and referred to Queen Victoria as ruler of India and "protectress of the whole Turkish empire in Asia." Henry Harris Jessup, *The Mohammedan Missionary Problem* (Philadelphia: Presbyterian Board of Publication, 1879), 108.
52. Avril Powell, "The Legacy of Henry Martyn to the Study of India's Muslims and Islam in the Nineteenth Century" (unpublished presentation at Cambridge Center for Christianity Worldwide, July 2017), https://www.cccw.cam.ac.uk/wp-content/uploads/2017/07/Powell-Dr-Avril.pdf.
53. Carey's work among Bengali Muslims along with William Ward has been overlooked. James Ryan West, "Evangelizing Bengali Muslims, 1793–1813: William Carey, William Ward, and Islam" (PhD diss., Southern Baptist Theological Seminary, 2014).
54. Clinton Bennett, "The Legacy of Karl Gottlieb Pfander," *International Bulletin of Missionary Research* 20, no. 2 (April 1996): 76–81; Avril Powell, *Muslims and Missionaries in Pre-Mutiny India* (Richmond, UK: Curzon, 1993). On other Lutherans working for the CMS, see Grafton, *Piety, Politics, and Power*, 94–95.
55. Deanna Ferree Womack, "Imperial Politics and Theological Practices: Comparative Transformations in Anglo-American and Russian Orthodox Missions to Syria–Palestine," *ARAM Periodical* 25, no. 1–2 (2013): 1–12; Grafton, *Piety, Politics, and Power*, 118–33. The bishopric became solely Anglican in 1887.
56. Michael Marten, *Attempting to Bring the Gospel Home: Scottish Missions to Palestine, 1839–1917* (London: I. B. Tauris, 2005); Michael Marten, "The Free Church of Scotland in 19th-Century Lebanon," *CHRONOS: Revue d'Histoire de l'Université de Balamand* 5 (2002): 51–106. The London Society for Promoting Christianity amongst the Jews, or the London Jews Society, had launched a mission in Palestine in 1823.
57. Congregationalists founded the ABCFM, but the society also included Presbyterian and Dutch Reformed missionaries.
58. In the 1870s those stations were in Ludhiana, Furrukhabad, and Kolhapur. Presbyterian Church of the United States of America, *The Thirty-Sixth Annual Report of the Board of Foreign Missions of the Presbyterian Church of the United States of America* (New York: Mission House, 1873), 4–5.
59. James McKinnis Balph, *Fifty Years of Mission Work in Syria: A Brief Compend of the Mission Work of the Reformed Presbyterian Church in Northern Syria, Asia Minor and Cyprus* (Pittsburgh: Murdoch, Kerr, & Co., 1913). By 1890, the UPCNA had twenty-three missionaries at five stations in Egypt and twenty-five in South Asia, with one station in North India and five stations in what became Pakistan. United Presbyterian Church of North America, *Thirty-First Annual Report of the Board of Foreign Missions of the United Presbyterian Church of North America* (Philadelphia: Edward Patterson, 1890), 3.
60. Eventually, British Quakers ran the mission in Lebanon, and Americans ran the one in Ramallah, Palestine. On British Quakers in India, see Siobhan Lambert-Hurley, "An Embassy of Equality? Quaker Missionaries in Bhopal State, 1890–1930," in *Rhetoric and Reality: Gender and the Colonial Experience in South Asia*, ed. Avril Powell and Siobhan Lambert-Hurley (Oxford: Oxford University Press, 2006), 247–81.
61. Their efforts, however, focused mainly on non-Muslim communities in these regions. David W. Scott, *Mission as Globalization: Methodists in Southeast Asia at the Turn of the Twentieth Century* (Lanham, MD: Lexington Books, 2016), 2, 10.
62. Grafton, *Power, Piety, and Politics*, 7, 237; Gardiner H. Shattuck, Jr., *Christian Homeland: Episcopalians and the Middle East, 1820–1958* (Oxford: Oxford University Press, 2023); Melanie E. Trexler, *Evangelizing Lebanon: Baptists, Missions, and the Question of Cultures* (Waco, TX: Baylor University Press, 2016).
63. E. J. Humphrey, *Gems of India: Or, Sketches of Distinguished Hindoo and Mahomedan Women* (New York: Nelson & Phillips, 1875); E. J. Humphrey, *Six Years in India: Or, Sketches of India and Its People as Seen by a Lady Missionary* (New York: Carlton & Porter, 1866). I am grateful to Arun Jones for alerting me to Humphrey's work.
64. Humphrey, *Six Years in India*, 203.
65. Zahur al-Haqq, *Autobiography of Rev. Zahur-al-Haqq: First Convert in the Mission of the Methodist Episcopal Church in India*, trans. E. J. Humphrey (New York: The Missionary Society, 1885). Arun Jones examined the accounts of Zahur al-Haqq's conversion in "Reshaping the American Evangelical Conversion Narrative in Nineteenth-Century North India," in *Godroads: Modalities of Conversion in India*, ed. Peter Berger and Sarbeswar Sahoo (New

Delhi: Cambridge University Press, 2020), 179-98; Arun W. Jones, *Missionary Christianity and Local Religion: American Evangelicalism in North India, 1836-1870* (Waco, TX: Baylor University Press, 2017), 139-57.
66. A. A. Cooper, "Syria and Palestine: Beyrout," in *The Ninety-Sixth Report of the British and Foreign Bible Society* (London: Gresham Press, 1900), 150; Emma R. Pitman, *Missionary Heroines in Eastern Lands: Woman's Work in Mission Fields* (London: S. W. Partridge & Co., 1884), 160; David D. Grafton, "The Legacy of Ion Keith-Falconer," *International Bulletin of Missionary Research* 31, no. 3 (July 2007): 148-52. The South Arabia Mission was operated first by the FCS and then by the United Free Church of Scotland (UFCS, a union of the FCS and the United Presbyterian Church of Scotland). Finally, it came under the Church of Scotland after the 1929 reunification. The UFCS described this as the church's only "purely Mohammedan mission" and sought to recruit more workers by advertising Aden's pleasant climate. James Robson, "'I Went into Arabia': Notes About the Pleasant Climate of Sheikh Othman," in *The Record of the Home Foreign Mission Work of the United Free Church of Scotland* (December 1920), 222.
67. For Jessup's account of Kamil's conversion, see Henry Harris Jessup, *The Setting of the Crescent and the Rising of the Cross, or Kamil Abdul Messiah: A Syrian Convert from Islam to Christianity* (Philadelphia: Westminster Press, 1898).
68. On Zahur's first experience preaching, see J. L. Humphrey, "Our First Convert in India a Mohammedan," *The Epworth Herald* 19, no. 15 (September 5, 1908): 35-36.
69. Susette Smith, "Notes from a Hareem Visitor at Beyrout," *The Missing Link* (August 1, 1876): 243-44.
70. Dana L. Robert, "Revisioning the Women's Missionary Movement," in *The Good News of the Kingdom: Mission Theology for the Third Millennium*, ed. Charles E. Van Engren, Dean S. Gilliland, and Paul Pierson (Eugene, OR: Wipf & Stock, 1993), 109-18.
71. Clara A. Swain, *A Glimpse of India: Being a Collection of Extracts from the Letters of Dr. Clara A. Swain [...]* (New York: J. Pott, 1909). Dr. Ara Elsie Harris worked in Syria, where her parents were missionaries, and later in India with her husband Burl Schuyler. On Harris and Eddy, see Womack, *Protestants, Gender*, 168, 299-301, 349.
72. The ZBMM formed from a preexisting zenana mission society after some members split off to establish the Church of England's Zenana Missionary Society.
73. The French colonized Algeria beginning in 1830, and the British occupied Aden, in the Arabian peninsula, in 1839 and Egypt in 1882.
74. Miriam Huffman Rockness, *A Passion for the Impossible: The Life of Lilias Trotter* (Grand Rapids, MI: Discovery House, 1999), 210-13. Lilias' mother was a low-church Anglican, and as a young adult Lilias was influenced by the Keswick Conventions (pp. 55-61). The AMB later became part of the North Africa Mission.
75. The Reformed Church of America (formerly known as the Dutch Reformed Church) took over the mission in 1894. John Hubers, "Samuel Zwemer and the Challenge of Islam: From Polemic to a Hint of Dialogue," *International Bulletin of Missionary Research* 28, no. 3 (July 2004): 118; J. Christy Wilson, Jr., "The Legacy of Samuel M. Zwemer," *International Bulletin of Missionary Research* (July 1986): 117-18.
76. Samir Boulos, *European Evangelicals in Egypt (1900-1956): Cultural Entanglements and Missionary Spaces* (Leiden: Brill, 2016), 76-77. These men who met in Belfast came from across Great Britain and belonged to several Protestant denominations.
77. The EGM also worked among Copts. On its history, see George Swan, *"Lacked Ye Anything?": A Brief Story of the Egypt General Mission* (London: EGM, 1932).
78. Boulos, *European Evangelicals*, 76, note 58; E. Sanders, "The Nile Mission Press," *The Moslem World* 34, no. 3 (July 1944): 209-13. Arthur T. Upson (1874-1958) of the North Africa Mission was the Nile Mission Press superintendent. Although some have described the press as being co-founded by Van Sommer and Upson together, its publications attribute the founding to Van Sommer. George Swan, "Miss Annie Van Sommer," *Blessed Be Egypt* 37, no. 151 (April 1937): 22-24. In 1912, Zwemer moved to Cairo, where he coordinated ecumenical efforts of American and British missionaries' work among Muslims. See Chapter 3.
79. The American Methodist Episcopal Mission began preparations for this new mission in 1907. Its first missionaries were two English women who had been running an independent mission in Algeria since the 1890s, Emily Smith and A. Dora Welch. J. H. C. Purdon, "Record of Operations of the Methodist Episcopal Church in Tunisia," 1920, North Africa Mission Papers (1459-2-2:29), United Methodist Church Archives—General Commission on Archives and History,

Madison, New Jersey (hereafter GCAH); "Algeria," North Africa Conference Handbook, 1939, North Africa Mission Papers (1459-2-2:15), GCAH.

80. The mission was also informally known as the Kurdish Missionary Society. The second issue of its journal called upon readers to support evangelistic work in the neglected area of Kurdistan, saying, "It remains now for the efforts of Christian men and women, filled with the spirit of missionary enterprise, to proclaim to the Mohammedan world the dawn of a brighter empire than that of the Saracen, or Great Mogul, or Tamerlane, or the ruler of the Turk." J. Telleen, "At the Closing Session," *The Kurdistan Missionary* 1, no. 2 (November 1910): 1.

81. Catriona Laing, "A Provocation to Mission: Constance Padwick's Study of Muslim Devotion," *Islam and Christian–Muslim Relations* 24, no. 1 (2013): 31–34; Sharkey, *American Evangelicals*, 93. Zwemer and Gairdner together established the Cairo Study Center for training missionaries to Muslims. Gairdner returned to Egypt in 1911 after an absence for Arabic study, and Padwick arrived there in 1912 and worked with the Nile Mission Press. On Gairdner and Padwick, see Richard Sudworth, *Encountering Islam: Christian–Muslim Relations in the Public Square* (London: SCM Press, 2017), 101, 138–39, 145.

82. See the chapters titled "Stemming the Mohammedan Tide" and "America's Part in Stemming the Mohammedan Tide" in *The Christian Occupation of Africa: The Proceedings of a Conference of Mission Boards Engaged in Work in the Continent of Africa* (New York: Committee of Reference and Counsel of the Foreign Missions Conference of North America, 1917); and Carl Meinhoff, "The Moslem Advance in Africa," in *Islam and Missions: Being Papers Read at the Second Missionary Conference on Behalf of the Mohammedan World at Lucknow, January 23–28, 1911*, ed. E. M. Wherry, S. M. Zwemer, and C. G. Mylrea (New York: Fleming H. Revell, 1911), 76–86.

83. Said, *Orientalism*, 114–15, 158, 174, 256.

84. Christine Leigh Heyrman, *American Apostles: When Evangelicals Entered the World of Islam* (New York: Hill and Wang, 2015), 71–94.

85. Masuzawa, *Invention of World Religions*, 179–206.

86. C. G. Pfander, *The Mizan Ul Haqq; Or, Balance of Truth*, trans. R. H. Weakley (London: Church Missionary House, 1866). Pfander wrote his tract in German, to be translated into Persian and Armenian.

87. Clinton Bennett, "The Legacy of Henry Martyn," *International Bulletin of Missionary Research* 16, no. 1 (January 1992): 10–15; Powell, "Legacy of Henry Martyn."

88. Powell, "Legacy of Henry Martyn"; Henry Martyn, *Controversial Tracts on Christianity and Mohammedanism. By the Late Rev. Henry Martyn, B.D., of St. John's College, Cambridge, and Some of the Most Eminent Writers of Persia*, trans. S. Lee (Cambridge: J. Sith, 1824).

89. Martyn, *Controversial Tracts*, 98, 100.

90. Asma Afsarrudin, *The First Muslims: History and Memory* (London: Oneworld, 2008).

91. Pfander, *Mizan Ul Haqq*, ix–x, 11–22.

92. Ibid., 78–84, 109–110.

93. Ibid., 122.

94. G. H. Rouse, *Tracts for Muhammadans*, 2nd ed. (London and Madras: The Christian Literature Society for India, 1897), v–vi. Rouse was head of the Baptist Mission Press in Calcutta and the translator of the mission's revised Bengali Bible, originally produced by William Carey. An announcement of his death and an obituary appeared in the *Baptist Missionary Society Report* (1909): 13, 97.

95. Islamic tradition holds that Jesus was not crucified but that someone else was crucified in his place and Jesus later died a regular human death.

96. Rouse, *Tracts for Muhammadans*, 137–42.

97. Frank W. Warne, "Methodists and Mohammedanism," *The Epworth Herald* 19, no. 15 (September 5, 1908): 36.

98. Other missionary women, like Fidelia Fiske (1816–1864) in Persia and Sarah Huntington Smith (1802–1836) in Syria, who were among the first to work in Islamic contexts of the Middle East, were recognized and introduced to Protestant readers through their memoirs and biographies. Yet these women engaged mainly with Middle Eastern Christians. See D. T. Smith, *Faith Working by Love: As Exemplified in the Life of Fidelia Fiske* (Boston: Congregational Publication Society, 1868); Edward William Hooker, *Memoir of Mrs. Sarah L. Huntington Smith: Late of the American Mission in Syria* (New York: American Tract Society, 1845).

99. Samuel M. Zwemer, *Islam: A Challenge to Faith* (New York: Student Volunteer Movement, 1907), 2. The book also featured Bishop Valpy French, Cornelius Van Dyck, and Benjamin Labaree.

100. Séverine Gabry-Thienpont and Norig Neveu, "Missions and the Construction of Gender in the Middle East," *Social Sciences and Missions* 34, no. 1–2 (2021): 15.
101. Ibid., 17.
102. Ibid., 15.
103. Joan Scott, "Gender: A Useful Category of Historical Analysis," *American Historical Review* (December 1986): 1056.
104. Ibid. Although the Protestants who are the subject of this study saw sex as a natural, predetermined category and enforced gender binaries, I note with Judith Butler that gender is not "conceived merely as the cultural inscription of meaning on a pre-given sex" but is the "apparatus of production whereby the sexes themselves are established." Judith Butler, *Gender Trouble: Feminism and the Subversion of Identity* (New York: Routledge 1990), 7.
105. Said, *Orientalism*, 41.
106. S. Hale, "Edward Said—Accidental Feminist: Orientalism and Middle East Women's Studies," *Amerasia Journal* 31, no. 1 (2005): 2. Among the many studies on this topic, see Rana Kabbani, *Europe's Myths of Orient* (Bloomington: Indiana University Press, 1986); Reina Lewis, *Gendering Orientalism: Race, Femininity and Representation* (London and New York: Routledge, 1996); Schueller, *U.S. Orientalisms*; Meyda Yeğenoğlu, *Colonial Fantasies: Towards a Feminist Reading of Orientalism* (Cambridge: Cambridge University Press, 1998); Madeleine Dobie, *Foreign Bodies: Gender, Language, and Culture in French Orientalism* (Stanford, CA: Stanford University Press, 2002).
107. Lila Abu-Lughod, *Do Muslim Women Need Saving?* (Cambridge, MA: Harvard University Press, 2013); Maryam Khalid, *Gender, Orientalism, and the "War on Terror": Representation, Discourse, and Intervention in Global Politics* (London and New York: Routledge, 2017). See also Alexis Tan and Anastasia Vishnevskaya, *Stereotypes of Muslim Women in the United States: Media Primes and Consequences* (Lanham: Lexington Books, 2022).
108. Kahf, *Western Representations*, 33; see also pp. 5, 30, 53, 63, 73.
109. Ibid., 158.
110. Sophia Rose Arjana, *Muslims in the Western Imagination* (Oxford: Oxford University Press, 2015), 9, 11.
111. Billie Melman, *Women's Orients: English Women and the Middle East, 1718–1918: Sexuality, Religion and Work* (Ann Arbor: University of Michigan Press, 1992), 7.
112. James A. Tebbe, "Kenneth Cragg in Perspective: A Comparison with Temple Gairdner and Wilfred Cantwell Smith," *International Bulletin of Missionary Research* (January 2002): 16–21.
113. Edward W. Said, *Culture and Imperialism* (New York: Vintage Books, 1993).
114. For example, Amira el-Azhary Sonbol, *Beyond the Exotic: Women's Histories in Islamic Societies* (Syracuse, NY: Syracuse University Press, 2005); Nikki R. Keddie, *Women in the Middle East: Past and Present* (Princeton, NJ: Princeton University Press, 2007).
115. I discuss this topic in Womack, *Protestants, Gender*.
116. On the first attempts of the United States to establish a diplomatic presence in the nineteenth-century Ottoman Empire, see Hans-Lukas Kieser, *Nearest East: American Millennialism and Mission to the Middle East* (Philadelphia: Temple University Press, 2010), 35–37.
117. The creation of women's missionary societies, however, led to new genres of missionary magazines for women and children that featured the writings of women missionaries. For early examples, see Dana L. Robert, *American Women in Mission: A Social History of Their Thought and Practice* (Macon, GA: Mercer University Press, 1997), 143.

2
Gender in Protestant Re-inventions of Islam from the Reformation to the Enlightenment

Echoes of some Reformation Protestant discourses about the Ottoman Turks have resurfaced in American cultural representations of Islam since the eighteenth century. Anglo-Protestants have repeatedly depicted *Muslim men* as tyrants—taking an old theme and recasting it for a new purpose. Yet during the Enlightenment period, Protestants set aside other Reformation-era narratives and re-invented Islam according to shifting western gender norms and rising colonial-imperial aspirations. In this way, neutral and even laudatory views of *Muslim women's* modest clothing that had circulated during the sixteenth century gave way to a new, highly critical discourse of the veil in the eighteenth. To explain the evolution of Protestants' views about Muslims, this chapter considers the centrality of gender in their engagements with Islam from the Reformation to the Enlightenment. Four points are important for understanding the context of Protestant–Muslim encounters at the beginning of this period.

First, sixteenth-century Protestants had little, if any, personal contact with Muslims. Thus, when the Reformers wrote and preached about Islam and about the expansion of Ottoman Turkish rule into southern and eastern Europe, they depended on ideas already in circulation and on reports from the battlefront between the Habsburg and Ottoman Empires.[1] Likewise, for the Protestant public in western Europe and especially in the more remote British Isles, this earliest interaction with Islam was impersonal and limited almost entirely to texts, oral narratives, and printed images, all produced or mediated by Christians. Second, Protestants used both positive and negative images of Islam as weapons to fight theological battles usually directed not against Islam but interestingly against internal, Christian opponents and even to admonish their own flocks. Only in cases in which the Reformers recognized an imminent threat of Ottoman invasion did Islam become the target of their discourse, and even then they concentrated primarily on preparing Christians to stand firm in their faith under Muslim rule.[2]

Third, on a related note, in the early decades of the sixteenth century it was conceivable that much of Christendom would come under Muslim control, raising questions about the survival not only of Protestantism but of European Christianity itself. Fourth, during this period, like other Europeans, the first Protestants treated the word *Turk* as synonymous with *Muslim* and with the other common identifiers at that time: *Mohammedan* and *Saracen*. In addition, they used the term *Moor* in reference to Africans generally but also specifically to designate North African Muslims.

In surveying notions about gender and sexual morality in Protestant images of Islam that set precedents for the modern missionary movement, in this chapter I turn first to the Reformation era in continental Europe, then to early Protestant England, and consider how Protestants adapted and re-invented approaches to Islam that they inherited from the medieval period. Finally, I explore the foundations of British and early American thought about Muslim women in the Enlightenment, when the discourse of the veil—an Orientalist re-invention of Islam—came to dominate Protestant discussions about women in Islam.

Reformation Images of Islam, Gender, and Violence

In their writings about Islam, medieval European Christian men focused mainly on theological disputes and on Muslim men's stereotyped behaviors and sexual practices. The latter discourse built upon negative portrayals of the Prophet Muhammad as "dishonest and insincere as a prophet, as a promoter of violence in order to establish his religion, self-indulgent concerning sexuality, and a Christian heretic and schismatic."[3] These critiques identified Islam as attracting and producing (male) followers for whom violence and licentiousness were innate behavioral traits. In today's terms, these western Christians denounced the "hypermasculinity" of Muslim men to uphold their own theological claims.

When medieval Christian texts spoke about Muslim women, the focus was often on how Muslim men treated them and not on the women's own activities. Thus, we find repeated tropes about Islam being "built upon a foundation of sexual license" and about the religion's expansion "by the sword"—tropes that critiqued male behaviors.[4] According to these texts, military violence generated plunder, slaves, and concubines, making Islam attractive to the Arab men who were Muhammad's first followers. The texts also frequently critiqued Islamic marriage practices—in terms which were then repeated for centuries—for positioning women as servants, for allowing four wives and male-initiated divorce, and for permitting men's sexual relations with slaves.[5] The infrequent and brief attention given to Muslim women themselves, by contrast, was strikingly positive. The escaped captive George of Hungary (1422–1502), for example, described Turkish women as "modest and honorable in contrast to the loose women of Christendom."[6]

The earliest Protestants built upon this gendered rhetoric when engaging with Islam, Muslims, and the material culture of the Ottoman Empire, using their medieval predecessors' work to re-invent Islam for Protestant theological and political purposes.

Critiques of Muslim Sexual Morality

In discussing Ottoman religious practices, social life, and culture, the Reformers sometimes offered positive commentary to reinforce their critiques of European Christianity. For instance, in his preface to George of Hungary's treatise, Luther affirmed the "good customs or good works" of the Turks, like the sharing of bread with those in need; and he complimented the "modesty and simplicity of their food, clothing, dwellings, and everything else, as well as the fasts, prayers, and common gatherings of the people."[7] Yet the Reformers also repeatedly condemned Islam for encouraging sexual immorality, though in this and their claims about Muslim violence the former conflated the nature of Islam with their sense of Muslim dispositions and social norms. In so doing, the Reformers elevated Protestant doctrinal critiques of Islam.

After reading Qur'an 6.101, which responds to Christian beliefs by asking how God could have a son without a female consort, Luther claimed in his loose German translation of Riccoldo of Monte Croce's *Confutatio Alcorani* that this verse's question about sexual behavior demonstrated how Muhammad was consumed by lust.[8] Building on such claims, Luther called the Qur'an Muhammad's "bed of harlotry." Of the prophet he asserted, "Thus, this contemptable filthy fellow boasts that God, that is, the devil, had endowed him with so much physical strength that he could be with as many as 40 women and yet remain unsatisfied."[9] Such comments exaggerated the number of Muhammad's wives and Islamic teachings on polygyny.[10] Luther spread similar misinformation by writing:

> It is customary among the Turks for one man to have ten or twenty wives and to desert or sell any of them he will, so that in Turkey women are held immeasurably cheap and are despised; they are bought and sold like cattle.[11]

In reality, Sunni and Shia religious laws permit men to marry up to four women at one time *if able to provide equitably* for all of them.[12] In an exception, the Prophet Muhammad had ten wives simultaneously after the death of his first wife, Khadijah, with whom he had a monogamous marriage. Whether the Reformers intentionally skewed such information or were themselves misinformed, their writings established a pattern of thought about Islam, gender, and sexuality that unfortunately still exists among Protestants today.

When assessing Islamic polygyny, Theodor Bibliander described it as contradicting the laws of God and violating marriage, "the most sacred institution among human beings." Ignoring the practices of polygyny in the Bible, the Hebrew scholar went on to explain biblical marriage, saying, "The Creator has instituted and consecrated it, so that human kind may live in the legal union of one husband and one wife.... The law of the Turks on polygamy has no justification, it is in contradiction to God's law."[13] Calvin similarly labeled Muhammad "a corruptor of conjugal faithfulness" and portrayed him as succumbing to lust and allowing men "to practice brute licentiousness when they collect wives by buying them."[14] Bullinger emphasized Islam's "shameful treatment of women and girls" and the promise to the faithful (men) of sensual pleasures in heaven, including beautiful maidens. He believed that the Qur'an "destroys marriage with its polygamy and subjects innocent women to the pleasure and whim of men."[15]

Such critiques were, as Katya Vehlow explained, also driven by European men's fascination with "the idea of polygamy and the sexual pleasure that it seemed to offer to Muslim men."[16] The Reformers claimed to defend the status of women and yet did not give substantial attention to the actual Muslim women they presumably wished to protect. Because their knowledge was based mainly on medieval texts and legends, translated or mediated by Christians, and not on personal contact with Muslims, the Reformers contributed little original insight on Islamic gender norms. Indeed, as

Vehlow argued, the medieval Christian writers' fixation on sexual promiscuity led them to misinterpret certain Qur'anic verses, like the instructions in Qur'an 2.223–24 on sexual intercourse after the wife's menstrual cycle. Though these verses resemble the Hebrew Bible's purity laws regarding sex after menstruation, Christians interpreted the Qur'an as alluding to sex postures or to sodomy.[17] To protect innocent ears, the Reformers refrained from mentioning these details and merely condemned the "horrifying impurities" and "vulgar and inappropriate" subjects discussed in the Qur'an.[18] Thus, without opportunity to consult Muslim interpreters, little changed in western Christian commentary on Islam and sexuality from medieval Catholicism to the Protestant Reformation. The Reformers simply recast old views to serve their own ends.

Reformation Commentaries on Islamic Violence and Apocalypticism

In an era which witnessed religiously motivated armed uprisings and brutal fighting between Protestants and Catholics in Europe, it is ironic that Reformation commentaries firmly established European Christian ideas about *Islam* as a religion of the sword. Such beliefs echoed earlier Christian writings on the rise of Islam and the first Arab empire of the seventh century. In addition, some of the Reformers simultaneously condemned the Ottoman military conquests and upheld medieval apocalyptic interpretations of Muslim rule as a God-ordained punishment for Christian sins. The first Protestants who wrote about Islam, however, distanced themselves from the violence they saw as innate in Islam and from the religiously sanctioned military campaigns of their Catholic rivals.[19] Luther characterized Muslims as doing everything "with the sword instead of with miracles."[20] Bullinger likewise critiqued the sword of the "Saracens and the Turks after them" and explained that Muhammad taught his followers to "take the sword into their hand and take all earthly kingdoms into possession."[21]

The Protestant Reformers understood the victory and prosperity of Muslim empires as God's punishment of Christian laxity. Bullinger viewed Ottoman imperial expansion as a sign of evil Christian lives, similar to God's punishment of the Israelites, while he also associated Islam (and Catholicism) with the antichrist.[22] Luther followed medieval eschatology to interpret Islamic armies as a sign of the last days, with Muhammad as a forerunner of the antichrist.[23] Philip Melanchthon (1497–1560), a Lutheran theologian, depicted Islam itself as the antichrist in his apocalyptic commentary on Daniel.[24] Calvin saw the papacy and Islam as holding apocalyptic importance too, depicting them as "two horns of the Antichrist."[25] While Zwingli did not believe that Ottoman expansion signaled the end times, he did assume that the Turks elicited the "vengeance of God."[26]

These early Protestant comments on Islam and violence elucidate two key points. First, following earlier apocalyptic interpretations, the Reformers incorporated Islam into Protestant eschatology, establishing a theological narrative about Islam that still lingers in Evangelical thought today. Second, what the Reformers saw as the clash between the truth of Protestantism and the evil of Islam was also, for them, a contest between men. Protestant men scrutinized Muslim manhood just as they scrutinized Islamic theology. Indeed, their cyclical logic suggested that Muhammad and his followers were prone to take both military violence and sexual pursuits to the extremes. At the same time the Reformers represented Islam as sanctioning and even encouraging these behaviors. Accordingly, their critique was not merely theological but also cultural: they denigrated Muslim men in an attempt to refute Islamic doctrine. Sixteenth-century ideas about Turkish or Arab men being the negative counterimage to European Christian men formed the basis upon which Orientalist and racist notions about the Middle East would develop in the coming centuries.

Muslim Women and Men in Reformation Images

What little the first Protestant theologians had to say about Muslim *women's* lives and behaviors was, by contrast, positive, both because it reinforced their critique of Catholicism and because what they knew about Muslim women matched their own gendered ideas about morality.[27] Luther repeatedly complimented Turkish women's modesty, noting that they veiled their heads and entire bodies. He was particularly impressed with their behavior at religious gatherings where he said they were as reverent as the men, and he regarded their reserve, humility, and devotion as surpassing that of European Christian women.[28] This matched the popular images circulating in sixteenth-century Germany, as Gregory Miller established in his study on German pamphlets of that period. The pamphleteers identified (male) Turks as characteristically lascivious in their practices of both polygyny and homosexuality—the latter accusation being an attempt to emasculate Turkish power. Yet the pamphleteers praised Turkish wives for their "silence, modesty, and obedience,"[29] thus echoing the approval with which George of Hungary and others wrote about Muslim women before the sixteenth century. Such remarks, however, reveal more about these European men's views of *Christian womanhood* than they do about the actual lives of Turkish women.

Positive or non-judgmental portrayals of Turkish women were apparent also in printed images of the Turks circulating in sixteenth-century Europe, as Charlotte Colding Smith's pioneering study confirmed. New print technology enabled much more rapid and inexpensive dissemination of illustrations, enabling northern Europeans with varying degrees of literacy to encounter images of Islam in travel literature, costume books, illustrated accounts of Ottoman battles, and even Bibles. Similar to the ways in which European Christians' writings and preaching recast ideas about Muslims for new purposes, the printing press enabled

> the same images to be reused in many contexts, either in their original form or as a close copy. This made certain images of Ottoman Turks more recognizable to viewers, but again reinforced older images rather than creating new ones from personal experience.[30]

Images of Turkish men in Smith's work reflect the masculinist focus in medieval writings about Islam and accompanying illustrations. Indeed, images of Muslim men had a prominent place in both medieval and Reformation-era printed literature, such as the *Nuremberg Chronicle*'s woodcut depicting the Prophet Muhammad on a throne (published in Latin in 1493 and later in German)[31] and images of Ottoman Muslims featured alongside European Christian rulers in Paolo Giovio's *Vitae Illustrium Virorem*, a volume first published in 1549 featuring the lives and portraits of notable men, including Sultan Suleiman I (circa 1494–1566; Figure 2.1). This masculinist focus continued in religious images of the Reformation. For example, the woodcut of the "Four Horsemen of the Apocalypse" that Lucas Cranach the Elder (1472–1553) designed to illustrate Luther's German Bible featured a Turk as the horseman representing pestilence.[32] Though Cranach's woodcuts did not picture Muslim women as biblical characters, Turkish women did appear in costume books and other illustrated texts showcasing the dress norms of both men and women in different ethnic groups.

Figure 2.1 Ottoman Sultan Suleiman I (1578)
Source: Paulo Giovio, *Novocomensis episcopi Nucerini Vitae illustrium virorum: Tomis duobus comprehensae, & proprijs imaginibus illustratae* (Basel: Petri Pernae typographi, 1578), 177. Courtesy of Special Collections and Archives at Pitts Library, Candler School of Theology, Atlanta.

One such image in Bernard Von Breydenbach's 1486 *Journey to the Holy Land*, the first illustrated work of travel literature documenting the appearance and habits of Muslims, Christians, and Jews, included a group of "Saracens." The men wore turbans, and one of the two women was fully veiled, while the other wore a hat.[33] The illustration depicted the women without conveying any judgment about their clothing. Another reprinted and widely circulated set of travel illustrations, by Nicolas de Nicolay, first published in French in 1567 and then translated into English in 1585 as *The Navigations, Peregrinations and Voyages Made into Turkie*, similarly displayed a variety of Muslim women's dress styles without critiquing them. Based on his visit to Constantinople, Nicolay's costumes included figures of men and women from all walks of life, with costumes specific to each: a female slave in Algiers, the wife of a sultan, a Turkish woman and her maid walking to the public baths. Some wore hats, others had their hair covered with scarves, and still others had their faces completely veiled. The variety in these images was the result of the broad personal contact the artist had with a diversity of Muslims of different social classes and cultural groups all present in Constantinople.[34] From these illustrations and from the positive commentary of Luther and his contemporaries about Muslim women's dress norms, it is apparent that the critique of veiling, which would become so prominent by the nineteenth century, had no place in the sixteenth.

Only a limited number of images featuring Muslim women were circulated in Reformation-era Europe, both because artists lacked access to women in the Ottoman Empire and because of Europeans' more extreme interest in the Turks' military might. Turkish soldiers were the most commonly depicted images of the Ottoman Empire in modern German prints, for example. What stereotypically signaled that the men in the images were Turkish was that their garb included a turban and scimitar, sometimes along with other symbols of warfare: bows and arrows, battle horses, crescent flags, and the hat (or *bork*) worn by the janissaries, the elite Ottoman military corps. As the threat of Ottoman expansion grew in German-speaking areas, images rather than merely text descriptions of Turks appeared in pamphlets and broadsheets, visually reinforcing prejudices of Turks as violent and bloodthirsty soldiers. As Smith explained:

> The German representation of the Turkish soldier highlighted the horror and catastrophe in gory printed images depicting pillaged villages, burned cities, adults chained and sold as slaves, garroted babies and human remains displayed on spears and paraded as proof of military might. The encroaching threat of those perceived as the "infidel" Turk made the Ottoman warrior a monstrous devil, and such images by Northern European artists exhibited awe, fear, excitement and loathing.[35]

Nonetheless, other representations showed Turks as worthy opponents without emphasizing such horrific violence. Genealogies of Ottoman rulers, in particular, commemorated "the power, glory and victories of previous and current eras" rather than presenting the Ottoman sultans as enemies of Christendom.[36] Still other images placed Turks alongside other Muslim men, as cartographer Sebastian Münster (1488–1552) did in his 1550 *Cosmographiae Universalis*. The volume's title page included four prominent woodcut images labeled *Turk*, *Sufi*, *Tartar*, and *Sultan*. Interestingly, none

Figure 2.2 Title page of *Cosmographiae Universalis* (1550)
Source: Sebastian Münster, *Cosmographiae Universalis* (Basel: Petri, 1550), title page. Courtesy of Special Collections and Archives at Pitts Library, Candler School of Theology, Atlanta.

of these figures wore the typical turban, but all carried weapons and shields (Figure 2.2).

While the violent images reinforced ideas about the Muslim Turk as Europe's counterimage and reflected fears of Ottoman expansion, the images of Turkish military achievements revealed European awe in the face of Ottoman power and the reality that the Habsburg Empire was in the weaker position. As this geopolitical power balance shifted in the coming centuries, so too would Protestants' conceptions of Muslim women.

Post-Reformation England's Theological Pronouncements and Cultural Engagement with Islam

Although English Protestants paid less attention to the Turks in their preaching and theological writing than did Luther or the Swiss Reformers, as the sixteenth century progressed Protestant leaders in the British Isles increasingly re-invented Islam for their constituents. They not only produced new English texts and translations of continental Protestant writings on Islam for a wider readership, but through their sermons they also brought discourses about the Turks to illiterate churchgoers. Outside the theological arena, other Britons contributed personal accounts of their encounters with Muslims as merchants, mariners, diplomats, and captives of North African corsairs (pirates or privateers). The increasing contact between the British Isles and the Ottoman Empire also generated cultural engagement with Islam, as seen in English Renaissance literature and plays performed on the London stage. And as a result of trade agreements that Elizabeth I (r. 1558–1603) undertook with the Ottoman sultans, luxury Ottoman goods such as coffee and carpets became permanently incorporated into English life and culture.[37]

Within this context, what ideas did English Protestant scholars, clergy, playwrights, and other public figures convey about the gender norms in Islam in the sixteenth and seventeenth centuries? The writings of Protestant men in England differed little from their predecessors' writings in Germany and Switzerland. Indeed, existing European discourses that equated Muslim masculinity with horrific warfare and violence, and that saw Islamic practices of polygyny as confirming Muslim men's irrepressible lust, strongly influenced the English. Like the continental Reformers, English men fixated on Muslim men's activities, but they gave little attention to the actual situations of Muslim women in Islamic societies. Nevertheless, gender broadly remains a salient lens through which to consider how English Protestants transmitted images of Muslim men because their concerns about the Turks most often focused on the lures and dangers that these formidable foes posed for English men.

English Theology and Cultural Critique of Islam

Until large numbers of Britons began making personal contact with Turks through travel and commerce, the textual information available to English Protestant readers about Islam came to them mainly by way of continental European publications or through English scholarship that itself relied on German, French, and Latin texts.[38] Among those who conveyed such European thought in English was the polemicist John Foxe, who fled to the Continent during Mary Tudor's reign and spent most of his exile, from 1555 to 1559, among Calvinists in Basel, Switzerland, working as a proofreader for the Protestant printer Johannes Oporinus (1507–1568). Foxe's engagement with continental writings and his correspondence with Heinrich Bullinger made him conversant with Reformed thought and shaped his perception of the Turkish threat. Two Latin martyrologies which Foxe published in Basel formed the basis of his immensely influential text, *Actes and Monuments*, published in England in 1563 after Elizabeth's ascension to the throne.[39] The book, popularly known as "The Book of Martyrs," enjoyed "the status of the second most popular book following the Bible" in Elizabethan England and went through three more editions during Foxe's lifetime.[40] The second edition was revised for a broader audience, and this time it included the first English history of the Ottoman Empire, in a section known as *The Turkes storye*. Read by scholars and clergyman, *Actes and Monuments* was also read aloud to the illiterate, so popular was it. Thus, along with its lasting influence in subsequent British works, *The Turkes storye* was among the first Reformation-era texts in English to influence the broader public's view of Islam.[41]

With its goal to vindicate Protestantism, Foxe's work was, according to historian Christopher Toenjes, the most aggressive anti-Muslim text in sixteenth-century England and did not reflect the views of all his contemporaries. Missing, for example, were the aforementioned positive assessments of Turkish culture and Muslim women's modesty that the Reformers used to shame Catholics.[42] Missing, as well, were the perspectives of English diplomats and merchants who cultivated cordial trading relationships with Muslims and, as a result of personal contact, transmitted more humanizing portraits of Muslim society.[43] Nevertheless, this single text and its extremely negative judgments of Islam had a tremendous influence on English audiences through its multiple printings, public readings, and other texts that cited Foxe.

In the second half of the sixteenth century, when English ships had frequent encounters with North African corsairs,[44] Foxe highlighted the misery of captured Christians in servitude to the Turks (without, however, showing similar concern for people whom Europeans captured and enslaved).[45] He played on the widespread notion of the Ottoman sultan as a slave master, whose subjects were all essentially enslaved.[46] Foxe's concern (and that of many other English clergy and theologians after him in the early seventeenth century when hundreds of ships were being taken by North Africans) was the pressure captives felt to convert to Islam, or "turn Turke."[47] Foxe lamented that the misery of these captives included their physical subjugation and their apostasy from Christianity.[48] He drew from the captivity narratives produced on the Continent, and when considering other forms of Muslim violence, he echoed existing images of the turbaned Turkish soldier, describing Islam as a menace and claiming that Muhammad spread his teachings by force of the sword.[49]

The narrative of Ottoman cruelty in battle in *The Turkes storye* included the slaughter and rape of Christians,[50] thus tying together military and sexual violence and emphasizing European presumptions about the Turks' libidinous nature. Additionally, for Foxe, the unbridled Turkish (male) sexual appetite was an affront to Christian concepts of marriage because it led to polygyny.[51] Beyond the battlefield, Foxe highlighted such ideas in an account of a Christian virgin who was martyred for resisting the advances of Sultan Mehmed II, who desired her as his concubine. As Toenjes explained Foxe's claim, "The young maiden was the victim of the Sultan's bestial and carnal desires. Because the followers of Muhammad were associated with every possible venereal vice, simply using the adjective 'Turkish' automatically evoked images of this kind of depravity in the mind's eye of the reader."[52] Thus, like other Protestant polemicists, Foxe made references to Turkish culture and Muslim social behavior to critique Islam as a false religious tradition.

English Protestant Worldviews in the Theater and Pulpit

Elizabethan theater similarly influenced English conceptions of two forms of Turkish violence: the public and uncontrolled brutality of the battlefield and the sexual oppression that occurred in private spaces behind the sultan's palace walls or in Muslim harems. With regard to military violence, in two of the most closely studied plays featuring Muslim characters, Christopher Marlowe's Tamburlaine and William Shakespeare's Othello both led armies against the Turks, Christendom's ultimate enemies.[53] Warning against the Ottoman menace and the dangers of conversion to Islam, in *Othello* and *Tamburlaine the Great, Parts I and II*, the main characters themselves end up embodying the stereotypical features of the Turk, although the historical Tamerlane was not an Ottoman and Othello was North African. These characterizations included "aggression, lust, suspicion, murderous conspiracy, sudden cruelty masquerading as justice, merciless violence rather than 'Christian charity,' wrathful vengeance instead of turning the other cheek."[54] Of his own Christian soldiers involved in a drunken brawl, Othello asks early in the play:

> Are we turn'd Turks, and to ourselves do that
> Which heaven hath forbid the Ottomites? (2.3.169–70).[55]

Yet by the play's conclusion even the "noble Moor," Othello, exhibits these aggressive qualities, by murdering his wife, Desdemona, in a jealous rage and returning to "the spiritual condition of reprobation that was identified with the 'pagan' Moors and the 'infidel' Turks."[56] In addition, Othello's epileptic seizures—understood as the physical manifestation of his devilish transformation—recall the apocryphal legend, widely disseminated in Europe, that the Prophet Muhammad was epileptic, thus linking Othello to Islam's founder (4.1.60). In the end, explained English literature scholar Daniel Vitkus:

> Shakespeare's tragic hero is a Moorish warrior whose public militarism becomes, in the privacy of his bedroom, a version of the sultan's overprotective absolutism in his imperial harem. By the time Othello murders Desdemona, he has converted to erotic, Islamic evil and conformed to the European stereotype of an irascible, libidinous Muslim.[57]

Presumptions about the sexual excesses of Turks (as representative Muslim men) are apparent elsewhere in Shakespeare. *King Lear*'s Edgar boasts in one scene, for instance, that he had "in women out-paramoured the Turk" (3.4.92), this time referring to tales about the Ottoman sultan and others in the Muslim ruling classes whom the English thought to be wholly promiscuous.[58] Muslims also appear in other, lesser known, plays with Turkish characters at the center. In addition to *Othello*, Vitkus named fifteen such English plays written between 1588, when Marlowe completed the second part of *Tamburlaine*, and 1630.[59] Muslim female characters appear in some of these, although they do not conform to a particular European trope about Turks in the same way that the Muslim male characters do. Rather, following English expectations about femininity, Muslim women on the stage might be virtuous, like Donusa in *The Renegado* (1630), who converts to Christianity after marrying a Venetian Christian. Or, on the other hand, Muslim women might be essentially evil, like the temptress Voada in *A Christian Turned Turk* (1612), who ultimately brings the protagonist John Ward "to his conversion and ruin."[60]

In most cases, Muslim women characters—like those in *Tamburlaine*, where most of the cast is at least nominally Muslim—appeared as "trophies and accessories to men and rarely budge from rather wooden roles." These suppressed roles did not reflect an English understanding of different norms for women in Muslim society, however; and apart from their religious identity, the Muslim women portrayed on the English stage acted in ways that European women characters also acted in plays and other literature.[61] Indeed, in the first half of the seventeenth century there was no unified model of the Muslim woman in western literature or theology, although seeds were planted by the end of the century that would lead to the Orientalist depictions of a later era. Neither did English writers make a firm distinction between Muslim and Christian women. Rather, within the "patriarchal modes of control" operating throughout Europe and the Mediterranean during the Renaissance period, women's bodies—regardless of religious identity— were like exchangeable commodities.[62] Late sixteenth- and seventeenth-century English men portrayed Christian and Muslim women similarly but considered Muslim men—with their purportedly innate sexual and military excesses—as the true representatives of Islam.

During the reigns of James I (1603–1625) and Charles I (1625–1649), anxieties about the Turks led Protestant leaders to condemn "renegades"— those British men who traveled to Turkey, the Levant, and North Africa as merchants or sailors and were lured by Ottoman wealth to "turn Turk" or who were captured and enslaved but were later granted freedom after converting to Islam. The number of such converts during the seventeenth century remains unclear, but Britons at the time believed that apostasy to Islam was a frequent occurrence. Certainly more Europeans converted to Islam than Muslims converted to Christianity. Thus, as Nabil Matar claimed, between 1558 and 1685, "Aware that the attraction of the Ottoman Empire sometimes proved irresistible to their compatriots, Britons tried to undermine this attraction in three areas of writing and activity: theological polemic, drama and evangelism."[63] In an imaginative field of action like the stage, such undermining entailed Muslims in the end converting to Christianity or suffering some form of ultimate punishment, as did also the renegades in these plays. Similarly, Matar described the pulpit as an imaginatively controlled environment in which apostates and Saracens alike could be condemned so that in the audience's perception the Christians won every time.[64] These accounts were far from the truth, for sermons also showed the anxieties of preachers who faced returned renegades in their congregations whose souls they felt were in danger. The uneasy rhetoric surrounding these renegades' circumcision (a requirement when converting to Islam) also disclosed that the primary concern was the loss of Christian *men*.[65]

Preachers and theologians interpreted the physical sign of rejecting Jesus Christ by the blood of circumcision as a return to Mosaic law,[66] and their discourses on this subject also reinforced English impressions of the sexual excess of Muslim men, "the reduction of the phallus signifying the need to curtail raging lust."[67] Thus, in his study of the Turk in English theater, Vitkus argued that during Othello's suicide scene, the audience would have understood the circular motion of his blade as an allusion to circumcision. It was an indication that the jealous, murderous Moor had either turned Turk or reverted to his original Islamic faith.[68] Othello's monologue suggests as much, for as he stabs himself he indicates that he is re-enacting his previous killing of a "malignant and turban'd Turk," recalling a "circumcised dog" he once took by the throat and smote in Aleppo (5.2.404–7).[69] Thus, after Othello murders Desdemona for suspected adultery:

> His identity as "the noble Moor of Venice" dissolves as he reverts to the identity of the black devil and exhibits the worst features of the stereotypical "cruel Moore" or Turk—jealousy, frustrated lust, violence, mercilessness, faithlessness, lawlessness, despair.[70]

Othello recognizes that unless he repents or turns back to God, he is "damn'd beneath all depth in hell" (5.2.164), and then he damns himself again by "killing the Turk he has become."[71] That the play called Othello a Black Moor and that White English actors in blackface portrayed him on the London stage signaled a western pattern of racializing Islam that would become more prominent in the colonial-imperial era.[72]

British–Ottoman Contact in the Seventeenth Century

Contact between the British and Ottomans increased so exponentially over the course of the seventeenth century, largely due to collaborations in trade, that by 1685 Islam had "left its mark on Britain in a way that was unparalleled by any other non-Christian civilization which Britons encountered."[73] Although, as Matar explained, widespread feelings of "philo-Islamism" never developed in Britain,[74] the sheer frequency of personal encounters between Britons and Muslims, and the growing familiarity of English people with continental scholars' writings on Islam, made a mark on English Protestant theology and scholarship, as well as on wider British culture.

For one thing, British–Ottoman encounters generated more firsthand facts about Islam for English-speaking audiences. For another, although many of the negative ideas that John Foxe had transmitted in the Elizabethan period persisted over the next century, other English scholarship was not so decidedly hostile toward the Turks. As an example, while the first English book that focused specifically on Ottoman history, Richard Knolles' *The General Historie of the Turkes* (1603), described the Qur'an as a "fear-inducing chronicle . . . filled with accounts of atrocities, rape, pillage, and torture," it also recognized positive features, like "Turkish determination, courage, and frugality."[75] This signaled the awe and reverence many Europeans felt in the face of Ottoman power.

That British scholars and clergy were becoming more conversant with continental European thought on Islam is apparent in the number of texts translated into English in the seventeenth century, during which more thorough study of Arabic was beginning at English universities and chairs of Arabic were established at Cambridge (1632) and Oxford (1636). Prior to this time, scholars who studied Islam and Arabic had access to few manuscripts.[76] In 1650, however, Edward Pococke, the first chair of Arabic at Oxford University, published his impressions of Islamic religion and history in *Specimen historiae Arabum*, a revolutionary text for Arabic studies in England.[77] Pococke capitalized on knowledge gained while serving as a chaplain for the Levant Company, and although his study was motivated by concern for propagating the Protestant faith, his account of the origins of Islam is recognized as being "largely impartial and well-documented."[78] The Qur'an, available previously in Latin and German, was translated into English by Alexander Ross in 1649, although the more precise translation that George Sale completed in 1734 would become the preferred version.[79]

This more accurate and plentiful information—for example, specifying that Muslim men can marry up to four wives rather than an unlimited number—did not necessarily result in more favorable theological treatments of Islam, although authors like John Bunyan (1628–1688) and Henry Stubbe (1632–1676) took appreciative approaches. Bunyan, a Puritan preacher, modeled toleration by asking whether Christians alone knew the right way to heaven or should be considered blessed in comparison to the many others in the world; and Stubbe, who studied with Pococke and worked at Oxford's

Bodleian Library, actually sought to vindicate Islam, calling Muhammad a great lawgiver and praising Muslims' devotion. Stubbe also compared Islamic marriage customs to biblical polygyny.[80] Thus, even though Stubbe was an outlier, his example indicates that British Protestant discourses about Islam have never been uniform, and some displayed genuine interest in and admiration for the tradition.

English preachers' rhetoric in the seventeenth century, however, often echoed Luther's 1529 injunction in "On War Against the Turk" that Christ would bring down the last judgment against both the Turks and the pope.[81] Around the year 1670, Isaac Barrow's "Of the Impiety and Imposture of Paganism and Mahometanism" was among those widely circulated sermons that recycled negative judgments about Islam. Several decades later, Humphrey Prideaux (1648–1724) took up the same theme in *The True Nature of Imposture Fully Displayed in the Life of Mahomet* (1697). English Protestants also adapted the arguments that the Reformers used to defame their internal religious rivals by linking them with Muslims. Anglicans did so when they applied such critiques to Unitarians, whose theology resembled Islam's committed monotheism. This was the primary purpose of Prideaux's work.[82]

As cultural historian Anders Ingram's study on English ballads during the 1683 Ottoman siege of Vienna demonstrated, images of the Turks were also frequently put to use in religiously inflected internal political debates. In ballads produced after the Habsburg Empire routed the Turks in Vienna, English Whigs and Tories—two opposing political parties—used this celebratory occasion to advance their positions on the succession crisis that began in the late 1670s. The Whigs opposed the succession of James, Duke of York, who was heir to Charles II (r. 1660–1685), and the Tories (also known as royalists) upheld King Charles' right to choose his successor.[83] Their politicized ballads resembled seventeenth-century accusations against those renegades who had "turned Turk," implying "faithless and treacherous behavior" if not actual conversions to Islam.[84] One Tory ballad titled "Vienna's Triumph" (1683) described the Whigs thus:

> To the Turks they no Martyrs
> but Converts would be,
> But in time we may see
> Them all dye by the Tree.[85]

The imagery in these ballads also reflected the high level of cultural contact and economic exchange occurring between Britons and Ottomans. Another Tory ballad, for instance, pitted royalist wine against Whiggish beer (usually "small beer," containing a low percentage of alcohol).[86] It critiqued the Whigs first by playing on the idea of Islam's prohibition of wine and then by referring to Turkish coffee:

> MAHOMET was a sober Dog,
> A Small Beer drouzy senseless [rogue] . . .
> Weak Coffee can't keep its ground
> Against the force of Claret . . .[87]

The final line above refers to a type of wine, indicating that the victorious European forces who broke the siege of Vienna drank royalist wine, while the Turks drank weak coffee and Muhammad drank Whiggish "small beer."[88]

This language reveals how frequently images of Muslims appeared in common English discourse. It also reflects the growing British–Ottoman cultural contact facilitated through the Levant Company, which introduced goods like coffee from the Ottoman realms.[89] Some Protestants denounced coffee's physiological effects and, seeing it as contrary to Protestant values, identified it as "Satan's drink, concocted with the Turk's assistance to destroy Christendom." Nevertheless, along with other commodities like sugar supplied through eastern trade routes, coffee quickly became popular in London in the second half of the seventeenth century.[90] It was therefore economic ties with the Ottomans, and the diplomatic efforts made to secure this trade relationship, that defined British–Muslim contact between 1558 and 1685.

Despite the attention the British gave to news from the Habsburg–Ottoman battlefront, their early imperial ambitions were largely commercial. The British did not engage militarily against the Ottomans, and only in the late seventeenth century did its naval fleet grow strong enough to enforce the treaties it made with the North African regencies to protect British vessels from piracy. The first British victory against Tangier in 1680 prompted a shift whereby Britons no longer saw Muslims as being "undefeatable adversaries." By the eighteenth century, Matar explained, the admiration and awe with which the British had viewed the Ottoman sultans and Islamic civilization was giving way to a new confidence in British power.[91]

In continental Europe, changes were underway as well. The 1683 siege of Vienna was the first in a series of military defeats the Ottoman Empire suffered during this period, ending with the Treaty of Karlowitz in 1699 and its loss of Hungary and other regions on the frontier.[92] Even though the Ottomans regained some of that territory in the subsequent decades, this unprecedented defeat was a turning point that shifted European Christians' demeanor toward Islam.

Enlightenment Orientalism in Britain and North America

In the wake of Said's *Orientalism*, some scholars sought to uncover the roots of European Orientalist thought in medieval or early modern Europe. They suggested that the phenomenon Said defined as a post-Enlightenment "Western style for dominating, restructuring, and having authority over the Orient" was operative in an earlier period.[93] Yet most scholars now agree, especially when it comes to the British Protestant context, that Orientalism, as Said described it,[94] came into full force only in the eighteenth century with new developments in scholarship and the European colonial-imperial enterprise.[95] In fact, the western vision of the world as divided into Orient and Occident did not exist prior to the eighteenth century. Originally, academic Orientalism—the formal field of study focusing on Islam and Middle Eastern cultures and languages from which Said coined the broader concept of Orientalism[96]—was an Enlightenment activity. It had roots in the seventeenth-century establishment of Arabic chairs at European universities but took on a distinct form in eighteenth-century Great Britain in response to people's increased travel to the Middle East and access to European texts on Islam and Arabic.[97]

Further, as Vitkus explained, "Before the latter half of the seventeenth century, England's 'colonial' discourse was merely the premature articulation of a third-rank power."[98] The British had not yet gained the economic or military might to build an empire (in comparison to Spain and Portugal), and indeed during the sixteenth and seventeenth centuries both Britons who traveled in the Mediterranean and residents in the British Isles alike recognized their political insignificance in the shadow of Ottoman power. The British only developed a theory of empire at the beginning of the eighteenth century,[99] and although they may have critiqued Islam and the Turks before that period, they "did not express either the authority of possessiveness or the security of domination," orientations that would be central to the birth of Orientalism.[100] Instead, Britain's inferiority complex generated an "imperial envy."[101] Incapable of conquest in the Mediterranean, the British eventually developed a commercial empire built on naval power and wealth gained through exploitation of the resources of the New World and other commodities gained through trade across Asia.[102]

This commercial and naval strength transformed Britons' views of the Ottoman Empire in the eighteenth and nineteenth centuries as they recognized themselves as equal or even superior to it in power. Until that point, however, we cannot speak about British Protestant Orientalism because Orientalist discourse presupposes a position of power. Protestant critiques of Islam, therefore, carried more intrinsic weight after the eighteenth century when backed by political and military force. One of the key re-inventions of Islam in this period—the discourse of the veil—is best understood in the context of imperialism.

Although some scholars, like Matar, have implied that Britain's imperial ascendancy in the eighteenth and nineteenth centuries put it in a position of superiority that the Turks themselves recognized,[103] I instead emphasize the Orientalist imaginings of mastery over the "Near Orient," a mastery that European nations attempted but never actually realized in the late Ottoman period. Napoleon's ill-fated invasion of Egypt in 1798 merely established the possibility and desire for colonization of Ottoman realms. As for Protestant powers, even in the high imperial era of the late nineteenth century, the only Ottoman principality Britain managed to take was Egypt, which it occupied in 1882 and administered through a semi-colonial government that remained nominally under the Ottoman umbrella. Of the Ottoman Empire's central lands, Anatolia remained independent, and the Arab Levant was not colonized until the aftermath of World War I, when the empire dissolved.[104]

Like Said's work, my discussion of British and American Protestant Orientalism in this section is limited to images of Arab, Turkish, and Persian cultures of the Middle East and North Africa. These were the Islamic societies of concern for British scholars and colonial administrators in the eighteenth and first half of the nineteenth century, apart from those in South Asia. Likewise, Anglo-Protestants in colonial America and the early United States were introduced to Islam primarily through discourses about the Ottoman Empire and North Africa. Only in this period did images of Muslim women as passive victims of oppression materialize fully, images predicated on existing notions about Muslim men's sexual excess, aggression, and drive to spread Islam by the sword. In the process, the discourse of the veil took hold—just as Protestant women began re-inventing Orientalist comparisons for their own objectives.

The Sword and the Veil in Anglophone Protestant Orientalism

By the early eighteenth century, British scholars had begun laying the foundations for a more informed understanding of Islam, and by mid-century the field of study known as Orientalism was established in Britain.[105] At this point, British Protestant scholarly writing on Islam underwent a change. As Matar explained, "the works that were published about Islam toward the end of the seventeenth century and in the eighteenth century treated it not as a dynamic force but as a historical theology, not as a civilization, but as a monotheism that was misguided in its prophecy." British writers no longer engaged Islam as a living culture, but rather as

> a creed to be studied and documented. Orientalists such as Simon Ockley, George Sale, Edward Pococke the Younger and others focused on Arabic translations, textual editions and linguistic history: their interest was in Islam as a religious tradition of the past and in Arabic as a "dead" language.[106]

In contrast to the aforementioned illustrations of the population in Constantinople by Nicolas de Nicolay and in contrast to travel accounts, this formalized Orientalist scholarship showed an indifference to the actual people of Islam.[107] As Islam became the subject of academic study, a western elitist and patriarchal understanding of religion predominated, including a focus on texts instead of practices. Key texts in this period included *History of the Saracens* (1718) by the aforementioned Ockley (1678–1720), professor of Arabic at Cambridge University and the first to attempt a comprehensive history of the Arabs in English. In 1731, William Hinchcliffe translated Henri de Boulainvillier's popular *La vie de Mahomet* into English; and in 1732, George Sale (d. 1736) produced the first accurate English translation of the Qur'an.[108] Another notable work of scholarship was Edward Gibbon's six volume *The History of the Decline and Fall of the Roman Empire* (published between 1776–1788). Gibbon (1737–1794) was one of the few English scholars before the nineteenth century to offer a comparatively favorable view of Islam, describing Muhammad as a "good, unexceptional man." Gibbon went on to contend, however, that unfortunately the prophet of Islam "became an ambitious politician given to fraud, fanaticism, and cruelty."[109] Further, his work made apparent the growing Protestant attention to perceived racial characteristics and imperial Britain's sense of cultural superiority when it described the Qur'an as "most powerfully addressed to a devout Arabian, whose mind is attuned to faith and rapture; whose ear is delighted by the music of sounds; and whose ignorance is incapable of comparing the productions of human genius."[110]

Joseph White (circa 1746–1814), who delivered the Bampton lectures on Islam and Christianity at Oxford in 1784, similarly recognized Muhammad's positive qualities but also critiqued him, calling him "a political-military genius, talented, possessed of a great mind, skilled at overcoming adversity, yet driven by lust and greed."[111] Notably, Gibbon and White recognized Muhammad's admirable attributes alongside their derogatory comments. In another strain of Orientalist scholarship, Enlightenment political thinkers in both Europe and North America used conceptions of Islamic government in their reflections on political philosophy and spilled much ink on "Turkish despotism."[112] American revolutionaries took up this line of thought when they compared King George with both the Prophet Muhammad and the Ottoman sultan, representing all three as despotic tyrants who imposed their will and their religion by force and who denied their subjects freedom.[113] Positive images of Islam could also be used to make political arguments, however. Humberto Garcia's *Islam and the English Enlightenment* explored, for example, the writings of radical Protestants in eighteenth-century England who idealized Islamic republicanism, "in which the Prophet Muhammad, the wise legislator, restored constitutional rule" in contrast to the way in which Britain implemented democracy at home and in its colonies.[114]

While Garcia pointed to the varieties of Protestant engagements with Islam in the Enlightenment, such ideas were outside of mainstream Protestant thought. Instead, Protestant theologians, clergy, and popular writers were more likely to associate Islam with political tyranny, with the threat of captivity by North African pirates, and with the harem (or seraglio), understood as a related form of captivity and servitude. *Harem* is an Arabic word; but its first citation in the *Oxford English Dictionary* came as early as 1634, and the term's meaning by the colonial period was derived "more from European usage than from its Arabic roots."[115] The term *seraglio* is derived by way of Italian from the Turkish word for palace (*saray*), usually denoting the Ottoman court, where Europeans believed the sultan kept his wives and numerous concubines imprisoned to indulge his sexual appetite. More generally, the term referred to the confinement of women in any Muslim home, a custom most often practiced by wealthier families. As Mohja Kahf argued in *Western Representations of the Muslim Woman*, with some groundwork laid in European literary works of the late seventeenth century, by the mid-nineteenth century the variety of historical prototypes for Muslim women was "reduced to a single harem woman who combines the most rigidly controlling mythic elements of 'Orient' and Occident: submissive erotic willingness and domesticated female numinosity."[116]

In plays and literature, even by the eighteenth century the focus had already expanded beyond depicting exclusively aggressive and tyrannical Muslim men, who might seek to imprison or control their wives' sexuality (like Othello does to Desdemona). Instead, the Muslim woman as a victim of oppression became the subject of Enlightenment-era writing. Kahf explained, "If European culture in the seventeenth century discovered the seraglio or harem and located the Muslim woman in it, the Enlightenment declared her unhappy there."[117] In this same period, the veil came to symbolize the harem—an extension of the Muslim man's power over the female body when women ventured from home fully covered. Commenting on the assumed association between "the Orient and the freedom of licentious sex" based on such clichéd images of harems and princesses, as well as of "slaves, veils, dancing girls and boys, sherbets, ointments, and so on," Said contended that in the western male Orientalist gaze the world of Islam also became "a place where one could look for sexual experience unobtainable in Europe."[118]

The Enlightenment critique of the old order opened opportunities to approach Islam in a new way—in political thought, as described above, but also in debates about the place of women in western societies. Concurrent with the development of Orientalism as an academic discipline, the notion emerged between 1760 and 1820 of the ideal European woman having two sets of virtues: passive virtues, like modesty and "obedience to male authority," and active "domestic virtues of the competent housewife." In this context, "The Muslim woman and the imagined harem in which she was now definitively enclosed serve as a negative counterimage for the ideal Western female in the home."[119] This newer image joined the existing view that Islamic masculinity (as violent and licentious) was the polar opposite of the ideal western Protestant masculinity (as rational, disciplined, and self-controlled).[120] In addition to enhancing discourses of European superiority that legitimized colonialism, British (and later American) writers used the discourse of the veiled and oppressed Muslim woman to uphold their own ideals about Protestant womanhood.

This brings us to one final transformation in British Protestant Orientalist writing in the eighteenth century: a select few women began contributing to these discourses as recognized authors, paving the way for the much larger group of missionary women writing on Islam in the nineteenth and early twentieth centuries that we shall encounter in subsequent chapters. One pioneer of this new "female genre" was Lady Mary Wortley Montagu (1689–1762), wife of the English ambassador to the Ottoman Empire. The letters she sent home after traveling to Constantinople in 1717 were circulated across Europe and then published in 1763. Lady Mary's letters both defended the upper-class Islamic culture that she experienced in Turkey and critiqued early eighteenth-century English society, which she believed denied women recognition as rational beings.[121]

Lady Mary learned Turkish and tried out the dress styles of elite Ottoman women. The latter perhaps surprisingly led her to conclude that Turkish women had more liberty (including sexual freedom) than English women. She also suggested that when completely veiled, Turkish women could more easily pursue "the same kinds of liaisons as Englishwomen pursue but with more security from men's prying."[122] The veil, however, was not the defining symbol through which Lady Mary interpreted the lives of Muslim women, nor was it an object of voyeuristic fantasy as it was for some of her male contemporaries. She demystified the harem, as well, by arguing that few Muslim men kept four wives and by noting that if Turks were unfaithful in marriage, as she indicated English men tended to be, they would at least keep their mistresses privately in a separate house. To Lady Mary, the sultan's seraglio was comparable to any European court, but the wealthy Turkish women actually achieved more financial independence than their British counterparts. With a hint of envy, she explained that these women had their own money, which they took with them upon divorce.[123]

Lady Mary not only observed Ottoman women's lives but also commented on how they responded to her presence among them. She recounted that upon her visit to a bathhouse, she found that Turkish women had reversed the typical western narrative about Muslims, for they saw her as *imprisoned* in her skirts and stays, writing "they believed I was so locked up in that machine that it was not in my power to open it, which contrivance they attributed to my husband."[124] Contrary, then, to many writers of her time, Lady Mary did not present the harem, the veil, or the Muslim woman as a negative model to defend the superior place of Christian women in European society.[125] Neither, however, did her published letters change the prominent image in English society of the female Muslim victim, whose veil signified her enslavement in the harem and her need for rescue.[126]

As the idea of harem oppression became entrenched in late eighteenth-century British thought, it was put to a different use by female advocates for White Christian women's rights, like the English writer Mary Wollstonecraft (1759–1797), who used the analogy of the harem "to expose the injustice of Western men's treatment of Western women."[127] Rather than depicting the Muslim harem as the counterimage to the virtuous Protestant household, she equated the two, arguing that western women were essentially harem slaves confined within a private feminine sphere. Thus Wollstonecraft, like other Protestant writers before her, employed cultural representations of Islam to engage in a debate internal to her own society.

In Britain's American colonies and in the young United States, texts like Wollstonecraft's and works of Orientalist scholarship were available to a few; but for the general population, British and other European narratives of enslavement by Barbary pirates of the North African coast were extremely influential.[128] These spurred on a wildly popular and sensationalized genre of Anglo-American captivity writing that became prominent in the years leading up to and during the wars between the United States and Tripoli (Libya) from 1801 to 1805.[129] Drawing from such sensationalized historical narratives about Muslims, Anglo-Americans used characterizations of both the veil and the sword of Islam to shape the political direction of their new society and to set the parameters for Protestant masculinity and femininity.

Supporters of the American Revolution employed discourses about Muslim tyranny, for example, to defend their political ideals. Baptist leader John Leland (1754–1841) argued in 1791 against established religion, like that of England, by referencing Islamic states, saying "Mahomet called in the use of law and sword to convert people to his religion; but Jesus did not, does not."[130] Similarly, Jonathan Edwards (1703–1758) held that Islam was propagated by the sword, while Christianity spread through reason. He also believed that Islam brought debauchery and corruption and that it had spread by playing to men's "luxurious and sensual disposition."[131] In this regard, Protestant leaders also critiqued what they understood as the Islamic vision of a heaven full of sensual pleasures. John Walton (1694–1764), another Baptist leader, considered the belief that Muslims (meaning men) "should carnally enjoy beautiful Women in Heaven" to be a ridiculous idea that nevertheless aided the propagation of Islam. New Jersey revivalist Gilbert Tennent (1703–1764), in a sermon published in 1744, used comparable references to Muslim doctrines about "eternal Pleasures . . . as the reward of good works" against the works-righteousness orientations of his Christian anti-revivalist opponents.[132]

Such ideas about Islam's expansion through worldly motivations (promises of sensual pleasures or threats of death) rather than spiritual means (gospel preaching and heartfelt conversion) endured in the early American republic. When taking up this topic in the nineteenth century, one of the first female writers on the subject of world religions, Hannah Adams (1755–1831), argued in her *Dictionary of All Religions and Religious Denominations* (1817) that "Mohammed contrived by the permission of polygamy and concubinage to make his creed palatable to the most depraved of mankind; and at the same time, by allowing its propagation by the sword, to excite the martial spirit of unprincipled adventurers."[133] Notably, the orientalizing and racist assumptions evident in this statement showed up only in this reference to marital norms and violence but were otherwise absent from the rest of Adams' account on Islam, which focused mainly on the religion's beliefs and practices. Other texts, like John Hayward's *The Book of Religions* (1841), made such Eurocentric critiques more explicit, however. Hayward (1781–1869) wrote:

> [Muhammad's] law was artfully and marvellously adapted to the corrupt nature of man, and, in a most particular manner, to the manners and opinions of the Eastern nations, and the vices to which they were naturally addicted; for the articles of faith which it proposed . . . were neither many nor difficult, nor such as were incompatible with the empire of appetites and passions.[134]

Presumptions about Islam as a false religion that capitalized on carnal desires became standard in most Protestant texts on comparative religion as the nineteenth century progressed. Even a scholar like Anglican theologian Frederick Dennison Maurice (1805–1872), who found value in the Islamic faith, argued in 1847 that "[Islam] can only survive while it is aiming at conquest" and would "fall to pieces" without the practice of polygyny.[135] Thus, the available scholarship comparing Christianity and Islam during the rise of nineteenth-century Anglo-Protestant missions engaged in cultural critique by denouncing Islam as built on military and sexual oppression or by describing Muslims as innately inferior to White Christians, or combined the two critiques.

Conclusion

This chapter has provided a framework for understanding the role of gender in the Protestant discourses about Islam that British and American missionaries of the nineteenth century would inherit and re-invent, as we shall see in the next chapters. What ideas did the pioneering Protestant mission societies receive from their predecessors and apply to their efforts in South Asia and the Middle East? American and British Protestants, along with other western Christians, made the Muslim woman's veil into a symbol of her oppression, using it to reinforce existing notions about Muslim men as tyrants and to elevate ideals of Protestant masculinity and femininity. This symbol was so powerful that it not only propelled modern missions to Muslims but also continues to fuel American Islamophobia today.

Yet, the transmitted Protestant narrative was not uniform, nor entirely negative. Although less prominent in theological treatises, Protestant textual and material engagements with Islam contained glimmers of admiration and tolerance that later generations would harness for Christian–Muslim dialogue. A foundation for this endeavor was also laid when basic doctrines and practices of Islam that some Protestants understood and appreciated became common knowledge—like prohibitions against alcohol and idolatry. Likewise, Protestant and Muslim cultures became entangled as Ottoman commodities, such as coffee, were integrated into British and American life. By the nineteenth century, as historian Timothy Marr explained, American elites frequently purchased Ottoman goods like carpets and displayed them in their homes, along with portraits of themselves wearing Turkish clothing.[136]

Protestant images of Muslim women varied, and in the first two centuries after the Reformation these resembled images of European Christian women more than images of an exotic or oppressed "other." In contrast, there were far fewer outlying portrayals of the traits and behaviors of Muslim men, beginning with the Prophet Muhammad. For even when Protestant men voiced admiration for the prophet's religious charisma or the Turks' military glory, they recycled medieval tropes about Muslims' masculine excesses. By the eighteenth century among British and American Protestants (and other western Christians), these persistent stereotypes had combined with colonial-era racism and shifting ideals about European womanhood to produce yet another re-invention of Islam: the veiled Muslim woman imprisoned in sexual servitude to her husband.

Notes

1. During the sixteenth century especially, the defense of Christendom against the expansion of the Ottoman Empire was a major concern of the Habsburg emperors, who held the title of Holy Roman Emperor.
2. Stephen Fischer-Galati, *Ottoman Imperialism and German Protestantism, 1521–1555* (Cambridge, MA: Harvard University Press, 1959).
3. Gregory J. Miller, *The Turks and Islam in Reformation Germany* (New York and London: Routledge, 2018), 13.
4. Ibid., 18.
5. Ibid., 18–19.
6. Ibid., 159.
7. Quoted in Sarah Henrich and James L. Boyce, "Martin Luther—Translations of Two Prefaces on Islam: Preface to the *Libellus de ritu et moribus Turcorum* (1530), and Preface to Bibliander's Edition of the Qur'an (1543)," *Word & World* 16, no. 2 (Spring 1996): 259.
8. Adam S. Francisco, *Martin Luther and Islam: A Study in Sixteenth-Century Polemics and Apologetics* (Leiden: Brill, 2007), 115.
9. Martin Luther, "On the Last Words of David" (1543), vol. 15, p. 343 in *Luther's Works,* vols. 1 – 30, ed. Jaroslav Pelikan (St. Louis: Concordia Publishing House, 1955–1976); vols. 31–55, ed. Helmut Lehmann (Philadelphia: Fortress Press, 1957–1986) (hereafter LW).
10. I use the term *polygyny* to emphasize that Islamic practice allows men to marry up to four wives at one time (whereas Muslim women may only marry one husband at a time).
11. Luther, "On War Against the Turk" (1529), LW 46:182.
12. Some Muslims interpret such equity to be unachievable and therefore see the Qur'anic teaching as limiting or discouraging polygyny. Others pursue legal ways within Islamic jurisprudence to prohibit polygyny. Kecia Ali, "Progressive Muslims and Islamic Jurisprudence: The Necessity for Critical Engagement with Marriage and Divorce Law," in *Progressive Muslims: On Justice, Gender and Pluralism,* ed. Omid Safi (London: Oneworld, 2003), 176–77.
13. Bibliander is quoted in Katya Vehlow, "The Swiss Reformers Zwingli, Bullinger and Bibliander and Their Attitude to Islam (1520–1560)," *Islam and Christian–Muslim Relations* 6, no. 2 (1995): 243–44.
14. These quotations from Calvin's *Opera* 41:270 and *Praelectiones in Danielem* 11:37 appear in Jan Slomp, "Calvin and the Turks," *Studies in Interreligious Dialogue* 19, no. 1 (2009): 62.
15. Bullinger is quoted in W. P. Stephens, "Understanding Islam—In the light of Bullinger and Wesley," *Evangelical Quarterly* 81, no. 1 (2009): 25. See also Vehlow, "Swiss Reformers," 238.
16. Vehlow, "Swiss Reformers," 243, 247.
17. Ibid., 243.
18. Ibid., 240, 243.
19. While not opposed to Germans defending themselves against Turkish armies, Luther railed against Catholic efforts to mount a crusade against the Ottomans. For him, military defense was a secular matter and not a cause for Holy War. Francisco, *Martin Luther and Islam*, 131; Vehlow, "Swiss Reformers," 247. Calvin also rejected the idea of military crusade. Slomp, "Calvin," 54.
20. Vehlow, "Swiss Reformers," 248, note 77.
21. Ibid., 240. See also Stephens, "Understanding Islam," 25.
22. Stephens, "Understanding Islam," 25; Vehlow, "Swiss Reformers," 232.
23. Vehlow, "Swiss Reformers," 245.

24. Jon Balserak, "Philip Melanchthon," in *Christian–Muslim Relations: A Bibliographical History*, vol. 7, *Central and Eastern Europe, Asia, Africa and South America (1500–1600)*, ed. David Thomas and John A. Chesworth (Leiden: Brill, 2015), 248–49.
25. Calvin's *Opera* 27:502 is quoted in Slomp, "Calvin," 60. See also Stuart Bonnington, "Calvin and Islam," *Reformed Theological Review* 68, no. 2 (August 2009): 81.
26. Vehlow, "Swiss Reformers," 236.
27. Psychologists Susan Fisk and Peter Glick's ambivalent sexism theory helps explain why this was the case. Reformers judged Muslim women positively because they saw their behavior and dress norms as a reflection of women's proper place and (subordinate) role in a society in which men were rightfully dominant. Peter Glick and Susan T. Fisk, "The Ambivalent Sexism Inventory: Differentiating Hostile and Benevolent Sexism," *Journal of Personality and Social Psychology* 70, no. 3 (March 1996): 491–512.
28. Francisco, *Martin Luther and Islam*, 111–12, 160.
29. Miller, *Turks and Islam*, 84.
30. Charlotte Colding Smith, *Images of Islam, 1453–1600* (New York: Routledge, 2018), 17.
31. Hartmann Schedel, *Liber Chronicarum* (Nuremberg: Anton Koberger, 1493), 146v. Courtesy of Special Collections and Archives, Pitts Library, Candler School of Theology.
32. Denise Alexandra Hartmann, "The Apocalypse and Religious Propaganda: Illustrations by Albrecht Dürer and Lucas Cranach the Elder," *Marginalia* 11 (October 2010): 10.
33. Smith, *Images of Islam*, 33.
34. Ibid., 103–5. The original French text was *Les navigations peregrinations et voyages, faits en la Turquie* (1567).
35. Smith, *Images of Islam*, 68.
36. Ibid., 167.
37. Anders Ingram, "The Ottoman Siege of Vienna, English Ballads, and the Exclusion Crisis," *The Historical Journal* 57, no. 1 (2014): 70; Nabil Matar, *Islam in Britain, 1558–1685* (Cambridge: Cambridge University Press, 1998), 110, 113.
38. In small numbers, Muslims had become permanently present in London by the sixteenth century, but only in the imperial period did growing numbers of Muslims from across the Islamic world arrive in pursuit of political, educational, and economic aims. Siobhan Lambert-Hurley and Sunhil Sharma, eds., "Introduction," in *Atiya's Journeys: A Muslim Woman from Colonial Bombay to Edwardian Britain* (Oxford: Oxford University Press, 2020), 6.
39. Christopher Toenjes, *Islam, the Turks and the Making of the English Reformation: The History of the Ottoman Empire in John Foxe's Acts and Monuments* (Frankfurt: Peter Lang, 2016), 3, 43–46.
40. These three later additions came out in 1570, 1576, and 1583. Toenjes, *Islam*, 4. Foxe's book is recognized as aiding in Elizabeth's "efforts to remake England in a Protestant image" as it placed the persecution of the Protestants under Elizabeth's predecessor and half-sister Mary Tudor within a history of Christian martyrdom dating back to the early church. Carla Gardina Pestana, *Protestant Empire: Religion and the Making of the British World* (Philadelphia: University of Pennsylvania Press, 2009), 44.
41. Toenjes, *Islam*, 5–7. Between 900 and 1200 copies of *Actes and Monuments* were produced for each edition. Although expensive, the text was accessible to readers in a number of churches and city halls.
42. Ibid., xv, 228, 246.
43. On the efforts of Queen Elizabeth's representatives during this period to pursue trade agreements with Ottomans and North Africans, see Jerry Brotton, *The Sultan and the Queen: The Untold Story of Elizabeth and Islam* (New York: Viking, 2016).
44. The North African regencies, which benefited from and to some extent exerted control over these corsairs, fell under the wider Ottoman umbrella.
45. In the early modern Mediterranean, Christians and Muslims enslaved each other. Britons theologically justified enslaving those who were non-Christians or were captives in a just war. Pestana, *Protestant Empire*, 96.
46. Toenjes, *Islam*, 348–49.
47. Matar, *Islam in Britain*, 6–7.
48. Toenjes, *Islam*, 352.
49. Ibid., 229.
50. Ibid., 262, 264, 272, 290.

51. Ibid., 288–89. Foxe spent little attention on polygyny itself and was inconsistent in his description of this practice.
52. Ibid., 263.
53. Daniel J. Vitkus, "Introduction," in *Three Turk Plays from Early Modern England: Selimus, A Christian Turned Turk, and The Renegado*, ed. Daniel J. Vitkus (New York: Columbia University Press, 2000), 2.
54. Ibid. In Marlowe's *Tamburlaine the Great, Parts I and II*, Tamburlaine's religious identity as a Scythian shepherd is ambiguous, possibly pagan; but he takes on stereotypical qualities of Turkish military aggression and lust for power. At one point he also converts to worshipping "Mahomet" but then sets out on an anti-Islamic quest and burns the Qur'an in the second play. The actual Tamerlane, or Timur, was of Turkic and Mongol descent, hailing from present-day Central Asia. On depictions of Islam in Marlowe's *Tamburlaine* plays, see Sophia Rose Arjana, *Muslims in the Western Imagination* (Oxford: Oxford University Press, 2015), 70–72.
55. This statement likens the soldiers' aggression to that of the Turks, although Islam prohibits alcohol.
56. Vitkus, "Introduction," 2.
57. Ibid.
58. Ibid., 13.
59. Ibid., 2–3.
60. Ibid., 14.
61. Mohja Kahf, *Western Representations of the Muslim Woman: From Termagant to Odalisque* (Austin: University of Texas Press, 1999), 67. See also Ibid., 69–70.
62. Ibid., 58, 64.
63. Matar, *Islam in Britain*, 19.
64. Ibid., 20.
65. Ibid., 64, 68. In order to be accepted back into British society, some returned renegades claimed they had received circumcision of the flesh but not of the heart. On views of Ottoman circumcision, see also Miller, *Turks and Islam*, 169. Fear of circumcision as emasculation, confused with castration and therefore associated with eunuchs, took on a comic rendition in the English play *The Renegado*. Vitkus, "Introduction," 5.
66. Matar, *Islam in Britain*, 64.
67. Daniel Vitkus, *Turning Turk: English Theater and the Multicultural Mediterranean, 1570–1630* (New York: Palgrave Macmillan, 2003), 104.
68. The play's opening presents Othello as a noble Christian general.
69. Ibid., 104.
70. Ibid., 106
71. Ibid.
72. Ian Smith, *Black Shakespeare: Reading and Misreading Race* (Cambridge: Cambridge University Press, 2022).
73. Matar, *Islam in Britain*, 184.
74. Ibid.
75. Frederick Quinn, *The Sum of All Heresies: The Image of Islam in Western Thought* (Oxford: Oxford University Press, 2008), 57. On Knolles, see Anders Ingram, "'The Glorious Empire of the Turkes, the Present Terrour of the World': Richard Knolles' *Generall Historie of the Turkes* (1603) and the Background to an Early Modern Commonplace," in *Explorations in Cultural History*, ed. D. Smith and H. Philsooph (Aberdeen, UK: BPR Publishers, 2010), 197–216.
76. Quinn, *Sum of All Heresies*, 64. William Bedwell, a scholar at Cambridge, began to study Islam and Arabic in the 1580s and visited the Arabic manuscript collection in Leiden. On the establishment of Arabic chairs at European universities, see Jack Goody, *Islam in Europe* (Cambridge: Polity Press, 2004), 79.
77. Quinn, *Sum of All Heresies*, 64–65.
78. Justin J. Meggitt, *Early Quakers and Islam: Slavery, Apocalyptic and Christian–Muslim Encounters in the Seventeenth Century* (Eugene, OR: Wipf & Stock, 2013), 35.
79. Quinn, *Sum of All Heresies*, 66.
80. Ibid., 68, 70. Stubbe's text was titled *An Account of the Rise and Progress of Mahometanism with the Life of Mahomet and a Vindication of Him and His Religion from the Calumnies of the Christians* (1676).
81. Quinn, *Sum of All Heresies*, 68; Luther, "On War Against the Turk," LW 46:207.

82. Quinn, *Sum of All Heresies*, 68–70. On the influence of Prideaux's text on Americans, see Thomas Kidd, *American Christians and Islam: Evangelical Culture and Muslims from the Colonial Period to the Age of Terrorism* (Princeton, NJ: Princeton University Press, 2009), 6, 12.
83. Ingram, "Ottoman Siege," 59–60.
84. Ibid., 69.
85. Ibid., 71. The reference to death by the tree recalls the execution of prominent Whigs after the alleged plot to assassinate King Charles II and his brother, James.
86. Ibid., 73–74.
87. Ibid., 73. Ingram quoted from the ballad titled "An Excellent New Song on the Late Victories over the Turks" (1684).
88. Ibid., 73.
89. Ibid., 70.
90. Matar, *Islam in Britain*, 110, 113. Sugar was introduced to Britain through trade with the Muslim world in the sixteenth century, being brought from India through the Levant. Goody, *Islam in Europe*, 78.
91. Matar, *Islam in Britain*, 185.
92. Ingram, "Ottoman Siege," 57. Beginning in July of 1683, the Habsburg forces held out for two months under siege in Vienna until forces led by Polish king Jan Sobieski III (1629–1696) arrived and routed the Ottoman army.
93. Edward W. Said, *Orientalism* (New York: Vintage Books, 1978), 3.
94. Said described two interconnected forms of Orientalism, an academic tradition and an imaginative "style of thought based upon an ontological and epistemological distinction made between 'the Orient' and (most of the time) 'the Occident.'" The latter, general form of Orientalism also included romantic, sympathetic appropriations of eastern cultures. Ibid., 2, 118.
95. Kahf, *Western Representations*, 56; Vitkus, *Turning Turk*, 3; Matar, *Islam in Britain*, 11.
96. On western engagements with Asia broadly and with religions other than Islam, see Richard King, *Orientalism and Religion: Postcolonial Theory, India and 'The Mystic East'* (London and New York: Routledge, 1999).
97. After 1707, England, Scotland, and Wales together became known as Great Britain.
98. Vitkus, *Turning Turk*, 3.
99. Rowan Strong, *Anglicanism and British Empire, c. 1700–1850* (Oxford: Oxford University Press, 2007), 10–40.
100. Matar, *Islam in Britain*, 11. According to Pestana, England had colonial-imperial designs, as seen in the establishment of colonies in North America beginning in 1607 and in its conquest of Ireland in the late sixteenth century. Yet, English rule could not expand militarily into continental Europe or the Mediterranean. Pestana, *Protestant Empire*, 66.
101. Vitkus, *Turning Turk*, 21.
102. Ibid. The British Empire relied on its own merchant-privateers to compete with North African corsairs and European rivals. On this British piracy, see also Pestana, *Protestant Empire*, 65, 73.
103. Matar, *Islam in Britain*, 11, 190.
104. Britain also occupied major ports in the Arabian Peninsula, expanded its influence in Persia, and colonized the Sudan. On British imperialism in the Middle East, see Wm. Roger Louis, *The British Empire in the Middle East, 1945–1951: Arab Nationalism, the United States, and Postwar Imperialism* (Oxford: Oxford University Press, 1984); H. Lyman Stebbins, *British Imperialism in Qajar Iran: Consuls, Agents, and Influence in the Middle East* (London: Bloomsbury/I.B. Taurus, 2016); Aimee M. Genell, "Empire by Law: Ottoman Sovereignty and the British Occupation of Egypt, 1882–1923" (PhD diss., Columbia University, 2013).
105. Quinn, *Sum of All Heresies*, 69; Kahf, *Western Representations*, 115.
106. Matar, *Islam in Britain*, 187.
107. Ibid.
108. Quinn, *Sum of All Heresies*, 57, 60, 66–67, 69. Ockley's *The History of the Saracens* appeared first in 1708 under the title *Conquest of Syria, Persia, and Egypt by the Saracens*.
109. Quinn, *Sum of All Heresies*, 71.
110. Edward Gibbon, *The History of the Decline and Fall of the Roman Empire* (New York: J. J. Harper, 1831), 3:378.
111. Quinn, *Sum of All Heresies*, 72. White was named Laudian Chair of Arabic at Oxford in 1774.
112. Timothy Marr, *The Cultural Roots of American Islamicism* (Cambridge: Cambridge University Press, 2006), 20–24. Charles Montesquieu's *The Spirit of the Laws* (1748) was one influential

text that addressed "oriental despotism" and was of interest to Americans when formulating their own arguments for democratic republicanism.
113. Marr, *American Islamicism*, 20.
114. Humberto Garcia, *Islam and the English Enlightenment, 1670-1840* (Baltimore: John Hopkins University Press, 2011), xi.
115. Kahf, *Western Representations*, 95. Harem relates to the Arabic word *haram* (forbidden), the opposite of *halal* (permissible), and refers to the fact that other men do not have access to women who are *halal* to male family members.
116. Ibid., 175. Kahf's book explores other earlier prototypes in which Muslim women exhibited agency.
117. Ibid., 111.
118. Said, *Orientalism*, 190.
119. Kahf, *Western Representations*, 115, 117.
120. Jeremy Gregory, "Homo Religiosus: Masculinity and Religion in the Long Eighteenth Century," in *English Masculinities, 1660–1800*, ed. Tim Hitchcock and Michelle Cohen (London: Routledge, 1999), 92. Although traditional ideals of manliness emphasized "physical strength, hardiness, courage and martial values," the ideal Christian man was identified as one who "treated his enemies with moderation" and had "all his passions under his command." English Protestant religious writings for young men in particular indicated, however, in warnings against "youthful lusts" and "lascivious pictures" that the ideal was not easily achieved (p. 88).
121. Kahf, *Western Representations*, 118–19.
122. Ibid., 120.
123. Ibid., 120–21. Lady Mary was describing *mahr* (dowry). Additionally, Muslim women have the right to keep what they earn.
124. Ibid., 122. Kahf quoted from Wortley Montagu.
125. Wortley Montagu wrote as "a woman contesting a male tradition which devalues her," but as a privileged, aristocratic woman she had "no interest in writing a new feminine ideal that would cut across class and factional affiliations." Ibid., 124.
126. In English literature such rescue typically came through conversion to Christianity and marriage to a European man. Ibid., 136. On Wortley Montagu, see also Quinn, *Sum of All Heresies*, 73–75.
127. Kahf, *Western Representations*, 148. In contrast to Lady Mary Wortley Montagu, Wollstonecraft critiqued both class and gender oppression in *A Vindication of the Rights of Woman* (1792).
128. The North African coast of the Mediterranean was known as the Barbary Coast.
129. Publications included *Louisa, A Novel* (1790); *Slaves in Algiers* (1792); *A Journal of the Captivity and Suffering of John Foss* (1798); *Narrative of the Captivity and Sufferings of Mrs. Maria Martin* (1800); *Narrative of the Captivity of John Vandike* (1801); *Humanity in Algiers* (1801); *The Algerine Captive* (1802); and *An Affective History of the Captivity and Sufferings of Mrs. Mary Velnet* (1804). Marr, *American Islamicism*, 45–65.
130. Kidd quoted from Leland's *The Rights of Conscience Inalienable* (1791) in *American Christians*, 18.
131. Ibid, 16. Kidd quoted from Edwards' "Notes on the Apocalypse."
132. Ibid., 13. Kidd quoted from Walton's *The Religion of Jesus Vindicated* (1736) and Tennent's *Twenty-Three Sermons upon the Chief End of Man* (1744). For Muslim perspectives on the afterlife, see Jane Idelman Smith and Yvonne Yazbeck Haddad, *The Islamic Understanding of Death and Resurrection* (New York: Oxford University Press, 2002).
133. Hannah Adams, *A Dictionary of Religions and Religious Denominations, Jewish, Heathen, Mahometan, and Christian, Ancient and Modern*, 4th ed. (Boston: James Eastburn and Co., 1817), 157. Other than this, Adams only mentioned gender again when describing Muslim views of heaven as full of beautiful women (p. 160). On Adams, see Thomas A. Tweed, "An American Pioneer in the Study of Religion: Hannah Adams (1755–1831) and Her 'Dictionary of All Religions,'" *Journal of the American Academy of Religion* 60, no. 3 (Autumn 1992): 437–64; Fuad Sha'ban, *Islam and Arabs in Early American Thought: The Roots of Orientalism in America* (Durham, NC: Acorn Press, 1991), 35–42.
134. John Hayward, *The Book of Religions: Comprising the Views, Creeds, Sentiments, or Opinions of All the Religious Sects in the World* [. . .], 2nd ed. (Boston: John Hayward, 1842), 229. The first edition appeared in 1841. See also Sha'ban, *Islam and Arabs*, 34–42.
135. Frederick Dennison Maurice, *The Religions of the World and Their Relations to Christianity* (Boston: Gould and Lincoln, 1854), 50, 52. The first edition of this text appeared in 1847.
136. Marr, *American Islamicism*, 262–66, 282–96.

3
Re-inventing Islam in Missionary Texts
"When Hagar Returns to Christ, Ishmael Shall Live"

From the late eighteenth century onward as European powers gained a foothold in regions that Muslim empires once controlled, British and American Protestants wrote about Islam with new boldness. Their sense of cultural superiority and Christian imperial power gradually replaced the reverent fear with which their Protestant forebears had once viewed the Ottoman Empire. Missionaries contributed significantly to the resulting religious and cultural critiques, especially regarding the status of Muslim women. Certainly they drew on their experiences of living in Islamic societies to author an outpouring of publications, and they maintained intricate networks of correspondence to support their evangelistic and humanitarian work among Muslims across Africa and Asia. But the information about Islam already circulating in the North Atlantic Protestant world also influenced missionaries' annual reports, articles, scholarly books, fictional works, and lectures. Through such textual media, they re-invented Islam to advocate for a Protestant duty to Muslim women.

Whereas Reformation-era Protestant theological discourses had largely repeated secondhand information from medieval Christian sources, nineteenth-century missionaries' personal contact with Muslims gave them some real expertise to confirm, deny, or expand upon earlier portrayals of Islam. They used that expertise and authority not just to inform but also to make Christian readers back home more sympathetic to the plight of Muslim women. Thus, when Annie Van Sommer, an English missionary in early twentieth-century Egypt, wrote that every Muslim female was "Unwelcome at birth, unloved in her life-time, without hope in her death," she placed upon her readers' shoulders the burden of saving a hundred million Muslim women from ignorance and degradation.[1] She urged her Protestant sisters in particular to read about Muslim women's lives and to respond in support of missions. Such work to uplift Muslim women, proclaimed Van Sommer, would regenerate the entire global Muslim population. For, in her words,

"When Hagar returns to Christ, Ishmael shall live."[2] Thus Van Sommer not only reinforced the traditional view of Muslims as the progeny of Ishmael but also identified Hagar as the prototypical Muslim woman whose salvation was key to winning Muslims for Christ.

Missionary literature is the most significant body of textual material—in quantity and influence—that conveys modern Protestant thought about Muslims from the nineteenth century to the mid-twentieth century. In this, the first of two chapters examining British and American missionaries' textual re-inventions of Islam, I read published missionary writings through the lens of gender, adding to several studies which have documented anglophone Protestant thought on Islam but which did not specifically examine the judgments such texts transmitted about the conditions of women and the behaviors of men in Muslim societies.[3]

Given the vast archive of missionary literature on Islam and this book's pan-Protestant focus, the range of nineteenth- and early twentieth-century texts I cover in this chapter and the next is necessarily limited. The sources I explore are not representative of all literature that circulated to British and American audiences in this formative period, but most texts did reach thousands of readers, if not tens of thousands. This material helps us both to discern the ways in which Protestant missionaries informed their audiences and to identify the common patterns in the publications that these audiences habitually read about Islam.

Because most studies on this subject focus on Protestant men, I give attention to the writings of missionary women in Muslim contexts, whose influence upon men, women, and children in nineteenth- and early twentieth-century Europe and North America has been overlooked. Women rarely produced the kinds of theological treatises and evangelistic tracts that missionary men wrote and that are featured in scholarship on Christian–Muslim relations. Yet women still left a substantial written record. Even beyond the volumes of correspondence and diaries in missionary women's archives, their literary output was immense, especially through women's missionary society publications. In the last quarter of the nineteenth century, when only a small number of missionary women were publishing books, they first carved out a space in periodicals; but by the early twentieth century their pamphlets, articles, non-fiction books, and novels had proliferated to such an extent that these women became key re-inventors of Islam.

This chapter examines the discourses of gender in texts that missionaries published to shape their adult audiences' understandings of Islam. But before turning to these missionary writings, I first comment on the prevailing gender norms for Anglo-Protestant missionaries. I next explore formative nineteenth-century texts about Islam authored mainly by missionary men, and then, in the last two sections, I consider women's contributions to the flood of missionary literature in the early decades of the twentieth century, decades which coincided with a push for ecumenical coordination of Protestant missionaries to Muslims.

Although mainline Protestant missionary thought generally reinforced traditional western polemics about Muslim women at least through the 1920s, I also identify some humanizing impulses that opened the way for later movements of interfaith dialogue—but did so without challenging established critiques of gender norms in Islam. For essentializing notions about masculinist Muslim violence and Islam's oppression of women in missionary texts often existed in tension with educational narratives that encouraged sympathy and cross-cultural understanding. In re-inventing Islam as an urgent concern for Protestant women, missionaries transmitted the unfortunately enduring stereotypes about Muslims that are at the root of present-day American Islamophobia, making use of biblical traditions about Hagar and Ishmael to do so. Nevertheless, they also laid the groundwork for more positive Christian–Muslim relations to come.

Gender in Anglophone Protestant Missionary Circles

Missionaries' gendered critiques of Islam rested on four key conceptions that shaped the strategies of Protestant missions. First, missionary men and women alike asserted that the freedom that western women enjoyed was a mark of Christian (or Protestant) superiority, in contrast with the oppression that non-Christian women in Asia and Africa experienced at the hands of male family members and religious leaders. This, then, was the wider context within which Protestant audiences read missionary texts about Muslim women.

According to historian Eliza Kent's examination of women's missionary encounters in South Asia, Protestant missionaries believed that uncivilized customs "would give way before the arrival of the evolutionarily subsequent and culturally superior form of [Protestant] religion."[4] Kent remarked further that missionaries were nearly always disappointed by their inability to impose western gender norms, and for all their talk about women's freedom, male and female roles on the mission field usually followed Victorian notions of complementarity. Even when some mission societies aimed for functional equality in theory between men and women in comparable roles as evangelists,[5] in practice women missionaries were assigned to "feminine" roles such as teaching or evangelistic work only among women. Thus, the conventions of Protestant patriarchy actually resembled quite closely the gender restrictions of Islamic societies that missionaries so frequently critiqued. Nevertheless, many of these women themselves transgressed gender barriers on the mission field,[6] even as most of their writings failed to emphasize how Muslim women similarly navigated patriarchy in their own contexts. As Saba Mahmood argued, Muslim women have asserted agency in defying the patriarchal norms of their societies but also by working within and even embracing those norms, as many Protestant missionary women did in their own societies.[7]

The constraints on Protestant women's activities are apparent in a second missionary pattern of idealizing the private, domestic sphere as a Christian woman's space. By the mid-nineteenth century in the United States, as Barbara Welter's study "The Cult of True Womanhood" explained, domesticity was one of the cardinal virtues for American Protestant women—along with piety, purity, and submissiveness. This ideology maintained that the woman's "proper sphere" was her home, where she could exercise religious influence as a good Christian wife and mother, while promoting the comfort, happiness, and moral uplift of her household.[8] Similarly, in Victorian England, middle- and upper-class women idealized the home as a female sanctuary.[9] On the mission fields, the Victorian-era woman's role of "homemaker"[10] translated into the duties of the missionary wife, who was entrusted with passing down the gospel to her children and being a "helpmeet" for her husband.[11] Although Protestant mission societies depended on the work of single women missionaries, they discouraged sending unmarried male missionaries into the field and instead supported missionary couples, who could model domestic virtue as an example for "native" Christians and "heathen" families.[12] British and American missionaries alike believed that female domestic labor was key to a family's religious uplift and would likewise enable the uplift of the nation. Thus, Van Sommer's aforementioned references to Hagar and Ishmael signified that converted Muslim mothers were key to saving the followers of Islam.

To Protestant missionaries, this understanding of female domestic labor in service to the nation was the cornerstone for transforming Asian and

African societies.[13] Accordingly, whereas missionaries believed that Muslim women were wrongly "sequestered" or "confined," both physically and spiritually at home (or behind a veil), they deemed both the home and modest clothing to be a refuge for Christian women.[14] The resemblance of such domestic gender norms in European and Middle Eastern societies actually led some English women travelers to compare the harem favorably to a bourgeois home.[15] Missionary literature, however, usually presented Muslim households and Protestant homes as opposites.

Based in part on this understanding of the Christian's woman's role in the home, a third practice emerged of assigning men and women to separate gendered spheres of mission work.[16] While men could serve as church pastors, teachers, itinerant evangelists, doctors, and mission press managers, in the nineteenth century women filled positions that matched the limited acceptable professional roles of middle-class Anglo-Protestant women who worked outside of the home. They therefore became schoolteachers, nurses, or administrators of girls' boarding schools that were understood as extensions of the home.[17] This "separate spheres" ideology fit the norms of most Muslim societies where the upper classes prohibited mixed-gender interactions outside of the immediate family. Missionaries therefore assigned American and British women to run girls' schools or to visit Muslim women in the Middle Eastern harem or South Asian zenana (women's spaces in the home) and justified such practices as a response to Islamic restrictions on women's freedom.[18] In fact, the (patriarchal) gender ideologies of Anglo-Protestant society had already predetermined that the proper sphere of missionary women's work was with other women. Thus emerged the aforementioned mission strategy of "woman's work for woman," through which Protestant women gained significant agency and authority within the missionary movement—albeit in the limited female sphere. They soon established independent women's missionary societies or separate women's boards within larger denominational societies, and women eventually became the majority within the Protestant missionary enterprise.[19] This system ensured, however, that male missionary ministers would continue to hold positions of religious authority and decision-making power, except in women's mission societies.[20] Thus, missionaries in Islamic contexts reinforced their own ideology of separate male and female roles in religious work while simultaneously critiquing the gendered spheres of Muslim life. They then used such critiques to justify their requests for more personnel and funding for "woman's work."[21]

Fourth and finally, missionary appeals for donor support not only rested on theological claims about Christian truth but also reinforced White western Protestant notions of superiority over other religions and over Asian and African cultures generally. In their representations of Muslim women and men, missionaries exhibited cultural imperialism, ethnocentrism, and deep racial prejudice. They justified such attitudes with references to philological and ethnological classifications of the peoples of the world within a racial hierarchy based on "objective" scientific assessments of physical features and allegedly innate moral, intellectual, and physical character traits. The accepted hierarchy placed White Christians at the top, Africans at the bottom, and inhabitants of Asia somewhere in between.[22] The implied racial distinction between White western women and "native" women in the mission fields lurked below the surface of missionary discourse if it was not explicitly linked to claims about the spiritual "darkness" of those whom missionaries felt a duty to save.[23]

As Kent put it, "The representations of indigenous society that filled missionary journals reveal that the dominant view of the relationship among gender, religion, and civilization was one in which 'barbaric' lands were those where women labored in dirty, difficult, or physically demanding occupations and where brides were bought or married off at a young age."[24] We see echoes of this, for instance, in the title of the magazine that the Woman's Foreign Missionary Society of the Methodist Episcopal Church published: *Heathen Woman's Friend*. Missionaries depicted *Muslim* women similarly, reflecting the Orientalist thought patterns that western Christians' sense of rising cultural and political power enabled and emboldened.

In this context, according to Mohja Kahf, shifting gender norms in Europe, fantasies about the Middle East, and strong Orientalist impulses led western Christians to critique the interrelated Muslim practices of veiling and women's seclusion.[25] Protestant missionaries followed up this prevalent cultural critique with a moral imperative: before Muslim women could be rescued, they urgently needed to hear the gospel. Gayatri Spivak's often-quoted reference to White men "saving brown women from brown men" applies here, except that in the missionary context White women took on the role of savior too and, in their view, true salvation came only through religious conversion.[26] Orientalism and a "savior" mentality merged, collapsing the distinctions between Muslim women of vastly different cultural backgrounds, nationalities, and social contexts, while at the same time masking the patriarchy that American and British women faced.

Missionaries' gendered discourses about Muslims were therefore shaped by 1) an emphasis on Christian women's freedom, 2) the idealization of women's roles in bringing the family and the nation to Christ, 3) the establishment of a separate sphere for women's missions, and 4) racist rhetoric reinforcing White Anglophone Protestant cultural norms.

(En)Gendering Nineteenth-Century Christian–Muslim Narratives

In addition to reflecting what missionaries wanted their constituents to know about Islam, missionary discourses about Muslims revealed their own Protestant sense of identity and habits, the nature of the wider missionary enterprise, and even the lived realities of their Protestant audiences. The aforementioned gender norms were in fact embedded in missionary practices, including their writing—an activity that became as central to missionary identity as the tasks of preaching or teaching. This section explores gendered discussions of Islam in nineteenth-century missionary texts, beginning with ethnographic-style travel accounts.

Ethnology, Travel Writing, and Missions

In the background of much nineteenth-century Protestant missionary writing about Muslims were two modern genres that sometimes blurred together: travel writing and ethnology. The latter was a precursor to modern anthropology that aimed to offer scientific descriptions of non-western peoples. This developing field had antecedents in costume books and other publications discussed in Chapter 2 that introduced European Christians to Ottoman Islamic society. In the nineteenth century, however, the notion of cultural difference took hold in British and American imaginations.[27] For Protestants writing about Muslim societies, ethnology and travel literature overlapped in their attention to customs and local inhabitants' appearances, including dress styles, physical features, and perceived racial characteristics. From the late eighteenth century onward, such accounts—by wealthy travelers, merchants, pilgrims, scholars, and missionaries—became more widespread in Britain and North America. This signaled a popular interest in the people, customs, and scenery of "the Orient," an ambiguous term applied to various parts of Asia and North Africa. As an example, the "Indian Journal" of Lady Charlotte Florentia Clive (1787–1866) included both written observations recorded during her British family's voyage to Madras in 1798 and watercolor paintings of Hindus and Muslims.[28] Such artistic renderings were linked to the same impulse for acquisition of knowledge and mastery over "others" that defined the world's fairs of the nineteenth century and the "curiosities" that wealthy travelers collected from the cultures they visited.[29] Missionaries both were influenced by and contributed to this body of discursive, pictorial, material, and performative knowledge about Islamic contexts.

Among the earliest Anglo-Protestant missionary accounts of travel to the Middle East are the British Anglican missionary William Jowett's *Christian Researches in the Mediterranean* (1822) and *Christian Researches in Syria and the Holy Land* (1826), both based on Jowett's explorations for the CMS. He aimed to document the region's social and religious conditions, systematically classifying the people in order to propose strategies for their conversion.[30] In *Christian Researches in the Mediterranean*, Jowett assessed Middle Eastern communities' doctrines and moral status, aligning the latter with cultural characteristics. Thus, Jowett described the different "races" of Muslims:

> The lordly Turk, fierce in arms, and patron of no other art; the sophisticated Persian, delighting in syllogism and verse; the Saracenic masters of literature and science; the wild Arab, never tamed or domiciliated; even the humble character of the industrious, trafficking Moor.[31]

He claimed further that the difficulty of introducing Arabs to Christianity was preordained in scripture, explaining "Whether in the steppes of Tartary, the sandy deserts of Arabia, or the mountains of Atlas, the Bedouin descendants of Ishmael, true to Prophecy, (Gen. xvi. 12. *He will be a wild man*,) have ever spurned restraint."[32] The immoralities Jowett perceived in Muslim lands—including "Ignorance, Apathy, and Crime"—were to him not merely social traits but "vices which the Creed of Mahomedans cherishes" and which were passed on through Ishmael's line as Genesis 16 foretold.[33]

Jowett's second volume presented his journey as a travel narrative describing biblical sites, people, and local costumes. With its attention to the region's "connection with all the great events recorded in the Holy Scripture," the book was a forerunner to William McClure Thomson's more widely read

The Land and the Book: Or Biblical Illustrations Drawn from the Manners and Customs, the Scenes and Scenery of The Holy Land (a two-volume set published in 1858 and 1860).[34] Because of its popularity, Thomson, a retired member of the American Syria Mission, expanded this work into three volumes between 1880 and 1886 and added more illustrations.[35] As David Grafton's study of American Biblical Orientalism explained, these volumes were "part of a larger explosion of American travel narratives that began to flood the markets in the middle to late nineteenth century."[36] Thomson's travelogue used conversational prose that invited readers to imagine themselves journeying alongside him across the Levant, and his illustrations facilitated such imaginings.[37] Descriptions of contemporary life—like a comparison of Arab Bedouin dress to that of the ancient Hebrews—primarily intended to help readers better comprehend scripture but also suggested that little had changed since Bible times.[38] Thus, when Thomson introduced Islam, he included "the followers of the Arabian Prophet in that multitude of Ishmael's descendants" and applied the words of Genesis 16:12 to Arab Muslims:

> [In] their long and varied career they have exhibited the very same characteristic traits ascribed to Ishmael. Their hand, also, has been against every man, and every man's hand against them, and yet they still dwell in the presence of all their brethren, in the center of the Old World, a defiance and a menace to the surrounding nations whether pagan or Christian. The promise to Hagar thus expanded is, to say the least, very suggestive and exceedingly impressive.[39]

Such repeated references to Ishmael reinforced longstanding views that Muslim men were innately violent. As for Muslim women, Thomson used a description of their dress to explain and critique the gender norms of Arab society:

> The dress of Oriental women is not so complicated as that of European ladies, and shows more the shape of the person, and they are not expected or allowed to mix in society with men, nor to be seen by them. Their indoor dress is not contrived to meet the demands of a public thoroughfare, and when they go abroad they are closely veiled from head to foot. The reasons—and such there are—for confining the women very much to their homes, and of closely veiling them when abroad are found in the character and customs of Oriental people; and the veils cannot be safely abolished,

nor their domestic regulations relaxed, until a pure and enlightened Christianity has prepared the way.[40]

This cultural critique of "closely veiling"—meaning the full covering of women's bodies—morphed into a theological judgment, as Thomson identified Christianity as the only way to mitigate against what he saw as improper gender norms. Thomson's assessment, however, failed to recognize the gender restrictions of his own time in Europe and North America—even for educated White Protestant women but more insidiously for Black women and others with family origins outside of western Europe.[41] Neither did he mention ways in which Middle Eastern women were even then working within the constraints of their own society to address gender disparities, nor the ways in which Islamic structures of gender segregation could actually protect and empower women.[42]

Thomson did not condemn Islam explicitly. Instead, he blamed the "customs of Oriental people," a long-practiced "system of domestic regulations and compensations" that both Middle Eastern Christian and Muslim communities followed.[43] Regardless of the origins, Thomson believed that such practices would not change until the people of the Holy Land accepted the (Protestant) gospel. Ironically, then, Thomson lamented the region's static customs when speaking about the treatment of women, even as he also romanticized contemporary life in the region as preserving the ways of the Bible. Significantly, like Jowett, Thomson did not just name contemporary Muslims as Ishmael's heirs but more definitively recast them as embodying Ishmael's unruly nature.[44] Considering that in its time *The Land and the Book* was second in popularity only to Harriet Beecher Stowe's *Uncle Tom's Cabin* in the United States,[45] Thomson's work brought this critique of Islamic gender norms to vast numbers of American readers, priming them for the flurry of missionary discourses about Muslim women to come.

Before turning to such missionary publications, however, it is important to recognize that travel writing and ethnographic accounts were not the purview only of western Christians. Muslims traveled abroad during this period too and wrote about their experiences in significant enough numbers that we can actually speak of "a literary sub-genre of *Muslim women's foreign travel writing* dating from the late nineteenth century."[46] The accounts of two South Asian women, for example—Atiya Fyzee (1877–1967), who traveled unveiled to London in 1906 and published accounts of her visit in an Indian newspaper, and Sikandar Begum (1817–1868), a ruler who completed the hajj (pilgrimage) to Mecca and wrote a book about her journey—defy many of the missionary discourses about Muslim women examined below.[47]

British and American Missionary Re-inventions of Islam

Nineteenth-century missionary publications often re-invented Islam for English-speaking Protestants by resurrecting familiar tropes and introducing new ones to solicit support for missions to Muslim societies.[48] The close contact missionaries had with Muslims did broaden their understandings of Islamic culture over time and did prompt some appreciative representations of Islam, yet these rarely related to gender norms. A sense of cultural and religious superiority nearly always extended to missionary rhetoric about Islamic violence, about Muslim male licentiousness, and about the condition of Muslim women—three interconnected areas of critique in British and American texts for mission supporters, to which I now turn.

First, nineteenth-century missionaries tied claims about violence to the prophet of Islam. Henry Martyn, the English Anglican chaplain and missionary in South and central Asia introduced in Chapter 1, was recognized for his relatively respectful approach to Muslims. Yet Martyn nevertheless described Muhammad in his *Controversial Tracts on Christianity and Mohammedanism* (1824) as "a man whose main object appears to have been ravage and war." He contended that conversions to the Islamic faith were "determined by the point of the sword," while the Arab military conquests offered a "violent motive" for keeping the Islamic faith in order to gain the spoils of war.[49] Later missionary writers shared this sentiment. Karl Pfander's *Balance of Truth*, which the CMS published in English in 1866, commented that Islam spread in a violent manner[50]; and Henry Jessup, the American Presbyterian in Syria, similarly asserted, "Whenever Islam holds the sword it uses it for the oppression and humiliation of all infidels."[51] Methodist missionary Emily Humphrey in India likewise wrote about Muslim armies ravaging South Asia and "crush[ing] the spirit of inquiry and improvement among the [Hindu] people."[52] When describing the 1857 Indian uprising against British rule, she depicted Muslims as "the *inciters* of the whole movement of rebellion." She continued, "Their *religious* enthusiasm, too, was far greater than that of the Hindoos, as the latter only wished to be let alone, and not have their religious superstitions infringed upon, while the Mahomedans longed to win back India for God and his prophet."[53] Such rhetoric not only defined Muslim men as threatening but also characterized Islam as a religion of male violence, harkening back to caricatures of both the Prophet Muhammad and Ishmael.

Second, when commenting on Muslim women's conditions in the nineteenth century, most missionary men focused on the sexual behaviors of Muslim men and not on actual women's experiences, following another long-established pattern. The Scottish Orientalist and mission supporter William Muir (1819–1905), for instance, found the medieval Latin version of the *Apology of al-Kindi* so informative for his contemporaries that in 1882 he produced an English translation of key excerpts, interspersed with his own commentary.[54] The text frequently mentioned the Muslim privilege of marrying four wives, in addition to owning slave girls. Muir's translation also reinforced the connection his predecessors had made between sexual deviance and violence in the character of Muhammad, arguing that his love of war, plunder, and women contradicted his claim to prophethood.[55] Thus, nineteenth-century missionaries embraced the same Latin polemic that had informed sixteenth-century Protestant writings on Islam. In his writing for The Christian Literature Society for India, British Baptist missionary George Rouse conveyed a similar message, despite his favorable view of Muhammad's early career, saying, "In time, as the number of adherents increased, Muhammad began to gain power, and with this immediately came deterioration of character. He would attack and rob caravans, ruthlessly slay his enemies, *add to his harem those who pleased his eye*, and bring revelations from God to justify him in all that he did."[56]

Henry Jessup built on such themes when he quoted from James Stobart's *Islam and Its Founder* (1877), saying, "In reality, the number of wives is practically unlimited, as divorce and exchange are allowed with little or no restraint," an exaggeration reminiscent of Luther.[57] Actually, legal evidence suggests that in the eighteenth- and nineteenth-century Ottoman Empire—Jessup's own mission context—divorce rates fluctuated according to social and political circumstances, and divorces could be undertaken by both men *and women* for a variety of reasons.[58] Furthermore, polygyny has never been universally practiced in Islamic societies, in part for economic reasons but also because Islamic tradition interprets the practice as a way to provide for women's social welfare and permits the taking of multiple wives only when the husband can care for them equitably. From the 1880s (when Ottoman courts began keeping marriage records) to the early twentieth century, "no more than two percent of the Muslim population was in such marriages."[59]

Nevertheless, the permissibility of taking up to four wives was enough to engender Jessup's vitriolic claim that "The Koranic doctrine of polygamy utterly destroys the sanctity and purity of the family, brutalizes the man and degrades the woman."[60]

Third, turning to a topic that was of little interest to the Reformers but that dominated nineteenth- and twentieth-century Protestant thought about Islam, Jessup also critiqued gendered seclusion, describing Muslim women in words reminiscent of Thomson as "closely veiled" and excluded from activities such as education and religious instruction.[61] Picking up on western fantasies about the Ottoman sultans, he depicted the harem of Sultan Abdulmejid I (1823–1861), where he imagined that for a thousand women and girls in the imperial family, "[t]he rod, the scourge, is the only instrument of discipline." Jessup's claims were unsubstantiated conjecture but nevertheless led him to conclude that Muslim women "are treated like animals, and behave like animals."[62] (In reality, women's memoirs from the Ottoman palace itself describe this harem not as a site of debauchery but as the home of a regulated and refined imperial family.[63]) Moving to another line of reasoning, Jessup blamed Muslims in India for instituting the zenana, where both upper-class Hindu and Muslim women resided, in this repeating the views of missionaries in South Asia like Humphrey. Jessup believed that "Hindoo women enjoyed vastly greater liberty" before the Mughals arrived in India. He concluded, "It is fair to judge any religious system by its fruits in the domestic family-life, by its treatment of woman; and, tried by this test, Mohammedanism is a failure."[64] One wonders whether nineteenth-century Christianity would fare any better if tried by the same test.

In her representations of Muslim women in India, however, Humphrey offered a different perspective on Muslim women, reminding us that missionary views were more nuanced than some of the more widely read works of male authors suggested. In her 1875 book *Gems of India*, Humphrey took a narrative approach, as she wrote about women in India "to make their past and present condition and capabilities matters of study and research."[65] She focused on individual Indian women, both Muslim and Hindu, and emphasized their bravery and leadership in positions of power. The book made neither sweeping claims about all Muslim women nor harsh judgments about Islamic teachings, even as Humphrey noted the general practice of seclusion and veiling of high-caste Indian women.[66] In fact, she found Muslim women to have more independence than Hindu women and, contradicting Jessup, confirmed that many of them were literate.[67] The Muslim "gems of

India" included Nur Jahan, a skilled tiger hunter who married Mughal emperor Jahangir Khan (1569–1627), and their son Shah Jahan's wife, Mumtaz Mahal, for whom Shah Jahan erected the Taj Mahal when he was emperor.

In her writings Humphrey also featured recent queens, or begums, of Bhopal, a princely state that the British governed through the Muslim Bhopal family. The Bhopal begums reigned independently of their male relations during much of the nineteenth century. As Humphrey narrated the lives of Sikandar Begum (r. 1860–1868) and her daughter Shahjahan Begum (r. 1844–1860, 1868–1901),[68] she complimented them for governing justly and for acting "a noble and wise part" in allying with the British during the Indian uprising of 1857.[69] Finally, Humphrey recounted Sikandar's hajj, teaching her readers about this pillar of Islamic faith and explaining that although Sikandar was "so faithful a friend to the English, she was still a devout believer in the Mahomedan faith."[70] This piety appeared to impress rather than to trouble Humphrey, despite her hopes for Indian women's conversion to Christianity.

Humphrey was critical of some Muslims, but she painted Sikandar Begum and Shahjahan Begum in a positive light. Although, like Jessup, she blamed the Islamic conquest and Muslim influence for degrading the status of Hindu women, she saw Muslim women as having a "superior faith" and "more hopefulness" than Hindus.[71] While reiterating understandings of monotheistic religions as superior to polytheism, her book also defied assumptions that all Muslim women were victims of oppression. Humphrey's stories of exemplary women did not suggest that women had never been mistreated in Islamic societies. Nor did *Gems of India* directly contest male missionary texts. But it did encourage a more balanced view in contrast to the prejudicial tropes that other Protestants circulated.

Muslim Women and Missionary Fiction

To convey the condition of Muslim women, other nineteenth-century missionaries began producing realistic fiction set in their mission fields.[72] In *Zeinab, the Panjabi: A Story Founded on Facts* (1895), Elwood Wherry, an American Presbyterian missionary in India from 1867 to 1923, tells of Zeinab, a Muslim woman in a village near Lahore (present-day Pakistan), who loses her husband and turns to a mission dispensary for assistance when her children fall ill.[73] Through the preaching of a Protestant convert from

Islam who runs the dispensary, Zeinab and both children embrace evangelical Protestantism and then face the anger of their "bigoted" and "fanatical" neighbors. The village imam soon hatches a conspiracy that lands Zeinab and her children in the harem of her brother-in-law in Lahore, essentially as captives. After enduring much abuse at his hands and at the hands of his wives, through intervention from the evangelist at the dispensary Zeinab and her children finally return home. The village Muslims recognize the family's hardships and vow to give the widow no further trouble. Shortly afterward, her brother-in-law becomes Christian as well.

While Wherry's purpose was to highlight the successful conversion of Muslims, the narrative format of this publication also allowed readers to imagine the conditions for Muslim women in India. The story was not concerned with Zeinab's attire and made no mention of the veil. Neither did it directly name the degradation of Muslim women. Yet, Wherry nonetheless emphasized the harsh situation for an Indian Muslim widow in a society where women were dependent upon men.[74] He introduced the concept of polygyny first when a kind neighbor considered marrying Zeinab to give her a place in his harem and later with reference to Zeinab living with her brother-in-law's wives. This signaled the Islamic practice of segregated gender spaces, which came into play also when Zeinab was effectively imprisoned in the women's quarters at her brother-in-law's home. The trope of the *Muslim home as a prison* contrasted with Protestant ideals of the *Christian home as a sanctuary* for women.[75] Therefore, although Wherry did not take up the discourse of the veil, his readers would have understood the practice of harem captivity as the private equivalent of public veiling.

Wherry depicted Zeinab as a helpless woman subjected to abuse. His story implied that missionary outreach not only saved her soul but also freed her from threatening Muslim men—including the imam and a dervish whose anti-Christian rhetoric incited Zeinab's brother-in-law to violence. Missionary literature like Wherry's text thus portrayed Muslim men as controlling and often abusive toward women but also as representatives of a "fanatical" and threatening religion. Like Thomson, Wherry described the system of Islam as leaving his characters little room to act. Some of the village men were inclined to show kindness toward the widow Zeinab—until the imam riled them up over her apostasy. Thus, the antagonist in this story was actually *Islam itself*, and for Wherry (like Thomson), Muslim men could leave their lives of unrestrained violence and religious rigidity only through conversion to Christianity.

Missionaries did not always think in such essentialist terms, however. Humphrey's nuanced narratives about individual Muslim women, for instance, presaged alternative approaches to Christian–Muslim relations that became more common in Protestant thinking in the twentieth century. While the longstanding gender tropes persisted, they stood in tension with narratives that today would be recognized as humanizing. This tension grew in the early twentieth century as Protestants launched a more concerted, united, and ecumenical movement for mission to Muslims.

Women and the Turn-of-Century Movement for Missions to Muslims

In 1893, the World's Parliament of Religions, held alongside the Chicago World's Fair, demonstrated a subtle shift in American and British Protestant theological views of other religions, foreshadowing the mid-twentieth-century emergence of western interfaith dialogue.[76] In the decades that followed the Parliament, the Protestant missionary movement exhibited a similar affinity for international gatherings and some hesitant signs of openness toward other religious traditions. Peppered throughout the proceedings of the ecumenical missionary conferences in Edinburgh (1910) and Jerusalem (1928), for example, was a new willingness to speak and write publicly about non-Christian faiths, including Islam, in more appreciative ways. At the same time, these gatherings also sought to unify missionaries across multiple societies working for "The Evangelization of the World in This Generation," the watchword that the Edinburgh Conference organizers adopted from the Student Volunteer Movement (SVM).[77] The ecumenical missionary spirit coalesced also in lesser-known regional gatherings during this period, like the conferences for missionaries to Muslims held in Cairo in 1906, Lucknow in 1911, and in five Middle Eastern locations in 1924.[78] Much more than the well-known meetings in Edinburgh and Jerusalem, these conferences demonstrated the growth of a unique global Anglo-Protestant movement for missions to Muslims.

In the first decade and a half of the twentieth century, this movement answered the call of the few individual missionaries and societies already devoted to converting the followers of Islam. In the religiously diverse context of the Punjab, Wherry was one of these. Samuel Zwemer and Lilias Trotter, whose missions focused exclusively on Muslims, stood out among the others.

Such efforts laid the groundwork for a more united movement by calling attention to what they saw as the overlooked field of missions to Muslims. Zwemer and his colleagues in the Arabian Mission (est. 1889) raised this cry in their quarterly periodical, which they renamed *Neglected Arabia* in 1902 to emphasize this point.[79] Trotter addressed what she saw as the equally neglected field of Algeria after her arrival there in 1888, beginning with the handwritten journals she circulated among supporters of the AMB in both the United Kingdom and United States.[80] In the mission's early years, she lamented that the number of workers was so small outside of Algiers that "the women and children in the far places were *untouched*" by the gospel.[81]

In the early twentieth century, others joined the chorus, especially missionaries working in the Middle East where the constitutional revolutions in Persia (1906) and Ottoman Turkey (1908) brought a new optimism about reaching previously inaccessible Muslim populations.[82] Zwemer has been recognized for orchestrating many of the international connections that facilitated this work, with the lesser-known Wherry as a key partner for convening and publicizing the conferences in Cairo and in Lucknow.[83] Zwemer is also remembered for mobilizing funds, missionaries, and evangelistic literature for Muslims after his return from Arabia to the United States in 1905 and for writing prolifically about Islam.[84] Yet the influence of missionary women like Trotter and Annie Van Sommer, the latter the English missionary who initiated the EGM and Nile Mission Press, is largely untold.[85] Women were instrumental to the missionary enterprise as a whole, but they showed particular interest in the narrative about oppressed Muslim women and girls. This narrative was central in the first three decades of the twentieth century as a rallying point for funds and personnel, and it also aided in uniting mainline denominational mission workers together with non-denominational "faith missions" like the AMB and EGM.

In the following, I examine the streamlined messages about Islam and gender in publications of the early twentieth-century movement for missions to Muslims.

Gender in the Movement for Missions to Muslims

In the early twentieth century, two events aided in formalizing a network of missionaries working among Muslims: the establishment of the Nile Mission Press in 1905 and the gathering known as the First Missionary Conference on behalf of the Mohammedan World in 1906. Both events occurred in Cairo, marking British-occupied Egypt as a center for this new effort. The Nile Mission Press quickly became the press of choice for Arabic evangelistic literature aimed at Muslims—literature which was often translated into other languages.[86] Although its visionary founder, Van Sommer, and its superintendent, Arthur Upson (1874–1958), were both British, the new press became known and gained support in the United States through the Nile Mission Press Auxiliary (in 1911 renamed the American Christian Literature Society for Moslems).[87] One year after the press's establishment, the Cairo Conference was the first in a series of international gatherings which called Protestant missionaries from Asia and Africa to unite toward a distinct goal: "The Moslem world for Christ, in this century!"[88] Sixty-two delegates (including ten women) from twenty-three Protestant mission societies converged on the CMS house in Cairo for this event. Most were British or American.[89]

What role did gender discourses play in the literature that this early twentieth-century movement produced for readers at home? First, the waves of publications solidified Protestant re-inventions of Islam, including the gender tropes. Second, women missionaries within this movement found opportunities to reshape the narrative and bolster their authority, capitalizing on their expertise about Muslim women and girls. The gender norms of Anglo-Protestant missionaries are apparent in the two official Cairo Conference volumes which the conveners produced in 1906. One, titled *Methods of Mission Work Among Moslems*, was edited by Wherry and intended for the private use of missionaries and their associates in developing strategies for missions. The other was a publicly circulated volume, *Mohammedan World of To-Day*, co-edited by Wherry, Zwemer, and James Barton, the latter an ABCFM missionary in Turkey. This volume contained lectures from the conference on the history, culture, and demographics of various Islamic societies.[90] Both books preserved assertions of masculine authority in ecumenical gatherings and in missionary publishing at a time when women had already become the majority in the Protestant missionary enterprise.[91] As reflected in the makeup of the attendees, in the skewed gender distribution of the presenters, and in the lack of voice given to women during conference discussions, such gatherings overlooked the "feminization" of missions. Apart from one session on "women's work" during the conference, at which women made brief statements, only one other woman speaker participated in the program: Anna Watson, a missionary doctor, who spoke about women's hospitals in Egypt at the end of the medical missions session.[92]

This gendered power differential also affected the subjects that the missionary men discussed in their lectures. The publicly available text, *Mohammedan World of To-Day*, covered intellectual arguments against Islam and recounted the history of Islam's advance. Both this and *Methods of Mission Work* also spent considerable time classifying the Muslim population in various regions and documenting strategies for converting Muslim subjects, who were usually gendered male in the lecturer's imagination. Much of the discussion in *Methods of Mission Work*, in fact, assumed that the Muslims in question were educated elite prepared to debate with their male missionary counterparts over the finer points of Islamic and Christian theology.

Missionary men did employ gender discourses purposefully, and several of them, like Jessup, Wherry, and Zwemer, published their own works on Muslim women.[93] Yet this was just one of their many areas of focus. Their lectures at the Cairo Conference left the development of a more robust discourse on Muslim women to their female counterparts and instead used the status of Muslim women to critique Muslim men and Islam. When the men at Cairo assessed the condition of Muslim women in mission fields from Africa to Southeast Asia, for example, they listed things Muslim men did to women—child marriage, arranged marriages, divorce, polygyny, concubinage, prostitution, adultery, veiling, and seclusion—and they described Muslim wives as slaves or "drudges" in the home.[94] The conference speakers presented the women themselves as having little agency, except in their willful ignorance and religious superstition that enabled their own oppression and prevented their men from modernizing.[95] One presenter described the low social development of Muslim countries:

> The social condition of Arabia is exactly what might be expected in a country where the women are almost wholly uneducated and are looked upon as mere animals whose sole purpose in life is to bear children for the husband, cook his food and fear his frown.[96]

Notwithstanding indications that Muslim women's lives differed according to context—like comments on women's relative freedom in West Africa and the lack of veiling or seclusion in Indonesia[97]—these assessments conformed to the typical narrative in other missionary men's writings about Muslim women. I include them here not to suggest their absolute truth through repetition but to exemplify the persistence of such transmitted re-inventions. In fact, Muslim men and women intellectuals in this same period sometimes also used such negative arguments to push for change from within.[98] Others, like the aforementioned Atiya Fyzee and the Indian Muslim reformists she met in London, advocated for women's education as consistent with their Islamic faith and, to support their arguments, "highlighted the numbers of 'famous, able, intelligent, and open–minded women' in Islamic history."[99]

In comparison to the men's presentations at Cairo, at the "women's work" session that was "hurriedly prepared by the ladies attending the Conference,"[100] women missionaries who had not been invited to give formal lectures offered abbreviated accounts of their work focusing not on Muslim men's actions toward women but on Muslim women's difficult experiences, including their "sense of degradation and inferiority ground into [them] by the veil," their use of stimulants to "deaden [their] misery," their fear of both marriage and divorce, and their endurance of physical abuse.[101] Like the men's presentations, these women's remarks also recognized some positive aspects of Islamic societies. For instance, Grettie Y. Holliday, a Presbyterian missionary in Persia, noted an increased appreciation for female education there; and an unnamed missionary in Turkey mentioned her surprise "at the amount of truth which the Moslems know, which harmonizes with what we believe."[102] The latter statement suggested possibilities of appreciation and understanding in Christian–Muslim encounters on the ground.

Our Moslem Sisters (1907): A Missionary Rallying Cry

In response to the inattention the Cairo Conference gave to women, in 1907 Van Sommer and Zwemer edited *Our Moslem Sisters: A Cry of Need from Lands of Darkness Interpreted by Those Who Heard It*. This seminal volume, which Fleming H. Revell published, included only three chapters by men and twenty-two by women, all of whom (except the co-editors) remained anonymous because the evangelization of Muslims was risky in many places. The publisher's identity offers one clue as to the text's pan-Protestant focus and wide distribution, for Revell was the most successful evangelical printing house at the time, with a growing list of titles on Islam.[103]

Our Moslem Sisters counterbalanced the official Cairo Conference volumes by focusing on the condition of Muslim women across the globe.

The idea for this book originated during the women's session in Cairo. Observers reported that "the time [there] was far too short nor had there been preparation for a full and free presentation and discussion of the condition and needs of our Moslem sisters."[104] In response to their exclusion from the conference program, some of the women who attended took initiative afterward under Van Sommer's leadership to compile the volume together with other missionaries not present at the gathering.[105] Women missionaries thus found an important way to engage in the essential missionary task of writing to inform and influence audiences at home. The book's introduction instructed British and American women: "Read for yourselves what is going on in the lives of a hundred million women in the world today and take this burden on your hearts before God."[106]

Our Moslem Sisters emphasized the missionary movement's perilous neglect of Muslim women, while calling for Christian women to answer their Muslim sisters' cries of need. Several themes tied the various chapters together: 1) spiritual and physical darkness as the common denominator for *all* Muslim females; 2) the veil, seclusion, and Muslim marriage as symbols of this darkness; and 3) Hagar as representing contemporary Muslim women, for whom women missionaries could fulfill biblical prophecy.

First, by printing the appeal that the women in Cairo drafted and that the whole conference endorsed afterward, the book's introduction stressed the urgent need for Christian missionaries in Muslim societies:

> The same story has come from India, Persia, Arabia, Africa, and other Mohammedan lands, making evident that the condition of women under Islam is everywhere the same—and that there is no hope of effectually remedying the spiritual, moral, and physical ills which they suffer, except to take them the message of the Saviour, and that there is no chance of their hearing, unless we give ourselves to the work. *No one else will do it.* This lays a heavy responsibility on all Christian women. The number of Moslem *women* is so vast—not less than one hundred million—that any adequate effort to meet the need must be on a scale far wider than has ever yet been attempted.[107]

Following this appeal, Van Sommer's opening chapter asserted that the contributors had not consulted with each other beforehand and that their resulting common message therefore only proved that the conditions for Muslim women were the same everywhere.[108] Likewise, although the book covered more than a dozen countries, Van Sommer emphasized that "one story is told and one cry heard everywhere" because all of the women for whom the missionary voices spoke lived "under Mohammedan law."[109] Indeed, many identical critiques, complaints, and calls for action appeared throughout the book. The editors may have shaped the accounts of their anonymous contributors to some extent, but the similarities also reflected the already well-established Protestant discourse about women and Islam.

We see signs of this basic discourse in the volume's second theme: the association of darkness with veiling/seclusion and Muslim marriage. Such topics were not new, but the authors re-invented them to advocate for Protestant women's mobilization on behalf of their "sisters." Key terms the authors recycled for this new purpose included *seclusion* as imprisonment (in the zenana, seraglio, or harem),[110] *veiling* as an experience of being shrouded or buried alive,[111] wives who endured beatings and treatment as *slaves*,[112] and frequent *divorce* as causing unhappy homes.[113] The authors claimed further that Muslim marriage was founded on *sensuality*,[114] and they described the detriments of *child marriage, loveless* arranged marriage, and *polygyny*.[115] The volume depicted these women as stuck in *degradation, ignorance*, and *superstition* and therefore unable to fulfill their God-given role as helpmeets and homemakers.[116] Such claims reinforced Victorian-era values of domesticity and linked the status of Muslim women to that of Muslims generally for, as Van Sommer emphasized, reiterating the views of her time, "the character of a nation cannot rise above the character of its women."[117]

When engaging the third theme of the book, however—the portrayal of Hagar as mother of the Arabs and as the prototype for Muslim women—these missionaries employed scripture to emphasize that hope remained. This biblical connection to Abraham's family distinguished Muslim women from those other subjects of "woman's work for woman." In her opening chapter titled "Hagar and Her Sisters," Van Sommer insisted that Hagar must return to Christ for Ishmael to live, playing on biblical expectations of her return to the fold of the faithful:

> The story of Hagar, the mother of the Arabs, tells us of a young girl sacrificed for the scheme and then jealousy of an older woman who should have loved and pitied her. And it seems to some of us that it needs the widespread love and pity of the women of our day in Christian lands to seek and save the suffering sinful needy women of Islam.[118]

While Van Sommer's chapter addressed the Hagar story most extensively, others picked up this narrative, calling Muslims the "lost sheep of the house of Ishmael" and the "children of Hagar."[119] The chapter titled "Darkness and Daybreak in Persia," in fact, used the story of Hagar and Sarah to condemn polygyny by citing the jealousy between wives and the effect on children who may see their mother (Hagar) treated with disrespect while another wife (Sarah) takes the place of honor.[120] The final chapter likewise returned to this theme, reiterating the readers' role in fulfilling the biblical promise. It announced that if only Christian women would rise to the occasion to "win the women and girls of Islam for Christ . . . we shall find the answer to Abraham's prayer for his son Ishmael begin to come true: 'As for Ishmael I have heard thee. Behold I have blessed him.'" The author concluded: "And to Our Moslem Sisters may come again the words that were spoken to Hagar: 'The Lord has heard thy affliction.'"[121]

Thus was the message drilled into mission supporters from all angles, using biblical imagery, the well-worn language about Islamic oppression, and assurances from missionary experts that all "our Moslem sisters" live in darkness. In fact the lives of Muslim women were far from the same everywhere. *Our Moslem Sisters* itself confirmed this whenever its authors offered observations of a more ethnographic nature unaccompanied by theological or cultural critique. Notably, the chapter on Egypt clarified that the poorest women there exercised the greatest freedom, for "strict seclusion" applied only to middle- and upper-class Egyptians.[122] Other chapters claimed that polygyny was dying as an institution,[123] that divorce was rare among Muslims in South India and China,[124] and that upper-class girls in Tunis were being married at more appropriate ages.[125] As for their commentary on Muslim men, the chapters reflected that there did exist loving marriages and men who were kind to their wives.[126] Several others identified positive changes in the outlook of Muslim men who wanted more freedom for their wives and daughters.[127] Contradicting the volume's theme of darkness, one author highlighted the bright sides,[128] while another contested universalizing claims about Muslim women saying that "the condition of women is of course not everywhere the same," even though, in her view, "the fundamental views [about women] are the same."[129] Another contradicted the discourse about seclusion:

> In Palestine the women have plenty of liberty. It is a mistake to say that they are shut up. To begin with, they live in large houses with gardens and

courtyards enclosed. They go out visiting one another, to the public baths, and to the cemetery regularly.... The girls go to school regularly. The richer Moslems have resident governesses for their daughters, and they are eager for education.[130]

Such pictures of Muslim life appeared often as the authors described their encounters with Muslims among whom they lived or worked, indicating that in the context of building personal relationships missionaries found many alternatives to the prevalent narrative about Muslim women's oppression. The authors interpreted these instances as *exceptions* that did not negate the dire need for more mission workers for Muslim contexts. Yet this commentary did show that personal contact shaped missionaries' views in more nuanced ways. For example, when the author of the chapter on Algeria (perhaps Lilias Trotter) affirmed the "qualities of endurance and sacrifice" that she perceived in the women there, she conveyed a human connection that her readers—who largely lacked contact with Muslims—would otherwise have missed. While reflecting on the unity of humankind as created by God, the author explained that Algerian "souls are the very same as other souls."[131] Such insights into Muslim life were even more prominent in the Lucknow Conference volume devoted to the subject of Muslim women.

Daylight in the Harem (1911): Optimism in the Women's Ecumenical Movement

In contrast to *Our Moslem Sisters*, the second volume that Van Sommer edited with Zwemer and published with Fleming H. Revell, *Daylight in the Harem: A New Era for Moslem Women* (1911), consisted of actual women's lectures from the Lucknow Conference of 1911. Avoiding a repetition of the haphazard women's session at Cairo, the Lucknow program included a "great company of women delegates" (43 out of 169) and thirteen women speakers. Twelve of these women gave addresses on work among women, most of which became chapters in *Daylight in the Harem*.[132] The tenor of this volume was decidedly more hopeful than that of *Our Moslem Sisters*, coming in the aftermath of the constitutional revolutions in the Ottoman Empire and Persia, which missionaries believed boded well for women's freedom. The book also included perspectives on Muslim women that were less unified than those of *Our Moslem Sisters*. Yet it is well not to overstate the differences between the two volumes. Having the same editors and publisher, the two books reflected the variety of ways in which missionaries from multiple denominations and mission societies interpreted the cultures within which they worked.

After a preface calling on Christian women to let the book stir their hearts "to the cause of Moslem Women," and following Zwemer's introduction,[133] Van Sommer's opening chapter proclaimed a "New Era for Moslem Womanhood" based on her experiences in Egypt and on information from contacts in Persia and Turkey. Emphasizing *daylight* rather than *darkness* as the increasing condition of the harem, the opening theme of this text was not a "cry of help" as in the 1907 volume but the optimistic assurance that circumstances were changing for Muslim women—because of the Protestant missionary movement in Islamic societies and other western influences. Taking up the discourse of the veil in a new way, Van Sommer described the veil's dwindling power as one sign of this hope: Turkish women were discarding their face veils, Persian women were doing away with the "house veil" and shifting from white muslin to a smaller black face covering for outdoors, and Egyptian elites had reduced their veils to "the merest pretence by using the finest gauze."[134] Thus, Van Sommer signaled the book's aim to demonstrate that both God and Protestant missionaries had been hard at work.

The related theme of revolution also permeated *Daylight in the Harem*. By and large, the ten authors—speaking on contexts including Turkey, Persia, Egypt, Algeria, and India—sustained the discourse of the veil/seclusion. Yet they also emphasized the revolutionary actions that Muslim women themselves were undertaking. Though "[s]till behind the veil, still restricted by religious law," women in Tehran had already established more than a hundred girls' schools and had organized societies for the promotion of female education, Holliday claimed.[135] In Turkey, likewise, Congregationalist missionary Mary Mills Patrick explained, a society of educated women had been created "for the elevation of those who are veiled."[136] These authors in their hopefulness for change gave Muslim women more agency than did the earlier narrative about Christian women saving Hagar's sisters, and although many of them focused on "woman's work,"[137] the repeated attention to shifts among reform-minded men softened the pervasive image of the irrationally violent Muslim man. This emphasis also appeared in many other missionary women's publications of this period. For instance, in January 1907 the Presbyterian women's mission magazine *Woman's Work for Woman* reprinted a cartoon from a Persian paper depicting a Muslim father walking his daughter to school. The caption read, "Furor for Education in Persia. The turbaned gentleman leads his daughter to the school-room door."[138] Such examples disclosed the plurality of views within the Protestant women's movement for missions to Muslims and indicated that missionaries were not the only—or even the primary—instigators of change in early twentieth-century Islamic societies.

The authors of *Daylight in the Harem* likewise demonstrated through their personal reflections that missionaries' methods and even beliefs could transform through contact with Muslims. Clara Wherry's chapter on the training of Indian women converts from Islam showed a sensitivity to accommodating the restrictive gender norms that both she and her husband Elwood had previously critiqued.[139] She had asked other missionary women in India whether missionaries should make "any special concessions to women converts, as to *purdah*," employing the term both Muslims and Hindus in South Asia used to describe the practice of female seclusion (including gender segregation and covering of the body).[140] One of Wherry's correspondents described Christian women wearing burqas (garments that fully cover the face and body) when passing through the streets but removing them upon arrival at church, where they nevertheless chose to retain their purdah practices by sitting separately from the men.[141] This missionary also believed that adherence to such customs at church "would be to the benefit of the Indian Christian Community" elsewhere.[142] Another missionary who wrote to Wherry recommended a "purdah arrangement for those who would like to use it" but not for all, since some Indians had begun giving it up.[143] A third correspondent described making provisions for baptizing Muslim women outside the view of men, noting that on one occasion a missionary woman had even performed the ceremony.[144] By suggesting that veiling and gender separation did not signify oppression if practiced by converts to Christianity, these missionaries and several others that Wherry cited from Syria and Egypt willingly accommodated the prevailing Islamic culture and carefully attended to the comfort of Muslim converts for whom such dress norms and seating arrangements were familiar.

The chapter that most strikingly disrupted the narrative about Muslim women's oppression was written by the aforementioned Mary Mills Patrick (1850–1940), president of Constantinople Woman's College, an American missionary school outside of Istanbul. An extraordinary figure, Patrick earned a PhD in Switzerland; and, as Carolyn McCue Goffman has demonstrated, she transformed during her years in Turkey from a missionary evangelist to a feminist educator who advocated for Muslim women's rights and supported Turkish nationalism. Evidence of Patrick's shift from "proselytizing Christianity to promoting cosmopolitan feminism" was apparent in her Lucknow address.[145] In it she argued directly against the Anglo-Protestant assumption that thick veils, heavy curtains, and seclusion were "the principal elements" of Muslim women's being—a view neglecting the various advantages "that are nevertheless connected with their legal and social relations."[146] Although Patrick was not wholly uncritical of Islamic society, unlike the other authors of the volume, she did not see hope only in the changes happening for contemporary Muslim women under the new Turkish regime. Rather, her lecture primarily informed her audience about the advantage of property rights that Muslim women had always had under Islamic law. Of these rights, Patrick explained:

> On her marriage, a Mohammedan woman does not lose her individuality. She does not merge her rights in those of her husband, but she may exercise many rights that may belong to any citizen. She may act as administratrix or executrix, or be appointed legally as governor of a charitable endowment, and she can make legal contracts with anyone.... If the wife earns money, the husband cannot control it or live upon it in idleness, without her consent. Marriage among the Mohammedans is merely a civil contract.... In many respects it regards the rights on either side, as neither has any control of the property and legal relations of the other.[147]

Patrick did not compare this Muslim practice to the situation of property rights in Christian marriage, but it was implied, nevertheless. We might also recall (from Chapter 2) Lady Mary Wortley Montagu's envy of elite Turkish women's financial independence in comparison to that of women of her own station in eighteenth-century England. While Patrick gave most attention to property rights, this was just one of several illustrations she offered to suggest that Islamic teachings on women did not conform to the western discourse about them. She insisted that such rights for Muslim women

> began with Mohammed, for when we consider the degraded condition of society in Mohammed's time, we see that his teachings enforced an increased respect for women, purified polygamy, although they did not destroy it, and demanded a degree of equity in marriage that was in advance of the teaching of that day among the Arabs.[148]

She noted further that by the third century of Islam, Qur'anic laws taught monogamy, that Muslim women historically had opportunities for professional life (including in medicine), and that, in an earlier era when Muslim women had greater freedom, there were female preachers who delivered sermons to other women in the mosques and marketplaces.[149]

What are we to make of such statements, which move so far beyond the positive observations of Muslim life that other missionary authors mentioned only as exceptions to the rule? Patrick not only directly contested the norms of missionary discourse; she also defended Islam in response to Protestant misperceptions. Although her lecture was included in the volume, the editor's remarks appended to her chapter attempted to diminish the impact of Patrick's radical claims.[150] According to the editorial note, property rights were necessary for Muslim women because marriage in Islam, unlike Christianity, was seen as "a temporary union terminable always at the will of the husband." Thus, the divorced wife needed to be able to take her dowry and other property with her to survive.[151] The editor also took issue with Patrick's claim that property rights for women originated with the prophet of Islam:

> The Quran does not provide for this right of woman to hold her own property, neither does it appear in the history of the founding of Islam. The inference is that fathers and brothers have devised it to protect the women of their families whom they give in marriage, and that instead of reflecting credit on Islam, it reveals the low ideas which underlie the Moslem conception of marriage.[152]

This editorial wrongly interpreted the right of women to "own, manage, and dispose of property," which Muslims enjoyed "centuries before women in the West"[153] as merely a social innovation disconnected from Islamic teachings and distant from the early years of the religion's founding. The editor stretched the truth here by emphasizing that women's property rights were not stipulated in the Qur'an. In fact, Muslim jurists did cite portions of the Qur'an when arguing that men and women have equal rights to property, but Islamic law (*shari'a*) is also based on the Hadith (accounts of the statements and actions of the Prophet Muhammad), which more explicitly provided for women's rights.[154] Thus, this skewed editorial note neglected the wider scope of Islamic teachings outside the Qur'an and encouraged readers' prejudices against Islam.

Nevertheless, in *Daylight in the Harem* the editors were unable to transmit a uniform message about Muslim women's lives like the one they put forth in the opening of *Our Moslem Sisters*. Rather, the 1911 text captured a range of missionary women's voices and acceptable views of gender norms in Islam from the perspective of the ecumenical missionary enterprise. More than its predecessor, the book also reflected the frank points of discussion and disagreement that arose at Lucknow among delegates hailing from a variety of Protestant traditions and mission societies.

Disseminating Missionary Women's Re-inventions

The first two volumes on Muslim women emerging from the ecumenical gatherings of the early twentieth century, *Our Moslem Sisters* and *Daylight in the Harem*, were key publications about Islam that gained attention in the outpouring of missionary literature that Protestant women helped disseminate during this period. These books effectively harnessed the ecumenical missionary spirit and gave the topic of "woman's work" for Muslim women a new urgency and legitimacy within the male-dominated international conferences of the period. These efforts were also tied to the successes of the wider women's missionary movement that had formed in Britain and the United States by the mid-nineteenth century and largely operated in spaces beyond male oversight. This women's movement facilitated the new push for missions to Muslim women by 1) providing a vocabulary upon which advocates for Muslim missions could build and 2) operating literary outlets through which this new cause and its accompanying publications could be made available to millions of Protestant men, women, and children.

First, twentieth-century advocates for the uplift of Muslim women built upon existing narratives about women of "the Orient." As Lisa Joy Pruitt argued in her study on nineteenth-century American Protestant women in Asia, messages about gender oppression, more than any other social factor, accounted for the rising activity of women missionaries working among non-western women.[155] This remained true in the early twentieth century, as we saw in Van Sommer's description of the typical Muslim woman as "Unwelcome at birth, unloved in her life-time, without hope in her death."[156] Adaptations of this same statement appeared several times in *Our Moslem Sisters* and were frequently repeated in other missionary literature.[157] In fact, Pruitt traced this discourse describing "Oriental" daughters as "unwelcomed at their birth" to the women's missionary boards of the late 1860s, and missionary women continued to employ this catchphrase into the early twentieth century. In an issue that *Woman's Work for Woman* published in 1900, for example, Mrs. Moses Smith, a representative of the Chicago-based Congregational Woman's Board of Missions of the Interior, wrote:

> One half of the women of the world are in seclusion. This may not always mean the actual imprisonment in Indian zenanas, lattice-closed houses of China and harems of Turkey, but it does mean that practically all the veiled, ghostly throng of the Orient are debarred from listening to the Gospel unless a Christian woman seeks and wins them. *Unwelcome at birth, married in childhood to men whom they have never seen, without love, without light, without hope, without home,* they live their lives and go the way of the earth, leaving their sons, as well as their daughters, their heritage of degradation.[158]

Thus seclusion (or veiling) symbolized for Smith the miserable condition of Asian women generally. Other missionary publications adapted the catchphrase to highlight the plight of Indian women specifically.[159] Still others applied it even more broadly:

> *Reader!* If you were one of the millions of heathen women: Unwelcome at birth; Untaught in childhood; Unloved in wifehood; Uncherished in widowhood; Unprotected in old age; Unlamented when dead—What would you ask the Christian women of America? *"Think on these things."* Philippians 4:8.[160]

Such language appeared so often in missionary literature that most American and British Protestant mission societies likely had disseminated some version of it by the time of the Cairo Conference.[161] In recasting this familiar refrain, then, *Our Moslem Sisters* drew upon the energies and convictions of the thriving women's missionary movement and primed Protestant audiences to take seriously its call for *woman's work for Muslim women*.[162]

Second, most Protestant mission boards in the United States, including women's boards, distributed and promoted the literature that came out of Cairo and Lucknow, as well as advertising other available American and British texts on Islam and missions. With rising frequency between 1906 and

1914 (when war broke out in Europe), they promoted such publications in book reviews, offered them through lending libraries, and integrated these resources into guides and curricula for women's and children's groups. Notably, *Woman's Missionary Friend*, the renamed periodical of the Woman's Foreign Missionary Society of the Methodist Episcopal Church in the United States, highlighted *Our Moslem Sisters* in 1907 as one outcome of the Cairo Conference. It concluded, with words similar to those of the book's introduction, "It is a pitiful story that is told by the twenty-five authors, and the unanimity of their testimony and unimpeachable character, make a strong appeal to the Christian World."[163] After several issues hailing the achievements at Cairo, *Woman's Work for Woman* also reviewed *Our Moslem Sisters*. Like the aforementioned Methodist review, this one emphasized the book's unanimous narrative, echoing Zwemer and Van Sommer to explain, "Writing independently, all the authors agree that 'Islam is the same everywhere' as regards polygamy, unhappiness in Moslem houses, degradation of the women and the part played by divorce."[164] The review noted with praise that, although the book demonstrated a great need, it still showed signs of hope. Significantly, the reviewer contended, the authors did not hesitate to "report 'grand exceptions' to the bad rule," and they demonstrated that "Moslem women *can* rise from the degradation of centuries."[165] Other women's periodicals republished portions of *Our Moslem Sisters*, bringing its message to those who might not have access to the book. In 1908, *The Women's Missionary Magazine* of the United Free Church of Scotland printed a four-page excerpt, titled "Not Dead, only Dry," and reprinted several images of North African women that had appeared in the volume's chapter of the same title.[166]

Following the Lucknow Conference, mission periodicals used reviews of *Daylight in the Harem* similarly to connect their readers with the ecumenical movement for missions to Muslims.[167] One such periodical, the ABCFM's *Missionary Herald*, recommended the 1911 volume, saying, "As showing brighter aspects of the picture, this book makes a good companion to 'Our Moslem Sisters,' the volume which, following the Cairo Conference, portrayed vividly the misery and shame of womanhood in Mohammedan lands."[168] While mission periodicals reinforced the basic narrative of these books, they also sometimes raised critical issues—like recognizing bright points, exceptions, and non-western women's agency for change. In short, Protestant readers (like the female missionary authors) did not all blindly accept the dominant discourse. In addition to this flurry of reviews, the circulation of book lists and titles available from mission libraries reflected efforts to make these women's volumes from Cairo and Lucknow available for readers,[169] along with other recent missionary publications on Islam.[170]

Women's missionary magazines best demonstrated the cohesion of the literature that Protestant societies transmitted to US audiences. Most drew on literature from the interdenominational Central Committee on the United Study of Foreign Missions (CCUSFM), an American committee founded during the Ecumenical Missionary Conference of 1900 in New York. The Federation of Women's Boards of Foreign Missions[171] operated the Central Committee and coordinated with the SVM to provide a series of annual textbooks for "united study." The eighth volume in the series was Samuel M. Zwemer and Arthur Judson Brown's, *The Nearer and Farther East: Outline Studies of Moslem Lands and of Siam, Burma, and Korea* (1908). Multiple mission societies used these textbooks and accompanying leaders' guides, even beyond the Central Committee's seven denominational members (Congregational, Episcopal, Methodist, Presbyterian, Baptist, Lutheran, and Dutch Reformed).[172] Women's magazines were an important means for promoting such resources. For instance, *Friends Missionary Advocate*, an American periodical that the Quaker Women's Foreign Union managed,[173] announced that their textbook for 1908–1909 was *The Nearer and Farther East*, the first part of which focused on "the terrible need and marvelous opportunity of the vast, almost untouched Mohammedan fields."[174] Starting in September 1908 with essays about the Prophet Muhammad and Islam, each monthly issue reprinted lessons from the textbook.[175]

Another American society that followed the CCUSFM series, The Free Baptist Woman's Missionary Society, printed the monthly study guides for *Nearer and Farther East* in its periodical, *The Missionary Helper*. For March of 1909, the section on "Helps for Monthly Meetings" suggested a Bible reading on "Hagar and Her Sisters" (Gen. 21:14–20) and included an excerpt from Van Sommer's chapter of the same title emphasizing, "When Hagar returns to Christ, Ishmael shall live."[176] This was one of the many ways in which *Our Moslem Sisters* influenced Protestant constituents beyond those who purchased the book. Meanwhile, the advertisement of such literature and the use of the CCUSFM textbooks also demonstrated the significant and deliberate Anglo-Protestant streamlining of educational and devotional materials related to Islam across multiple denominations and independent mission organizations in the pre–World War I era.

Conclusion

In the context of early twentieth-century ecumenical enthusiasm, missionary women found opportunities to reshape Protestant images of Islam through their published narratives. These women expanded the movement for missions to Muslims through their lectures and writings and through the literature that women's missionary societies distributed widely in the United States and Britain. In analyzing missionary women's textual re-inventions of Islam along with men's publications, this chapter has illustrated key shifts in Protestant discourses on Islam from the nineteenth to the early twentieth century. It has shown that the missionary movement gave more attention to Muslims than ever before and that, as Protestant women took on a larger role in defining and critiquing Islamic cultures, they focused on Muslim women's experiences, often expanding or countering information male writers had provided. Yet three points require further elucidation before I conclude:

1) Missionary women re-invented the Protestant discourse about Islam by focusing upon actual Muslim women's lives and by identifying Christian women as the saviors of these Muslim women.
2) British and American Protestant missionaries strategically used biblical accounts of Hagar and Ishmael in their messages to mission supporters.
3) Despite the persistent tropes, missionary texts also contained nuanced, even appreciative images of Muslim women and men—what amounted to positive re-inventions of Islam.

First, rather than using narratives about women's oppression primarily to condemn Islam or to mark Muslim men as immoral, as male writers usually did, missionary women more often shifted the discourse to the actual lived experiences of Muslim women. They followed the pattern that the women's missionary movement established in the nineteenth century—recasting the general emphasis on a Protestant woman's duty to other women to emphasize the pressing need to reach Muslim women specifically. Although not all women missionaries wrote about women's issues, those who did spoke with authority based on the access they had to Muslim women's spaces in homes and schools. In so doing, they recognized Muslim women as subjects in their own right. The perspectives offered in volumes like *Our Moslem Sisters* and *Daylight in the Harem* went only so far, however. For although these texts did not use the plight of Muslim women as a tool for theological critique, missionary women employed the discourse of the veil/seclusion to legitimize their work as equally important to that of missionary men. While empowering Protestant women's religious leadership, therefore, these texts also conveyed that most Muslim women were helpless victims needing (White) Christian women to rescue them. Missionary women underlined the urgency of this work through claims that Muslim mothers were the key to saving the entire Muslim population.

Second, in texts meant to inform mission supporters, raise funds, and recruit new workers, Protestant missionary men and women alike interpreted the narrative from Genesis about Hagar and Ishmael as an archetype for conceiving of modern Islam within God's plan for the spread of Christianity. These texts associated all Muslims—regardless of their ethnic heritage—with the assumed character traits of Hagar and her son, thus stretching the understanding (common to both Christians and Muslims) that the Arabs were Ishmael's descendants. While the story of the helpless Hagar fit the rhetoric of the women's missionary movement, references to the outcasts from Abraham's family tapped into the kind of biblical Orientalism that made William Thomson's *The Land and the Book* a bestseller.[177] Missionaries therefore not only employed the biblical narrative to reinforce religio-racial hierarchies (identifying Ishmael's descendants as innately wild and hostile); they also assigned Protestants a central role in fulfilling the promise that Ishmael would live and Hagar would return to the fold of God's people.[178] To spur her readers to action, Annie Van Sommer equated Hagar's story with the situation of all Muslim women: both "Hagar and her sisters" were abused and defenseless. Indeed, in Van Sommer's interpretation, although Hagar herself wept and God answered, Hagar's contemporary sisters needed Christian women to cry out for them:

> You cannot know how great the need unless you are told; you will never go and find them until you hear their cry. And they will never cry for themselves, for they are down under the yoke of centuries of oppression, and their hearts have no hope or knowledge of anything better.[179]

Despite the diverse contexts in which early twentieth-century Muslim women lived from North Africa to Southeast Asia and beyond, mission supporters likely accepted this statement based on the image that the women's missionary movement had already established of non-western women as passive victims. In light of this view, missionary narratives that characterized Hagar as the Egyptian foremother of Arab Muslims did not necessarily contradict the image of Hagar as an enslaved African that was common in nineteenth-century biblical interpretation.[180] Missionaries working in the Middle East saw the Egyptian Hagar as Arab, making this biblical analogy particularly strong. But within the broader discourse of women's missions, Hagar's story was just as relevant for all women of Africa and Asia who required western women's help to escape lives of misery. Thus, missionary women employed racist and Eurocentric ideas for their own advantage.

This powerless Hagar differs significantly from the image of Hagar in Islamic tradition, which honors her both for trusting in God and for actively seeking water in the desert to save her son.[181] When God provided a spring in response to Hagar's prayers, according to *Sahih al-Bukhari* (the foremost of the canonical Sunni collections of Hadith), she built a basin to control the flow of water, forming the sacred well known as Zamzam.[182] Located within the Masjid al-Haram in Mecca, which also houses the Ka'ba, the well is a pilgrimage site for Muslims who commemorate Hagar's decision "to keep running and looking and praying for help" and her "determination to fight for her beloved child's life to the last drop of her own strength."[183] Thus, the Islamic tradition emphasizes Hagar's agency for good, and not her passivity in suffering. In Riffat Hassan's words, "She is a victor who, with the help of God and her own initiative, is able to transform the wilderness into the cradle of a new world dedicated to the fulfillment of God's purpose on earth."[184] This contrasts starkly with the modern missionary's helpless Hagar.

Third, despite claims about the universality of Muslim women's oppression, missionary texts also mentioned happy Muslim marriages and instances in which Muslim women took action to change their circumstances, like the Islamic Hagar did. These reports were usually muted or passed off as exceptions, but it is important to acknowledge the nuances and alternate understandings even in texts aiming to draw in mission supporters because such understandings eventually led some missionaries toward interfaith dialogue efforts. Significantly, both Emily Humphrey's late nineteenth-century account of admirable Muslim women leaders in India and the optimistic portrayals throughout *Daylight in the Harem* of reform-minded Muslim men disrupted the discourse of the veil/seclusion.

In highlighting such perspectives, I do not intend to redeem the Protestant polemics that at the same time advanced racist notions of White Christian supremacy and turned the actual suffering of some Muslim women into a fundraising tool. Yet these narratives offer a fuller picture of American and British Protestant missionaries. The firsthand encounters upon which missionaries based their stories distinguished their writings from Reformation-era texts on Islam, for example, and led to ethnographic-type descriptions of Islamic societies. Because they built relationships with indigenous people and endeavored to learn local languages and customs, missionary writings humanized Muslims even as they also transmitted negative gender tropes. For instance, missionary women willingly accommodated practices of seclusion in Protestant schools and Muslim homes. Several missionaries in South Asia and the Middle East whose accounts appeared in *Daylight in the Harem* even recommended these practices within churches for Muslim converts. Such attention to Muslim women's preferences not only shifted missionary approaches over time but also changed their views on Islam, as we saw most clearly with Mary Mills Patrick's positive assessment of Muslim women's property rights.

These three points help to clarify how Anglo-Protestant missionaries simultaneously perpetuated longstanding tropes about Muslims and developed for themselves more appreciative images of Islam. Considering the widely disseminated literature from the early twentieth-century movement for missions to Muslims that aimed at fundraising and recruitment, it is not surprising that the gender critiques continued. For their part, a huge number of Protestants at home consumed such literature and incorporated it into their devotional lives. Mission-focused Bible study guides and common prayers, like one from the CMS Prayer Cycle that appeared at the conclusion of *Our Moslem Sisters*, provided a sense of unity with other mission supporters and modeled an appropriate Protestant orientation toward Muslims.[185] Protestant audiences who used such devotional materials internalized and incorporated missionary re-inventions of Islam into their lived religious practices and often became transmitters of missionary material themselves. They did so through lending libraries and mission auxiliary meetings or as authors for local newspapers, women's magazines, or even major book publishers. Mary Entwistle, a British supporter of the CMS whose children's books are featured in the next chapter and who was not a missionary, took on the latter role. I turn now to the ways that such authors of children's literature sought to instill a sense of missionary responsibility in Protestant children and youth.

Notes

1. Annie Van Sommer, "Hagar and Her Sisters," in *Our Moslem Sisters: A Cry of Need from Lands of Darkness Interpreted by Those Who Heard It*, ed. Annie Van Sommer and Samuel M. Zwemer (New York: Fleming H. Revell, 1907), 19.
2. Ibid., 15.
3. Studies upon which my work builds include Thomas Kidd, *American Christians and Islam: Evangelical Culture and Muslims from the Colonial Period to the Age of Terrorism* (Princeton, NJ: Princeton University Press, 2009), 37–95; Jane I. Smith, "Christian Missionary Views of Islam in the Nineteenth and Twentieth Centuries," *Islam and Christian–Muslim Relations* 9, no. 3 (2007): 357–73; Timothy Marr, *The Cultural Roots of American Islamicism* (Cambridge: Cambridge University Press, 2006), 82–133; Christine Leigh Heyrman, *American Apostles: When Evangelicals Entered the World of Islam* (New York: Hill and Wang, 2015). Of these, Heyrman's book gave the most attention to missionary writings about women and Islam.
4. Eliza F. Kent, *Converting Women: Gender and Protestant Christianity in Colonial South China* (Oxford: Oxford University Press, 2004), 11.
5. Dana L. Robert, *American Women in Mission: A Social History of Their Thought and Practice* (Macon, GA: Mercer University Press, 1997), 200–1; Rhonda Anne Semple, *Missionary Women: Gender, Professionalism and the Victorian Idea of Christian Mission* (Woodbridge, UK: Boydell Press, 2003), 11.
6. Single women carved out space for themselves on mission fields where they fulfilled roles different than those expected of missionary wives and mothers, making missionary work into a woman's profession by serving as teachers, directors of mission schools, and even evangelists and preachers. On the professionalization of women's missionary work, see Semple, *Missionary Women*, 6, 190–228.
7. Saba Mahmood, *Politics of Piety: Islamic Revival and the Feminist Subject* (Princeton, NJ: Princeton University Press, 2012). In the late nineteenth and early twentieth centuries, Zaynab Fawwaz was one such Muslim woman who argued that women could pursue any male profession, a radical idea for Christians and Muslims alike. Yet Fawwaz also followed Islamic norms of gender separation and veiling. Deanna Ferree Womack, *Protestants, Gender and the Arab Renaissance in Late Ottoman Syria* (Edinburgh: Edinburgh University Press, 2019), 178–79. See also Marilyn Booth, *The Career and Communities of Zaynab Fawwaz: Feminist Thinking in Fin-de-siècle Egypt* (New York: Oxford University Press, 2022), 11–12.
8. Barbara Welter, "The Cult of True Womanhood: 1820–1860," *American Quarterly* 18, no. 2, part 1 (Summer 1966): 152–53, 163–64.
9. Charlotte E. Weber, "Making Common Cause?: Western and Middle Eastern Feminists in the International Women's Movement, 1911–1948" (PhD diss., Ohio State University, 2003), 18; Sarah Frances Smith, "'She Moves the Hands That Move the World': Antebellum Childrearing: Images of Mother and Child in Nineteenth-Century Periodicals for Mothers" (PhD diss., University of Minnesota, 2006).
10. Amy G. Richter, *At Home in Nineteenth-Century America: A Documentary History* (New York: New York University Press, 2015), 214–15.
11. Robert, *American Women in Mission*, 65.
12. Lisa Joy Pruitt, *A Looking-Glass for Ladies: American Protestant Women and the Orient in the Nineteenth Century* (Macon, GA: Mercer University Press, 2005), 49; Semple, *Missionary Women*, 54; Robert, *American Women in Mission*, 67.
13. Welter, "Cult of True Womanhood," 171. On the transmission of such views to Protestants in the Middle East, see Womack, *Protestants, Gender*, 169–76.
14. Pruitt, *Looking-Glass*, 43, 49; Welter, "Cult of True Womanhood," 162; Claire Cooke, "Capping Power? Clothing and the Female Body in African Methodist Episcopal Mission Photographs," *Mission Studies* 31 (2014): 424, 426, 432, 437, 439.
15. Billie Melman, *Women's Orients: English Women and the Middle East, 1718–1918: Sexuality, Religion and Work* (Ann Arbor: University of Michigan Press, 1992), 137–64. Based on an extensive survey of women's magazines published between 1820 and 1860, Welter described the proper role of the woman as being a "hostage" in the home. Welter, "Cult of True Womanhood," 151.
16. Séverine Gabry-Thienpont and Norig Neveu, "Missions and the Construction of Gender in the Middle East," *Social Sciences and Missions* 34 (2021): 14.

17. In small numbers from the middle to late nineteenth century, women also found placements as missionary doctors, often focusing on medical care for women and children.
18. The same was true for upper-class Hindus who practiced purdah, or female seclusion in zenanas, and the covering of the body from male eyes.
19. On "woman's work for woman," see Chapter 1 and Robert, *American Women in Mission*, 130–37. On the growth of women's missionary societies and auxiliaries, see P. Hill, *The World Their Household: The American Woman's Foreign Movement and Cultural Transformation, 1870–1920* (Ann Arbor: University of Michigan Press, 1985), 3. The number of American women involved in missions rose to three million by 1915.
20. Even women-led societies like the British Syrian Mission (introduced in Chapter 1) depended on partnerships with missionary men in other societies in order to hold chapel services. Womack, *Protestants, Gender*, 169–76.
21. For one example in Ottoman Syria, see Womack, *Protestants, Gender*, 278–84.
22. Deanna Ferree Womack, "American Muslims, Arab Christians, and Religo-Racial Misrecognition," in *Alterity and the Evasion of Justice: Explorations of the "Other" in World Christianity*, ed. Deanna Ferree Womack and Raimundo C. Barreto, Jr. (Minneapolis: Fortress Press, 2023), 33–34.
23. This was implied in the title of the following: Annie Van Sommer and Samuel M. Zwemer, eds., *Our Moslem Sisters: A Cry of Need from Lands of Darkness Interpreted by Those Who Heard It* (New York: Fleming H. Revell, 1907).
24. Kent, *Converting Women*, 10.
25. Mohja Kahf, *Western Representations of the Muslim Woman: From Termagant to Odalisque* (Austin: University of Texas Press, 1999), 7, 15, 96–98, 112–13, 117, 177–79.
26. Gayatri Chakravorty Spivak, "Can the Subaltern Speak?," in *Marxism and the Interpretation of Culture*, ed. Cary Nelson and Lawrence Grossberg (Urbana: University of Illinois Press, 1988), 293. On the imperial rescue paradigm and Spivak's work in relation to Islamic feminism, see Miriam Cook, "Islamic Feminism Before and After September 11th," *Duke Journal of Gender Law & Policy* 9, no. 2 (2002): 227–35.
27. Christopher Herbert, *Culture and Anomie: Ethnographic Imagination in the Nineteenth Century* (Chicago: University of Chicago Press, 1991).
28. Charlotte Florentia Clive, "Indian Journal, 1798." Transcribed by W. H. Ramsey, circa 1857. Asia, Pacific, and African Collections (WD4235), British Library, London. Charlotte's father, Edward Clive, was governor of Madras, India, from 1798 to 1803.
29. See Chapters 5 and 6.
30. William Jowett, *Christian Researches in the Mediterranean, from 1815 to 1820, in Furtherance of the Object of the Church Missionary Society*, 2nd ed. (London: L. B. Seeley and J. Hatchard & Son, 1822); William Jowett, *Christian Researches in Syria and the Holy Land in 1823 and 1824 in Furtherance of the Objects of the Church Missionary Society* (Boston: Crocker & Brewster, 1826); Gareth Atkins, "William Jowett's *Christian Researches*: British Protestants and Religious Plurality in the Mediterranean, Syria and the Holy Land, 1815–30," *Studies in Church History* 51 (2015): 217–18. This information-gathering strategy in support of Protestant missions began with the widely received publication by Claudius Buchanan, chaplain of the British East India Company: *Christian Researches in Asia: With Notices of the Translation of the Scriptures into Oriental Language* (Boston: Samuel T. Armstrong, Cornhill, 1811).
31. Jowett, *Christian Researches in the Mediterranean*, 248–49.
32. Ibid., 256. Italics in original.
33. Ibid., 249, 252–53.
34. Jowett, *Christian Researches in Syria*, v; William M. Thomson, *The Land and the Book: Or Biblical Illustrations Drawn from the Manners and Customs, the Scenes and Scenery of The Holy Land*, exp. ed. (New York: Harper & Brothers, 1886). On Thomson, see David D. Grafton, *An American Biblical Orientalism: The Construction of Jews, Christians, and Muslims in Nineteenth-Century American Evangelical Piety* (Lanham, MD: Lexington Books, 2019), 147–80; Kidd, *American Christians*, 55–56.
35. Grafton, *American Biblical Orientalism*, 173.
36. Ibid., 154. Among other such narratives flooding the market was Mark Twain's *Innocents Abroad* (1859). Grafton also mentioned Edward Robinson's and Eli Smith's studies of the Holy Land, which were less popular in nature.

37. Grafton, *American Biblical Orientalism*, 155. See pp. 165 and 175–76 on Thomson's misleading use of images from William Edward Lane's *The Manners and Customs of Modern Egyptians* (1860) when representing Syria.
38. Thomson, *Land and the Book*, 83–84.
39. Ibid., 536–37.
40. Ibid., 86–87.
41. Ann Braude, *Radical Spirits: Spiritualism and Women's Rights in Nineteenth-Century America*, 2nd ed. (Bloomington: Indiana University Press, 2001); Kabria Baumgartner, *In Pursuit of Knowledge: Black Women and Educational Activism in Antebellum America* (New York: New York University Press, 2019); Tera W. Hunter, *Bound in Wedlock: Slave and Free Black Marriage in the Nineteenth Century* (Cambridge, MA: Belknap Press of Harvard University Press, 2017); Benson Tong, *Unsubmissive Women: Chinese Prostitutes in Nineteenth-Century San Francisco* (Norman: University of Oklahoma Press, 2000).
42. Other missionaries, like Mary Mills Patrick, recognized Muslim women's movements and the advantages of women's property rights in Islamic law. M. M. Patrick, "Among the Educated Women of Turkey," in *Daylight in the Harem: A New Era for Moslem Women*, ed. Annie Van Sommer and Samuel M. Zwemer (New York: Fleming H. Revel, 1911), 73–89. On nineteenth-century Muslim women engaging in debates on girls' education, marriage, divorce, and polygyny, see Booth, *Career and Communities*.
43. Thomson, *Land and the Book*, 87, 92.
44. Ibid., 536. For Thomson, the Bedouin Arabs most closely retained the traits of the Ishmaelites. See also similar references to the Bedouins' unruly "Ishmaelitic spirit" in Henry Harris Jessup, *Fifty-Three Years in Syria* (New York: Fleming H. Revell, 1910), 1:359.
45. Kidd, *American Christians*, 55–56.
46. Siobhan Lambert-Hurley and Sunhil Sharma, "Introduction," in *Atiya's Journeys: A Muslim Woman from Colonial Bombay to Edwardian Britain*, ed. Siobhan Lambert-Hurley and Sunhil Sharma (Oxford: Oxford University Press, 2020), 5. Italics added.
47. Ibid.; Siobhan Lambert-Hurley, ed., *A Princess's Pilgrimage: Nawab Sikandar Begum's A Pilgrimage to Mecca* (Bloomington and Indianapolis: Indiana University Press, 2008).
48. A portion of this section is adapted, with permission, from my article, Deanna Ferree Womack, "Protestant Portrayals of Islam: From the Reformation to Modern Missions," *Interpretation: A Journal of Bible and Theology* 76, no. 2 (2022): 140–55.
49. Henry Martyn, *Controversial Tracts on Christianity and Mohammedanism. By the Late Rev. Henry Martyn, B.D., of St. John's College, Cambridge, and Some of the Most Eminent Writers of Persia*, trans. S. Lee (Cambridge: J. Sith, 1824), 81, 88.
50. C. G. Pfander, *The Mizan Ul Haqq; Or, Balance of Truth*, trans. R. H. Weakley (London: Church Missionary House, 1866), 131.
51. Henry Harris Jessup, *The Mohammedan Missionary Problem* (Philadelphia: Presbyterian Board of Publication, 1879), 34.
52. E. J. Humphrey, *Six Years in India: Or, Sketches of India and Its People as Seen by a Lady Missionary* (New York: Carlton & Porter, 1866), 9.
53. E. J. Humphrey, *Gems of India: Or, Sketches of Distinguished Hindoo and Mahomedan Women* (New York: Nelson & Phillips, 1875), 144. Italics in original.
54. William Muir, trans., *The Apology of Al Kindy, Written at the court of al Mamun in Defense of Christianity Against Islam*, 2nd ed. (London: Society for Promoting Christian Knowledge, 1887).
55. Ibid., 2, 9, 10–11, 49.
56. G. H. Rouse, *Tracts for Muhammadans*, 2nd ed. (London and Madras: The Christian Literature Society for India, 1897), vi–vii. Italics added.
57. Jessup, *Mohammedan*, 35. See also J. W. H. Stobart, *Islam and Its Founder* (New York/London: Society for Promoting Christian Knowledge and E. S. Gorham, 1911).
58. Leyla Kayhan Elbirlik, "Negotiating Matrimony: Marriage, Divorce, and Property Allocation Practices in Istanbul, 1755–1840" (PhD diss., Harvard University, 2013), 13–14. A husband might initiate divorce when sent to war as a courtesy to his wife if he was unlikely to return home. Additionally, women in Ottoman society exercised agency in using Islamic courts (*shari'a* courts) to negotiate issues of marriage and divorce (pp. 160–72).
59. Ibid., 78.
60. Jessup, *Mohammedan*, 36–37.
61. Ibid., 40–41.

62. Ibid., 45.
63. Douglas Scott Brookes, *The Concubine, the Princess, and the Teacher: Voices from the Ottoman Harem* (Austin: University of Texas Press, 2008). See also Leslie Peirce, *The Imperial Harem: Women and Sovereignty in the Ottoman Empire* (Oxford: Oxford University Press, 1993).
64. Jessup, *Mohammedan*, 46. Compare to Humphrey, *Gems*, 176.
65. Humphrey, *Gems*, 7.
66. Ibid., 93–94, 176–77, 192.
67. Ibid., 92.
68. See Lambert-Hurley, *Princess's Pilgrimage*. Sikandar Begum was regent for her young daughter Shahjahan Begum from 1844 to 1860.
69. Humphrey, *Gems*, 139. On the Begums of Bhopal, see pp. 153–75.
70. Ibid., 160. Humphrey relied on Sikandar Begum's published account of her pilgrimage. See Lambert-Hurley, *Princess's Pilgrimage*. Another American missionary in India, Clara Swain, showed similar reverence for Muslim worship. Clara A. Swain, *A Glimpse of India: Being a Collection of Extracts from the Letters of Dr. Clara A. Swain* [...] (New York: J. Pott, 1909), 67.
71. Humphrey, *Gems*, 193.
72. On the attraction of fiction and novels for Protestant religious audiences drawn to adventure and exotic areas of the world, see Anna Johnston, *Missionary Writing and Empire, 1800–1860* (Cambridge: Cambridge University Press, 2003), 19.
73. E. M. Wherry, *Zeinab, the Panjabi: A Story Founded on Facts* (New York: American Tract Society, 1895). On Wherry, see Stanley E. Brush, "Presbyterians and Islam in India," *Journal of Presbyterian History* 62, no. 3 (Fall 1984): 215–22.
74. For Wherry's readers who were familiar with the Indian context, this widow's story likely brought to mind critiques of high-caste widowhood that missionaries circulated, like Pundita Ramabai Sarasvati, *The High-Caste Hindu Woman* (Philadelphia: J. B. Rodgers, 1887).
75. Weber, "Making Common Cause," 18.
76. Thomas Albert Howard, *The Faiths of Others: A History of Interreligious Dialogue* (New Haven, CT: Yale University Press, 2021), 79–135. Protestant missionaries were among the Parliament's speakers and attendees.
77. On the world missionary conference in Edinburgh in 1910, see Brian Stanley, *The World Missionary Conference, Edinburgh 1910* (Grand Rapids, MI: Eerdmans, 2009). On the delegates' engagement with Islam at the International Missionary Council conference in Jerusalem in 1928, see Deanna Ferree Womack, "A View from the Muslim Arabic Press, 1928: The International Missionary Conference in Jerusalem." *Exchange: Journal of Contemporary Christianities in Context* 46, no. 2 (2017): 180–205. SVM (founded in 1886) was instrumental in recruiting young adults to become missionaries.
78. The 1924 conferences organized by American ecumenical leader John Mott were held in Jerusalem, Baghdad, Constantine (Algeria), Helwan (Egypt), and Brummana (Lebanon). John R. Mott, *Conferences of Christian Workers Among Moslems, 1924: A Brief Account of the Conferences Together with Their Findings and Lists of Members* (New York: International Missionary Council, 1924).
79. Beginning in 1892, the Arabian Mission began publishing field reports and then shifted in 1898 to a periodical titled *The Arabian Mission: Quarterly Letters from the Field*. The title changed to *Neglected Arabia: Missionary Letters and News* in the publication for January to March 1902, and the publication continued until 1962.
80. By 1913, on its twenty-five-year anniversary, the AMB had four stations (Blida, Relizane, Miliana, and Mascara), a Council of Reference in London consisting of seven supporters, and an honorary secretary of the Algerian Women's Mission Band residing in Chicago.
81. Lilias Trotter, *Algiers Mission Band,* vol. 17 (1913): 5, in Arab World Ministries/Algiers Mission Band Papers (box 1), Special Collections, School of Oriental and African Studies, University of London. Italics added.
82. A Quaker missionary magazine saw the hand of God bringing liberty through both political events. "Turkish Post Card," *Friends Missionary Advocate* 24, no. 10 (October 1908): 6.
83. See the volumes Wherry edited for the Cairo and Lucknow conferences: E. M. Wherry, ed., *Methods of Mission Work Among Moslems* (New York: Revell, 1906); Samuel M. Zwemer, E. M. Wherry, and James L. Barton, eds., *The Mohammedan World of To-Day: Being Papers Read at the First Missionary Conference on Behalf of the Mohammedan World Held at Cairo April 4th–9th, 1906* (New York: Fleming H. Revell, 1906); E. M. Wherry, S. M. Zwemer, and C. G. Mylrea, eds., *Islam and Missions: Being Papers Read at the Second Missionary Conference on Behalf of the Mohammedan World at Lucknow, January 23–28, 1911* (New York: Fleming H. Revell, 1911).

84. The numerous texts Zwemer authored or initiated were considered essential readings for generations of missionaries. These included *The Moslem World* journal, which he founded in 1911 and edited until 1948.
85. Trotter has received acclaim in some Evangelical circles, and The Lilias Trotter Center was established in her honor. See https://www.liliastrottercenter.org. Van Summer also worked with the Prayer Union for Egypt and established the Fellowship of Faith for Muslims. She was the founder and editor of the mission magazine *Blessed Be Egypt*, published at the Nile Mission Press from 1899 until the year of her death in 1937. George Swan, "Miss Annie Van Sommer," *Blessed Be Egypt* 37, no. 151 (April 1937): 22–24.
86. Samir Boulos, *European Evangelicals in Egypt (1900–1956): Cultural Entanglements and Missionary Spaces* (Leiden: Brill, 2016), 76, note 58; E. Sanders, "The Nile Mission Press," *The Moslem World* 34, no. 3 (July 1944): 209–13. By 1928, the Nile Mission Press had issued more than six hundred Arabic publications for Muslims, in addition to books printed in other languages. It claimed that in 1927 the press distributed half a million books. This information was printed on the back page of Lilias Trotter, *The Debt of Ali Ben Omar* (Cairo: Nile Mission Press, 1928), 9.
87. Papers of the American Christian Literature Society for Moslems (Record Group 81, box 27, folder 19), Presbyterian Historical Society, Philadelphia; Charles R. Watson, "The American Christian Literature Society for Moslems," *The Moslem World* 8, no. 2 (April 1918): 178.
88. Van Sommer and Zwemer, *Our Moslem Sisters*, 193.
89. Wherry, *Methods of Mission Work*, 9, 12–16.
90. Zwemer, Wherry, and Barton, *Mohammedan World*.
91. At the start of the twentieth century, American missionary women outnumbered missionary men two to one. Dana L. Robert, *Christian Mission: How Christianity Became a World Religion* (Chichester, UK: Wiley-Blackwell, 2009), 128.
92. Six women gave short presentations on "women's work," and three others offered remarks during the discussion that followed. Zwemer, Wherry, and Barton, *Mohammedan World*, 110–26. Watson's statement appeared in Wherry, *Methods of Mission Work*, 109. No women were included among the officers and committee members who organized the conference (p. 12).
93. Wherry, *Zeinab*; Samuel M. Zwemer and Amy E. Zwemer, *Moslem Women* (West Medford, MA: Central Committee on the United Study of Foreign Missions, 1926); Henry H. Jessup, *The Women of the Arabs* (New York: Dodd & Mead, 1873). Zwemer also co-edited the Cairo and Lucknow women's volumes.
94. Zwemer, Wherry, and Barton, *Mohammedan World*, 25, 62, 139, 141.
95. William K. Eddy, "Islam in Syria and Palestine," in Ibid., 63. According to Eddy, women's "influence is conservative and acts to restrain any liberalism which men from their freer contact with Christians might favor." Similar views appear in Van Sommer and Zwemer, *Our Moslem Sisters*, 59, 254, 258; and C. W. P., "Islam and Christianity," *The London Friend* 47, no. 29 (July 19, 1907): 486.
96. J. C. Young, "Islam in Arabia," in Zwemer, Wherry, and Barton, *Mohammedan World*, 81.
97. W. R. Miller, "Islam in West Africa," in Zwemer, Wherry, and Barton, *Mohammedan World*, 48; Gottfried K. Simon, "Islam in Sumatra," in *Mohammedan World*, 211. Another speaker noted the interesting case of a woman in Persia who "acted as the Imam to a small gathering" of other women. W. St. Clair Tisdall, "Islam in Persia," in *Mohammedan World*, 116.
98. One example is Qasim Amin's 1899 text *Tahrir al-Mar'a*, published in English as "The Liberation of Women," in *The Liberation of Women and the New Woman: Two Documents in the History of Egyptian Feminism*, trans. Samiha Sidhon Peterson (Cairo: The American University of Cairo Press, 2022). On male and female reformists who critiqued their own Muslim societies while pushing for women's rights and education in the nineteenth and early twentieth centuries, see Nikki R. Keddie, *Women in the Middle East: Past and Present* (Princeton, NJ: Princeton University Press, 2007), 60–74.
99. Lambert-Hurley and Sharma, *Atiya's Journeys*, 72–73. The authors quoted from Abdullah Yusuf Ali, who is famous for translating the Qur'an into English and who included Atiya herself in a list of noteworthy Muslim women during a speech in London. Another reformist whom Atiya met there, Syed Ameer Ali, argued in *The Spirit of Islam* (1891) for giving Muslim women the full legal rights afforded to them in the Qur'an.
100. Wherry, "Women's Work," in *Methods of Mission Work*, 110. This editorial note in the "Woman's Work" chapter explained why the women's remarks were so brief.
101. Ibid. 111–12.

102. Ibid., 115, 120.
103. The volume went through three English editions in 1907 and was translated into Swedish. In addition to *Our Moslem Sisters*, Revell's list of "Latest Important Works on Mohammedanism" in 1911 included the following: Zwemer, Wherry, and Barton, *Mohammedan World of To-Day* (1906); E. M. Wherry, *Islam and Christianity* in India and the Far East (New York: Fleming H. Revell, 1907); Samuel M. Zwemer, *Arabia, the Cradle of Islam* (New York: Fleming H. Revell, 1900); Samuel G. Wilson, *Persian Life and Customs* (1899); John Kelly Giffen, *Egypt and the Sudan* (1905); George Smith, *Henry Martyn, Saint and Scholar* (1892); Robert E. Speer, *Missions and Modern History* (1904). See Wherry, Zwemer, and Mylrea, *Islam and Missions*, front matter.
104. Samuel M. Zwemer, "Introduction," in *Our Moslem Sisters*, 8. Zwemer was named as the author of the introduction, and Van Sommer was named as the author of the opening chapter and likely wrote the concluding chapter.
105. The book included chapters on Egypt, Tunis, Algiers, Morocco, Hausa Land, East Africa, Arabia, Palestine, Syria, Turkey, Bulgaria, Persia, India, Indonesia.
106. Van Sommer, "Hagar and Her Sisters," in *Our Moslem Sisters*, 16.
107. Zwemer, "Introduction," 9. Italics in original.
108. Van Sommer, "Hagar and Her Sisters," 17. Several of the anonymous chapter authors repeated similar claims. See "Light in Darkest Morocco," in *Our Moslem Sisters*, 99, 115; "Pen-and-Ink Sketches in Palestine," in *Our Moslem Sisters*, 152.
109. Van Sommer, "Hagar and Her Sisters," 17.
110. Van Sommer and Zwemer, *Our Moslem Sisters*, 33, 176. Muslim women were also described as inmates and as living in prison. Ibid., 208, 260, 298.
111. Ibid., 6, 28, 60, 176, 207 228.
112. Ibid., 29, 36, 64, 125, 155, 196, 214, 231, 250, 266. The terms *drudge* and *servant* were also common.
113. Ibid., 39–41, 95, 137, 147–48, 154, 166, 176, 183–84, 196, 229–30, 267, 284, 289, 290.
114. Ibid., 27, 30, 118, 178.
115. Ibid., 48, 40, 136, 220, 231, 251, 253, 276. Another theme emphasized less frequently was the preference of male over female children (pp. 50, 172, 263).
116. Ibid., 28, 54–56, 70, 128, 169, 222, 297.
117. Ibid., 46. See similar statements on pp. 70, 122, 140.
118. Van Sommer, "Hagar and Her Sisters," 15–16.
119. Van Sommer and Zwemer, *Our Moslem Sisters*, 159, 235.
120. Ibid., 235.
121. Ibid., 297.
122. Ibid., 35.
123. Ibid., 48–49, 164, 204–5, 253.
124. Ibid., 262, 276.
125. Ibid., 77. Present-day Tunisia was then known as Tunis.
126. Ibid., 119, 132, 133, 139, 147, 148, 169, 196, 214, 255.
127. Ibid., 70, 75, 122, 174, 185, 202, 228.
128. Ibid., 129.
129. Ibid., 263.
130. Ibid., 169–70.
131. Ibid., 92. The author quoted Acts 17:26, saying, "He hath made of one blood all the inhabitants of the earth."
132. Samuel M. Zwemer, "A Sketch of the Conference at Lucknow," in *Daylight in the Harem: A New Era for Moslem Women*, ed. Annie Van Sommer and Samuel M. Zwemer (New York: Fleming H. Revel, 1911), 15. Van Sommer wrote two of the book's chapters, and nine others came from the conference sessions on women's work. Just one woman speaker had a paper included in the regular Lucknow Conference volume: Jennie Von Myer, "Islam in Russia," in Wherry, Zwemer, and Mylrea, *Islam and Missions*, 249–72.
133. The preface listed the women members of the Committee of the Lucknow Conference as authors: Annie Van Sommer (Egypt), I. Lilias Trotter (Algeria), Grettie Yandes Holliday (Persia), and Agnes de Sélincourt (India), all unmarried missionaries.
134. Annie Van Sommer, "A New Era for Moslem Womanhood," in *Daylight in the Harem*, 23, 33, 50. Van Sommer attributed some of the shift in Egypt to interest in French fashions and noted this influence on the lengthening of Persian skirts (p. 33).

135. G. Y. Holliday, "Awakening Womanhood," in *Daylight in the Harem*, 125. Also working in Persia, the medical doctor Emmeline M. Stuart mentioned that the majority of women were not kept in seclusion but could go about with complete freedom as long as they kept "closely veiled in the streets." Emmeline Stuart, "The Ministry of Healing," in *Daylight in the Harem*, 142.
136. Patrick, "Educated Women," 83.
137. In her address at the Lucknow Conference, Trotter outlined general strategies for disseminating Protestant literature to Muslims, without focusing particularly on Muslim women. Lilias Trotter, "The Ministry of the Press," in *Daylight in the Harem*, 147–58. Later in her career when she wrote prolifically for Fellowship of Faith for Muslims, a Christian literature organization, Trotter's literature was not aimed specifically at Muslim women either.
138. "Furor for Education in Persia," *Woman's Work for Woman* 22, no. 1 (January 1907): 8.
139. See Elwood Wherry's book, *Zeinab*, discussed earlier in this chapter and, in Chapter 4, Clara Wherry's writings about Indian Muslims for a children's magazine.
140. Clara M. Wherry, "Training of Converts," in *Daylight in the Harem*, 172. Italics added.
141. Ibid., 172–73. Wherry reported that a similar practice of removing the veil when entering the church was common in Syria, where private baptisms were also performed for Muslim women converts. In Egypt, converts were not expected to remove their veils during worship "but to dress like their native sisters," and Protestant men and women there were usually separated in worship by a curtain (p. 175).
142. Ibid., 173. Here Wherry's correspondent referred to an *Armenian Christian* community from Afghanistan that observed purdah.
143. Ibid., 174.
144. Ibid., 175.
145. Carolyn McCue Goffman, *Mary Mills Patrick's Cosmopolitan Mission and the Constantinople Woman's College* (Lanham, MD: Lexington Books, 2021), xiv. Patrick was a missionary of the ABCFM, and she retired from her position as college president in the 1930s. See also Hester Donaldson Jenkins, *An Educational Ambassador to the Near East: The Story of Mary Mills Patrick and an American College in the Orient* (New York: Revell, 1925).
146. Patrick, "Educated Women," 74.
147. Ibid., 76–77.
148. Ibid., 74. She explained, "Koranic laws taught monogamy and not polygamy, a fact which is also claimed by many at the present time."
149. Ibid., 75, 78, 84.
150. The note was signed "Editor," indicating either Van Sommer or Zwemer.
151. Patrick, "Educated Women," 90.
152. Ibid.
153. Benjamin G. Bishin and Feryal M. Cherif, "Women, Property Rights, and Islam," *Comparative Politics* 49, no. 4 (July 2017): 501. I am grateful to Rahimjon Abdugafurov for pointing me to this resource.
154. Ibid., 506. For example, Qur'an 4:6: "if you perceive in them right judgment, deliver them to their property."
155. Pruitt, *Looking-Glass*, 6.
156. Van Sommer, "Hagar and Her Sisters," 19.
157. Pruitt, *Looking-Glass*, 156.
158. Mrs. Moses Smith, *Mission Studies: Woman's Work in Foreign Lands* 20, no. 5 (May 1902): 129. Italics added. Smith repeated this italicized line in Mrs. Moses Smith, *Woman Under the Ethnic Religions* (Chicago: Woman's Board of Missions of the Interior, 1910): 31.
159. "Religious Intelligence," *The Friends' Review* 46, no. 21 (December 15, 1892): 326. In the piece, the catchphrase was placed in quotation marks describing the Indian woman as "unwelcome at birth, untaught in childhood, enslaved when married, accursed as a widow, and unlamented when dead." The very same line was applied to a Hindu woman in Mary Louisa Carus-Wilson and Georgina Petrie, *Irene Petrie: Missionary to Kashmir* (London: Hodder and Stoughton, 1901), 169–70.
160. "If You Were a Heathen Woman!," *Missionary Review of The World* 40, no. 11 (November 1917): 855. Italics in original.
161. Variations on this catchphrase appeared in "The Miracles of Missions: The Land of Esther," *Missionary Review of the World* 12, no. 12 (December 1889): 911; "Religious Intelligence," *The Friends' Review* 46, no. 21 (December 15, 1892): 326; V. F. P., "About Foreign Hospitals and

Dispensaries," *Missionary Review of the World* 19, no. 9 (September 1896): 676; *The Missionary Helper* 15, no. 2 (February 1892): 59; "If You Were a Heathen Woman!," *Missionary Review of The World* 40, no. 11 (November 1917): 855; *The Missionary Survey: The Presbyterian Church in the U.S. at Home and Abroad* 8, no. 1 (January 1918): 54.

162. Also reflecting the growth and power of the woman's missionary movement was the popular book by Helen Barrett Montgomery, *Western Women in Eastern Lands: An Outline Study of Fifty Years of Woman's Work in Foreign Missions* (New York: Macmillan, 1910). The Central Committee on the United Study of Foreign Missions (CCUSFM) published this book, and women's missionary societies distributed it as the new textbook for 1911. See "Notes from Headquarters," *Woman's Work for Woman* 25, no. 12 (December 1910): 285.

163. "Books and Magazines," *Woman's Missionary Friend* 39, no. 6 (June 1907): 211. *Heathen Woman's Friend* was this periodical's former title. Zwemer described this testimony as "unimpeachable and unanimous." Zwemer, "Introduction," *Our Moslem Sisters*, 6.

164. "New Missionary Books," *Woman's Work for Woman* 22, no. 8 (August 1907): 179. Zwemer wrote that "the condition of women under Islam is everywhere the same." Zwemer, "Introduction," 9. Van Sommer wrote, "one story is told and one cry heard everywhere." Van Sommer, "Hagar and Her Sisters," 17. For the magazine's commentary on the Cairo Conference, see *Woman's Work for Woman* 21, no. 5 (May 1906): 101; "Letters from Missionaries," *Woman's Work for Woman* 21, no. 10 (October 1906): 37; F. E. Hoskins, "1906," *Woman's Work for Woman* 21, no. 12 (Dec. 1906): 271.

165. "New Missionary Books," *Woman's Work for Woman* 22, no. 8 (August 1907): 180. Italics in original.

166. "Not Dead, Only Dry," *The Women's Missionary Magazine of the United Free Church of Scotland*, no. 87 (March 1908): 64–67. See the chapter titled "Not Dead, Only Dry," in *Our Moslem Sisters*, 90–97.

167. Other missionary publications, like the following, cited *Daylight in the Harem* for its expertise: Mary Schauffler Labaree, *The Child in the Midst: A Comparative Study of Child Welfare in Christian and Non-Christian Lands* (West Medford: CCUSFM, 1914), 67, 162, 209; Agnes de Sélincourt, "The Place of Women in the Modern National Movements of the East," *The International Review of Missions* 1, no. 1 (1912): 104.

168. "The Bookshelf," *The Missionary Herald* 107, no. 2 (February 1912): 93–94.

169. The following publications featured both books: Margaret Ernestine Burton, *Woman Workers of the Orient* (West Medford, MA: CCUSFM, 1918), 231; "Loan Library: Books for the Times," *Life and Light for Women* 48, no. 9 (October 1919), backmatter; "The Bookshelf," *The Missionary Herald* 107, no. 2 (February 1912): 93–94; Emma Roberts, "Moslem Women," *The Missionary Survey* 5, no. 6 (July 1915): 525–27. The latter periodical's circulation in 1915 was 27,500 (p. 482). The Missionary Education Movement of the United States and Canada in 1912 highlighted *Daylight in the Harem* among the one hundred most popular missionary books and one of six listed under "Mohammedan Lands." *One Hundred Most Popular Missionary Books* (New York: Missionary Education Movement of the United States and Canada, 1912), 11. Advertisements and reviews of *Daylight in the Harem* also appeared in "Book Reviews," *The Moslem World* 2, no. 2 (1912): 194–95; "Bibliography," *The International Review of Missions* 1, no. 1 (1912): 183; "Remember Lucknow 1911," *The Outlook of Missions* 4, no. 1 (January 1912): 6; "The Bookseller's Diary," *The Bookman* 40, no. 241 (October 1911): 11; *The Bookman* Christmas supplement (1911): 35, 44; *The Bookseller: A Newspaper of British and Foreign Literature* (August 11, 1911): 1063, 1078; "Messrs. Oliphant, Anderson & Ferrier's New Books," *The Bookseller*, Christmas supplement (1911): 108; "New Books," *Missionary Review of the World* 24, no. 12, new series (December 1911): 960; "Books on Various Subjects," *The Indian Interpreter: A Religious and Ethical Quarterly* 14, no. 2 (July 1919): backmatter.

170. Other advertised texts included Zwemer, *Arabia, the Cradle of Islam*; Samuel M. Zwemer, *Islam: A Challenge to Faith* (New York: SVM, 1907); Wherry, *Islam and Christianity*; William H. T. Gairdner, *The Reproach of Islam* (London: SVM, 1909); Urania Latham Malcolm, *Children of Persia* (New York: F. H. Revell, 1911); M. E. Hume-Griffith, *Behind the Veil in Persia and Turkish Arabia* (Philadelphia: J. B. Lippincott, 1909); Hester Donaldson Jenkins, *Behind Turkish Lattices: The Story of a Turkish Woman's Life* (London: Chatto & Windus, 1911). On Zwemer's *Islam: A Challenge to Faith*, see: "Books and Magazines," *Woman's Missionary Friend* 40, no. 3 (March 1908): 96. Another review recommended Wherry's text

as "a good companion volume to 'Our Moslem Sisters.'" "New Missionary Books," *Woman's Work for Woman* 22, no. 8 (August 1907): 181.
171. "A New Series of Text-Books," *Woman's Work for Woman* 23, no. 8 (August 1908): 190; CCUSFM, *The Story of the Jubilee: An Account of the Celebration of the Fiftieth Anniversary of the Beginnings in the United States of Woman's Organized Work for Foreign Missions, 1860–1910* (West Medford, MA: CCUSFM, 1911), 3.
172. CCUSFM, *Story of Jubilee*, 3. The American Baptist Missionary Union used this study not just for American readers but for Burmese Christians associated with its mission. J. F. Smith, "A Mission Study Class in Burma," *The Baptist Missionary Magazine* 89, no. 12 (December 1909): 450–51.
173. *The Friends Missionary Advocate* encouraged Sabbath Schools to offer a missionary lesson each month, and it provided materials for a number of auxiliaries that had a junior society under its care. *The Friends Missionary Advocate* 24, no. 7 (July 1908): 10, 14, 85.
174. "Report of Department of Literature," *The Friends Missionary Advocate* 24, no. 7 (July 1908): 17. This was a direct quotation from the "Foreword" of the textbook. Samuel M. Zwemer and Arthur Judson Brown, *The Nearer and Farther East: Outline Studies of Moslem Lands and of Siam, Burma, and Korea* (New York: Macmillan; West Medford, MA: CCUSFM, 1908), v. Other such announcements of this CCUSFM text appeared in "Editorial," *Woman's Missionary Friend* 40, no. 3 (March 1908): 88; "A New Series of Text-Books," *Woman's Work for Woman* 23, no. 8 (August 1908): 190.
175. "The Man Mohammed," *Friends Missionary Advocate* 24, no. 9 (September 1908): 23–24; "Muhammedanism," *Friends Missionary Advocate* 224, no. 9 (September 1908): 24. Several of the lessons featured missionaries in Islamic contexts: Raymond Lull, Henry Martyn, Karl Gottlieb Pfander, Ion Keith-Falconer, and Hester Needham.
176. "Helps for Monthly Meetings," *The Missionary Helper* 32, no. 3 (March 1909): 86–87. The "Helps" recommended an opening hymn, Bible reading, and prayer for Muslim women, along with guidelines for the lesson based on readings from *Nearer and Farther East*.
177. Thomson, *Land and the Book*, 536–37.
178. Wherry wrote, "We do not believe any Christian can read the papers now published, without feeling in his heart a new joy in the belief that God is answering the prayer of Abraham for his son Ishmael: 'Oh, that Ishmael may live before thee.' (Gen. 17:18)." Wherry, "Introduction," in *Methods of Mission Work*, 11.
179. Van Sommer, "Hagar and Her Sisters," 16.
180. Nyasha Junior, *Reimagining Hagar: Blackness and the Bible* (Oxford: Oxford University Press, 2019). That is to say, regardless of Hagar's actual ethnic background, missionary women saw her as representing millions of oppressed women in Africa and Asia. African American biblical tradition, as Junior noted, stressed Hagar's agency and strength.
181. Hagar is not mentioned in the Qur'an, but the Hadith gives her considerable attention.
182. Riffat Hassan, "Islamic Hagar and Her Family," in *Hagar, Sarah, and Their Children: Jewish, Christian, and Muslim Perspectives*, ed. Phyllis Trible and Letty M. Russel (Louisville, KY: Westminster John Knox Press, 2006), 152–53.
183. Ibid., 154–55. During the *hajj*, Muslims also trace Hagar's journey running back and forth searching for water in the valley between the hills of Safa and Marwa.
184. Ibid., 155.
185. Van Sommer and Zwemer, *Our Moslem Sisters*, 299. The CMS prayer called upon God to "destroy the sword of Islam, and break the yoke of the false prophet Mohammed from the necks of Egypt, Arabia, Turkey, Persia, and other Moslem lands, so that there may be opened throughout these lands a great door and effectual for the Gospel, that the Word of the Lord may have free course and be glorified, and the veil upon so many hearts may be removed."

4

Islam Re-invented for Young Readers

Children's Work for Muslim Children

The turn-of-the-century ecumenical movement for missions to Muslims generated new material for young readers and for their teachers and Sunday school leaders. This literature introduced missionary re-inventions of Islam to Protestants at an early age, translating existing information about Muslims into a more accessible format for children. It also built on texts about Islamic cultures already available for children and youth, like the popular stories of the *1001 Arabian Nights* and Sunday school movement publications, such as the 1837 book *The Customs and Manners of Bedouin Arabs*.[1] Some missionaries included material for children within publications for adults, like the "Children's Chapter" in Henry Harris Jessup's *The Women of the Arabs* (1874).[2] But by the late nineteenth century, dedicated missionary magazines for children had become widely available sources of information for thousands of young readers. According to Hugh Morrison's study on Protestant missions and children's education, these "periodicals acted as a dialogical tool, giving power to children's agency both as interactive readers and missionary participants" while also forming "part of a wider global and imperial swirl of goods, ideas and information by which children learned or thought about the wider world."[3] Often with attractive illustrations, such works not only described but also pictured the lives of Muslims and other inhabitants of global mission fields. One such early magazine in Britain was the *Church Missionary Juvenile Instructor*, which the Church Missionary Society (CMS) established in 1842. The CMS replaced it with *A Quarterly Token for Juvenile Subscribers* in 1856.[4] Another similar periodical, *Children's Work for Children* (*CWC*, est. 1876), was a publication of the Woman's Foreign Missionary Society of the Presbyterian Church of the United States of America (PCUSA), a testament to the ways in which women's missionary societies affected and influenced Protestant readers. In the early twentieth century, these women's organizations played an important role in publishing

Re-inventing Islam. Deanna Ferree Womack, Oxford University Press. © Oxford University Press 2025.
DOI: 10.1093/9780197699195.003.0004

and distributing the growing variety of fiction and non-fiction books for young people, in addition to magazines. Like my examination of literature for adults, British and American missionary publications for children must be studied in tandem because the missionaries cobbled together their messages about Islam by borrowing material from one another and by summarizing or reproducing the work of other Protestant mission societies, regardless of national origin or denomination. The London-based magazine *The Wesleyan Juvenile Offering*, for example, carried a series titled "Notes from Syria" in the mid-1870s that featured anecdotes about Muslim women and children excerpted from *The Women of the Arabs*.[5]

Such missionary books and periodicals for young readers emphasized the success of Protestant work in Islamic contexts and taught that children ought to do their part to support this work through *juvenile* or *junior* mission bands and fundraising.[6] Often the authors endeavored to motivate readers to do so by informing them about the plight of children in global mission fields. Through periodicals, books, and short stories aimed at children and at their parents and teachers, missionaries sought to cultivate a disposition of work, prayer, giving, sympathy, self-denial, and faithful labor among the youngest generation. *Wesleyan Juvenile Offering*, for instance, urged readers to show their love to Jesus by becoming a "little missionary."[7] Periodicals also called children to act for missionary causes in specific regions of the world with appeals like the following, printed in *Quarterly Token*:

> Dear Children, will you not help to enlighten the Turks? The Church Missionary Society has commenced a good work amongst them. Will you not strive to promote it? Is it not the desire of your heart,
> "That Turkish women soon may know
> What blessings Jesus can bestow?"[8]

Similarly, one *CWC* article on Syria emphasized that children could support missions in the same land where Jesus journeyed by taking up a collection. It read, "Ah, we need your pennies and your prayers too, dear boys and girls, for the many boys and girls of Syria."[9] The *CWC* editors also invited its readers to send in letters for publication, through which they could encourage other children to give.[10] One such young author, Susie Hogan, the secretary of a Presbyterian children's mission band in Indiana called Willing Workers, wrote about a missionary heroine:

We have learned so much of Miss [Fidelia] Fiske's work, and those girls she taught in Oroomiah, that some of us are looking forward to going to Mt. Holyoke Seminary when we are older; and perhaps we may go from there to Persia, as Miss Fiske did.[11]

Thus, missionaries became role models for young readers at the same time as these magazines taught them about Islamic contexts.

This chapter explores how British and American missionaries and mission organizations presented material about Muslims and Islamic societies to children and youth. This subject has received little attention in mission histories and can shed light on the ways in which the basic Protestant discourse about Islam became embedded in American imaginations early on. In the first section, I focus on children's magazines and educational, non-fiction books from the late nineteenth and early twentieth centuries. In the second, I examine several works of missionary fiction for children that became more readily available in the 1920s; and in the third, I analyze the ideas that these various works transmitted about Islam and gender. Fourth and finally, I consider the shifting emphases in missionary fiction for children over time and the more humanizing portrayals of Muslims that emerged toward the mid-twentieth century.

Islam in Children's Magazines and Non-Fiction

I turn first to periodicals, focusing on the CMS's *Quarterly Token* and the PCUSA's *CWC* as two prominent British and American missionary periodicals for children that began in the nineteenth century and extended into the twentieth. While the former publication most often featured Muslims in the CMS fields of South Asia, the latter reported on Presbyterian mission work in Persia and Syria. Through such magazines, young readers learned about Islam alongside stories about other religions and cultures. A considerable number of American and British children had access to such publications through their own subscriptions or through Sunday schools. The CMS offered free magazine issues as a gift to children who donated one shilling (twelve pennies) a year or one penny a month. Based on these calculations, in its first year of operation in 1856 when juvenile associations had contributed £3,000, this could have funded up to 60,000 copies of each issue. By 1865, the contributions of young subscribers given through juvenile associations and Sunday schools had doubled.[12] As for *CWC*, at the end of its first year of publication in 1876, its editors noted that over 4,000 boys and girls were already subscribers to the magazine; and they encouraged readers to help raise those numbers to 10,000. By 1912, this magazine, which by then had been renamed *Over Sea and Land: A Missionary Magazine for the Young* (*OSL*), reported 19,000 subscribers and an additional 1,181,000 children who had access to the publication in Presbyterian Sabbath Schools but were not yet individual subscribers.[13]

Quarterly Token presented stories about particular mission stations and the people whom British missionaries encountered there, often with accompanying images. The magazine's first issue mentioned a Muslim man in South Asia named Abdool Messeeh (Abd al-Masih) who converted under the influence of Henry Martyn.[14] The magazine offered no negative commentary on Islam in this first issue, and this was also true for the first article on Islam in *CWC*, which explained Muslim beliefs without rendering any judgment.[15] This reflected the educational aim of missionary publications, which generated descriptive, ethnographic accounts on global mission contexts that appeared not to be explicitly motivated to do anything other than inform readers. Yet both magazines soon took up the same themes that were central in missionary publications for adults: the violence of Muslim men and the low status of Muslim women. In its third issue, *Quarterly Token* asserted that its missionaries in Peshawar (in contemporary Pakistan) found that "the Mussulmans are even more bitterly set against the Gospel of Jesus Christ than the heathen," and the Protestants were afraid to preach publicly because the "Mussulmans of that city are fiercest among the fierce."[16] The CMS periodical made such stereotypes more explicit when detailing the experiences of a converted couple being pressured to return to Islam by "a hundred furious and savage-looking men, with drawn swords, ready to inflict torture."[17] With such statements, missionary writers perpetuated alarming and graphic depictions of Muslim men's violence to young readers.

In *CWC*, Presbyterian missionary in Persia William Levi Whipple (1844–1901) conveyed similar ideas when emphasizing his view that the prophet of Islam chose the way of violence and that this became the norm for the whole religion:

Mohammed and his followers put many hundreds and thousands to death with the sword, because they would not accept him and his religion. But many more, however, to save their lives forsook their own religion and accepted his. By this cruel method and by other means was this religion of "the false prophet," as Mohammed is called, spread, and thus it gained many converts. But it has lost very much of its power and influence, and is gradually giving place to the religion of our blessed Lord and Saviour.[18]

After thus drawing on the same trope about the Prophet Muhammad and violence that had been passed down among Protestants since the Reformation, Whipple adopted another common missionary discourse that contrasted the worldly violence of Islam with the spiritual conquest of Christianity:

> Would you not, dear children, love to see the religion of Jesus conquer this false religion of Mohammed, and convert those 150,000,000 souls (more than three times the entire population of the United States), not by the aid of the sword of steel, such as Mohammed used in making his converts, but by the "sword of the Spirit" which is the Word of God, and by the power of Jesus' love? If you do so desire, you can pray to God and ask Him to do this, and to bless the missionaries who are working among the Mohammedans to bring about this very end. You can also have a *share* in this work by giving your contributions of money.[19]

What effect would such a statement have had on young readers? Whipple sought to establish in their minds the idea that Muhammad's purportedly violent nature was the essence of Islam and a trait his followers naturally shared. Further, Whipple contrasted his assessment of Muhammad with a picture of Jesus who conquered only by the spirit, assuring these children of the superiority of their own religion while also calling on them to aid in this spiritual warfare through prayer and by giving money to the missionary cause. Whipple's assessment—coming in the aftermath of the brutal American Civil War (1861–1865) and a few years prior to Britain's violent occupation of Egypt in 1882—failed to recognize that Anglo-Protestants did not actually restrict their warfare to the spiritual realm. Such publications also unfortunately neglected to offer their young readers examples of Muslim men who defied such gross mischaracterizations, although on occasion in other settings missionaries did praise Muslim men—like the Algerian emir Abd al-Qadir (1808–1883)—precisely because of their military interventions on behalf of suffering populations.[20]

As for references to Muslim women and girls in children's magazines, the following statement from *CWC* is instructive:

ISLAM RE-INVENTED FOR YOUNG READERS 117

In Persia, very few of the children go to any school, and hardly ever a girl among the Mohammedans, unless she belong to a noble family. They think it is unnecessary for girls to learn to read, and so they grow in ignorance, to become wives and mothers and teachers in their own houses; for mothers are the real teachers in all countries.[21]

Similarly, in an article titled "Girls of Turkey," *Quarterly Token* described all Turkish girls as "strangers to education," who were treated as having no soul and therefore having no need of religious instruction and who were "kept in bondage of the most debasing kind." The article included an image of an elite Turkish daughter with her slave girl (Figure 4.1) and described each one as living under the "false religion of Mohammed [that] degrades and oppresses her, making her the mere slave of man." The lives of Turkish girls, as presented here, were the exact opposite of the lives of "happy little girls in England" whose Christian faith "exalts the female sex, and gives woman her

Figure 4.1 "Girls of Turkey" (1864)
Source: "Girls of Turkey," *A Quarterly Token for Juvenile Subscribers*, no. 35 (October 1864): 4. Courtesy of National Library of Scotland, Edinburgh.

proper place in society."[22] Before appealing to the readers to help, the article contended:

> At an early age—when about twelve years old—she will be betrothed to some husband, chosen by her father, whom she will not see until her wedding-day, and who will probably have many other wives. Then begins her life of slavery, as it may now justly be called. Jealousy, envy, and other evil passions are sure to rise and embitter her existence. And, alas! she knows no better remedy than revenge. Oh how different are the dark abodes of these poor Turkish women to a happy English home![23]

Thus, while naming typical themes of child marriage, polygyny, and domestic slavery, the Anglican magazine critiqued the ignorance and misbehavior of women in Islamic societies and alluded to the domineering and licentious nature of Muslim husbands. This pattern of missionary discourse that blamed non-western cultures for oppression of women while also portraying the women themselves in a negative light was common also in *CWC*. For example, an article by Henry Jessup described Bedouin Arab men sitting around lazily while the women labored to draw water at the wells, where they often quarreled, cursed, and fought.[24] A missionary in South Asia, Clara Wherry, explained in another article that a Muslim man may "have four wives, free women, and as many concubines or slaves as he can buy"; and she also encouraged her audience to imagine the quarrelling that must ensue in a household of "such jealous and selfish people." Of Muslim women's status in India, she concluded: "A woman in this country is equal to only *half* a man!"[25] Such critiques reinforced the need for mission schools for girls, while promoting the idea of western Christian civilization as superior in its treatment of women. Thus, similar to missionary reports for American and British adults, articles like Wherry's blatantly ignored the existing inequalities between men and women (and boys and girls) in western societies.

By the early twentieth century, when *CWC* became *OSL* and its distribution reached tens of thousands of children, the publication reflected that in fact such messages had spurred the growth of children's mission bands. Magazine issues consequently now catered to the needs of mission band leaders and Sunday schools, suggesting activities for gatherings of children and youth and offering cut-outs of "Muslim Types" and instructions for primary classes to act out the magazine's stories. One issue included a Persian

Figure 4.2 "Paper Doll—A Little Girl from Persia" (1907)
Source: J. E. Hyde, "Paper Doll—A Little Girl from Persia," Over Sea and Land 32, no. 10 (October 1907): 81. Courtesy of Presbyterian Historical Society, Philadelphia.

paper doll meant to resemble a Muslim girl, whose story the magazine featured in a previous issue (Figure 4.2).[26] The OSL also regularly published advertisements for newly published children's literature.

Two such educational, non-fiction books were *Topsy-Turvy Land: Arabia Pictured for Children* (1902) and *Children of Persia* (1911), which appeared regularly in the recommended books section of women's and children's missionary magazines before World War I.[27] While mission magazines were targeted at readers within particular denominations, such books were intended for a broader Protestant readership and were made available across multiple denominations and organizations by way of the ecumenical missionary movement. Notably, both of these books were published by Fleming H. Revell Company, the largest and most influential independent Christian publisher in the United States at that time. Along with many of Revell's other books on Islam, the Scottish publisher Oliphant, Anderson, and Ferrier carried *Children of Persia*, extending the American evangelical publisher's international reach.

Samuel Zwemer and his wife, Amy, co-authored *Topsy-Turvy Land*. Amy Zwemer went on to write several other books for young readers and may have been the primary author for this text as well.[28] Based on their residency on the Arabian peninsula, the Zwemers presented the volume as "a book of pictures and stories" intended "for all who love Sinbad the sailor and his strange country," referring to a popular story from *1001 Arabian Nights*. They noted that "The stories are not as good as those of the Arabian Nights but the morals are better" because these stories were *true*.[29] Arabia, as the Zwemers presented it, was a *topsy-turvy* land because "all the habits and customs are exactly opposite to those in America or England."[30] They claimed, "Everything seems different from what it is in a Christian country."[31] Thus, in such statements and in the title itself, the book emphasized the same western Christian norms that children's missionary magazines elevated, and it painted Islam and Christianity as opposites.

Although the book described many of the *cultural* differences in neutral terms,[32] it presented Islam as a "crooked" *religion* and portrayed Islamic gender norms in a consistently negative light.[33] For example, the Zwemers wrote:

> In your country boys learn the lesson of politeness—ladies first; but it is not so over here. It is *men first* in all grades of society; and not only men first but men last, in the middle, and all the time. Women and girls have a very small place given them in Topsy-turvy Land. The Arabs say that of all animal kinds the female is the most valuable except in the case of mankind! When a baby girl is born the parents are thought very unfortunate. How hard the Bedouin girls have to work! They are treated just like beasts of burden as if they had no souls.... They are very ignorant and superstitious, the chief remedies for sickness being to brand the body with a hot iron or wear charms.... How very thankful girls should be that in all Christian lands they have a higher place and a better lot than the poor girls and women of Arabia![34]

Sometimes the book described gender-based customs like the bride price for marriage and women's figure-concealing robes and veils in uncritical, informative terms.[35] Yet repeatedly, the authors also echoed negative tropes like those the aforementioned children's magazines introduced. They presented upper-class Arab women and girls as enclosed in their homes and afraid "to show their faces to strangers,"[36] while lower-class Bedouin women and girls were slaves to the men who lived lazy lives smoking pipes and drinking coffee.[37] Even in such statements disclosing that not all Muslim females faced the same life circumstances, the Zwemers taught children that their situation was dire. This basic "fact" was drilled into young readers, a pattern that other early twentieth-century books for children repeated.

One of these was the British missionary Dr. Urania Latham Malcolm's *Children of Persia*.[38] Malcolm's 1911 text, based on her work as a medical missionary for the CMS in Yezd (in present-day Iran), reiterated the tropes found in *Topsy-Turvy Land*, while presenting them within a different regional and cultural context. Instead of an educational overview of life in Arabia, Malcolm introduced children to the customs of Persia, which she considered to be equally "topsy-turvy," although not necessarily wrong in every case.[39] As for the practices of Islam, Malcolm's preface warned that, out of concern for her young audience, she had not fully described

> how bad Muhammedanism is, for a great deal of its sin and cruelty is too terrible to tell to young folks. But I hope enough has been said to show you that Persian children do need to be rescued from Muhammedanism and brought to the Lord Jesus Christ.[40]

From what did Malcolm think these children needed to be saved? Her response followed the usual pattern critiquing the age of marriage, Muslim men's mistreatment of women, Muslim families' preference for boys, and the seclusion and restrictive clothing proscribed for Persian women. Many Persian mothers, Malcolm said, were too young to know how to take care of their babies, a subject she expanded further in a chapter on "Child Wives."[41] She claimed that in Muslim countries "the men are allowed to treat the girls and women very badly," while in contrast Jesus "cares for us all equally." Thus, a Persian girl "has a much more secluded and restricted life than girls in Europe."[42]

Yet Malcolm's portrayal of the situation for Persian women and girls was not entirely negative. When explaining women's indoor and outdoor attire, she remarked on the "pretty prayer chadar" (or *chador*, the Persian term for a woman's head covering) worn indoors that did not cover the face, in contrast to the large black outdoor chador that completely covered the head, face, and body when Persian women went out in public.[43] She admitted, as well, that Persian families were very fond of their little girls, and noted that although few parents would invest in their girls' education, Persia exceeded other Muslim countries in education of girls, an indication that Muslim women had opportunities for education outside of Protestant mission schools, contrary to some missionary claims.[44]

Although in these ways Malcolm provided a nuanced picture of Muslim life in Persia, her book stood out from the other children's texts considered here for the insidious way ideas about race colored her descriptions of Persian Muslim life. She first brought up skin tone in a chapter on Persian clothing, noting that "Persian boys and girls are white, almost as white as ourselves, though they generally have black hair and dark eyes." The chief difference she noted between Persian and European children was their style of dress, a statement which emphasized commonalities and appeared to neutralize any negative impressions her readers may have had about racial difference.[45] After thus encouraging her target audience of young White Christians to think positively about Persians as members of the White race, just a few pages later Malcolm suggested that Islam had stunted the growth of Persians and other Muslims because it forced children to grow up too soon, making "the grown-ups too childish." She made this argument through a troubling comparison with animal development:

> You will find, that roughly speaking, if you look at animals that the higher the animal, the longer its childhood lasts, because it has more growing up to do. . . . [M]ice grow up in a few weeks, horses in a few years, and man takes longer to grow up than any animal. Now Muhammad, the false prophet whom the Persians believe and obey, had . . . no such high ideal for them to grow up to, as our Lord Jesus Christ set before his followers and enables them to grow up to; and so his religion provides only a short time for growing up, and stunts instead of assisting the growth both of individual Muhammadans and of Muhammadan nations.[46]

Thus, Malcolm described what she viewed as the successful growth of individual Christians and western civilization, while depicting Muslim societies as underdeveloped. Although she explicitly blamed this childlike state on the teachings of Islam, this was not merely a theological critique. In a chapter that began with commentary on skin tone, her statements must also be understood within the context of early twentieth-century biological racism, which Europeans and Americans mapped onto a hierarchy of bodies. This worldview that justified western colonialism also informed British and American Protestant missions.

When speaking later about mission schools in Persia, similar themes arose as Malcolm explained the difficulties of teaching "people whose intelligence and memory have never been developed by study of any kind, whose minds and brains have never grown up properly."[47] To such racializations of Muslims, Malcolm also added ideas about gender when arguing that Muslim girls who became wives and mothers at an early age would never reach adulthood. Their persistent ignorance and improper behavior, in the author's view, rendered them perpetually unable to manage their children or their homes.[48] Therefore, Malcolm concurred with the author of the aforementioned *CWC* article who claimed that "mothers are the real teachers in all countries."[49] For Malcolm, the backwardness identified in Islamic society was largely a result of the women's lack of education. These arguments led up to an appeal for American and British children to support missions to Muslims through prayer, gifts, and service.

Like children's magazines, both *Topsy-Turvy Land* and *Children of Persia* used depictions of Islam and Muslim life not just to inform but also to assure young readers of the supremacy of their own religion and culture and to nurture in them a missionary zeal. Such books, aiming to reach beyond a particular denomination, were part of the pan-Protestant efforts that gained momentum with the aforementioned Central Committee on the United Study of Foreign Missions (CCUSFM), founded in 1900 to unite the work of American women's mission boards.[50] The committee provided reading materials and educational guides for men, women, and children, believing that by reading the same literature, people in various churches and organizations would be better able to serve a common mission. As the CCUSFM work picked up again following World War I, on a rotating basis it designated Muslim lands as an area of focus for united study. In 1927, for instance, when the general textbook was Amy and Samuel Zwemer's *Moslem Women* (1926), the book for juniors was Amy Zwemer's *Two Young Arabs: The Travels of Noorah and Jameel* (1926).[51] I turn now to this widely advertised fictional tale and several others featuring Muslim characters.

Fictionalizing Islam for Young Readers

By composing short stories and novels featuring Muslim characters, missionaries expanded the growing body of missionary fiction, some of which focused on the transformation of women and children.[52] These texts drew in adults but were often aimed at younger readers, adding to the educational books and magazines that mission societies produced for children and youth. In addition to demonstrating what missionaries, mission auxiliaries, and Sunday schools were teaching children about Islam, such narratives captured Protestant gender ideals.

Although missionary men like Elwood Wherry wrote fiction, in the remainder of this chapter I focus on novels and short stories by missionary *women*, and this for several reasons. First, proportionally, men published many more theologically and scholarly oriented books and non-fiction accounts of Islamic societies than did women and less fiction. Women missionaries had less access to scholarly publishing, but a significant portion of the books that these women wrote were works of fiction.[53] Therefore, attending to fiction is particularly important for understanding the ways in which missionary women contributed to literature on Islam. Second, such stories that aimed to reach women readers, youth, and children had more popular appeal than theological texts and were widely used for teaching the British and American public about Muslim mission fields and for recruiting support. This is doubly important when considering that women on the home front largely orchestrated the fundraising and promotion of missionary causes, often as part of auxiliaries or church circles that used such materials in programming for men, women, and children. These women's stories were therefore geared toward a wider audience than most writings of missionary men, and they reached readers at an earlier age.

Because their role in educating children was deemed appropriate for Christian women, leaders of Protestant women's missionary movements could capitalize on the opportunity to inform audiences back home about their work for women and children and to solicit funds. In so doing they created a publishing niche for women. The four fictional accounts I examine below emerged from this context. All four stories were produced during the 1920s and emphasized the role of Protestant missions in improving the lives of Muslim women and girls, while simultaneously assuring readers that efforts to evangelize Islamic societies were proving successful but needed ongoing support.

The first is Helen Moody Stuart's *Fatmeh: A Common Story of Mission Schools for Moslem Girls*, which the British Syrian Mission (BSM) distributed in booklet form and published as a chapter in J. Edith Hutcheon's 1920 book *Pearl of the East*.[54] The stand-alone booklet was intended to be shared with young readers, while *Pearl of the East* was a largely non-fiction text geared toward an older audience.[55] The tale of this Fatmeh (there were several characters so named in other stories), a Syrian Muslim girl, is set in Damascus, where both Stuart and Hutcheon worked for the BSM.[56] It begins with young Fatmeh accompanying her cousin to a mission school where Muslim girls can learn from female teachers in complete seclusion from men.[57] Delighted by the Bible stories she hears at school, Fatmeh recounts them to the women of her household and then brings a Biblewoman (Syrian female evangelist) from the mission to teach her older sister Badriyeh how to read. The women in the harem reluctantly allow the Biblewoman to teach from the New Testament, and quickly all of them become drawn to the gospel.

Fatmeh soon confesses her faith in Jesus Christ, but when her father discovers this, he bans her from attending the school and forbids any further contact with Biblewomen or missionaries. Cut off from this Protestant influence, both daughters eventually marry Muslim men. Stuart concludes with an explanation that Fatmeh and Badriyeh do not represent actual Muslim girls but "are types of multitudes who reach a certain point in mission schools, or under the Biblewomen's teaching in the homes" and then are never seen again.[58] The author appeals to the reader for prayer and support of the BSM work among Muslims in Damascus so that it might carry on past such a limit. An editorial note on the last page is more optimistic, however, emphasizing that even such a limited amount of influence "does bear fruit in the afterlives of the girls and women" because even though the girl is "outwardly a Moslem, she secretly brings up her children as Christians."[59] This focus on mission schools as a means for reaching Muslim children with the gospel, and thereby influencing Muslim families, is prominent in the other children's stories considered below.

I turn next to two books by Mary Entwistle, *Habeeb: A Boy of Palestine* (1924) and *Musa: Son of Egypt* (1927), both of which feature Muslim boys as main characters. Entwistle (b. 1878) was British and a prolific writer of Christian children's literature, including many publications on global missions for American and British audiences. The CMS published *Habeeb*, and Entwistle dedicated *Musa* (which was published by the CMS and several other presses) to her friends in the CMS in Cairo.[60] A variety of Protestant mission societies recommended and distributed these books to readers in Britain and the United States.[61] *Habeeb* follows the life of a seven-year-old boy in Palestine whose name means Beloved and who longs to be old enough to stay out in the fields all night tending his father's flocks. Such pastoral scenes and other biblical imagery—like that of Habeeb's baby sister Fatmeh swaddled and sleeping in a manger—remind readers that this is the land of Jesus' birth. Yet the Christians whom Habeeb encounters in the story are not

Middle Eastern Christians who have maintained the faith since the time of Christ. Instead, the young Palestinian is introduced to Christianity through Protestant missionaries. Despite the claims of his mother and the mosque preacher (*khatib*) that Christians are infidels, Habeeb comes to recognize the missionaries as healers and friends. Their medical knowledge relieves baby Fatmeh from an illness, and Habeeb's older cousin, Hassan, benefits from attending Mount Zion School in Jerusalem, a CMS institution. From Hassan, Habeeb learns about a prophet named Jesus, who lived in Galilee, healed people, and fed the hungry.

Just as Habeeb seems unaware of the indigenous Christians in Palestine, this appears to be the first time he has heard about the prophet 'Isa, as Jesus is known in the Qur'an. In order to emphasize how learning about Jesus could transform Habeeb's life, Entwistle thus simplified the Islamic tradition for her young readers. She neglected to explain that Muslims revere Jesus as a prophet and that a boy like Habeeb would likely have known of 'Isa. As the two cousins read the Bible, Habeeb becomes drawn to the Christian faith and longs to attend a Christian school too. He is too young for Mount Zion School, but a new Christian school opens in his village and his parents decide to send him there. Habeeb does not want to disappoint his parents by forsaking their religion, and there is no formal conversion scene in this story. Yet Habeeb intends to continue his education at the CMS school in Jerusalem, and readers can expect that he will embrace the gospel by the time he graduates.

In *Habeeb*, Entwistle spent significant time informing her young readers about Islam and Palestinian Muslim life, reflecting that one of the book's aims was educational. Another aim—to encourage financial support for the CMS—was apparent in Entwistle's descriptions of CMS endeavors in Palestine and appeals for prayers and donations for the Mount Zion School, the Bishop Gobat School, and five mission hospitals. Entwistle's endearing depictions of Habeeb's loving family suggested yet another, more subtle aim: to prove that many Muslims are open to missionaries' educational and medical resources and to the gospel message itself.

Published three years later, in 1927, Entwistle's *Musa: Son of Egypt* followed a similar trajectory, featuring an Egyptian boy, Musa (or Moses), who, like Habeeb, has a sister named Fatmeh.[62] The story opens with the two siblings awaiting their father's return from his pilgrimage to Mecca, a sign that this is a devout Muslim family. More than Habeeb, Musa has a negative view of Christians and sees women and girls as inferior. When their father sends the children to a Christian school, Musa is shocked to find that his teacher is a woman, and he is outraged that he must share a desk with a Christian boy. Soon, however, he learns to respect his teacher (and all women) and makes friends with his Christian classmate. Musa's positive encounters with Christian missionaries continue throughout the story as he falls ill and receives treatment at a missionary hospital; as he meets the son of a British missionary, Bob; and as Musa and Fatmeh spend time in Bob's home. Like Habeeb, Musa hears "of a wonderful Prophet who lived many years ago in the land of Palestine," and the missionaries give him and Fatmeh children's books telling them more about this prophet named Jesus.[63] Entwistle concluded: "And they are learning to be like Jesus, to have compassion, and to do kindness, away in that far-off land, Bob and Musa and Fatmeh."[64] This story, like *Habeeb*, reinforced the need for and successes of missionary institutions, it humanized Muslims to show their openness to the gospel, and it informed readers about the Middle Eastern context through a section at the end of each chapter titled "Things You Would Like to Know." Thus, in both texts, Entwistle transmitted knowledge about Islam and Muslim life while also encouraging her readers' support of missions and grounding them more deeply in (the superiority of) their faith.

The fourth and final text under consideration, Amy Zwemer's *Two Young Arabs*, is the most straightforward about its aim to educate and influence young readers. After mentioning Entwistle's *Habeeb* in the acknowledgments as one book upon which her own story builds, Zwemer explains:

> *The Aim* of [*Two Young Arabs*] is to picture what the Mohammedans believe and to show how they practice this religion which came from the desert in Arabia. *The Purpose* is to enlist the sympathy of the juniors of this country in the eighty millions of juniors in the Moslem world. These boys and girls love the things that make life so joyous and happy for you. Will you share your best with them?[65]

The main character of the story, six-year-old Noorah, is an earnest seeker after the truth, who has an older brother named Jameel. Soon after the death of their mother, the siblings travel with their father, Abu Jameel, to Islamic pilgrimage sites in Mecca, India, Persia, Algeria, Egypt, and Jerusalem. As the book gives young readers a tour of various Muslim societies, describing these key sites and the religious history of each region, none of the holy shrines satisfies Abu Jameel. Zwemer uses the father's spiritual quest and eventual conversion to Christianity as a backdrop for telling Noorah's story as a young Arab Muslim girl.

Abu Jameel desires for his children to have better lives, and his hope for Noorah, in particular, comes to fruition through the opportunities she finds to attend missionary schools in the various cities where the family settles temporarily. In contrast to the unruly Muslim girls, Noorah finds that the girls in these Christian schools have learned to "be obedient and to play together without quarreling."[66] Noorah, an astute child, discerns the goodness in Christian teachings and missionary institutions before her father and brother do, and their love for Noorah eventually leads Abu Jameel and Jameel to become Christian. For they are drawn to the positive way that Christians treat women and girls. Thus, in the end, Zwemer urges her young readers to take up the missionary cause as "Christ's Crusaders" especially for the sake of Muslim girls.[67] Like Stuart and Entwistle, Zwemer highlights the role of children in mission schools in bringing their families to Christ and emphasizes that such Protestant work can be successful among Muslim families like Noorah's who want what is best for their children, have open minds, are truth-seeking, and can think critically about their own Muslim traditions.

Islam and Gender in Early Twentieth-Century Children's Stories

Turning now to the strong emphasis that Stuart, Entwistle, and Zwemer all placed on the situation for women and girls in Muslim societies, I analyze four prominent themes in these texts: 1) education, 2) veiling/seclusion, 3) marriage, and 4) behavior of Muslim men and boys. For these and other similar stories, education is the author's goal for female protagonists, and early marriage, women's seclusion, and male behaviors are seen as barriers to these goals.

First, mission schools play the primary role in bringing the gospel to Muslim children in Stuart, Entwistle, and Zwemer's stories. These authors, like other women who wrote about missions, stressed the importance of educating Muslim girls despite resistance from families who saw this as a waste of resources. In the American and British Protestant understanding, women were the key to raising a Christian family. At the same time, missionary discourses blamed uneducated Muslim women for holding back their societies. According to *The Pearl of the East*, for example, "'If you get the girls for Christ,' said an Egyptian official, 'you get Egypt for Christ,' and so it is everywhere. The dark, ignorant, superstitious womanhood of the East has done more than anything else to retard the spread of Christ's Kingdom."[68]

In the four stories reviewed here, objections to Muslim female education reflected the ways in which missionaries understood Islam as undervaluing and mistreating women and girls. In *Fatmeh*, the protagonist's mother initially asks, "What do you want with reading?" when she learns of her daughter's interest. She tells Fatmeh to come and help with the housework instead.[69] Yet Fatmeh's father permits her to attend the mission school because he recognizes the advantage that literacy can bring to his daughter's marriage prospects. Noorah's father in *Two Young Arabs* and Fatmeh's father in *Musa* both also see the benefit of educating their daughters. Musa, however, objects to his sister's desire for schooling, and his father rebukes him for exclaiming, "A girl, wanting to be wise! ... Everybody knows that girls are the silliest."[70] Musa is repeating the ideas of his former teacher at the mosque school, while his father's response reflects the changing views of modern Muslim men that twentieth-century missionaries often cited. Noorah's father falls somewhere in between. While he values what mission schools can offer, he hesitates to denounce his own society. Thus, when Noorah tells their dinner hosts that she likes the Bible stories more than those in the Qur'an, an embarrassed Abu Jameel responds, "Please excuse her, she is only a girl and ignorant." Yet their female host replies:

> Well, we women and girls may be ignorant and we are, but somehow the Words of Jesus (upon Him be peace), and the good works of the Christian ladies are very comforting in the times of trouble.[71]

Thus, Zwemer indicates that Muslim women who recognize the attractions of Christianity are not actually ignorant at all. Instead, in this book and in other missionary texts Muslim women are considered ignorant only when they persist in beliefs that the authors deem unfounded. In *Habeeb*, for instance, when baby Fatmeh becomes sick, her mother initially relies on a blue bead threaded into the baby's hair and a necklace with a bead in the shape of a hand, both intended to protect her from evil spirits. In the end, however, because these folk remedies do not work, her mother makes the wise choice to consult a neighbor who had learned some basic medical knowledge from missionary doctors.[72]

A major barrier to addressing such ignorance among women is the second theme emphasized in all four stories: Muslim women's seclusion, as symbolized in their confinement at home and in the wearing of the face veil. *Fatmeh* describes the various levels of seclusion in women's spaces and the way veiling was practiced in Muslim communities, first by introducing Fatmeh as a little girl in an ankle-length dress "with a coarse white muslin veil twisted about her head and shoulders, hiding the fair hair in its tight little pigtails."[73] The picture on the opposite page of three "Moslem women in outdoor dress" with bodies and faces completely covered also sets the tone for the story, which takes place in women's spaces of the home and the school. Stuart describes Badriyeh, Fatmeh's sister, as a "poor girl" because she "was not free to go even the few steps to her uncle's house without carefully covering herself up, face and all," while Fatmeh could go there "with no more protection than what was afforded by her muslin scarf."[74] The caption for the accompanying photograph of two women with their faces and bodies completely covered emphasizes that this is "How Badriyeh looks when she goes out of doors."[75]

Fatmeh and her young cousin are allowed to attend the mission school in their white scarves and brightly colored dresses because they assure their families that it is *harim*, or a female space where they will not be seen by men. While there, they find a Muslim girl their age dressed "as if she were a grown-up lady" with a black cloak covering all but her face, indicating that some families enforce an even stricter dress code on their girls than Fatmeh's does.[76] The accompanying photos of the BSM's Saint Paul's School in Damascus show a variety of dress norms for young girls—some with no head coverings, some with scarves like Fatmeh's, and some older girls wearing longer cloaks that fully cover their heads and arms. In each case, Stuart emphasizes the difficulty such seclusion poses for young women and girls and indicates her disapproval of these norms. At the same time, she shows that the BSM's female mission still worked within those norms by offering educational services in female-only spaces.

In Entwistle's first story, the text follows Habeeb into men's spaces like the mosque, rather than centering on the experiences of his mother or sister. Yet women's reduced place in Muslim society is a prominent theme. Habeeb is disturbed to notice how some of his friends disrespect their mothers, and he asks his father why his own mother does not pray, since she does not accompany them to the mosque.[77] This question critiques the absence of women in public worship, since congregational prayer is obligatory only

ISLAM RE-INVENTED FOR YOUNG READERS 131

for men in Islam, a stipulation related in part to women's need for exemption from prayers during menstruation. A similar critique is offered in *Two Young Arabs* when Noorah and her hostess pray in the house and do not think of accompanying the men to prayers in the mosque. Zwemer explains this by stating that "Islam is a man's religion."[78] Thus, she echoes a recurring Protestant discourse that condemns Islam while detracting attention from Christian patriarchy. As noted in *Topsy-Turvy Land*, however, Muslim women and girls do have agency to pray in private spaces—a reality that Habeeb's father also confirms when he explains that women pray at home.[79] The veil is not a topic of discussion in *Habeeb*, but the appearance of Habeeb's mother only in the home emphasizes the public separation of genders. Palestinian Muslim women, like Habeeb's mother, are pictured in the illustrations with their heads, but not their faces, veiled (Figure 4.3). *Musa*, by contrast, mentions women's face veiling in the author's commentary on Egyptian clothing at the end of one chapter.[80]

The typical western discourse of the veil is most prominent in Zwemer's *Two Young Arabs*. From the start, on the way to Mecca Noorah is

Figure 4.3 Habeeb's mother and baby Fatmeh, in *Habeeb: A Boy of Palestine* (1927)
Source: Mary Entwistle, *Habeeb: A Boy of Palestine* (London: Church Missionary Society, 1927), frontispiece. Illustration by Elsie A. Wood.

uncomfortably confined with the women travelers in a "cage strapped onto the back of a camel" with curtains pulled tightly closed, while her brother and father ride out in the open.[81] Zwemer regularly critiques such gender separation because it also prevents families from sitting down to eat together: the women serve the men and take their meals separately later. In this she picks up on a theme she previously addressed in *Topsy-Turvy Land*, which criticizes Arab Muslim society for putting men first, citing as an example the practice of men eating first and the women eating the leftovers.[82] She does not, of course, encourage her young readers to consider how often women's roles as food-preparers in Anglo-Protestant homes also hindered their ability to enjoy a leisurely meal with their families.

Although Noorah must follow the prevailing customs when visiting other Muslim families, she does not cover her face. She just covers her hair with a veil. This contrasts with the garb of a young girl she meets in Persia, who can only leave the house with a veil thrown over her head so that her entire face is covered. Yet the girl relishes these few opportunities to escape the walls of her house.[83] For readers who may be disturbed by such practices, Zwemer asserts:

> A change is coming over the people, and some of the educated women and men are working for freedom from the veil and other things, and a few are daring to walk out unveiled. They are very brave to do this, because some of the rougher people of the streets follow them making unpleasant remarks.[84]

A change is also coming, Zwemer implies, for those like Noorah's father Abu Jameel, who observes that "Christians honor their women and girls and let them go about freely."[85]

Although these depictions might suggest that practices of face veiling will only change through Christian influence, Zwemer notes that women from the city are the ones "shrouded from head to foot," whereas women in rural areas commonly go out unveiled "in costumes entirely different from those worn in the city."[86] Through her descriptions of veiling and dress styles in different regions,[87] like comments Entwistle offered about women's attire throughout Egypt, Zwemer reveals how missionaries educated readers about the nuances of Muslim women's lives, even while using discourses about veiling and seclusion to advance their own work.

A third hurdle that missionaries critiqued for inhibiting women's education was the marriage of girls at a young age. Unlike discourses aimed at adult readers and some of the reports in children's magazines and non-fiction, the fiction examined here does not focus on themes of Muslim male licentiousness or polygyny. Of the four stories considered, only *Two Young Arabs* mentions polygyny briefly when Noorah reflects that she's lucky not to be born into a family that is "always changing families and mothers whenever the fathers want to marry a new wife."[88] Noorah's main fear of being married off at a young age is a more prominent theme. The women she meets in different Muslim contexts keep discussing her marriage prospects, "for girls in Moslem lands are often married off by their parents when they are very young."[89]

In *Fatmeh*, the topic of marriage comes up as soon as Badriyeh, Fatmeh's older sister, appears on the scene and is introduced as being "grown-up and engaged to be married, though she was only fifteen."[90] Then marriage prospects emerge again as a family concern when Fatmeh's father recognizes the progress she has made in school and states, "I wish Badriyeh had been sent to school when she was younger. Her bridegroom said to-day that he wanted a wife who could read, but she is too big to send to school now."[91] Their mother later emphasizes that Badriyeh must learn to read, even if the Biblewoman teaches her from the *injil* (gospel), "for we must please this bridegroom."[92] Thus, both parents indicate their support of women's literacy in order to make a good match for their daughter, while Stuart also signals that times are changing: Muslim men now value an educated bride. This is an argument that missionaries made for girls to continue their education in order to secure a good match later, rather than being married off early. Yet for both Badriyeh and Fatmeh, Stuart's story concludes with their marriages to Muslim men, in homes where they are presumably cut off from missionary influence—an unhappy ending that the author promises will await many more Muslim girls without increased missionary efforts.

Neither of Entwistle's books focus on marriage, as the protagonists are young boys. More important for Entwistle is the way in which Muslim males treat women and girls, a fourth and final theme that arises in these stories. Because Entwistle and Zwemer feature Muslims who are receptive to Christianity, they make little use of the discourse about violent Muslim men. The fathers in these stories care deeply about their daughters and have thoughtful, gentle manners. *Two Young Arabs* depicts Abu Jameel and Jameel both as loving toward Noorah, rather than aggressive or controlling. The only indication of the violent lives they purportedly gave up by embracing Christianity appears in the first image of the story, a photograph of an Arab man handing his small son a rifle, with a caption that describes the boy's future: "Mahomet taught war, not peace—some day [the boy] will have a gun" (Figure 4.4). The conclusion of *Two Young Arabs*, however, calls Christian children to "join the army of Christ's Crusaders" fighting sin with the "Sword of the Spirit," indicating another way in which Zwemer (mistakenly) believes Christianity is the mirror opposite of Islam.[93]

Although Zwemer and Entwistle's stories include some Muslims who rigidly oppose Christianity and some men who disparage women, the trope of the violent, domineering Muslim man is only prominent in *Fatmeh*. Describing the enraged response of Fatmeh's father after he learns of his household's interest in Christianity, Stuart writes, "Strong words were spoken, hard blows were struck, Fatmeh never went back to school, the Biblewoman was never again permitted to cross the threshold, [and] in due course both girls were married to the Moslem husbands selected by the family."[94] She depicts the father as an authoritarian who allows Fatmeh's education only because he hopes it will increase her chances of a lucrative marriage. He ultimately exhibits no real openness to Christianity, making him a prototype for the violent Muslim patriarch.

Figure 4.4 "Someday he will have a gun" (1926)
Source: Amy E. Wilkes Zwemer, *Two Young Arabs and the Travels of Noorah and Jameel* (West Medford, MA: Central Committee on the United Study of Foreign Missions, 1926), frontmatter.

Mid-Twentieth-Century Shifts in Missionary Fiction

By the 1920s, when missionaries published the aforementioned literature for children and youth, the basic Protestant discourse about Islam and gender was firmly embedded in missionary culture and in American society. Missionaries contributed to the widespread ideas about Islam as a religion that sanctioned masculinist violence and the oppression of women, and they capitalized on such claims to gain support for their work and to reinforce Protestant theological claims over and against Islamic doctrine. Yet, as I shall explain in the final chapter, during the interwar period and after World War II, some mainline Protestants, including missionaries, began rethinking polemical approaches to Islam and other world religions. Such shifts appeared, for example, in the 1932 Laymen's Foreign Missions Inquiry that recommended less emphasis on evangelism and more on education and humanitarian services.[95] More inclusive theologies of religion and efforts at formal interfaith dialogue in Europe and North America emerged during this period in both Protestant and Catholic circles. To demonstrate how these changing views affected mainline Protestant missionaries' gendered discourses about Islam, this final section examines two fictional accounts of the mid-twentieth century by Congregationalist missionaries—a short story and a novel. Set in different Islamic contexts, both featured Muslim girls of marriage age and were aimed at youth and young adult readers. When compared to earlier works of missionary fiction, these two texts show how missionary storytelling about Islam transformed over time, reflecting debates within the Protestant ecumenical movement about the proper approach to Christian-Muslim engagement.

Modern Muslim Women: Lindao and Filiz

The story "Lindao's Dowry" is a short unpublished work written in the 1950s by Margaret Hamm, an American Congregationalist who worked for the ABCFM on the island of Mindanao, a largely Muslim area of the Philippines. In addition to sharing the written text, Hamm may have narrated the tale to listening audiences.[96] Set in the Lake Lanao region, the story introduces Lindao as a fourteen-year-old Maranao Muslim whose father, "a wise and kind man," had ensured her education through sixth grade, the traditional age of engagement. This level of education was uncommon for girls in her village.

Lindao dreams of her future and desires a modern marriage, in which she would be her husband's first and only wife, "according to the newer custom." Thinking of marriage only as an "obligation to her family," however, she does not expect to fall in love.[97] Soon the village imam approaches Lindao's family with an offer of marriage to his educated son, Mustapha. Mustapha has already completed four years of high school and two years of pre-medical study at a mission school. He is now studying medicine at a university just outside of Manila and wants to take his new wife back there, where he would finish his degree and she could continue her education. Wishing Lindao to remain in the village, however, her father knowingly demands a dowry (or bride price) higher than Mustapha's family can pay, so as to prevent the marriage.[98] Although it is not appropriate for the young couple to meet before the engagement, they see each other from a distance during a village celebration and fall in love. When Lindao's father learns of his daughter's feelings for Mustapha, he regrets increasing the bride price; but he cannot retract his decision. Meanwhile, Mustapha tells his father that although he had not wanted an arranged marriage, he now realizes that Lindao is the only one he wants to marry. To the delight of all, a wise old matriarch soon orchestrates a clever way for Mustapha's family to pay the otherwise unattainable bride price, so the two young people become engaged after all.

American Congregationalist missionary Dorothy Blatter's 1961 novel *Cap and Candle* also involved an arranged marriage. Published after Blatter had worked for decades with the ABCFM in Turkey, in American book reviews this story was promoted as a "romance" novel for readers over twelve.[99] The second edition was released in 1964, and the multiple reviews and letters to the author contained in Blatter's personal papers show the keen interest that librarians, educators, and church people of the time showed in the novel.[100] Blatter's main character, Filiz, grows up in a traditional Muslim home in a rural Turkish village but then attends an American missionary boarding school in Istanbul. Her education and exposure to the modernization efforts in urban Turkey lead her to pursue a public career in nursing, to set aside outdated cultural practices for Muslims, and, unveiled, to embrace modern clothing and hair styles. Although her mother, grandmother, and sisters protest that she is meant to marry and raise children, Filiz delays the marriage that her parents arranged for her to a young army officer from her village named Hasan. Instead, she completes five years of nursing training after graduating from the mission school. Only after her sister dies of typhoid and Filiz calls a nurse to save her nephew from the same fate do the women of her family recognize the value of modern medicine. Filiz also proves her worth through diligent work when skeptical male doctors question her abilities, and after she finally marries Hasan she continues with her career. They are not married long, however, before Hasan is killed in the line of duty. At the close of the book, Filiz has been assigned to a new medical project in a rural village where she reconnects with an old friend, Orhan, a modern-thinking agricultural developer who is more highly educated than Hasan was. Orhan shares Filiz's goals for modernizing the village and, Blatter suggests, will someday soon make a better life partner for her.[101]

In both of these stories, marriage is a primary concern, education is the author's goal for the female protagonist, and women's seclusion is the traditional gender norm that the young women face. Though this critique of Islamic gender norms is consistent with the other writings discussed in this chapter, these mid-twentieth-century stories also showed some differences in approach.

We might recall, in the early twentieth-century story of *Fatmeh*, Stuart's negative interpretation of the sisters' fate. This stands in contrast to the way Blatter and Hamm, writing several decades later, presented the matches of Filiz to Orphan and Lindao to Mustapha as results of the mutual attraction between modern, educated Muslim young people. In both *Cap and Candle* and "Lindao's Dowry," the protagonists' wishes conflict with the longstanding customs in their villages. Filiz delays her engagement and wedding and then continues working after marriage, despite her mother's hope that she will return to their village to raise a family. Lindao wishes to marry and accompany Mustapha to Manila, and she desires further education in order to become the ideal wife for Mustapha—the "only wife" and not the first of several wives like in her father's polygynous marriages.[102] Meanwhile, Lindao's father insists that it is customary for a daughter to remain near her family for the first year of marriage. Both Lindao and Filiz win out in the end, and their families are content with the resulting marriages, even though the young women leave their villages. On the topic of marriage age, Blatter's account aligns more with Stuart's, which emphasizes that Badriyeh is too young at age fifteen to be considered "grown-up" and engaged. Blatter likewise suggests that Filiz chooses the right course in not marrying directly after high school, while Hamm presents Lindao's marriage as the best choice available to her at age fourteen. Although Hamm's story does not fit with missionaries' typical critique of child marriage, it notes that otherwise the second-best marriage prospect for Lindao would have been her friend's uncle, Hadji Abdul, an old man. Hamm emphasizes this point with a comment from Lindao's younger brother that "she will not really be alive again" if she marries Hadji Abdul.[103]

In these stories, the seclusion of Muslim women is featured in different ways. "Lindao's Dowry" does not mention Maranao women's head coverings or veils when it describes traditional clothing worn for occasions like the engagement ceremony. Rather, Hamm shows the community's customs by noting the separation of genders with physical barriers—like the curtain behind which, at her father's suggestion, Lindao watches the first engagement negotiations or the space separating the men and women seated in the same room during the second engagement meeting. In addition, Hamm explains that young women are expected to refrain from interacting with young men. During an outdoor village gathering, Mustapha can speak with Lindao's brother, Amin; but although Lindao is near enough to hear the conversation, Mustapha never speaks to her, and she refrains from looking directly at him. Amin also has more freedom, as a young man, to leave the home to solicit the aid of a wise old female relative, Kaka Salam, while Lindao remains at home. Only once the engagement terms have been agreed upon can Lindao and Mustapha sit together and hold a conversation in the same room as, but at a distance from, their watching family members.

Cap and Candle likewise emphasizes that young Turkish women like Filiz are expected to refrain from contact or conversation with the opposite gender unless closely supervised. Her grandmother reminds her of this code of conduct, warning her before she goes to school in Istanbul not to talk to boys.[104] Later her family worries that Filiz's reputation will be ruined because she traveled on her own on a rescue mission to a flooded village with "all kinds of men around!" The family is relieved when Hasan tells Filiz that he is proud of her courage, while assuring her parents that she will not "go out unprotected like that" ever again.[105] They conduct the engagement ceremony as planned, and at the party Hasan mingles with the men and Filiz with the women, according to custom.

Like Hamm, Blatter does not take up the discourse of the veil.[106] However, she makes clear that Filiz adopts the modern clothing she encounters in Istanbul, rather than retaining her village dress. Filiz's choice of headgear is the nurse's cap she receives after completing her exams, followed by taking the Florence Nightingale pledge (see two different images of Filiz on the front covers of *Cap and Candle*: Figures 4.5 and 4.6). In short, the cap signals

ISLAM RE-INVENTED FOR YOUNG READERS 139

Figure 4.5 Cover image of *Cap and Candle* (1961)
Source: Dorothy Blatter, *Cap and Candle* (Philadelphia: Westminster Press, 1961).

Figure 4.6 Cover image of *Cap and Candle* (1964)
Source: Dorothy Blatter, *Cap and Candle* (Philadelphia: Westminster Press, 1964).

her status as a professional, and its contrast to the headgear of "closely veiled" Muslim women would be apparent to Protestant readers who had been exposed to earlier missionary discourses.[107]

In both stories, as in much of the missionary writing about Muslim women and girls, issues of education are closely tied up with concerns about marriage and the seclusion or protection of girls. In each story, the father as patriarch of the household voices the strongest desire for his daughter(s) to be educated, aligning with the commentary in mission reports about the changing perspectives of modern Muslim men. Hamm presents Lindao's father as one of the most educated men of his village, having completed one year of high school and being the only one of them who knows English. It is he who insists that Lindao should go to school with the village boys, starting at age eight, while Hamm notes that "the women had chattered and murmured and muttered! 'A girl, educated?'"[108] Similarly, he objects to the marriage not because Mustapha wants his wife to gain higher education but because Lindao would have to leave the village. Yet eventually Lindao's father admits, "I know that new days are coming. Before long many young girls will go away for schooling. Perhaps it really would be better for her to go now, and if she were with Mustapha he would guard her well."[109]

Similarly, in *Cap and Candle* Filiz's father is the driving force behind her mission school education. It is his ambition to send a daughter to the American Girls' School, and he fervently wishes for Filiz to learn English.[110] Filiz's female family members object to her continued schooling and delayed marriage, while her father calls her mother "a wee bit old-fashioned" because she continues to believe in superstitions.[111] Filiz's mission to break through such superstitions in the medical arena supports Blatter's general claim (consistent with other missionary writings) that men in Islamic societies are advancing through education, while greater efforts must be made to educate women. In contrast to the image of the violent patriarch seen in *Fatmeh*, these two mid-twentieth-century stories also offer a picture of Muslim men who appreciate and give their daughters access to modern education. Like Stuart, however, who has Fatmeh's mother object at first to her daughter's desire to learn how to read, both Hamm and Blatter give women what we might call *negative agency*. In their stories, it is not Muslim men nor Islamic teachings that keep females uneducated but rather the cultural traditions carried on by Muslim women—traditions that the authors contend can be broken through mission education.

Shifts in Twentieth-Century Muslim Societies

Written in the 1950s, Margaret Hamm's story suggested more strongly than the missionary writings of the early twentieth century that the old cultural practices and newer modern ones could go hand in hand. Her character, Lindao, is hesitant at first about arranged marriage and certainly does not want to be one of many wives. But she falls in love with Mustapha when she watches from behind the curtain while the fathers and male village elders conduct the betrothal negotiations with him, sitting on floor mats and wearing the customary belted *malongs* (fabric wrapped around the waist).[112] Likewise, the missionary-educated Mustapha, who typically wears western attire and once vowed to choose his own wife, also quickly gives up that modern notion when he glimpses Lindao's beauty. Theirs becomes a modern "love marriage" yet manages to do so without casting aspersions on customary family negotiations.

Americans who read or listened to Hamm narrate "Lindao's Dowry" gained insight into the traditions and shifting practices of Maranao Muslims in the Philippines. Similarly, Blatter's readers in the 1960s would have learned something about Turkish society and its recent changes through the eyes of Filiz. Yet, even more than Hamm's story, *Cap and Candle* narrates the life of the Turkish young woman in accordance with modern western ideals, as seen in Blatter's description of the day before Filiz's wedding. Readers learn about the custom of staining the bride's nails and hair with henna, which the Turkish bride resisted, saying, "It wouldn't be suitable with my uniform, and I expect to be back at the hospital in less than a week."[113] Her friends bemoaned the fact that they could not cut her already-short hair to make bride's locks[114]; and Filiz, who already knew her future husband, Hasan, remarked to a friend, "[I]t must have been awful in the old days when ... the bride and groom hadn't met before the wedding day.... We've got lots to be thankful for, Suzan, that we weren't born sixty years ago."[115] Although Filiz had turned from many of the "old ways," out of respect and obligation to her family at the age of sixteen she endured the typical family-to-family betrothal negotiations. She also allowed some of the customary wedding preparations, opting for a religious ceremony and a large family celebration complete with displaying her trousseau, rather than only the private civil ceremony that the Turkish government required.

So, what did readers learn from these texts? Alongside potentially inflated evidence that young Muslims in both societies were embracing western habits, the stories contained details about sacred and mundane customs. This was especially apparent in the works of Hamm and Blatter, which took on an educational tone in contrast to missionary texts that emphasized Muslim girls' dire needs in order to raise funds for the cause. That Hamm and Blatter carefully studied their respective missionary contexts is apparent in their accounts of marriage and engagement practices. It is also clear from their descriptions of clothing (of girls' dress styles in rural and urban Turkey or of the gold coins adorning the clothing of engaged Maranao couples), of songs and dances (the Turkish *zeybek* folk dance and the *kulintang*, a Southeast Asian instrument), and of religious holidays like the end of the pilgrimage (*hajj*) that both cultures shared yet celebrated differently.[116]

At the end of Hamm and Blatter's stories, the happy Filipino couple marry and move to Manila, while the equally happy Turkish couple wed and then return to their jobs in separate regions of the country. This contrasts with the ending of Stuart's early twentieth-century story, which gave readers little assurance that Fatmeh and Badriyeh lived enjoyable lives after their arranged marriages to Muslim men. *Cap and Candle* and "Lindao's Dowry" contrasted as well with the aforementioned stories by Mary Entwistle, Amy Zwemer, and Elwood Wherry, which all depicted Muslim characters either converting to Christianity through contact with missionaries or taking steps in that direction.

In mainline denominational mission societies like the Congregational ABCFM in Turkey and the Philippines, the emphasis had changed since the early decades of the twentieth century. These missions did not focus as much attention on evangelism but had expanded their existing educational, medical, and other humanitarian services. Such mid-twentieth-century accounts demonstrated that mainline missionaries transformed over time through cultural immersion and relationships with Muslims and Christians in Islamic contexts, and because their home societies and worldviews were changing following World War II. In contrast to missionary writers in earlier periods, and particularly male missionary-scholars like Samuel Zwemer and Henry Jessup, Blatter and Hamm expressed appreciation for Turkish and Filipino customs, something that was missing from Stuart's story. *Cap and Candle* and "Lindao's Dowry" gave no indication that Filiz or Lindao left Islam or even that the authors hoped the young women would someday embrace Christianity. Yet the intent to change the host society is central to missions. While this is clearest before World War II in stories like Stuart's, even Blatter and Hamm, who appeared uninterested in turning their fictional Muslims into Protestants, still enthusiastically supported the modernization (meaning westernization) of Turkey and the Philippines in the mid-twentieth century. They glorified American Protestant gender norms as they used the heroines of their stories to critique what they identified as outdated cultural practices in Islamic societies.

Gaining a wide popular audience, such accessible stories influenced views of Islam in ways that missionaries may not have intended. Notably, Blatter painted modern Turkey in a generally positive light as she noted how the society was changing for the better, while Hamm repeatedly showed Mustapha and Lindao moving away from old customs. Nevertheless, these stories reinforced earlier missionary notions of rigid Muslim–Christian and "East–West" divisions by evoking American readers' sympathy only for Muslims who upheld western norms regarding marriage and women's roles in the public sphere. Essentialist notions that other missionaries disseminated through critiques of veiling—implying that Islam was oppressive while Christianity was liberating—persisted easily alongside Blatter and Hamm's affirmation of Muslims who became "modern."

Conclusion

In illuminating how Protestant missionaries and their supporters reinvented Islam for American and British children and youth, this chapter has unearthed some tensions inherent in missionary literature about Muslims. On the one hand, negative gender discourses appeared repeatedly in Protestant writings, implicitly or explicitly reinforcing the missionary interpretations that I am challenging in this book. On the other hand, missionary texts also included neutral and appreciative assessments of Muslim contexts that at times even contradicted their own harsh critiques of Islamic gender norms. This was apparent in material for young readers, revealing the key ideas that missionaries wanted to pass on to the next generation. The humanizing impulses prominent in missionary fiction elucidate these tensions further. By identifying the ways in which missionary narratives led readers to build empathy for Muslim subjects we can do justice to the complexity of missionaries' views without excusing the patterns of dehumanization that the missionary enterprise also perpetuated. The children's literature I have examined encouraged intercultural awareness and interreligious understanding in two notable ways.

First, to make Muslim life understandable to young readers, missionaries produced informative, ethnographic-style accounts with neutral observations about the societies in which they lived. This reflects the educational nature of the children's missionary movement.[117] In contrast with its harshly critical narrative about the unequal status of males and females in Islam, the educational thrust of books like *Topsy-Turvy Land*—covering geography, sayings, food, and stories about individuals' daily lives—humanized Muslims and at times was even laudatory and comical.[118] Furthermore, children's mission magazines like *Quarterly Token* and *CWC* were packed with informative material about history and culture, and in their fictional accounts Amy Zwemer, Mary Entwistle, and Helen Stuart all offered details about the lifestyles of Muslims in various parts of Africa and Asia. Missionaries' provision of such cross-cultural knowledge in later works like Dorothy Blatter's and Margaret Hamm's—which offered detailed, neutral observations about engagement and marriage customs in Turkey and the Philippines and the way some of these were changing—would eventually aid in the establishment of formal interfaith movements after the mid-twentieth century. Yet even the early twentieth-century authors disclosed the diversity within Muslim communities worldwide that contradicted prevailing tropes about Muslim men and women. Sometimes these humanizing re-inventions pertained directly to gender.

For instance, missionary authors described how Muslim women's dress norms and public activities differed based on social status, family circumstance, and nationality, among other factors. The CMS children's magazine indicated such differences in its aforementioned article titled "The Girls of Turkey," with the following description of an accompanying image:

> The two Turkish females in the picture occupy different positions in life. The young girl, about twelve years of age, belongs to the richer class, as her dress indicates. Her attendant, whose face is partially concealed, is, in fact, her slave.[119]

In the image, the wealthy Turkish girl wears no face covering and a small hat that does not conceal her hair (recall Figure 4.1). In Syria, however, according to a *CWC* article, it was the lower-class women who left their faces bare and only draped their veils over their heads. Only Syrian women of the "higher classes" covered their faces in public.[120] Alternately, readers learn from *Children of Persia* that *all* women wore face veils when leaving their homes, which purportedly was a common occurrence except among the most elite families whose women stayed secluded.[121] Still other authors emphasized the difference between the dress norms of urban and rural Muslim women in the same country. Zwemer spoke of city women as being "shrouded," while those in the countryside went about with faces "unveiled."[122] In Egypt, as well, Entwistle maintained,

> When they go out it is the custom for Egyptian women to cover themselves all over with a black garment of cotton cloth called a *melayya*, and to veil the mouth and lower part of the face. But village women do not veil their faces for they all work very hard on the land and in their houses.[123]

Musa's Egyptian family was urban, we learn, as his mother wore a long veil to hide her face when outside of the house but laid it aside at home.[124] Entwistle offered this information without critiquing these practices, and such evidence that not all Muslim women's experiences were the same contradicted the missionary discourse about Muslim women's oppression, at least to a certain extent. For accurate descriptions of diverse veiling norms did not prevent gross generalizations about Muslim women's lives.

Contemporary scholarship on nineteenth- and twentieth-century Islamic societies, however, supplements missionaries' ethnographic-type writings, not only confirming the diversity of Muslim women's experiences but also demonstrating how these women understood their own gender norms in different and far more nuanced ways than did their British and American counterparts. For one compelling example, we can turn to Marilyn Booth's research on Zaynab Fawwaz (circa 1860–1914), a Shia Muslim in Ottoman Syria whose published writings and gender activism defied missionary characterizations of Muslims in the late nineteenth- and early twentieth-century Middle East. Fawwaz advanced notions that we would today describe as radically feminist for that time, contradicting the ideas about female domesticity that American and Arab Protestants held. She also defied western generalizations while critically resisting patriarchal norms in ways that fit her understandings of Islamic faith and cultural practice.[125] As Booth explained, for instance, in her published articles and novels Fawwaz challenged the "separate spheres" approach that many of her Arab Protestant interlocutors and missionaries in the Middle East upheld:

> Fawwaz described sex difference as generative of social differences which had disprivileged women of every social class and environment.... [S]he

rejected notions of hierarchical difference sanctioned by "Nature." She did not celebrate women's "special" qualities or argue that they were different-but-equal, though she did insist that women's reproductive work be respected and valued as *labour*. She insisted that there was no realm of work that women as a category could not perform.[126]

Although Fawwaz was by all accounts a unique figure for her time, missionaries in Islamic contexts encountered many Muslim women whose diversity of experience and social activities informed their ethnographic and fictional accounts.[127]

A second way these authors sought to help children understand Islam, and thereby encouraged interreligious awareness, was by relating Muslim life to their readers' own lives in Europe and North America. Though they presented Islamic cultures in a playful manner as "topsy-turvy," their stories nevertheless portrayed Muslim characters as not very different from Christian men, women, and children. The children in these stories acted much like American and British children might in their excitement about school, travel, and meeting new friends or their love for their siblings and parents. This emphasis on commonalities and the fictional narrative drew readers into the characters' lives and helped them sympathize with Muslims in ways that missionaries' non-fiction texts did not. Zwemer, Entwistle, and Stuart, for example, presented their main characters favorably and reserved judgments only for the teachers of Islam or ignorant devotees who upheld intolerant practices. Likewise, of all the Muslim characters in Entwistle's *Habeeb*, the author critiqued only those Muslim boys who disrespected their mothers and the teacher at the mosque, who informed Habeeb's initial negative view of non-Muslims. These figures, however, were peripheral to the story. Thus, *Habeeb* avoided the trope of violent and domineering Muslim men in order to disprove another common early twentieth-century stereotype that Muslims were so rigid and unyielding in their beliefs that they could not be won for Christ. *Topsy-Turvy Land* similarly concluded with hopeful words: "I believe God loves these sons of Ishmael and will yet bring them back to Abraham's faith. Don't you think so too?"[128] Notably, however, as they sought to inspire children's work for Muslim children, the four fictional accounts of the 1920s only presented Muslims in a favorable light when they were under the influence of Christianity and on the path to conversion.

Blatter and Hamm also softened the traditional missionary image of Muslim men, but they did so in a different way in mid-twentieth-century texts that aimed to educate and show the social change occurring in Islamic societies where Protestant missionaries had long labored. Ignoring the topic of conversion altogether, they both depicted Muslim fathers who were loving and understanding toward their daughters and open to missionary education and western gender norms. Such stories may still have inspired young readers to become missionaries, but responses to Blatter's widely read novel, in particular, also demonstrated that affirming depictions of Muslim characters could make *them* into positive role models for American Protestant readers. One eleven-year-old wrote to Blatter of her dream to follow in Filiz's footsteps, saying, "I love the book and want to be a nurse."[129] While Blatter's approach to Islam and Turkish life encouraged such a statement, the earlier examples of missionary fiction also contributed to a situation in which young readers no longer saw Muslim lives as strange or threatening but could recognize commonalities with their own lives. Missionaries' humanization of characters like Noorah, Fatmeh, Musa, and Habeeb in the 1920s opened up the possibility for the mid-twentieth-century stories about Filiz and Lindao that neither condemned Islam nor depicted Muslim women as oppressed but rather gave them agency to follow their own dreams without converting to Christianity. Such literature did not fully negate the discourse of the veil or stop its use in missionary circles. It did, however, at least offer American audiences a more nuanced and appreciative picture of Muslims by the mid-twentieth century—a re-invention of Islam built on human connections.

Notes

1. *The Customs and Manners of Bedouin Arabs* (Philadelphia: American Sunday-School Union, 1838). The first translation of *1001 Arabian Nights* into English was made from the French version Antoine Galland produced between 1703 and 1713. A more popular, revised version came out in the 1880s. C. Knipp, "The 'Arabian Nights' in England: Galland's Translation and its Successors," *Journal of Arabic Literature* 5 (1974): 43, 46.
2. Henry Harris Jessup, *The Women of the Arabs* (New York: Dodd & Mead, 1873). The "Children's Chapter" consisted of 135 pages and appeared after the final chapter.
3. Hugh Morrison, *Protestant Children, Missions and Education in the British World* (Leiden: Brill, 2021), 36. For a few other studies on missionary literature for children, see Christine Weir, "'Deeply Interested in These Children Whom You Have Not Seen': The Protestant Sunday School View of the Pacific, 1900–1940," *The Journal of Pacific History* 48, no. 1 (2013): 43–62; Divya Kannan, "'Children's Work for Children': Caste, Childhood, and Missionary Philanthropy in Colonia India," *The Journal of the History of Childhood and Youth* 14, no. 2 (Spring 2021): 234–53; Karen Li Miller, "The White Child's Burden: Managing the Self and Money in Nineteenth-Century Children's Missionary Periodicals," *American Periodicals* 22, no. 2 (2012): 139–57.
4. *Quarterly Token* bore the subtitle "A gift from the Church Missionary Society." Subscribers were considered to have contributed financially to the missionary cause, and the magazine was recommended for use by officers of juvenile associations, Sunday schools, local libraries, and families.

5. See "Notes from Syria," *The Wesleyan Juvenile Offering: A Miscellany of Missionary Information for Young Persons* 8, no. 96 (November 1874): 123–26; *Wesleyan Juvenile Offering* 9 (1875): 20–22, 28–30, 87–88. Organizations like the Wesleyan Missionary Society, which did not establish stations in the Middle East, thus used the writings of fellow Anglo-Protestants to inform their own readers about this region.
6. Various mission societies referred to juvenile mission bands or simply to "juniors" when mentioning children and youth who subscribed to their periodicals or were members of clubs that studied and raised funds for missions. For one overly optimistic picture of missionary success, which quoted the ABCFM's *Missionary Herald*'s statement that thousands of Muslims in Damascus desired to become Christian, see "Christian Revival in Damascus," *Wesleyan Juvenile Offering* 4, no. 68 (August 1872): 88.
7. "The Little Missionary," *Wesleyan Juvenile Offering* 2, new series (March 1868): 47.
8. "Girls of Turkey," *A Quarterly Token for Juvenile Subscribers*, no. 35 (October 1864): 4.
9. "Syria," *CWC* 1, no. 12 (December 1876): 184. Such missionary magazines emphasized that children could do odd jobs to earn money for missions. See "What Children Can Do," *Wesleyan Juvenile Offering* 4 (January 1870): 9–10.
10. Other children's magazines, like *World Comrades*, published by the Women's Missionary Union of the Southern Baptist Convention in the United States, encouraged children's participation in various mission bands including Girls' Auxiliaries, Royal Ambassador Chapters, and Sunbeam Bands by placing noteworthy members' names on an honor roll. The honor roll for 1924 listed nine members from seven states. "World Comrades Honor Roll," *World Comrades* 3, no. 3 (December 1924): back page.
11. "News from the Bands and Circles," *CWC* 1, no. 4 (April 1876): 94. On Fidelia Fiske, a missionary of the ABCFM in Persia, see Heleen Murre-van den Berg, "'Dear Mother of My Soul': Fidelia Fiske and the Role of Women Missionaries in Mid-Nineteenth Century Iran," *Exchange* 30, no. 1 (January 2001): 34–48.
12. "Juvenile Associations," *Quarterly Token*, no. 1 (June 1856): 7; "Juvenile Contributions from the Various Counties," *Quarterly Token*, no. 36 (January 1865): 2.
13. "A Talk with Our Young Friends," *CWC* 1, no. 12 (December 1876): 179; "Not to Be Read by Lazy People," *Over Sea and Land: A Missionary Magazine for the Young* 37, no. 9 (September 1912): 86. The magazine, which had been retitled in 1900, continued to encourage its readers to find other subscribers.
14. "Abdool Messeeh's Hymns," *Quarterly Token*, no. 1 (June 1856): 4.
15. "Persia," *CWC* 1, no. 10 (October 1876), 150.
16. "Our Mission in Peshawur," *Quarterly Token*, no. 3 (October 1856): 6.
17. "Gopenath Nundy," *Quarterly Token*, no. 24 (January 1862): 2–3.
18. W. L. Whipple, "Pilgrims on their Way to Mecca," *CWC* 4, no. 3 (March 1879): 45. The Prophet Muhammad was commonly called the "false prophet" in missionary texts, including texts for children. See this phrase's use in Urania Malcolm, *Children of Persia* (New York: F. H. Revell, 1911), 27; "Missionary Intelligence," *The Children's Missionary and Sabbath School Record* 1 (1844), 94; "Turkey and the Turks," *Baptist Children's Magazine and Juvenile Missionary Record*, new series 4 (1857): 141; "Dilawar Khan," *Quarterly Token*, no. 63 (October 1871): 4; "Notes from Syria," *Wesleyan Juvenile Offering* 8, no. 96 (November 1874): 123–26.
19. Whipple, "Pilgrims on Their Way," 45–46. Italics in original.
20. Abd al-Qadir fought against French colonialism in Algeria and then intervened to prevent massacres of Christians in Damascus, Syria, in 1860. When describing this intervention during a time of severe civil strife, Jessup claimed, "God had prepared a deliverer." Henry Harris Jessup, *Fifty-Three Years in Syria* (New York: Fleming H. Revell, 1910), 1:196.
21. G. W. Coan, "A Mohammedan School," *CWC* 1, no. 10 (October 1876): 150. A later article in *CWC* emphasized that only Muslim men and boys, and not females, were taught to read the Qur'an in Arabic. "A Moslem School," *CWC* 4, no. 9 (September 1879): 134. However, the October 1876 article included an accompanying photo of a male teacher and three pupils, one of whom is a girl, seated on the floor with books, captioned "A Mohammedan School," (p. 151).
22. "Girls of Turkey," *Quarterly Token*, no. 35 (October 1864): 4.
23. Ibid.
24. Henry H. Jessup, "The Well of Water," *CWC* 3, no. 8 (August 1878): 121–22.
25. Mrs. E. M. Wherry, "An Afghan Wedding in India," *CWC* 3, no. 11 (November 1878): 162, 163. Italics in original. The latter comment came after her explanation that either two men or one man and two women were required in Islamic law as witnesses for the wedding contract. Clara

Maria (Buchanan) Wherry was married to Elwood Morris Wherry, the author of *Zeinab, The Panjabi*. She authored a chapter on Muslim women in India in *Daylight in the Harem*. Clara M. Wherry, "Training of Converts," in *Daylight in the Harem: A New Era for Moslem Women*, ed. Annie Van Sommer and Samuel M. Zwemer (New York: Fleming H. Revel, 1911), 167–82.

26. J. E. Hyde, "Paper Doll—A Little Girl from Persia," *Over Sea and Land* 32, no. 10 (October 1907): 81. The caption read: "Make the veil white, the cape dark blue and the skirt of bright colors. (The readers of *Over Sea and Land*, for October, 1906, will remember the story of this little girl. Her name is Sharbanu.)"
27. *Topsy-Turvy Land* was listed in "Books Received," *Over Sea and Land* 27, no. 10 (October 1902): 187; "Topsy-Turvy Land," *Over Sea and Land* 30, no. 10 (October 1905): 80; "Topsy-Turvy Land," *Over Sea and Land* 34, no. 12 (December 1909): 91–92. Both *Topsy-Turvy Land* and *Children of Persia* were recommended in women's missionary society magazines like the following from the American Congregational Woman's Board of Missions: "Missionary Circulating Library," *Life and Light for Heathen Women* 44, no. 12 (December 1914), backmatter. These texts were available from the women's society circulating library.
28. Samuel M. Zwemer and Amy E. Zwemer, *Topsy-Turvy Land: Arabia Pictured for Children* (New York: Fleming H. Revell, 1902). Amy likely wrote Chapter 10, titled "Noorah's Prayer," as it described women's spaces in Muslim homes that Samuel would not have visited.
29. Zwemer and Zwemer, *Topsy-Turvy Land*, 9.
30. Ibid., 16. This statement signaled the book's broad intended readership.
31. Ibid., 18.
32. While the book was most critical of gender norms, the introductory chapter also described the religion of Arabia as "all upside down too," emphasizing the poor children who had not heard about Jesus and encouraging the young readers to "help to turn that land of Topsy-turvy right side up" through their prayers and offerings. It also described the religion practiced in Arabia as worshipping God "in such an ignorant and idolatrous way." Ibid., 19, 25.
33. Ibid., 67.
34. Ibid., 18–19. Italics in original.
35. Ibid., 43, 55–57.
36. Ibid., 32.
37. Ibid., 62–63.
38. Malcolm, *Children of Persia*. Urania Latham Malcolm (1870–1952) was a medical doctor, and her husband Napier Malcolm (1870–1921) was an Anglican priest.
39. Malcolm, *Children of Persia*, 62, 67. While using the term *topsy-turvy* to describe Persian life, Malcolm emphasized the children in Persia "have a very different life from you and me" (p. 13).
40. Ibid., 4. Malcolm was critical of the Prophet Muhammad when comparing him to Jesus Christ (pp. 10–11).
41. Ibid., 18–19, 79–84. See also Malcolm's discussion on girls marrying young (p. 23).
42. Ibid., 23, 24, 28. On treatment of wives like slaves, see p. 84.
43. Ibid., 68, 70.
44. Ibid., 26.
45. Ibid., 24.
46. Ibid., 26–27. At the end of this same chapter, Malcolm explained further her view that Islam's rules about clothing and washing before prayer treat Muslims like children: "Here again we see Muhammad giving his people what we may call 'nursery rules,' treating them as children, while our Master expects us to grow up so that we can arrange these matters for ourselves" (p. 30).
47. Ibid., 68.
48. Ibid., 79–81.
49. Coan, "Mohammedan School," 159.
50. Central Committee on the United Study of Foreign Missions (CCUSFM), *The Story of the Jubilee: An Account of the Celebration of the Fiftieth Anniversary of the Beginnings in the United States of Woman's Organized Work for Foreign Missions, 1860–1910* (West Medford, MA: CCUSFM, 1911), 3.
51. Amy E. Wilkes Zwemer, *Two Young Arabs and the Travels of Noorah and Jameel* (West Medford, MA: CCUSFM, 1926); Samuel M. Zwemer and Amy E. Zwemer, *Moslem Women* (West Medford, MA: CCUSFM, 1926). The *Friends Missionary Advocate*, the periodical of the Woman's Missionary Union of Friends in America (and United Society of Friends Women), which had recently begun a juniors department within the magazine, recommended *Two Young Arabs*, calling Amy Zwemer "the author of other well-known books for boys and girls."

"Department of Literature," *Friends Missionary Advocate* 42, no. 4 (April 1926): 115. Among the other mission organizations that used *Two Young Arabs* and *Moslem Women* for 1927 were the Women's Missionary Society of the Augustana Lutheran Synod and the Woman's Foreign Missionary Society of the Methodist Episcopal Church. "Young People and Juniors," *Mission Tidings* 21, no. 6 (December 1926): 265; Woman's Foreign Missionary Society of the Methodist Episcopal Church (WFMSMEC), *Year Book: Being the Sixtieth Annual Report of the Society* (Boston: WFMSMEC, 1929), 130.
52. Hyaeweol Choi, *Gender and Mission Encounters in Korea: New Women, Old Ways* (Berkeley: University of California Press, 2009), 121–23.
53. Nineteenth-century missionary women also wrote many magazine articles, especially for women's missionary societies, but few published books. Emily Humphrey, author of *Gems of India* and *Six Years in India*, was among the exceptions.
54. Citations here are from the original booklet: Helen I. Moody Stuart, *Fatmeh: A Common Story of Mission Schools for Moslem Girls* (London: BSM, circa 1920), in Middle East Christian Outreach archive (box 10), Centre for Muslim–Christian Studies, Oxford. The story was published sometime during or before 1920 as it also appeared that year as a chapter in *Pearl of the East*, a book centered on the BSM in Damascus. J. Edith Hutcheon, *The Pearl of the East* (London: BSM, 1920), 43–56.
55. The only fictional chapter was the one featuring Stuart's story.
56. Three of the stories examined here included a girl named Fatmeh.
57. The school in the story is modeled after Saint Paul's School in Damascus, which is featured in *Pearl of the East* and where Hutcheon and Stuart taught. Hutcheon, *Pearl of the East*, 41.
58. Stuart, *Fatmeh*, 37–38.
59. Ibid., 39. This additional commentary added by the BSM did not appear at the end of the story in *The Pearl of the East*.
60. Mary Entwistle, *Habeeb: A Boy of Palestine* (London: CMS, 1927); Mary Entwistle, *Musa: Son of Egypt* (London: Edinburgh House Press, 1927). The first edition of *Habeeb* appeared in 1924, and the CMS also published an edition of *Musa* in 1927. Other titles included Mary Entwistle, *Little Children of Mission Lands* (New York: G.H. Doran, 1925); Mary Entwistle and Elizabeth Harris, *The Call Drum: African Stories and Studies for Primary Children* (New York: Friendship Press, 1928); Mary Entwistle, *The Bible Guide Book: A Companion to Bible Study for Young People and their Teachers* (London: Student Christian Movement Press, 1936). Several of Entwistle's books were also translated into other languages, including Dutch, German, Chinese, Swedish, Danish, Finnish, French, Russian, and Xhosa, thus serving evangelistic purposes.
61. This was true for others of Entwistle's books as well, like *The Book of Babies* (1913), which was advertised by the Congregational Women's Board of Missions in the United States. "Missionary Circulating Library," *Life and Light for Heathen Women* 44, no. 12 (December 1914): backmatter.
62. WorldCat lists an earlier co-authored version of the book: Mary Entwistle and Jeanette Perkins Brown, *Musa: Son of Egypt, Programs and Stories for Primary Children* (New York: Friendship Press, 1926). This chapter examines the 1927 edition attributed solely to Entwistle.
63. Entwistle, *Musa*, 50.
64. Ibid., 76.
65. Zwemer, *Two Young Arabs*, 9.
66. Ibid., 64.
67. Ibid., 216.
68. Hutcheon, *Pearl of the East*, 37–38.
69. Stuart, *Fatmeh*, 4.
70. Entwistle, *Musa*, 33.
71. Zwemer, *Two Young Arabs*, 208.
72. Entwistle, *Habeeb*, 44–45. Malcolm also critiqued the use of clay beads and ideas about the "evil eye" in Malcolm, *Children of Persia*, 59.
73. Stuart, *Fatmeh*, 3.
74. Ibid., 8–9.
75. Ibid., 9.
76. Ibid., 20.
77. Entwistle, *Habeeb*, 42–43.
78. Zwemer, *Two Young Arabs*, 73.
79. Entwistle, *Habeeb*, 42. *Topsy-Turvy Land* introduced a girl named Noorah who would pray privately outside with her sister. Zwemer and Zwemer, *Topsy-Turvy Land*, 64–67.

80. Entwistle, *Musa*, 16.
81. Zwemer, *Two Young Arabs*, 25.
82. When the family visits a Muslim home for dinner, the mother and Noorah serve the men and boys and eat their meal afterward. Zwemer, *Two Young Arabs*, 206. Similarly, in *Habeeb*, the mother Jameelie prepares supper first for the "men-folk" and waits on them. Entwistle, *Habeeb*, 56, 79.
83. Zwemer, *Two Young Arabs*, 82.
84. Ibid., 83.
85. Ibid., 57.
86. Ibid., 105.
87. Ibid., 155. Zwemer described some of the veils worn by Egyptian women, explaining that country women wear a round nosepiece covered with gold and affix a thick, black, crocheted veil to that. Women in town, however, wear veils of white georgette, just covering the lower part of the face and making the wearer's brown eyes attractive, according to Zwemer.
88. Ibid., 28.
89. Ibid., 44. Zwemer offered the example of a ten-year-old girl who did not want to get married but relented to her parents' wishes in the end. Ibid., 87.
90. Stuart, *Fatmeh*, 7.
91. Ibid., 28–29.
92. Ibid., 30.
93. Zwemer, *Two Young Arabs*, 216.
94. Stuart, *Fatmeh*, 37.
95. William Ernest Hocking, *Re-Thinking Missions: A Layman's Inquiry After One Hundred Years* (New York and London: Harper & Brothers, 1932). Hocking chaired The Commission of Appraisal, which produced this report. See also Peggy Bowler Lindsey, "Around the World in 283 Days: Traveling with the Laymen's Foreign Missions Inquiry Commission of Appraisal," *International Bulletin of Mission Research* 46, no. 4 (2022): 492–503.
96. Margaret J. Hamm, "Lindao's Dowry," circa. 1950s, Hamm Family Papers (MS 4849, box 4), Congregational Library & Archives, Boston. This story is filed in a folder titled "Academic Papers and Speeches, 1954–1958." Margaret and her husband lived in the southern island of Mindanao for about thirteen years and ran Danislan Junior College.
97. Hamm, "Lindao's Dowry," 1, 6.
98. Although the story spoke of a dowry—a concept perhaps more familiar to English readers—the negotiations actually center on a *bride price*, a payment made from the groom's family to the bride's family (not the wealth or property the bride's family gives to the groom or his family).
99. Dorothy Blatter, *Cap and Candle* (Philadelphia: Westminster Press, 1961). Blatter first published the book in Turkish as *Alninin Yazisi* in the 1950s. Blatter (1901–1977) entered the ABCFM's mission field in Turkey in 1931 and retired in 1967. In 1945, Blatter began working for the ABCFM's Publication Department, and she was the author of other shorter children's books, several of which were published in both English and Turkish: *Uncle Ali's Secret: A Story of New Turkey* (1939), *Sleepy Sami* (1946), *The Thirsty Village* (1950), *Who Is My Neighbor?* (1964), *The Stranger's Good News; and the Farmer's Four Sons* (1964), *A Father's Love* (1964). Blatter also translated into English several Turkish texts by other authors, including Cahit Ucuk, *The Turkish Twins*, trans. Dorothy Blatter (London: John Cape, 1956). In 1968 Blatter married Frank Ross. See Figure 6.9 for Blatter's image during her early years in Turkey.
100. Blatter's personal papers at the Congregational Library reflect this interest. The documents include letters from readers and numerous news clipping advertising the book for school libraries. One clipping lists the book under "Socio-Romantic Novels for Older Girls." Another review calls it a counterpart to Najmeh Najafi's *Persia Is My Heart* (1953), which introduces young readers to Persian culture and, in appreciative terms, to Islam. Dorothy Blatter Ross, "Miscellaneous Manuscripts," circa 1960s, Iain Campbell Papers (RG 0043-3-9, LF22), Congregational Library & Archives, Boston. The 1964 edition of *Cap and Candle* was published by E. M. Hale in Eau Claire, Wisconsin, and by Collins in London and Glasgow.
101. One review showed that readers were attuned to the commentary Blatter was making in "killing off" the more traditional husband. Ross, "Miscellaneous Manuscripts."
102. Hamm, "Lindao's Dowry," 2.
103. Ibid., 10–11.
104. Blatter, *Cap and Candle*, 10.

105. Ibid., 129, 130.
106. While Maranao Muslim women did not traditionally cover their heads, the secular-oriented government of the Republic of Turkey, established in 1923, discouraged religious headgear; and it became less common there by the mid-twentieth century.
107. Blatter, *Cap and Candle*, 83–84.
108. Hamm, "Lindao's Dowry," 1.
109. Ibid., 15.
110. Blatter, *Cap and Candle*, 15, 50.
111. Ibid., 27.
112. Hamm, "Lindao's Dowry," 7.
113. Blatter, *Cap and Candle*, 149.
114. Blatter refers to the practice—a coming of age ritual—of cutting locks of hair from the front of the bride's head before the wedding.
115. Blatter, *Cap and Candle*, 149.
116. Ibid., 13, 22–26, 64, 138; Hamm, "Lindao's Dowry," 2–3, 6.
117. On the wedding of philanthropy and pedagogy in the children's missionary movement in Britain, which had parallels in the United States, see Morrison, *Protestant Children*.
118. The Zwemers described Arabs as more hospitable than people of western countries. Zwemer and Zwemer, *Topsy-Turvy Land*, 25.
119. "Girls of Turkey," *Quarterly Token* (October 1864): 3.
120. "Syrian Woman and Baby," *CWC* 1, no. 12 (Dec 1876), 184. Describing a picture of a Syrian Muslim woman without a face veil, the author explained further, "If she speaks to a man, she will draw the veil around so as to cover her lips, as this is a sign of humility."
121. Malcolm, *Children of Persia*, 83.
122. Zwemer, *Two Young Arabs*, 105.
123. Entwistle, *Musa*, 16.
124. Ibid., 46.
125. Marilyn Booth, *The Career and Communities of Zaynab Fawwaz: Feminist Thinking in Fin-de-siècle Egypt* (New York: Oxford University Press, 2022), 5–6. See also Deanna Ferree Womack, *Protestants, Gender and the Arab Renaissance in Late Ottoman Syria* (Edinburgh: Edinburgh University Press, 2019), 147, 178–79.
126. Booth, *Career and Communities*, 11. Italics in original.
127. Halide Edib Adivar (1884–1964), a Turkish nationalist author who was educated in an ABCFM school, also defied stereotypical portrayals of Muslim women's lives. See Halide Edib, *Memoirs of Halidé Edib* (London: John Murray, 1923).
128. Zwemer and Zwemer, *Topsy-Turvy Land*, 63.
129. Ross, "Miscellaneous Manuscripts."

5
Recasting the Protestant Gaze
Missionary Images of Islam as Material Religion

Along with the outpouring of American and British Protestant writings about Islam, the late nineteenth and early twentieth centuries generated an equally significant flow of non-textual material depicting Muslims. Missionaries disseminated this media, including images, religious objects, and articles of clothing, giving their western Christian consumers more visual, tactile, and material modes of encounter with Islamic societies than they had experienced before. Since the sixteenth century, Protestants had been producing artistic and theatrical portrayals of Muslim life and had been adopting and appropriating Ottoman luxury goods for themselves. Yet for several centuries, access to such items of material culture in Great Britain and the United States was limited to the elite. In the nineteenth century, for example, it became popular for White upper-class Americans to don Islamic garb for portraits or everyday wear and to incorporate Turkish furniture, carpets, and other aspects of Islamic culture into their homes—demonstrating a form of "American Islamicism," as Timothy Marr termed it.[1] A wider audience was drawn into such material practices between the 1890s and the 1930s as new technologies increased global travel and tourism, facilitated the transnational exchange of goods and print media, and enabled the production of millions of photographs of Muslims and their wide dissemination across Europe and North America.[2]

This chapter and the next turn to such sources of material culture held in archives of American and British churches and mission societies. These material representations of Islam, Muslims, and Islamic cultures fall into four categories: images, costumes, objects in museums or private collections, and live exhibitions by missionaries.[3] Whereas the costumes, objects, and exhibitions are the focus of Chapter 6, this fifth chapter examines images that British and American Protestant missionaries collected, preserved, and used to galvanize support for the evangelization of Muslims from North Africa to Southeast Asia. The images include photographs, paintings, and sketches of individuals, groups, landscapes, and ancient sites, all of which were themselves forms of material culture that missionaries captured and developed as amateur photographers or purchased in photography studios or tourist shops. Missionaries sent these images as postcards, affixed them to scrapbooks and travel journals, displayed them at churches in albums and slide shows, and reprinted them as illustrations for books, mission reports, or magazines. Protestant missionaries used such tangible items alongside texts to re-invent American cultural understandings of Islam.

Because most studies on American views of Islam depend on texts that only reached a certain segment of the population,[4] my examination of material culture is significant. While the written discourses that I analyzed in the preceding chapters conveyed Protestant leaders' views and influenced mission supporters and churchgoers, non-textual sources of knowledge could reach a much wider audience and often had a more intimate effect than texts alone. A women's mission auxiliary member, for example, might keep a photograph of a sponsored Muslim child in her Bible as a reminder to pray for that child daily. In addition, missionary lectures and theatrical performances drew audience members who were not already active mission supporters. Such presentations of Islam in the late nineteenth and early twentieth centuries were also important precursors to mass media depictions of Muslims later in the twentieth century, such as blockbuster films.[5]

This chapter considers how missionaries used such material culture for *Protestant* purposes to convey messages about Islam, Muslims, and Islamic societies. In light of the earlier patterns of Protestant thought explored in this book, here I ask: What did missionaries intend to convey about Islam through the images they collected, displayed, and sent home? Although pictures alone may not convey the same meaning for each viewer, postcard captions and other accompanying commentary reinforced the common theological claims of missionary texts, asserting Christian religious superiority and western civilizational preeminence. The images conveyed such messages primarily through religiously inflected cultural critique, reflecting Protestant gender constructs and racialized notions about Islam. Yet since Protestant perceptions of Islam have never been monolithic, such material sources are also open to wider interpretation. Indeed, even when reinforcing cultural tropes, images of Muslims could also have a humanizing effect, which in many cases missionaries also intended in order to cultivate sympathy.

In the first section below, I introduce my analytical framework, and in the second I explain Protestant missionary practices of creating and collecting postcards and photographs of Muslims and Muslim-majority regions. The remainder of the chapter then examines three types of images that missionaries repeatedly used: "vacant" landscapes, portraits of Muslims, and images of Islamic rituals.

Interpreting Protestant Performances and Collections of Islamic Material Culture

Before turning to the actual images, I offer a word about my interpretive method for this chapter and Chapter 6, a method which differs from that of most studies on missions and Islam. First, as a contribution to the critique of Orientalism, I consider the transmission of ideas about Islam. Focusing on the knowledge missionaries constructed and how they guided their audiences to view Islam, I identify prominent patterns in Protestant missionary representations of Muslims that were similar across various denominations and mission agencies. Without claiming that all Protestants adopted these missionary views, I maintain that the images and performances of missionaries were a key force, along with Protestant missionaries' writings and speeches, in shaping both nineteenth- and early twentieth-century Protestant culture in the United States and American understandings of Islam.

Second, I approach material culture as an overlooked yet significant source for understanding historical Christian–Muslim encounters.[6] While most studies on missions, including books on Protestant missions in Islamic contexts, employ mainly textual sources, I focus on tangible items of material culture as key historical evidence of Protestant missionary practices, demonstrating the choices missionaries made when presenting information to their constituents. Photographs—and the costumes and artifacts examined in Chapter 6—reveal much about the missionaries who collected them. Missionaries sought to shape a historical narrative through "choosing, making, and using material things to preserve and regulate knowledge," thereby employing material culture to re-invent Islam.[7] Though Protestants emphasized the power of the written word, texts were not the only way in which missionaries communicated their theological beliefs and what they wanted their audiences to think about Islam. Besides, attention to material culture is also an avenue for understanding the histories of marginalized individuals or communities who were not major producers of texts.[8] The sources used in this chapter were among the forms of communication that women missionaries commonly used to transmit their ideas about Islam outside the male-dominated sphere of Protestant publishing.

Third, I approach Protestant missionaries' act of re-inventing Islam as a performative practice.[9] Why? Because at a basic level, the reports, stories, and images that missionaries sent to mission supporters were ones they wrote or chose with an audience in mind, carefully crafting or curating the information their readers or viewers received—just as they did when preparing for live performances. Even their so-called private correspondence, journals, and diaries were not truly private: they were copied, circulated among loved ones, passed down within families, and eventually preserved in historical archives according to the missionaries' own intentions. The photographs that missionaries selected for their supporters resembled the images one might expect western travelers or tourists to collect—except Protestant propriety usually prevented them from publicly displaying the genre of pornographic harem photography available to tourists in North Africa and elsewhere.[10] The creators of photographic images and works of art are also rightly understood as performers, and there was a performative element to missionaries' presentation of photographs and their display of clothing and other material objects from Islamic contexts for mission supporters.

Fourth and finally, I follow a material theory of religion to discern the meaning and implication of such Protestant engagement with material objects. Arguing against the idea that religions can be understood primarily through the interpretation of texts, Manuel Vásquez challenged the traditional Christian, and specifically Protestant, approach to religion as doctrinal belief—an approach that has shaped the western study of theology and religion. Vásquez argued instead that religions ought to be appreciated in their *full materiality*. The challenge of overcoming dichotomies within the study of religion—which falsely privilege "belief over rituals, the private over the public, text and symbol over practice, and mind and soul over body"—can be overcome, he explained, "if we contextualize and historicize [religions], if we approach them as phenomena produced, performed, circulated, contested, sacralized, and consumed by embodied and emplaced individuals."[11] The "material turn" underway in religious studies has not yet taken hold within the study of mission history in the same way it has for ethnographies of religion. Although my research does not focus on typical forms of Protestant material culture (like objects used in formal worship settings), Vásquez's theory can still be applied to the material things Protestant missionaries used or created. This allows for a more capacious understanding of missionaries' own religious practices and their influence upon the material realities of Protestant audiences, beyond the narrow ways that Protestants have typically conceived of religion.

With these four points in mind, how does one detect what messages the missionaries themselves intended to convey in the photographs they sent home of Muslims? Here, the captions or commentaries that often accompanied printed images help. I also interpret missionaries' use of images in the context of the writings on Islam explored in the previous chapters and within the wider context of western production and consumption of Islamic culture during the late nineteenth and early twentieth centuries. Although missionary motives may have differed from those of tourists and other western visitors to the Middle East and South Asia, they participated in the same activities of postcard collection and amateur photography— two pastimes enabled and influenced by European colonial domination of Muslim societies. This context shaped missionary actions, for missionaries were among those nurtured by the same sorts of colonial photographs and travelogues that also provided cultural conditioning for their Protestant viewers' interpretation of missionary images. Christian missions were a part of the western colonial "network of practices, institutions, and relations that made possible the production of these images in the first place, as well as the politico-cultural context that led them to be so rapaciously consumed as visual and exotic objects."[12] Thus, even when contrary to missionaries' own humanitarian intentions, the images they transmitted often reinforced White Protestant supremacy, marked Muslims of all different ethnic and cultural backgrounds as racially inferior, and assessed non-western gender norms according to a religio-racial hierarchy that Sahar Aziz described as the central factor in Americans' historical treatment of Muslims.[13]

Capturing the Muslim Image: Photography and Postcards

Photographic images of Muslims became increasingly available in the west after the 1839 invention of the daguerreotype made commercial photography viable.[14] By the late nineteenth century, missionaries had found that images held just as much power as printed texts for gaining support at home for the work they sought to accomplish abroad. Images of strange and exotic places drew onlookers who otherwise might not have read a missionary magazine, and photos of the poor and destitute touched the emotions and opened the wallets of potential donors. Photos could both humanize and essentialize otherwise unknown people on a scale that had not been possible before the nineteenth century. Thus, missionary images became tools to reinforce or reshape existing discourses, in the process displaying the intertwining altruistic and imperialistic character of missionaries' activities.

Missionaries collected and created all sorts of images of Islamic contexts. Their desire to record and transmit new knowledge to fellow Christians—similar to nineteenth-century ethnologists' work to document and categorize cultures[15]—was apparent in their use of stock photos. Missionaries reprinted these generic images from tourist shops in their periodicals and on postcards to deepen the connection between mission supporters and the men, women, and children who were objects of missionary work. Thus, their intentions differed from those of imperial administrators who described Muslims, Arabs, or Indians as a collective in order to maintain Europeans' detachment from the human experiences of colonial subjects they sought to control.[16] Although missionaries perpetuated tropes about Islam, their messages to constituents often focused on named individuals whose souls they sought to save, whom they hoped to educate in Protestant schools, or to whom they offered medical care.

In the Middle East and South Asia—key locations for American and British missions to Muslims—missionaries took their own photographs of mission schools, churches, and Christian converts. But to describe eastern society, Muslim life, or Islamic religious practices, they often relied on the widely available work of "colonial photographers," who used staged photos to represent everyday life and customs.[17] This industry arose in European colonial contexts because of new photographic technology, access to European markets, rising tourism, and Orientalist interest. Due to European public demand, the colonial photography industry also extended beyond the colonized regions of North Africa and South Asia to capture on film the peoples and lands of the Ottoman Empire, including Turkey, Syria/Lebanon, and Palestine. In his study of photography in the Middle East, Ali Behdad identified four common forms of such photographic representation: panoramas of landscapes or city views, photos of historical monuments, images of the exotic (representing racial, ethnic, and professional types of photographed subjects), and images of the erotic (photos of the harem, of women veiled and unveiled, and of partially dressed women, girls, and adolescent boys).[18]

The first three categories are well represented in missionary archives. Ethnological photography in particular echoed the impulse of European philologists to determine an "Oriental type," a pseudo-scientific activity of scrutinizing human characteristics that Edward Said argued dehumanized Arabs as objects of study disconnected from history.[19] Colonial photography reinforced the religio-racial hierarchies upon which scholars established such essentialist typologies, and the industry thrived because of the European and North American public's fascination with what they regarded as strange and unknown. Thus, ideas about the insurmountable distance between "East" and "West" or between Christians and Muslims were transmitted widely as visual media, and missionaries used such images for their own purposes.

Those purposes were largely to report on their missionary work and to appeal for financial and spiritual support. Mission societies, as historian Paul Jenkins described them, functioned as "communication systems linking people in the West with situations in the non-western world, and depending on the financial commitment of their supporters at home."[20] From the 1850s onward, most American and British missions embraced photography as a communications technology and began gathering their own supply of photographs from Asia and Africa by producing, purchasing from studios, and exchanging photos with other mission societies for publicity use—a practice apparent in the number of missions using the same images in their publications.[21] In the Middle East and North Africa, such photos as well as sketched illustrations fed a growing picture postcard industry that began in the 1880s and peaked between 1900 and 1930. Similar practices of postcard production and collection during this period took place in South Asia and other Islamic contexts, facilitated by colonial power and fueled by a western desire for the exotic.[22] The picture postcard was a modern and popularly accessible visual genre whose life cycle of transnational production and travel uniquely reflected western Christian encounters with Islam in the heyday of European imperialism and often expressed "the triumph of empire in colonial space, the *work* of civilization," according to Saloni Mathur, a scholar of South Asian visual cultures.[23] Of the colonial postcard's transnational nature, Mathur explained that:

> a photograph might be shot in India, produced as an image by a publisher in Britain, sent to Germany to be printed as a postcard, sold to a colonial officer or traveler back in India, returned to Europe as a souvenir or greeting, only to find its place on display in a private collection in a European home.

... Mass-produced, dispersed, and always in motion, it was the quintessential traveler of the modern age.[24]

In the early twentieth century, postcard writing and collecting became a fashionable hobby across Europe and North America, with a record number of 860 million cards sent through British post alone in 1908.[25]

The images that missionaries distributed on postcards, preserved in scrapbooks and albums, or printed in books and magazines became a way of reproducing and disseminating "new forms of knowledge, new regimes of 'seeing,' organizing, measuring, and categorizing the physical and metaphysical world."[26] Commenting on French photography in the nineteenth century, Middle East studies scholar Stephen Sheehi explained that "European studios in the Ottoman east during the Second Empire [of Napoleon III] and the Victorian era produced character-types, landscapes, architectural photography, and tableau vivant genre scenes that were particularly useful for postcards, stereoscopes, and exotic tablature," activities which cannot be disconnected from colonial and imperial expansion.[27] A similar point can be made for British and later American imperial endeavors.[28] Photographic portraiture objectified African and Asian peoples using "powerful claims to scientific objectivity and truth," while postcard factories mass-produced images of what were commonly called human "types" or "specimens," signaling scientific classification. These were part of a genre known as "scenes and types" which European and American collectors could readily possess, circulate, or discard based on their own whims.[29]

The following sections focus on such images produced or collected by Protestant missionaries in which Muslims or Islamic societies were the subjects, including landscapes, portraits of individuals and groups, and photos or drawings depicting religious rituals.

The Sacred Topography of "Vacant" Landscapes

When American Protestants looked toward Muslim-majority societies in the nineteenth century, their gaze often rested upon the Middle East. Before advances in photography brought professional and amateur photographers to the region in droves, nineteenth-century American painters traveled there and produced panoramas and easel paintings of "sacred topography." These Holy Land scenes connected American Protestant viewers to the contemporary land of the Bible while also advancing ideologies of American exceptionalism and (White) western Christian superiority.[30] In the process, the region's inhabitants—Muslims, Jews, and eastern Christians—became supporting actors in scenes of "American Biblical Orientalism," as David Grafton put it. Indigenous peoples were "replaced with model images of biblical characters that were more properly a reflection of American evangelical Bible-based piety than reality."[31] Such images were popular among missionaries who collected photographs and postcard images that allowed their viewers to believe that time had stood still in the land of Jesus' birth, cultivating what Simon Goldhill called the "biblical gaze."[32]

In the late nineteenth century, historian John Davis explained, the means of feeding the American public appetite for "virtually any scrap of information about the traditional biblical territories" shifted from painted panoramas to photographs, which "could provide the all-important sense of documentary verisimilitude, the unmediated 'truth' demanded by a public yearning to be persuaded."[33] This Protestant Holy Land mania was one starting point for Americans' pictorial encounters with the Islamic Middle East, encounters that often undergirded American Protestant conceptions of Islam. Through photography or illustrated volumes like William Thomson's enormously popular *The Land and the Book* (first published in 1858), the Middle Eastern landscape became familiar to Americans, who posited their own special relationship with the lands of the Bible, styling "the United States as a new Israel, a New World promised land reserved for members of a favored nation."[34] Landscape photos devoid of inhabitants played a special role in the imagination of the Holy Land as pristine and unchanged since the time of the Bible. These images transported the viewers to the land where Christ walked, and the experience became even more real through the use of the stereoscope, a handheld device for viewing photographs that was popular in the United States and Europe after the 1860s because it submerged the viewer in the photographed scene. The stereoscope was a precursor to more immersive experiences like the Palestine Park, built in Chautauqua, New York, and the Street of Cairo at the World's Fairs in Chicago (1893) and St. Louis (1904). Over five million stereographic negatives were produced in the United States in the last quarter of the nineteenth century, with the Holy Land images being among the most popular.[35]

Protestant missionary archives are filled with blank landscapes of the Levant and of scenes in North Africa and South Asia—images that effectively erased, displaced, or neglected these regions' inhabitants.[36] In other landscape photos of the Middle East, local people were present but were not the central focus. Instead, the photographers had arranged human figures like props for showcasing spiritually inspiring scenes, for indicating the scale of buildings and archaeological remains, or for anchoring contemporary practices in the biblical past, as was the case for most of Thomson's illustrations. In drawings and photographs of the Middle East printed on missionary postcards, the captions focused on Bible scenes or on verses of scripture, ignoring the cultural particularities and religious identities of the people.[37] Amateur photographs followed a similar practice. For example, Elihu Grant, an American Methodist minister and biblical scholar who superintended Quaker mission schools in Jerusalem and Ramallah, depicted Palestinian men and boys in photographs of his 1930 archaeological expedition at Bet Shemesh, a town west of Jerusalem, in order to convey the size of cisterns and walls. Evoking the biblical era, he wrote on the back of one, in reference to a Palestinian boy, "A little Canaanite lad working his way down the excavated side of the pottery kiln in which we found so much" (Figure 5.1). On another he explained that the interesting items

Figure 5.1 "Canaanite Lad" at Bet Shemesh (1930)
Source: Elihu Grant photographs and manuscript collection (HCS.001.014), Quaker & Special Collections, Haverford College, Haverford, PA.

Figure 5.2 "Modern Canaanite" at Bet Shemesh (1930)
Source: Elihu Grant photographs and manuscript collection (HCS.001.014), Quaker & Special Collections, Haverford College, Haverford, PA.

found discarded at the bottom of the cistern included "the knife in the belt of the modern Canaanite," referring to a man pictured cleaning out the debris (Figure 5.2).[38] Davis identified such practices of inserting local people into photos of landscapes and architectural structures as "treating human bodies as formal adjuncts to the architecture and topography, arranging them into pleasing patterns based on symmetry and tonal values."[39] Despite reinforcing notions of American Biblical Orientalism for those who viewed his photographs or attended his lectures, Grant also built relationships of trust with Palestinians, like the Quaker educator Khalil Totah, for whom he was a significant mentor.[40] Here, then, we see the disconnect between relationships on the ground and the ideas that Protestants in the Middle East like Grant transmitted to American audiences.

Many of the images Protestant missionaries collected or sent to supporters on postcards similarly portrayed contemporary people of the Middle East standing in for biblical figures. These images were part of the biblical landscape genre because they disguised the subjects' identities so that viewers would see them not as contemporary Muslims (or Jews or Christians) but as living connections to the Bible. As Davis explained, "To the degree that they demonstrated the unchanged, biblical way of life, then, indigenous residents were allowed representation as part of the complete organic testimony sought by Americans."[41]

Among the frequently depicted biblical figures in missionary images was the Samaritan woman at the well, typically shown with a scarf over her head and holding a water jug.[42] Given the dwindling Samaritan population, the women in these images were likely not Samaritans, but their actual identity was not important to the photographers or their viewers. Other repeated images in missionary albums and postcard collections were related to Jesus' parables, or they connected contemporary occupations in the Holy Land to those of biblical times: shepherds, workers gleaning wheat, plowmen, sowers, fishermen, vineyard workers. Postcard and scrapbook captions reinforced this connection, often through scriptural references. One postcard produced by the London Jews Society showed Palestinian peasant men eating together in a scene reminiscent of the Last Supper (Figure 5.3).[43] Unlike the scenes of landscapes or ancient buildings that discounted or rendered invisible the people in the peripheries of the scene, these images did not erase local identities but did deliberately transform them. Missionary postcards in a sense converted Middle Eastern men and women into symbols that edified the faith of western Christian viewers while also prefiguring the actual religious conversions that Protestant evangelists hoped to inspire in Islamic contexts.

Protestant missionaries used the fantasy of the pristine Holy Land depicted in biblical landscape imagery to draw attention to their cause but then turned the focus back to the local people who they believed had lost the truth of the gospel. Missionaries and their supporters testified to the reality that the rise of Islam had altered the Middle Eastern landscape, language, culture, and religious practices. Protestants sought to convert Jews and eastern Christians but were decidedly critical of the Islamic faith in the Holy Land, which posed the "most obvious threat to its possession by Christian civilization."[44] When it came to Islam, therefore, many of the photographs in mission archives reflected a different purpose akin to that of Orientalist scholars and anthropologists of the time documenting the culture and cataloguing the people they believed were in need of both salvation and civilization.

RECASTING THE PROTESTANT GAZE 165

Figure 5.3 "Evening Meal Among the Fellaheen"
Source: Missionary Postcard Collection (Record Group 101, box 87, item 5), Special Collections, Yale Divinity School Library.

Staged Portraits and Colonial Photography

The prevalence of individual and group portraits in missionary collections and publications signaled an important reality of missionary work that some Protestants back home had overlooked—in part through the vacant landscapes just described: the Holy Land was not an empty, pristine place preserved since biblical times but one inhabited by religious "others"—especially Muslims—whom Protestant missionaries sought to convert *and* to reform socially. Landscape photography, therefore, might appeal to missionaries' spirituality and attract the attention of their constituents at home, but portraits allowed missionaries to make a different sort of appeal, cultivating a Protestant gaze that connected their supporters to the people among whom the missionaries worked overseas.

Many of the photographs that missionaries used to describe their mission fields visually they purchased from professional photographers—like the famous studio of French photographer Félix Bonfils that operated in Beirut from 1867 to 1938 and identified people according to physical and cultural characteristics or "type." This focus of colonial photography on racial types matched the impulse of ethnology during that period, which documented, categorized, and compared the peoples of the world and their religions.[45] Such pictures became stock photos that missionaries used to illustrate their descriptions of Islam—often anonymous images (here of Muslims) with no reference to the subject's name or personal history. When printed for albums or displayed as postcards, however, the images were usually generically labeled, making the individual representative of all Muslims or of a certain region or tribe.

For example, photos from a Bonfils studio collection on Palestine and Syria that Auburn Theological Seminary theology professor James Stevenson Riggs (1853–1936) compiled in the late nineteenth century bore the following titles: "Bédouines du Moab devant leur tente," "Groupe de Bédouines syriennes," and "Fils de Cheikh Diab" (Bedouins of Moab in front of their tent, Group of Syrian Bedouins, and Sons of Shaykh Diab; Figures 5.4, 5.5, and 5.6, respectively).[46] The third image—of three men in headdresses held in place with a thick black rope (*agal*) and carrying swords and daggers—was not generically labeled but resembled another staged photo in an album that American Presbyterian missionary Kate Hill brought home on furlough from India after a tour of Palestine and Egypt in 1904 (Figure 5.7). The single man in Hill's image was labeled as a Bedouin, visually capturing ideas about

Figure 5.4 "Bedouins of Moab" (circa 1880–1890)

Source: Photographs of Palestine and Syria, vol. 3, circa 1880–1890. Burke Library at Union Theological Seminary, Columbia University, New York City.

Figure 5.5 "Group of Syrian Bedouins" (circa 1880–1890)

Source: Photographs of Palestine and Syria, vol. 3, circa 1880–1890. Burke Library at Union Theological Seminary, Columbia University, New York City.

Figure 5.6 "Sons of Shaykh Diab" (circa 1880–1890)
Source: Photographs of Palestine and Syria, vol. 3, circa 1880–1890. Burke Library at Union Theological Seminary, Columbia University, New York City.

fierce Arab warrior tribes that contrasted with the first two Bonfils photos of needy Bedouin families.[47] Such photos of Muslim men in traditional garb bearing weapons also bring to mind Reformation-era woodcuts of Turks with scimitars, as well as Protestant claims that the Prophet Muhammad

Figure 5.7 "Bedouin" (1904)
Source: Furlough Journey Album 1904, Kate Alexander Hill Papers (Record Group 53, box 2, folder 12), Presbyterian Historical Society, Philadelphia, PA.

himself "taught war." (Recall the caption claiming just that alongside the picture of a boy with a gun in Amy Zwemer's *Two Young Arabs* [Figure 4.4].)

Parallel to the way in which missionaries misrepresented Middle Easterners in Holy Land scenes, the individuals in such colonial photos came to represent a timeless practice and unchanging way of life.[48] This was particularly true for staged photos that skewed the diverse realities on the ground in Muslim societies from Africa to South and Southeast Asia. Many such staged shots of Muslim women in the early twentieth century represented the colonial photographer's own fantasies. Pictorial Orientalism was at play in scenes of Turkish or North African harem life recreated in a studio where local women were paid to pose for the photographer (sometimes pornographically). Malek Alloula, for instance, critiqued a series of colonial postcards of the same woman model that purported to represent three different "types" of women in Algeria.[49] Similarly, Behdad found that many models posing in photographs of Muslim women in Turkey during the late Ottoman period were actually Armenian or other Christian women.[50] Such staging practices expose the skewed nature of these images that pretended to offer scientific documentation of Islamic societies. Christians from those societies have commonly been mistaken for Muslims, and at times have used such assumptions for financial gain, as these photographed women presumably did.[51]

The English evangelical Lilias Trotter (1853–1928) was one of many missionaries who made use of such staged photographs in her annual reports and mission magazines.[52] Trotter, founder of the Algiers Mission Band (AMB), collected picture postcards from tourist markets and sent them to her British and American supporters to convey how Algerians, especially the women and children, looked. Taking advantage of the plentiful stock photos of veiled women, Trotter affixed a postcard labeled "Blida Woman in Outdoor Dress" to an issue of the AMB periodical (Figure 5.8). Reinforcing missionary writings about "shrouded" Muslim women, she used this image of a woman with just one eye uncovered to represent all the women of the city of Blida and its surrounding region (south of Algiers).[53]

In a later report describing the Algerian town of Bou Saada, Trotter reported, "I have looked through the Algiers shops to see if Bou Saada faces are to be found among the 'types,' and here are just a few."[54] The postcards attached to Trotter's report were of unveiled women and were similar to the sort that Alloula critiqued; one actually featured the *exact same* Algerian model who appeared in the same clothing but with a different pose in Alloula's collection.[55] Trotter's colonial postcards intended to represent Algerian women, whose portraits mission supporters might presumably interpret variously as destitute, oppressed, or sensual, depending on clothing and expression. Yet, in commenting that viewers must not allow such women to "be left to a Christless future," she used images to facilitate religious judgments too.[56]

Figure 5.8 "Blida Woman in Outdoor Dress" (1908)
Source: Lilias Trotter, *Algiers Mission Band,* vol. 8 (March–April 1908), Arab World Ministries/Algiers Mission Band Papers (box 1), SOAS Special Collections, University of London. Courtesy of Arab World Ministries.

Trotter disseminated such picture postcards as a tactic to introduce readers to *specific* individuals or groups the mission served who shared the physical characteristics of those photographed, in her view. Consider the following four postcards from the pages of AMB periodicals in the early 1900s:

1. One postcard represented a girl named Aissha, whom Trotter described as one of the mission's new "little housemaidens" who was "raw from the country." Next to the postcard she wrote, "This head is so like her!" (Figure 5.9).[57]
2. In a second, Trotter described a girl named Hadia, whom she met in a rural village during an evangelistic tour. Under the accompanying postcard she wrote, "This [photograph] found afterwards in Algiers has such a look of her, in couture, expression and garb" (Figure 5.10).[58]

172 RE-INVENTING ISLAM

Figure 5.9 "Aissha" (1909)
Source: Lilias Trotter, *Algiers Mission Band*, vol. 10 (May–December 1909), Arab World Ministries/Algiers Mission Band Papers (box 1), SOAS Special Collections, University of London. Courtesy of Arab World Ministries.

Figure 5.10 "Hadia" (1907)
Source: Lilias Trotter, *A Week in a Strong City* (September 18, 1907), Arab World Ministries/Algiers Mission Band Papers (box 11), SOAS Special Collections, University of London. Courtesy of Arab World Ministries.

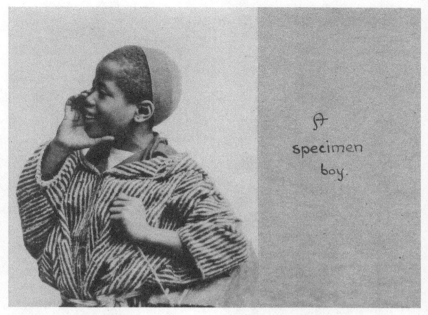

Figure 5.11 "A Specimen boy" (1912)
Source: Lilias Trotter, *Algiers Mission Band*, vol. 15 (1912), Arab World Ministries/Algiers Mission Band Papers (box 1), SOAS Special Collections, University of London. Courtesy of Arab World Ministries.

3. A third postcard labeled simply "A Specimen boy" illustrated a report on the AMB's work with young boys (Figure 5.11).[59]
4. Finally, a card strikingly labeled "Specimen 'wild elephants'" represented the sort of children who might attend the mission's new classes for "the little waifs that run wild in the streets." The image of one boy carrying another on his back represented for Trotter the energetic and unruly Algerian street children that she compared to wild elephants (Figure 5.12).[60]

Like the child sponsorship photos that became the norm in later missionary humanitarianism, these images enabled Trotter's western supporters to encounter North African Muslims as individuals, many of whose names and background stories Trotter provided through a series of journal entries. Such steps toward humanization of the "other" are noteworthy. Trotter, who had studied painting with art critic John Ruskin, saw beauty in much of North African life even as she critiqued Islam. As reflected in the sketches

Figure 5.12 "Specimen 'wild elephants'" (1912)
Source: Lilias Trotter, *Algiers Mission Band*, vol. 15 (1912), Arab World Ministries/Algiers Mission Band Papers (box 1), SOAS Special Collections, University of London. Courtesy of Arab World Ministries.

and paintings she affixed to AMB reports along with stock photos, she wanted her supporters to glimpse this beauty too, including the vivid colors that she described or illustrated with her artist's palette.[61] Nevertheless, with strong links to biological racism and the categorization of national and ethnic groups according to "type" during this period, missionaries like Trotter treated the anonymous individuals in these photos as "specimens." Although these were common terms of the period that might be applied to western individuals too, such wording suggested practices of categorizing and showcasing cultural and natural history objects in cabinets of curiosity and museums. The fact that Trotter—and many other European and American missionaries and travelers—collected and displayed snapshots of Muslim men, women, and children gave these terms a sinister tone.

As evident in Trotter's photo captions, picture postcards racialized Muslims, marked them as different, and exoticized Muslim women, especially when missionaries appropriated colonial photography for their own purposes. The same was true in the stock photos printed in *Our Moslem Sisters*, the volume Annie Van Sommer and Samuel Zwemer edited. Among these images were several labeled "Types in Tunis and Algiers."[62] One of these women was the same Algerian model featured in both Alloula's study and Trotter's mission journal—demonstrating that Protestant missionaries in the early twentieth century often drew from the same pool of North African "specimen" photos. Referring to another stock photo of a young Algerian woman, the book urged, "Look at the awful and fierce sadness of this face: more like a wild creature than a woman." Imagining the destitute nature of the woman's life and her need to be freed from "the social yoke of Islam," the author assured the readers that "God's 'season' comes when all has gone down to despair."[63] Thus, in words reminiscent of those Trotter used in her journals, Van Sommer and Zwemer's volume cultivated their readers' gendered and racialized gaze upon Islam in order to enlist support for the evangelism of Muslim women and girls.[64] This was apparent also in a portrait in the book of "A Bedouin girl from North Africa," showing a young woman with one breast exposed, which appeared in the volume's chapter on Morocco without comment from the author.[65]

Related to this use of colonial portrait photography were several other categories of images that missionaries produced with their own cameras. Common in all missionary archives were photographs of individuals and groups connected to the mission. Shots of mission employees, groups of schoolchildren, or patients at missionary clinics demonstrated the work of the mission in action; and these were central to annual reports and fundraising campaigns. The related photos of "native" Christians or preachers and their families, in particular, demonstrated the spiritual outcome of mission work. These converts were clearly meant to show evidence of successful evangelism and signs of hope for continued conversions to come.

The Protestant identity of such photographed figures was often reinforced by the Bibles they held, signaling the importance of vernacular scripture and literacy. In many such missionary photos shown in scrapbooks, on postcards, or in published reports, neat and clean western clothing also distinguished converts from non-Christians in their communities, marking them not only as saved but as civilized. Photos of school pupils in uniforms also signaled the reforming influence of such work, even on students who were not Protestant. For example, in the early 1880s, the Methodist Episcopal Mission of India sent out to supporters in the United States a photo card of a Sunday School class of boys in Lucknow titled "The Hope of India" (Figure 5.13). On the

Figure 5.13 "The Hope of India" (circa 1882)
Source: Thomas Craven, "The Hope of India," circa 1882, Badley Family Collection (Record Group 1554-2-5), United Methodist Church Archives – General Commission on Archives and History, Madison, NJ.

back of the card missionary Thomas Craven described the students—most of them not yet Christian—as the hope of India, detailing how well they had learned their lessons and telling about the conversion of one Muslim pupil, Zuhur ud Din, the oldest boy seated in the second row holding a book. Craven urged his audience to help sell copies of the photo to support the mission and "Rally to the rescue of India's children."[66]

Such mission institution photos contrasted with the generic "specimen" photos and the photographs that missionaries took on their own cameras to show locals in need of missionary assistance. In late-1920s Palestine, for instance, Eva Marshall, an American Quaker missionary who would soon marry Khalil Totah, wrote about her attempt to take candid photos of Muslim women with water jugs atop their heads who covered their faces to prevent her from capturing their pictures. "Snap" went the Kodak camera anyway, Marshall said, "catching shepherd, goats, black covered [women] figures and all."[67] Similarly, the Augustana Lutheran Church's mission society described a photograph it published of two "heavily veiled" Egyptian Muslim women in 1923, saying, "They did not want their picture taken, but tried to get away. They did not succeed!"[68] In Kuwait during the same period, the medical missionary Eleanor Calverley was so intent on showing her supporters what Muslim life looked like in the Arabian Mission's field that she also took snapshots of individuals who declined to be photographed, noting how one man feared that if his printed picture were destroyed, he would die and that another, who covered his face, was "reluctant to be photographed."[69]

Scrapbooks and photo albums documenting Calverley's work showed a student who had converted, a man who confessed Christ but then returned to Islam, and many shots of poor Bedouin families with desert tents and what Calverley regarded as unsanitary health practices. The latter resembled the aforementioned Bonfils photos (recall Figures 5.4 and 5.5).[70] As Mathur noted in missionary photographs from India, the contrast between the "before" picture of impoverished non-Christian locals (representing backwardness and spiritual darkness) and the "after" photos of local converts in crisp, western attire (representing progress and the evangelical faith) signaled visually the extraordinary transformation missionaries were accomplishing in these regions. For missionaries working among Muslims, some of the "before" pictures also portrayed Islamic practices.

Depicting Islamic Rules and Rituals

While ethnological portraits featured physical characteristics and cultural dress, another genre of colonial photography informed viewers about Muslim religious practices, especially the five daily prayers. Missionaries used such images but did not take many of their own, perhaps because photographs of Islamic practices were already so plentiful. Picture postcards of Muslim prayers were particularly popular with Europeans, as attested in William Christian, Jr., and Amira Mittermaier's study of 2500 prayer postcards that French soldiers and visitors purchased in North Africa between 1900 and 1960.[71] Mittermaier and Christian categorized these postcards into three groups, all of which had prototypes in earlier French paintings: great prayer, desert prayer, and daily prayer. The great prayer images were often taken during holidays that drew large crowds. These showed many rows of people (mostly men) praying outside, bowing or prostrating themselves in unison.[72] Often these postcards did not indicate the prayer's location so that snapshots from Algeria, Tunisia, or Morocco became part of a wealth of North African "scenes and types" and might be used to represent Muslim prayer practices even outside of that region.[73] The second type of postcard featured desert scenes of a small group of travelers with a caravan or of a single man with a camel, often at sunset. The third category of daily prayer photos intended to educate the audience and included staged photos of individuals demonstrating various prayer postures: bowing, standing, sitting, and prostration.[74]

These daily prayer postcards had precursors in French paintings. For example, the 1875 painting titled *Prière dans la Mosque* (Prayer in the Mosque) by Jean-Léon Gérome (1824–1904) appeared as part of his Orientalist series depicting Muslim men praying in various scenes.[75] Unlike such coveted artwork, however, the prayer postcards were widely available for purchase, singly or in tear-out booklets. Those purchased in North Africa were frequently bought by French soldiers or tourists and ended up in private collections. Yet French postcards had a much larger audience, including British and American Protestant missionaries, who used the same types of images as did their Catholic missionary competitors and showed marked interest in the third category of prayer postures.

Daily prayer images served a didactic purpose to introduce audiences to Muslim practices, as depicted in Thomson's *The Land and the Book* and in Amy and Samuel Zwemer's book for children, *Topsy-Turvy Land*. Thomson's text featured two images of men praying—one of prayers in a mosque and the other showing six individual prayer postures. The accompanying text described each movement along with the words spoken during the prayers.[76] The Zwemers' book included a sketch of eight prayer postures in sequence, showing "How a Moslem boy prays" (Figure 5.14). A similar image in Yale Divinity School's extensive missionary postcard collection showed four men outside, each performing a different prayer posture. It was labeled in English, French, and German as "Muslims praying" (Figure 5.15).[77] This image was merely informative, but *Topsy-Turvy Land* both explained the prayer postures and described a blind child who was praying as "doubly blind because her religion is false."[78] Likewise, *Children's Work for Children* assessed the prayers of Islam after depicting six postures. The magazine described the prayers with a mix of judgment and admiration as being undertaken "in a thoroughly ritualistic spirit, with many marvelous particularities, and with a mixture of simplicity and devotion quite surprising."[79]

One specific daily prayer image that Protestant mission organizations in the Middle East used frequently in publications in the early 1900s shows two men at prayer in a mosque, one kneeling with hands resting on his knees and the other prostrate, with his forehead touching the prayer rug (see the image on the right in Figure 5.16). Based on the popularity of this genre in

RECASTING THE PROTESTANT GAZE 179

Figure 5.14 "How a Moslem boy prays" (1902)
Source: Amy E. Zwemer and Samuel M. Zwemer, *Topsy-Turvy Land: Arabia Pictured for Children* (New York: Fleming H. Revell, 1902), 45.

Figure 5.15 "Muslims praying" (1905)
Source: Missionary Postcard Collection (Record Group 101, box 87, item 96), Special Collections, Yale Divinity School Library.

French North Africa and the many originals of this early twentieth-century postcard still for sale today in France, this photograph may have been widely available in North Africa, although the columns match those of the Umayyad Mosque in Damascus.[80] My random search in December 2021 generated fourteen postcards with this same prayer image available from French sellers on Delcampe.com, an online collectors' marketplace. Of these, two were dated (1903 and 1904). On the same day, two copies of the postcard were also available on eBay from American and British sellers. The postcards labeled with French captions variously identified the location as Syria, Cairo, Alexandria, or Morocco. My search revealed that the image was actually part of a set of three photographs with the same background. In a second photo of the two men, they are performing the prayer in standing positions, one upright and the other bent at the waist in a bow (see the image on the left in Figure 5.16). Only one of the men appears in the third photograph, where he is seated as a teacher with two young boys and a girl near him on the prayer rug (Figure 5.17). The card was labeled "Syrie—Maître d'école musulman" (Syria—Muslim schoolteacher). Postcards showing the praying men far outnumbered the school images for sale online, and I also repeatedly found the daily prayer cards featuring these two men in Protestant missionary publications and archives.[81]

Figure 5.16 "Greetings from the Orient: Muslim Prayer, Morocco" (circa 1903)
Source: Author's private collection.

RECASTING THE PROTESTANT GAZE 181

Figure 5.17 "Syria—Muslim schoolteacher" (circa 1903)
Source: Author's private collection.

When the same illustration of the kneeling and prostrating men appeared in the 1906 Cairo Conference volume, *Mohammedan World of To-Day*, the Muslims were said to be at prayer in Egypt.[82] Without noting the location, the Church Missionary Society (CMS) in London also printed this photograph in its "Picture and Fact" postcard series to offer a general commentary on Islam. The "fact" printed beside the praying men emphasized the rigid enforcement of Muslim prayer posture. It read: "Of Mohammedanism it has been said that the minutest change of posture in prayer would call for much heavier censure than outward profligacy or absolute neglect."[83] This echoed Protestant critiques of Islam for ritualism and works-righteousness, dating back to the Reformation. Indicating that the outward form of the prayer was unimportant, the CMS suggested that Islamic worship practices were empty rituals. The idea that a slight imperfection in prayer posture would invite heavy censure also reinforced Protestant views of Islam as a religion of masculinist dominance in which adherents were kept in line by the threat of violence.

The British Syrian Mission (BSM), a female-led society in Ottoman Syria, used the photo of these two men standing at prayer in the 1903 publication *One Hundred Syrian Pictures* alongside a photograph of two women fully veiled and bundled in long robes. Thus, the prayer photo the CMS disseminated as a generic representation of Muslim practice became Syrian for the BSM. *One Hundred Syrian Pictures* told the British mission's story, illustrated with a range of missionary-produced and professional, staged images. These included photos of mission buildings and groups of employees and students, as well as stock photos of scenery and of Muslim men and women to illustrate the broader Syrian context in which the missionaries labored. The BSM printed side by side the photos of the two praying men (Figure 5.18) and the two veiled women in a section devoted to its work in Damascus (Figure 5.19). This placement of the photos on the same page is significant, as is the appearance of two figures in each image. Thus, the BSM presented the image of veiled and secluded Muslim women as the counterpart to the photo of the Muslim men's rigidly formulaic prayer, giving a fuller Protestant conception of the Islamic faith than the prayer postcard would alone. The prayer photo caption reads, "Moslems at Prayer," and in more objective terms than the CMS postcard, the booklet explains,

> During prayer, the shoes are removed, and the carpet is spread towards Mecca. On Fridays there is congregational worship in the Great Mosque [the Umayyad Mosque in Damascus]; but on other days, the devout pray each independently of his neighbor.[84]

The photo of the women is titled "Mohammedan Women in Town Costume," indicating that the full covering would be worn by urban Muslim women when appearing in public. It reflects the western fascination with and concern for Muslim veiling practices, explaining, "Out of doors it is difficult to recognize our Moslem lady friends, unless we are well acquainted with their garments. Both form and face are shrouded, and all that is generally visible is a pair of high-heeled slippers."[85]

The image of the two men standing at prayer (this time titled "In the Great Mosque") also appeared next to the same image of "Moslem Women in Outdoor Dress" in another BSM publication focusing on Damascus: J. Edith Hutcheon's *The Pearl of the East* (1920), the same publication that included *Fatmeh's Story* (see Chapter 4).[86] Recalling tropes about oppressed Muslim women, such photos of "shrouded" women were intended to convey religious

Figure 5.18 "Moslems at Prayer" (1903)
Source: One Hundred Syrian Pictures: Illustrating the Work of the British Syrian Mission (London: S. W. Partridge & Co., 1903). Courtesy of Oxford Centre for Muslim-Christian Studies.

Figure 5.19 "Mohammedan Women in Town Costume" (1903)
Source: One Hundred Syrian Pictures: Illustrating the Work of the British Syrian Mission (London: S. W. Partridge & Co., 1903). Courtesy of Oxford Centre for Muslim-Christian Studies.

rigidity, similar to the interpretation of the Muslim men's prayer in the CMS postcard. Thus, under the Protestant gaze, Muslim religiosity was an oppressive system of control that held both men and women captive, while encouraging male violence and the abuse of women. Missionaries saw Muslim women as physically imprisoned, while Muslim men were in bondage to a false doctrinal system. Yet, even while vilifying Islam, the BSM booklet's reference to Muslim "friends" may have humanized Muslims for some readers and signaled that the individuals whom missionaries came to know in Muslim communities were not merely objects of proselytization, although the term might also have intended to signal the possibility of their conversions.

Images of Muslims at prayer also circulated in colonial India, where western travelers collected them.[87] Photographs of prayers in the outdoor courtyard of the Jama Masjid, a famous Mughal-era mosque in Delhi, India, drew attention, for example, because the outdoor space allowed a full view of those praying, including in the women's section behind a barrier at the back. Like the "great prayer" shots Mittermaier and Christian described, this scene was often photographed with large crowds filling the entire courtyard. An early twentieth-century Jama Masjid photo appeared in a British library collection, and another like it was affixed to Letha Daubendiek's 1930 MA thesis on Islam and missions at Hartford Seminary. Her caption read, "Notice that the women must worship behind the curtain."[88] This statement suggested that the act of worship itself reinforced gender inequality, making the image of Muslim women's prayers behind a barrier a truer counterpart to the prayer posture postcards featuring Muslim men. Although photos of Muslim men praying—like those in the desert at sunset—might have evoked beauty or devotion for some Christian viewers, images of Muslim women inevitably reinforced tropes of oppression, seclusion, exploitation, or sensuality. Those who read missionary texts were already conditioned to think in such terms. Such Orientalist images tell more about the mindsets of those who produced, distributed, and consumed them than about those depicted. In this case, the images reflect the nature of American Protestant material culture in the pre–World War II period and its use in spreading re-invented ideas about Islam.

Conclusion

Protestant perceptions of Islam have always been nuanced and varied, even if some views dominated public discourse more than others. This chapter gave evidence that missionaries pictured Islam in gendered and racialized ways that often reinforced longstanding prejudices and masked realities on the ground across diverse Islamic contexts. At the same time, the chapter also showed that missionaries' dissemination of visual material gave American audiences humanistic points of contact that were absent from many textual representations of Islam and Muslims and from other colonial discourses.

Capturing images on film or securing photographs from local studios became a central missionary routine in Islamic societies (and elsewhere) by the early twentieth century.[89] Missionaries like Eva Totah, Lilias Trotter, and Eleanor Calverley understood the sharing of images with family and friends, with financial supporters, and with wider Protestant audiences as essential to their evangelistic and humanitarian pursuits. By the 1930s, as Joseph Ho's study of missionary photography in China demonstrated, missionaries commonly packed cameras when embarking on a new assignment.[90] Yet in the late nineteenth century, before most missionaries owned photographic equipment, they were already using images in lectures, publications, and correspondence. As this chapter has demonstrated, such images were often supplied somewhat artificially through staged colonial photography and the tourism industry.

By attending to images as evidence of the visual, material culture of missions, I have sought to give a more capacious account of the ways in which missionaries shaped American conceptions of Islam and gender. Missionaries implicitly and at times intentionally connected gender oppression to Eurocentric perceptions of Muslims as racially inferior. At other times they humanized Muslims in ways not possible at a popular level before the mechanical reproduction of images. Protestant missionary collections of images point to the material and embodied dimensions of Islam, for example, in snapshots of individuals in Islamic clothing or kneeling on prayer rugs. The missionaries in this study distanced themselves from such material practices, which they interpreted as ritualistic or even oppressive (in the case of Muslim women's dress norms). Perhaps this is one reason why studies on missions have gravitated toward missionary writings, recognizing the Protestant emphasis on doctrinal teachings and the power of the printed word. The photographs and illustrations examined here therefore signal overlooked ways that missionaries and their supporters believed and lived out their religious identities outside of traditional worship spaces. They point to several material dimensions of Protestant practice in the late nineteenth and early twentieth centuries.

First, this chapter reinforced David Morgan's argument that far from rejecting images or only using them for "secular" purposes, nineteenth- and early twentieth-century Protestants enthusiastically embraced and employed photographs as a new way of expressing their religious identities (and others' very different identities). In this period, missionaries and their constituents were among those for whom, in Morgan's words, "looking at mass-produced images was an act imbued with the power of belief or to make one believe." He continued:

> [N]ineteenth-century Protestantism participated in a cultural economy in which belief was converted into graphic information and disseminated cheaply over great distances by virtue of a mass-produced medium and an ever-expanding infrastructure of distribution.[91]

Despite Protestants' iconoclastic leanings and their insistent view of religion as a set of doctrinal teachings,[92] Protestantism has always had its own materiality—a materiality that through the modern missionary enterprise came to incorporate both images of Muslims and items of Islamic material culture. Images emphasizing Muslims' civilizational, theological, and racial difference not only established Islam as inferior and opposed to Christianity; such images also activated Protestant belief and practice by inspiring a sense of spiritual calling to support missions and by orienting Protestants on how to gaze upon, think about, and act toward such needy, oppressed, or violent religious "others." Thus, Protestant visual culture nurtured and reinforced these dispositions and influenced the everyday practices of both missionaries and their audiences in the pre–World War II period.

Second, then, the images in Protestant missionary collections and publications offered evidence of missionaries' tangible faith practices in pursuit of their religious vocations. If belief is, in Morgan's words, "what people do, how they do it, where, and when,"[93] then missionary beliefs were embodied in their activities as creators, collectors, and distributors of an uncountable number of images of Islam, Muslims, and Islamic societies. As we shall see further in Chapter 6, missionaries performed their beliefs publicly before a watching, listening, and reading audience, of whom they were always conscious during the day-to-day workings of the mission. They represented themselves and the mission for their constituents as a routine part of the missionary vocation—one that typically also included multiple modes of evangelism, medical or other social services, teaching, publishing, fundraising, and recruitment of new missionaries. Images of Islam aided especially with the last two activities and with the task of educating audiences at home. Recall, for example, Lilias Trotter urging her supporters to imagine the "Christless future" that would be the fate of needy Muslim women pictured in her magazine without the AMB. The Protestant missionary gaze on these images was similar in many respects to the gaze Goldhill described in his study of Holy Land photo albums: "The pastoral, the backward, the simple, the humble, the poor, are not simply subject to the superior gaze of the civilized Western traveller, but are invested with the historical significance of the Christian message." For Goldhill, the biblical gaze evokes "memories of the foundational moments of religious truth" tied to the Bible.[94] The missionary gaze sees religious truth as well and invests in the images of Muslims a spiritual message to be conveyed to the Protestant viewer. The missionary's religion was not just assent to belief in Christ but a felt urgency to introduce Muslims to Jesus Christ (as Christians knew him and not according to Islamic tradition). This shared Protestant sense of urgency led to actions—like the aforementioned routines—which became just as central to missionaries' lived religious practices as their doctrinal claims.

Third, and finally, this chapter explored how missionaries' pictorial messages about Islamic societies aimed to influence an audience of mission supporters and other Americans. Although missionaries could not control their audiences' interpretations, the images examined here reinforced understandings of Muslims as inferior and exotic religious "others," particularly for those viewers who also read mission literature or attended missionary talks. Images of landscapes, portraits, and Islamic rituals were didactic—and not only in introducing the basics of Islam. For by highlighting differences in theology and gender norms, missionary images also signaled the superiority of Protestant culture and warned their constituents against heterodox religious practices. Some images also lent themselves to devotional use, inviting prayer for the Muslim individuals or groups pictured. Like their missionary contacts, many who received images became collectors (and thereby strengthened their connection to the missionary enterprise), saving photographs enclosed in missionaries' letters or cutting them out of mission magazines. Eva Totah enabled friends and family to do just that by encouraging them to review the photographs she sent and, before returning them to her by mail, to mark their names on the backs of those they wished her to have copied.[95]

As missionaries found new ways to energize the practice of tithing and donating by using images to prompt a sentimental response, recipients of such missionary photographs used financial contributions to express their devotion to the Protestant cause—and to Christ, whom they served by caring for the "least of these." Photographs of destitute people in foreign places, especially of famished children, recalled these words of Jesus in Matthew 25:40 and may also have reminded viewers of the gaunt Christ figure on the cross.[96] Although in early twentieth-century missionary humanitarianism such images were not focused primarily on starving Muslims, the idea that service to the hungry and impoverished was service to Christ helped counteract dehumanizing rhetoric about non-Christian and non-western cultures generally, because the recipient of aid and not the missionary worker stood in the place of Christ in such images. In response, those who received missionary images became involved as missionaries themselves, as organizers of mission auxiliaries at home, or as distributors of missionary reports and photographs to church circles or newspapers. Totah's family members, for instance, took seriously their role in publicizing her work in their local papers and in Quaker periodicals.[97] In collecting, curating, and distributing images of Muslims and Islamic life, by the early twentieth century missionaries had thus not only solidified their re-inventions of Islam but also shaped new practices of Protestant material culture in the United States.

With a foundation built, at least in part, by the ideas missionaries had disseminated, images of Arabs and Muslims (often conflated as one and the same) would proliferate in the United States after World War II when the American film industry emerged as the most powerful in the world. Racial stereotypes and orientalization of Muslims appeared in film by the late nineteenth century and became more prominent in the twentieth century.[98] Typical views of Muslim women as captives in the harem and of Muslim men as dangerous surfaced repeatedly, for example, in several different films with the title *Harem Scarem*. One of these is the oldest surviving Walt Disney cartoon, produced in 1928, in which a rabbit named Oswald falls in love with a dancing girl in Morocco and rescues her from a hostile Arab, played by Pete the cat. *Harem Scarem* is also the title of a 1932 film, in which a White protagonist named Al visits "a phony black prophet wearing Arab garb" in Harlem and, entranced by a crystal ball, imagines himself in a palace harem in Baghdad. He fights and defeats Arab and African guards and rescues a blonde maiden who has been captive in the ruler's harem. Similarly, in the 1932 Disney cartoon *Mickey in Arabia*, an Arab potentate (again Pete the cat) kidnaps Minnie Mouse. Mickey rescues her from Pete's desert palace after fighting the pajama-clad cat who comes at him with a saber, a blade associated with Muslims.[99] In such ways films offered similar messaging about Muslim violence and mistreatment of women, aimed at audiences of adults and children.

Several decades later another adaptation on this theme, *Harum Scarum* (1965), starred Elvis Presley as an American movie star kidnapped in the Middle East by a man who wants help assassinating the king of Bar Esalaam, a fictional city. Elvis falls in love with the king's daughter, however, and ends up fighting against the assassins. In the end, he returns to the United States with the princess as his bride and several of her dancing girls.[100] Although in this film the American hero does not save the princess from her Arab oppressors, it still paints a violent picture of the Muslim Middle East, and it sexualizes Arab women. Such ideas endure in American Protestant culture today in implicit, invisible biases that shape responses to Islam even outside of Protestant contexts, as seen in the Hollywood films and other American mass media to be examined in the final chapter. First, however, I consider how Protestant missionary materiality included not only images but also Islamic cultural objects.

Notes

1. Timothy Marr, *The Cultural Roots of American Islamicism* (Cambridge: Cambridge University Press, 2006), 262–66, 282–96.
2. On the proliferation of travel photo albums and picture postcards from the Middle East and South Asia, see Simon Goldhill, "Photography and the Real: The Biblical Gaze and the Professional Album in the Holy Land," in *Travel Writing, Visual Culture, and Form, 1760–1900*, ed. Mary Henes and Brian H. Murray (New York: Palgrave, 2015), 87–111; Saloni Mathur, *India by Design: Colonial History and Cultural Display* (Berkeley and Los Angeles: University of California Press, 2007), 109–32; Joseph A. Boone, "Vacation Cruises; Or, the Homoerotics of Orientalism," *PMLA* 110, no. 1 (January 1995): 89–107; Malek Alloula, *The Colonial Harem*, trans. Myrna Godzich and Wlad Godzich (Minneapolis: University of Minnesota Press, 1986).
3. I follow Gaskell and Carter's maximalist definition of material culture as "physical entities that resonate with communities of humans." Ivan Gaskell and Sarah Anne Carter, "Introduction: Why History and Material Culture?," in *The Oxford Handbook of History and Material Culture* (Oxford: Oxford University Press, 2020), 2.
4. For example, see Thomas Kidd, *American Christians and Islam: Evangelical Culture and Muslims from the Colonial Period to the Age of Terrorism* (Princeton, NJ: Princeton University Press, 2009).

5. Until mid-century, at least, the Protestant missionary movement remained a primary producer of knowledge about Islam for American audiences. For the changing scene after the mid-twentieth century, see Melanie McAlister, *Epic Encounters: Culture, Media, and U.S. Interests in the Middle East since 1945* (Berkeley: University of California Press, 2005).
6. On historians' use of material culture, see Gaskell and Carter, "Why History and Material Culture?," 12.
7. Ibid., 10.
8. Ibid., 4.
9. On performance analysis and religion, see Joy Palacios, "Introduction: Performing Religion," *Performance Matters* 3, no. 1 (2017): 1–6. John Fletcher defined performance broadly, explaining, "Given that *to perform* combines the sense of both *presenting* (for an audience in accordance with a planned, rehearsed, or ritualized pattern) and *doing*, performance can encompass not merely formal theater but practically any discrete expressive act directed toward and for the benefit of someone else." John Fletcher, *Preaching to Convert: Evangelical Outreach and Performance Activism in a Secular Age* (Ann Arbor: University of Michigan Press, 2013), 17.
10. Alloula, *Colonial Harem*.
11. Manuel A. Vásquez, *More than Belief: A Materialist Theory of Religion* (Oxford: Oxford University Press, 2011), 321.
12. Ali Behdad, *Camera Orientalis: Reflections on Photography of the Middle East* (Chicago: University of Chicago Press, 2016), 21.
13. Sahar Aziz, *The Racial Muslim: When Racism Quashes Religious Freedom* (Oakland: University of California Press, 2022), 4–5, 19–20, 25–33.
14. Stephen Sheehi, *The Arab Imago: A Social History of Portrait Photography, 1860–1910* (Princeton, NJ: Princeton University Press, 2016), xx.
15. Christopher Herbert, *Culture and Anomie: Ethnographic Imagination in the Nineteenth Century* (Chicago: University of Chicago Press, 1991). On the connection between ethnology and colonialism, see Mark Brown, "Ethnology and Colonial Administration in Nineteenth-Century British India: The Question of Native Crime and Criminality," *British Journal for the History of Science* 36, no. 2 (June 2003): 201–19.
16. Deanna Ferree Womack, "Edward Said and the Orientalized Body: A Call for Missiological Engagement," *Swedish Missiological Themes/Svensk Missionstidskrift* 99, no. 4 (2011): 447–48.
17. Such images available in tourist shops were often of much higher quality than those that missionaries produced and were easily accessible at a time when many missionaries did not have photographic equipment. Following studies on this topic by Ali Behdad and Malek Alloula, I use the term *colonial photography* to refer to an industry that was independent of colonial administrations but which, through the circulation of images between the colony and the imperial center, often served the aims of empire. Behdad, *Camera Orientalis*; Alloula, *Colonial Harem*.
18. Behdad, *Camera Orientalis*, 45–67.
19. Edward Said, *Orientalism* (New York: Vintage Books, 1978), 97, 150, 231. See my analysis on this subject in Womack, "Edward Said and the Orientalized Body," 447–49.
20. Paul Jenkins, "The Earliest Generation of Missionary Photographers in West Africa and the Portrayal of Indigenous People and Culture," *History in Africa* 20 (1993): 92. For more on missionary photography, see Joseph Ho, *Developing Mission: Photography, Filmmaking and American Missionaries in Modern China* (Ithaca, NY: Cornell University Press, 2021).
21. Jenkins, "Missionary Photographers," 92.
22. Alloula, *Colonial Harem*, 4–5; Mathur, *India by Design*, 109–32.
23. Mathur, *India by Design*, 117. Italics in original.
24. Ibid., 115.
25. Ibid., 114. An astonishing 786 million postcards were sent in Germany in 1900, and annual production of postcards in France reached 123 million in 1910.
26. Sheehi, *Arab Imago*, xix.
27. Ibid., xx–xxi.
28. It was not only westerners who took these photographs, however. By the mid-nineteenth century we can speak of Arab photography. For instance, in 1861 an Egyptian amateur photographer, Muhammad Sadiq Bey (d. 1902), became the first person to photograph the holy sites and pilgrims of Mecca and Medina. Sheehi, *Arab Imago*, xvii–xx, 163–70. On Iranian, Turkish, and Arab photography studios that traded in Orientalist imagery, see Behdad, *Camera Orientalis*.

29. Mathur, *India by Design*, 82, 110–11. As scholars like Malek Alloula, Saloni Mathur, and Joseph Boone demonstrated, both genres—studio photographs and picture postcards produced in or about colonial environments—brought millions of images to western viewers from the late nineteenth century onward. Mathur, *India by Design*, 109–32; Boone, "Vacation Cruises," 89–107; Alloula, *Colonial Harem*.
30. John Davis, *The Landscape of Belief: Encountering the Holy Land in Nineteenth-Century American Art and Culture* (Princeton, NJ: Princeton University Press, 1996).
31. David D. Grafton, *An American Biblical Orientalism: The Construction of Jews, Christians, and Muslims in Nineteenth Century American Evangelical Piety* (Lanham, MD: Lexington Books, 2019), 3.
32. Goldhill, "Photography and the Real," 92–97.
33. Davis, *Landscape of Belief*, 73. See also Stephanie Stidham Rogers, *Inventing the Holy Land: American Protestant Pilgrimage to Palestine, 1865–1941* (Lanham, MD: Lexington Books, 2011), 24–26.
34. Davis, *Landscape of Belief*, 3; William M. Thomson, *The Land and the Book: Or Biblical Illustrations Drawn from the Manners and Customs, the Scenes and Scenery of the Holy Land*, exp. ed. (New York: Harper & Brothers, 1886). See also Grafton, *American Biblical Orientalism*, 176.
35. Davis, *Landscape of Belief*, 74–75.
36. Sheehi spoke about French colonial photographers' "photographic rejection of contemporary Middle Eastern life" and denial of the existence of the inhabitants that facilitated colonial rule in North Africa and the Levant. Sheehi, *Arab Imago*, xxi.
37. This was true in mission-produced postcards, in the published photography books of American Protestant origin that John Davis analyzed, and in the photo albums in Simon Goldhill's study. Davis, *Landscape of Belief*, 84; Goldhill, "Photography and the Real."
38. Photographs of "Canaanite Lad" and "Modern Canaanite," 1930. Elihu Grant photographs and manuscript collection (HCS.001.014), Quaker & Special Collections, Haverford College, Haverford, PA.
39. Davis, *Landscape of Belief*, 84.
40. Eva Marshall Totah mentioned this relationship between her husband, Khalil, and Elihu Grant in letters to her family. Eva Marshall to Frank and Myrtle Marshall, December 14, 1928, Khalil A. Totah and Eva Marshall Totah Papers (MC 1210, box 4, folder 2) (hereafter *Totah Papers*), Quaker & Special Collections, Haverford College, Haverford, PA.
41. Davis, *Landscape of Belief*, 83. See also Goldhill's treatment of tableau vivant pictures of the biblical story of Ruth in Goldhill, "Photography and the Real," 95.
42. Two such images appear in Missionary Postcard Collection (Record Group 101, box 87, item 5), Special Collections, Yale Divinity School Library (hereafter *YDS*).
43. "Evening Meal Among the Fellaheen," circa 1920s–1960s, Missionary Postcard Collection, YDS 101-87-5. Postcards of multiple other biblical scenes can also be found in YDS 101-87.
44. Davis, *Landscape of Belief*, 88.
45. Charles D. Orzech, *Museums of World Religions: Displaying the Divine, Shaping Cultures* (London: Bloomsbury, 2020), 18–24.
46. Félix Bonfils, Photographs of Palestine and Syria, vol. 3, circa 1880–1890. Burke Library at Union Theological Seminary, Columbia University, New York, NY.
47. Furlough Journey Album 1904, Kate Alexander Hill Papers (Record Group 53, box 2, folder 12), Presbyterian Historical Society, Philadelphia (hereafter *PHS*). This image was labeled as originating in the American Colony Jerusalem. Henry Jessup employed both contrasting portrayals of the Bedouin when he commented, "While in the one sense they are simple-minded, hospitable, true children of nature, they show they are also the children of Adam, superstitious, suspicious, and revengeful to the last degree." Claiming that "midnight raids upon hostile camps" were ingrained activities for the Bedouin tribes, he also commented that "the old Ishmaelitic spirit is wrought into the very fibre of their being" and then cited Genesis 16:12. Henry Harris Jessup, *Fifty-Three Years in Syria*, vol. 1 (New York: Fleming H. Revell, 1910), 359–60.
48. Grafton, *American Biblical Orientalism*.
49. Alloula, *Colonial Harem*, 62–65.
50. Behdad, *Camera Orientalis*, 63, 66.
51. Linda K. Jacobs, "'Playing East': Arabs Play Arabs in Nineteenth-Century America," *Mashriq & Mahjar* 2, no. 2 (2014): 79–110.

52. On Trotter, see Lisa M. Sinclair, "The Legacy of Isabella Lilias Trotter," *International Bulletin of Missionary Research* 26, no. 1 (January 2002): 32–35; Constance E. Padwick, "Lilias Trotter of Algiers," *International Review of Mission* 21, no. 1 (January 1932): 119–28.
53. Postcard labeled "A Blida Woman in Outdoor Dress," in Lilias Trotter, *Algiers Mission Band*, vol. 8 (March–April 1908), Arab World Ministries/Algiers Mission Band Papers (box 1), SOAS Special Collections, University of London (hereafter *AMB*). Trotter attached postcards to this handwritten journal that circulated among supporters, including those in the United States where the AMB had an auxiliary.
54. Lilias Trotter, *A Week in a Strong City* (September 18, 1907), AMB box 11.
55. Alloula, *Colonial Harem*, 56.
56. Trotter, *Week in a Strong City*.
57. Trotter, *Algiers Mission Band*, vol. 10 (May–December 1909), AMB box 1.
58. Trotter, *Week in a Strong City*.
59. Trotter, *Algiers Mission Band*, vol. 15 (1912), AMB box 1.
60. Ibid.
61. Examples of Trotter's earliest sketches and paintings from Algeria have been published in Lilias I. Trotter, *Lilias Trotter's 1889 Sketchbook: Scenes from North Africa, Italy & Switzerland* (Lilias Trotter Legacy, 2020).
62. Annie Van Sommer and Samuel M. Zwemer, eds., *Our Moslem Sisters: A Cry of Need from the Lands of Darkness Interpreted by Those Who Heard It* (New York: Fleming H. Revell, 1907), 90.
63. Ibid., 96–97.
64. The anonymous author who contributed the chapter containing images of Algerian women was British and may indeed have been Trotter herself. The photo of the Tunisian woman and infant pictured at the front of the book also appeared in one of the first biographies of Trotter after her death, I. R. Govan Stuart's *The Love that Was Stronger* (London: Lutterworth Press, 1958).
65. Van Sommer and Zwemer, *Our Moslem Sisters*. The picture was printed between pages 102 and 103.
66. Thomas Craven, "The Hope of India," circa 1882, Badley Family Collection (Record Group 1554-2-5), United Methodist Church Archives—General Commission on Archives and History, Madison, NJ.
67. Eva Totah, "We Like Our School," circa 1928–1930, Totah Papers MC 1210-4-10.
68. The photo appeared in Joshua Oden, "Mohammedanism from the Viewpoint of One Who Has Seen It," *The Missionary Calendar of the Augustana Foreign Missionary Society* 3 (Rock Island, IL: Augustana Book Concern, 1923), 87.
69. Scrapbook of "Calverley Picture Collections," circa 1920s, Edwin E. Calverley Papers (box 375), Hartford International University Library Archives, Hartford, CT (hereafter *Calverley Papers*). On the back of the second photo, it read, "Bedouin man reluctant to be photographed." Calverley Family Photographs, Calverley Papers, box 376.
70. Describing the practices of an Arab barber leeching a sick patient, with an accompanying photograph, Calverley noted that Kuwait lacked a board of health. Scrapbook of "Calverley Picture Collections."
71. William A. Christian Jr. and Amira Mittermaier, "Muslim Prayer on Picture Postcards of French Algeria, 1900–1960," *Material Religion: The Journal of Objects, Art and Belief* 13, no. 1 (2017): 25–51.
72. Ibid., 27.
73. Ibid., 28.
74. Ibid., 30–33. Some of these postcards conflated Arab identity and Islam, describing the scene as "Arab prayers."
75. Gerald M. Ackerman, *The Life and Work of Jean-Léon Gérôme* (New York: Sotheby's, 1986).
76. Thomson, *Land and the Book*, 65–66.
77. The number of prayer postures depicted in these images varied. The International Mission Photography Archive of the University of Southern California Libraries also holds a number of images of Muslim prayer postures and congregational prayers, many of them originating in the Swiss Protestant Basel Mission between 1906 and 1960. See "No. 107. Muslim at Prayer III," http://tiny.cc/IMPA1; "Mohammedans at Prayer," http://tiny.cc/IMPA2; "Muslims at Prayer," http://tiny.cc/IMPA3. Accessed January 7, 2024.
78. Samuel M. Zwemer and Amy E. Zwemer, *Topsy-Turvy Land: Arabia Pictured for Children* (New York: Fleming H. Revell, 1902), 46.

79. Cyrus Hamlin, "The Mussulman at Daily Prayer," *CWC* 3 (1878): 184. Hamlin was an ABCFM missionary in Turkey.
80. Missionaries in Syria claimed the image was of the "Great Mosque" in Damascus. See *One Hundred Syrian Pictures: Illustrating the Work of the British Syrian Mission* (London: S. W. Partridge, 1903). The image is of the Umayyad Mosque, but the photographer may have superimposed the images or staged the photo in front of a backdrop that resembled the mosque.
81. Marketplace search by the author on Delcampe.com and Ebay.com on December 10, 2021.
82. Samuel M. Zwemer, E. M. Wherry, and James L. Barton, eds., *The Mohammedan World of To-Day, Being Papers Read at the First Missionary Conference on Behalf of the Mohammedan World held at Cairo April 4th–9th, 1906* (New York: Fleming H. Revel, 1906). The image was printed between pages 36 and 37.
83. "Mohammedans at Prayer," Missionary Postcard Collection, YDS 101-87-114. This popular photograph appeared a second time in the YDS postcard collection, with no caption or indication of which mission society used it. Missionary Postcard Collection, YDS 101-87-109.
84. *One Hundred Syrian Pictures.*
85. Ibid.
86. J. Edith Hutcheon, *The Pearl of the East* (London: BSM, 1920), 7. Another frequently used missionary photo of a Muslim man praying, facing the camera with his hands raised beside his ears, appeared in Hutcheon's volume (p. 21). The BSM used this image in several other publications, including its monthly magazine, *Daughters of Syria*, special seventieth anniversary number (1930): 53. The two men standing at prayer also appeared in Helen I. Moody Stuart, *Fatmeh: A Common Story of Mission School for Moslem Girls* (London: BSM, circa 1920), 34.
87. Mathur, *India by Design*, 120.
88. "Jama Masjid Prayer Meeting," circa 1900, Asia, Pacific, and African Collections (Mss Eur E267/189(64)), British Library, London; Letha Idell Daubendiek, "The Christian Approach to Muslim Women in India" (MA thesis, Hartford Seminary Foundation, 1930).
89. For one comprehensive study of the ways Protestant and Catholic missionaries used visual media—including photographs and film—to document and advance their work on China, see Ho, *Developing Mission.*
90. Ho, *Developing Mission*, 59–94.
91. David Morgan, *Protestants and Pictures: Religion, Visual Culture, and the Age of American Mass Production* (Oxford: Oxford University Press, 1999), 6. Missionaries were part of this distribution infrastructure.
92. Morgan noted that Protestantism intensified further the general Christian emphasis on belief as connected to religious teachings. David Morgan, "Introduction: The Matter of Belief," in *Religion and Material Culture: The Matter of Belief*, ed. David Morgan (London and New York: Routledge, 2010), 1. The critique of such Protestant views of religion has been important for the material turn in religious studies. On the influence of Protestant theories of religion, see Webb Keane, *Christian Moderns: Freedom and Fetish in the Mission Encounter* (Berkeley: University of California Press, 2007), 6–7; Vásquez, *More Than Belief*, 1, 3, 31–34, 87–122.
93. David Morgan, "Preface," in *Religion and Material Culture*, xiv.
94. Goldhill, "Photography and the Real," 106.
95. Eva Marshall to Family, June 11, 1928, Totah Papers MC 1210-4-2; Eva Marshall to Family, September 30, 1928, Totah Papers MC 1210-4-3.
96. See, for example, Heather D. Curtis, *Holy Humanitarians: American Evangelicals and Global Aid* (Cambridge, MA: Harvard University Press, 2018), 128–59. On the development of humanitarian photography, see Heide Fehrenbach and Davide Rodogno, eds., *Humanitarian Photography: A History* (Cambridge: Cambridge University Press, 2014).
97. Eva Rae Marshall to Father and Mother, February 14, 1929; Eva Marshall to Father and Mother, February 24, 1929; and Eva Rae Marshall to Bud and Myrtle, February 24, 1929, Totah Papers MC 1210-4-4. In the letter to her brother Frank Marshall (known as Bud), Eva complained that "father keeps clambering [sic] for articles for the paper and prints my hasty personal ones when I can't comply." Eva's letters and articles were published in the *Wessington Springs Republican* and the *Wessington Springs Independent*, the Marshalls' local newspapers in Wessington Springs, South Dakota.

98. McAlister, *Epic Encounters*, 31.
99. Jack Shaheen, *Reel Bad Arabs: How Hollywood Vilifies a People* (New York: Olive Branch Press, 2001), 233. The scene in *Harem Scarem* is supposed to take place three thousand years in the past, signaling the historical inaccuracy of this attempt to depict a Muslim harem over a millennium and a half prior to the Prophet Muhammad's birth.
100. Ibid., 211–34.

6

Performative Re-inventions

Missionary Costumes, Curios, and Comparative Religion

The objects that missionaries sent back or brought home for display in churches, schools, curiosity cabinets, mission museums, and international exhibitions included Islamic material culture. Missionaries also sent photographs of themselves in Muslim garb to their supporters and wore such costumes during performances and presentations when home on furlough. Thus, by adapting the long tradition of western actors portraying Muslims in the theater and of western elites wearing Ottoman costume, missionaries added a new dimension to the images of Islam already circulating in the United States and Britain. In so doing, they used tangible material strategically to re-invent Islam for an audience that was now more knowledgeable about Muslim societies and eager to support Protestant work among Muslims financially.

This chapter considers how missionaries' use of material objects reinforced critiques of Islamic gender norms and how they promoted ideas about Muslims' racial otherness among American audiences before World War II. While keeping transnational British–American connections in view, I focus more closely here than I did in previous chapters on missionary displays and performances for audiences in the United States specifically. I locate the activities of Protestant missionaries in Islamic contexts within wider colonial and Orientalist networks that generated the growth of museums, the development of anthropology, and the establishment of comparative religion.

As they invited viewers to move imaginatively into the world of Islam without actually leaving their home societies, missionary performers cultivated an audience that desired entertainment along with factual reports. Missionaries were not the only peddlers of such voyeuristic experiences. The American public's attraction to the "exotic East" generated funding both for missions and for an entertainment industry in which Middle Eastern migrants in the United States could make a living in the late nineteenth and

Re-inventing Islam. Deanna Ferree Womack, Oxford University Press. © Oxford University Press 2025.
DOI: 10.1093/9780197699195.003.0006

early twentieth centuries by representing their own cultures on the stage.[1] Yet, between 1880 and 1930 especially, Americans were strongly invested in missionary campaigns, making missions "an activity that exceeded other reform or benevolent organizations in size and resources."[2] The rising enthusiasm for evangelization of Muslims during this same period meant that American audiences were attuned to missionary messaging about Islamic societies. Drawing on Manuel Vásquez's materialist theory of religion, it is important to consider how this messaging involved not only truth claims, texts, and printed images but also material artifacts and performative practices.[3]

I focus here on performative transmissions of knowledge about Islam through two forms of material culture: 1) religious and cultural objects displayed in a wide range of settings and 2) costumes worn by missionaries purporting to represent Muslim dress styles. While missionary "dress up" carried a stronger theatrical dimension, both material forms were performative in the sense that missionaries selected the medium and mode of displaying items they collected for a target audience. Aiming to educate and elicit support for their work, missionaries transmitted ideas about Islam in what might be considered an early instance of "performance activism," as John Fletcher termed it, meaning that these performances intended to provoke religiously motivated social action.[4] Indeed, missionary performances aimed to inspire financial contributions, to encourage the educational and fundraising work of mission auxiliaries on the home front, or to convince the audience members to enter the mission field themselves.

Notably, because of the intricate relationship between the performer and the audience, the performer's needs, and the audience's expectations, performances do not always reveal the actors' full beliefs or understandings of the topic at hand.[5] Thus, the messages that Anglo-Protestant missionaries hoped to convey when using Islamic material culture fell within the limits of American and British cultural expectations.[6] These expectations were shaped by broader colonial and Orientalist endeavors to document, and in many cases control, Muslim populations. Just as the missionary photographs examined in Chapter 5 resembled the images other western travelers collected, so too did missionaries' use of material objects in performances fit with the patterns of western appropriation of eastern dress, early museum curation practices, and the colonial materiality of world's fairs.

Perhaps it is because of Protestantism's inclination toward textualism that the study of Protestant missions has given so little attention to missionaries' use of material culture, in comparison to the significant number of studies on missionary preaching, writing, and translations of scripture.[7] This is true of research on Protestant missions in Muslim societies, which has gravitated toward missionaries' polemical arguments and their comparisons between Christian and Muslim doctrines or between the Bible and the Qur'an.[8] Yet regardless of the context, few studies on missions move significantly beyond a focus on textual transmission of ideas and doctrinal beliefs to consider the material culture of missions or the links between Protestant missionaries and material religion.[9]

Scholars have long recognized the connections between missionary activities and the production of western knowledge about religious and cultural "others." Some scholarship has focused on missionary museums and their role in exposing their constituents to religious artifacts from around the world, using various performative techniques, from local church displays to international exhibitions. Little attention, however, has been given specifically to the objects brought back from Islamic contexts. Building on my argument in the previous chapter about missionaries' incorporation of images into Protestant material culture, I show how the curation and viewing of Islamic artifacts and Muslim clothing became a regular practice for missionaries and other mission-minded Protestants in the early twentieth century.

Notions of difference and impulses toward comparison significantly shaped Protestants' collection and display of non-western religious and cultural artifacts.[10] Comparison necessitated categorization of objects and people groups, and this, in turn, facilitated (often negative) judgments about alternate ways of being. When Protestant missionaries compared their own evangelical faith to Islam, especially before the twentieth century, they usually found the latter sorely wanting, just as they also found Middle Eastern, African, and Asian societies inferior to western civilization. Missionaries' display of Muslim objects was therefore not only didactic and centered on fundraising or personnel needs: their re-inventions of Islam were also assertions of Protestant identity and White Christian superiority.

The shaping of Protestant self-understandings occurred during missionary performances through the encounter with and rejection of religious and racial difference. This fits with Katheryn Gin Lum's study on the formative role that the concept of "the heathen" played in shaping White American Protestant discourse and identity formation from the colonial period to the twentieth century (and even into the present). The term *heathen* signaled not just racial and religious difference but inferiority, based on the ideal of a Christian Caucasian racial "type" from which the non-Christian and non-western people of the world had purportedly degenerated—both in terms of deviating from Christianity and in terms of "inferior" bodily features and behaviors.[11] While western theologians distinguished more clearly between "heathens" as polytheists and Muslims as monotheists than did ordinary people, nevertheless the Christian arguments against all of these religious "others" were similarly laden with racist pronouncements of cultural superiority. We might note, for example, the way women's missionary societies applied statements like "unwelcome at birth" and "unlamented when dead" to all African and Asian women, regardless of religious, cultural, or national context.[12]

These practices emerged at a time when notions about race and religion were becoming linked in scientific studies of non-western cultures, as seen in the religio-racial taxonomies followed in museums, in anthropological studies, and in missionaries' writings and images.[13] It is significant for this study, as well, that the scientific racism of the nineteenth century typically categorized non-western societies according to the perceived characteristics and behaviors of the men (as actors) and the status of the women (as passive). Both portrayals contrasted with the dominant image "of a white self-sufficient man, his self-sufficiency defined by possession, control, and mastery," as Willie James Jennings described it.[14] Thus, missionary exhibitions and performances not only reinforced Protestant critiques of Islamic beliefs as false but also characterized Muslim women as oppressed, heightening the missionary discourse of the veil when theatrically displayed for Protestant audiences on western women's bodies. In contrast to images of Muslim men as violent oppressors, however, missionary men's use of Islamic costume more often transmitted romanticized ideals of eastern wisdom and scholarship, similar to the ways in which elite western men of the time appropriated Islamic clothing.

The first section below begins with the imperial context of the nineteenth century in which missions became intertwined with the converging activities of museums, colonial exhibitions, amateur collections, and performances in exotic costumes. The subsequent two sections focus on common ways in which missionaries offered performative displays of Islamic material culture: through collections of "curiosities" and through dressing up in Muslim costumes.

Material Connections: Curiosity Cabinets, Museums, and Great Exhibitions

Protestant missionaries in the nineteenth century existed in a symbiotic relationship with empire. Like western scholars who sought and produced knowledge about non-western cultures and religions during this period, missionaries did not always support their own nations' colonial-imperial pursuits. Nevertheless, missionaries were shaped by and benefited from empire, and they contributed to such pursuits through the information they transmitted back to the imperial centers. Scholars and missionaries were part of an ethos of western travelers venturing out to strange and exotic lands for whom it was only natural to document and collect information about religions, often motivated by a humanistic pursuit of knowledge.[15] In addition to taking photographs and creating travel journals, western travelers collected objects, artifacts, and "curiosities"—known as curios or strange and interesting souvenirs. Such collections took two prominent forms: 1) cabinets of curiosities that evolved into public museums and 2) international exhibitions at world's fairs.

From Curio Cabinets to Museums

In the sixteenth and seventeenth centuries, members of the ruling classes and wealthy gentry in Europe began exhibiting objects from their travels to Africa and Asia in their own private collections. Spurred on by increased scholarly activity after the Renaissance and during the Enlightenment, along with the growth of the middle classes and European exploration, collectors stored these items in "cabinets of curiosities"—sometimes arranged in actual cabinets and sometimes in entire rooms devoted to showing off exotic artifacts. Offering a "miniature sampler of the world," these private collections proliferated as European empires expanded.[16] The objects were usually arranged haphazardly, showcasing treasures acquired from all over.[17] As Michael Ames explained in his study of museum anthropology, in these European collections

> the material properties of tribal peoples were classed with strange flora and fauna, as objects of wonder and delight, to be collected as trophies,

souvenirs, or amusing curiosities during one's travels to far and distant lands.[18]

These curio cabinets, which became a common feature in noble and royal households, eventually evolved into the earliest European museums as families donated collections for public display. In England, the first public museum was Oxford's Ashmolean, founded in 1683. The British Museum was opened to the public in 1759 after several individuals and organizations turned over their curios.[19]

A major shift from private collections to museums came in the early nineteenth century with the systemization of public museums. Such museums reflected two key scholarly fields that developed throughout the century: anthropology and comparative religion (also called the *science of religion* or *history of religions*), areas of study which were entangled in European colonial pursuits.[20] As Ames maintained, "A typical objective of early anthropological displays was, therefore, to present artefacts from 'primitive societies' as if they were specimens akin to those of natural history." Anthropologists classified and presented human societies "according to similarity of form, evolutionary stage of development, or geographical origin."[21] Museums echoed this scholarship by introducing systems of scientific classification and interpretation of artifacts. Through this process, former "objects of curiosity or glory became scientific specimens, and scholars devoted themselves to their study and classification." They consequently started to organize and group collections "according to what at the time were thought to be universal themes, such as race or evolutionary stage."[22] These ostensibly objective scientific presentations of human development were, however, in fact strongly guided by ideologies of White western Christian superiority. The systematization of racial categories, along with the curated display of objects under glass and in cases, put foreign cultures and religions under the control of both the curators and the viewers. As Ames explained, to "museumify" other cultures is to "exercise a conceptual control over them."[23] Notably, Orientalism emerged from and participated in the same desire for physical control or intellectual mastery through which the subordination of eastern and Islamic values could be upheld scientifically and the Orientalist scholar, colonial administrator, or Christian authority could define reality.

Museums also supported and benefited from the comparative study of religion, a field that Charles Orzech described as an "adjunct to empire" which "originated as the shadow of Protestant Christianity" with the aim of studying the divine.[24] Although scholarly collections were not usually established explicitly on behalf of Protestantism, religion was a focus of museum collections, and western Christian worldviews were often imposed. As Orzech explained, "Collections of objects were enmeshed in knowledge regimes that preceded and contributed to the production of 'religions' in the context of Empire."[25] For example, because they had such close contact with local customs, missionaries were instrumental in documenting and gathering material objects for display in museums and for the comparative examination of religions.[26] Thus, these global emissaries of Protestantism were among the network of colonial officials, scientists, traders, collectors, and other agents "through which the raw materials of the ruled territories were turned into 'intellectual manufactured goods' and funneled for display, discussion, and consumption" in museums and at scholarly gatherings.[27] Comparative religion evolved within and was dependent upon these varied modes of anthropological classification, collection, and comparison. Implicit—and sometimes glaringly explicit—in modern museums, as well as in the great exhibitions explored below, was the drive to judge between western civilization and the rest of the world, and between Christianity and other religions.[28]

Great Exhibitions

International exhibitions have a shorter history than do modern museums but can be traced to similar religio-racial thought patterns. Like the comparative science of religion, the so-called great exhibitions were imperial endeavors that "collected, condensed, and displayed the empire as a sign of its global scope and domination."[29] The link between empire and comparative religion could be seen prominently in the coinciding meetings of the Chicago World's Fair (World Columbian Exposition) and the World's Parliament of Religions in 1893. The "paradigmatic" exhibition, however, was England's Great Exhibition of 1851, also known as the Crystal Palace Exhibition, which sparked a series of world's fairs in Paris (1867 and 1889); Philadelphia (1876); South Kensington, England (1886); and Chicago (1893).[30] These massive gatherings rendered empire visibly and materially in a colonial theater of sorts with costumes, backdrops, and props.[31] Such expositions have been called "living museums,"[32] but in more sinister terms Orzech compared the world's fair of 1893 to a "human zoo" because of the numbers of people brought in from the non-western world in an attempt to represent entire cultures materially for the millions of Americans who came not just to gaze upon but to be immersed in "traditional" life within the fair's Asian, African, and Middle Eastern facades.[33]

Anthropologists contributed to such exhibitions. For instance, the German-American pioneer of modern anthropology Franz Boas (1858–1942) supervised arrangements for the Chicago World's Fair, and "popularized a different form of anthropological display, exhibiting artefacts in fabricated settings that simulated the original cultural contexts from which they came, rather than as natural history specimens representing some typology or evolutionary sequence."[34] This was a step toward deeper appreciation of global cultures, yet the immersion in an exotic experience was also a draw, indicating the truth in Orzech's claim that such exhibitions resembled human zoos. As Walter Putnam wrote when critiquing the 1889 Universal Exhibition in Paris, which put several hundred Africans on display, these widespread

> spectacles of radical alterity placed European and North American audiences in direct contact with "specimens" (for that is the term that was commonly used) from exotic lands . . . for the amusement and edification of their western audiences.[35]

Noting that European empires controlled nearly eighty-five percent of earth's inhabitable land by the start of the First World War, Putnam continued, "Human zoos served ideological and propagandist purposes by attempting to convince a skeptical metropolitan population that the colonial adventure was working and that it was worth the cost."[36] Such voyeuristic experiences claimed to capture authentic and timeless traditions but actually erased context.[37]

In contrast to photographic images of distant people that could only facilitate a limited sense of familiarity, these living museums or human zoos "shrank distance to the space of a cage, a roped-off area, an arena or a stage, sometimes even allowing for direct physical contact to take place between observed and observer." This enabled viewers to act as eyewitnesses of the wider world who could confirm through their firsthand experience of these staged scenes the taxonomies of religious and cultural hierarchy upon which the scientific racism of the nineteenth century rested.[38] In addition to positing the racial inferiority of the peoples on display, these exhibitions often reinforced western gender norms, affirming the supposed self-sufficient superiority of White Christian men and the freedom and honor afforded to White Christian women, in contrast to the degradation of Asian and African women.[39] Through the exhibitions' living displays of difference, Protestant onlookers who were already used to colonial and missionary images depicting the pitiful status of non-western women became, in Putnam's words, active "participants in a parade of radical alterity." They were invited to gaze voyeuristically upon "the exotic other," reinforcing "the power differential across the divide between spectator and spectacle,"[40] between civilized and uncivilized, and between Christian women and Muslim women.

Islam and Muslim cultures were not the only focus at such international exhibitions, of course; but considering the expanding western presence in North Africa and Asia by the late nineteenth century, Muslim societies were prominently featured at these world's fairs. Audiences in Chicago in 1893 flocked to an exhibit called "The Street of Cairo," the largest money-making venue of the entire fair. Complete with belly dancers, twenty-six edifices representing premodern Cairo, and Arab vendors, the exhibit transported visitors to an imagined world of Islam. This effect would not have been achieved without Middle Easterners dressed up in what purported to be their own native Egyptian costumes.[41] Some of these costumed performers were Muslims, but as Linda Jacobs noted, many Syrian and Lebanese Christian migrants came to the United States for the world's fair and worked in Egyptian, Turkish, and Persian venues, where American visitors would likely have understood them to be Muslims. Some Arab Christians who settled in the United States after the fair capitalized on this market for theatrical display of Islam and voyeuristic experiences of "the Orient" through careers in belly dancing, acrobatics, and simulations of Muslim prayers, sword fights, or weddings on stage.[42] The situation for Syro-Lebanese vendors and performers was distinct because their homelands remained under Ottoman rule and were not colonized by European powers, but the choice to travel to the world's fair and—for some—to reside in the United States thereafter points to the agency of Middle Eastern actors in these venues who used the exhibitions as an opportunity for financial gain and to see the world.

Although "exotic" aspects of Islamic cultures drew crowds in late nineteenth- and early twentieth-century America, when it came to displays of explicitly religious artifacts, more attention was drawn by polytheistic traditions that diverged far more from Christianity than did Islam.

Islam on Display in Missionary Exhibits and Museums

Objects that missionaries brought or sent back to Europe and North America found their way into national expositions, public museums, and private touring collections. After considering ways in which Protestant missionary societies adapted the performative practices of colonial exhibitions, this section provides background on the first Protestant missionary museum and others that followed in its wake. It then examines two collections aimed at Protestant viewers in the United States, which missionaries established for educational and fundraising purposes.

Mission Society Expositions

Some mission societies put on their own displays at international fairs, like the Exposition Universelle in Paris in 1867, which included a pavilion of Protestant evangelical missions that many of the exposition's eleven million visitors viewed during the six months of the fair.[43] Individual missionaries also spoke at events held in conjunction with great exhibitions, like the World's Parliament of Religions during the 1893 Chicago World's Fair.[44] Building on the world's fair model and on practices of displaying curiosities during annual meetings and at ecumenical missionary gatherings, in the early twentieth century Anglo-Protestant missionaries also initiated their own version of world's fairs for the public. The first took place in Britain in 1908, and American mission societies soon followed suit. In her study of American missionary expositions in the early twentieth century, Erin Hasinoff described the first such event in the United States in 1911, a gathering known as The World in Boston, as the culmination of a "national interest" in missionary objects at a time when Americans were adopting new patterns of consumption and relying "heavily on commodities to know and define themselves and structure and give meaning to their lives."[45] The material things displayed at missionary exhibitions, therefore, shaped the way in which early twentieth-century American Protestants perceived Islam but also how they understood themselves, viewed their relationship to the world, and practiced their faith.

The exhibits featuring Muslim societies at The World in Boston are instructive. These included Persian, Turkish, Egyptian, and Arabian "courts" as well as scenes from Palestine in the exposition's "Mohammedan Lands" exhibit—all of which claimed to give the audience a firsthand experience of life in these contexts, peppered with information about the need to support missions. As visitors toured the exhibits, they heard missionaries who worked in these regions inform them about Islam as the "faith most strongly opposed to Christianity."[46] The exposition guidebook explained:

> As the visitor passes from this part of the Exposition, he will carry with him an impression of the great need of the Moslem world for that which Christianity and the Christian civilization has to offer. May he now and in the days to come offer this prayer of intercession: "O God, to whom the Moslem world bows in homage five times daily, look in mercy upon its peoples, and reveal to them Thy Christ."[47]

Like the great exhibitions, the scenes at The World in Boston were peopled with costumed attendants whose presence added to the audience's sense of being on a world tour. Unlike the colonial expositions, however, the parts were played primarily by American actors, including missionaries and stewards who volunteered to assist particular mission societies with their assigned scenes.[48] The Islamic lands exhibits included a Bedouin tent, around which American performers acted out the daily lives of the Arab Muslims of the desert.

Although the guidebook's commentary on this and other Muslim scenes in Boston suggested that the exposition focused less on critiquing Islam than on advocating for missions, the descriptions of daily life echoed familiar tropes about Muslim gender norms. The commentary described Bedouin women as having to make, set up, take down, and move the tents while their husbands "lie down to smoke," signaling that these Muslim wives were essentially servants, similar to statements in the Cairo and Lucknow conference volumes explored in Chapter 3. The guidebook mentioned as well that a separate apartment within each tent was intended for the seclusion of women.[49] It also commented on the status of women in upper-class and peasant homes in Turkey, the former including a "harem, or woman's apartment, which no male guest ever enters," while the latter had only one room for the entire family.[50] Such references signal the common sexual critique of Muslim men engaging in polygyny, while also emphasizing the passive and oppressed status of women imprisoned in female-only spaces. The guidebook's comments on Bedouins also repeated another prevalent trope, that Muslim women labored in public while their lazy husbands contributed little to the family's welfare—a statement that contradicted the book's other claims about Muslim women being confined to the home.

Although these representations implied that the situations for Muslim women varied according to social context, Muslims' own understandings of women's seclusion and ways of confronting patriarchy were absent from such missionary material, as were understandings of the harem as a place of protection and honor.[51] In addition, while the exhibits at The World in Boston showcased a diversity of Muslim cultures within the Middle East, they also transmitted misleading information, reflecting tendencies to lump all Muslims together and to render racial as well as religious judgments against them. Under the guidebook's description of the Turkish court, for example, appeared an image of two men in Bedouin attire, labeled "Arab types."[52] In addition to racial typecasting, the image blurred the ethnic, cultural, and linguistic differences between Turks and Arabs, as well as obscuring the existence of Arab Christians. Thus, despite missionary exhibitions' more explicitly religious motivations in comparison to imperial exhibitions, these performative displays of Islam revealed Protestant missionaries' enmeshment in the colonialist mentality of this high imperial period.

Missionary Museums

Also reflecting missionaries' links to the colonial and scholarly networks that Orzech described, numerous missionaries collected cultural objects and religious artifacts from the fields in which they worked[53]; and some mission societies also created their own museums. That was the case for the first missionary museum, which the London Missionary Society (LMS) founded in England in 1814. From the very beginning, the collection was intended for "public inspection."[54] The mission transferred its Pacific Island collections to the British Museum in the early 1890s, and when the LMS museum closed in 1910, some of the artifacts went to the Pitt Rivers Museum in Oxford.[55] Although at its closing the mission indicated a waning of public interest in the collection, missionary museums continued elsewhere into the mid-twentieth century.

Chris Wingfield described the LMS museum as driven by the "accumulation of 'curiosities' brought to Europe for display, including specimens of natural history, items of local dress, and examples of local religious and superstitious practices."[56] Besides attracting public attention to the missionary endeavor through its inclusion on tourist maps and guidebooks of London, LMS missionaries and affiliates visited the museum during the mission's annual meetings to inspect what they saw as false gods, as a way to bolster confidence in the urgency and successes of missionary endeavors.[57] Many of the items displayed were deities and "rejected idols" that converts to Protestantism had relinquished, and therefore, as Rosemary Seton emphasized, "The presence of these 'trophies of Christianity' proclaimed the victorious nature of successful Protestant missionary activity."[58] Early on, the LMS featured items of natural history, such as handmade baskets, clothing, a stuffed zebra, and a rhinoceros head, with captions relating such animals of Africa to biblical references.[59] However, as it became dominated toward the end of the nineteenth century by "discarded symbols of tribal and animist beliefs" in the Pacific Islands, Africa, India, and China, the collection might also be considered the first comparative religion museum. Thus, the LMS performed Protestant supremacy through displaying and comparing religions, including Christianity, in an increasingly common practice that other mission societies followed.[60] Nevertheless, missionaries had other reasons for collecting such objects beyond Protestant theological pronouncements and fundraising, including educational goals, political motives, and "romantic interest in salvaging material that was rapidly disappearing due to the increasing use of imported goods and changing local practices."[61] As has often been the case in the history of Protestant–Muslim encounters, humanistic aims for learning were at play alongside other impulses, none of which were mutually exclusive.

After the LMS museum closed, in Britain the offices of the CMS and the Methodist Missionary Society both housed significant displays of objects that missionaries had collected, and dozens of missionary museums were established in German-speaking regions of Europe.[62] "Missionary curiosities" also formed the basis for similar collections of the Board of Foreign Missions of the Presbyterian Church in New York and the ABCFM in Boston, among other prominent mission organizations in North America.[63] Still other museums were established in the mission fields themselves, aiming to support the faith of recent converts and to attract new ones.[64] Their systematization, classification, and display in glass boxes drained what missionaries saw as idols "of their natural and supernatural agencies and enchantments and, once purified, resituated [them] for modern contemplation and aesthetic inspiration."[65] Protestants thus put notions of empire and control to use in their own museum collections but with more theological framing than usually found in anthropological museums. Like anthropologists, comparative religion scholars, and great exhibition organizers, missionaries provided comparisons that typically reinforced the superiority of western Christianity in contrast to the falsehood of other traditions. Following the pattern of the anthropological museums in Europe and the United States, these missionary museums moved beyond mere colonial collections of "curiosities" with an intent to preserve, classify, study, and educate.[66]

Although missionary collections proliferated with "heathen" idols and fetishes, tending to emphasize cultures and religions more extremely different from Christianity than Islam, missionaries in Islamic societies collected material culture too; and some of those items made their way into permanent exhibits and Protestant museums. Samuel Zwemer contributed to one such museum at the library of Princeton Theological Seminary, called the Museum of Religion and Missions. He curated the collection after taking a position at the seminary as professor of history of religions. Similar to the way in which Zwemer had brought together networks of Protestant missionaries working across multiple Muslim societies, he capitalized on these global missionary ties to display a broader view of world religions for seminary students who might one day enter the mission field. The museum aimed, in Zwemer's words, at "Visualizing Non-Christian Religions." Its opening was announced in newspapers across the United States in August 1931: "A missionary museum has been opened at Princeton Theological Seminary. The museum is intended rather for study than for exhibition purposes."[67] The museum remained until the 1950s.

As historian of religion Richard Fox Young explained in his study of this library museum, visitors could see "alterity being constructed, theologically" behind the museum glass that encased objects from religious communities that Zwemer believed were "dying and disintegrating."[68] Despite Zwemer's focus on Islam as a missionary and scholar, this seminary museum was not devoted to showcasing only the religious artifacts of Islam. Indeed, the "Pantheon of Strange Gods" exhibit was the most striking, Young noted; and despite the museum's emphasis on academic study, it likely attracted visitors in the same way that the idols and fetishes of so-called pagan religions drew popular attention to the LMS museum. Nevertheless, the Museum of Religion and Missions also featured Islamic material in its collection of rosaries, or prayer beads, which Muslims use to remember God's attributes. The ninety-nine attributes or names for God in Islam resemble the ways Christians understand God. Yet although Zwemer noted the beauty of these rosaries and affirmed Muslims' devotional practices, his criticisms of Islam persisted over the years.[69] Zwemer's collection also displayed objects of Islamic culture that had no apparent religious relevance but which suggested the diversity of Muslim societies and, for discerning observers, might have disrupted notions of Islam as a monolithic force: dozens of shoes and other footwear from different Muslim societies.[70]

Hartford Seminary not only educated many missionaries for work among Muslims but also operated a library museum by the late 1800s. Eventually disbanded in the 1960s, Hartford's museum similarly featured many "missionary curiosities" and "a great variety [of articles] illustrating the customs and worship of races among which missions have been established."[71] As a Congregational institution, Hartford Seminary had inherited the ABCFM collection from the mission board headquarters in Boston. The original collection had been created through the contributions of missionaries and was intended to reflect the various fields within which Congregationalists worked, including parts of the Middle East. Despite the distinctive focus on the work of missions and the accompanying theological judgments that upheld the superiority of (Protestant) Christianity, these mission institutions shared with other museums of the time a belief in scientifically provable racial hierarchies and the view that within such hierarchies, inferior cultures and religions went alongside the degraded status of women.

Missionaries' Personal Collections

Beyond such permanent institutional exhibits, some missionaries sent objects of material culture home for display or sale at fundraising fairs and church bazaars, offering mission supporters tactile ways to learn about and contribute to their work. Like international expositions, as Hasinoff explained, for Protestant audiences these events were a form of religious entertainment, "intended to deepen Christian identity by charitable transfers of wealth."[72] The American Quaker missionary Eva Marshall Totah sent packages of Palestinian needlework to her mother to sell in church circles, and mission auxiliaries often raised funds for missions by selling "curios" or holding educational events and exhibitions that showcased objects of interest from the mission field.[73] Other missionaries like Kate Hill (1873–1960), an American in the Punjab, took their own personal collections on the road during furloughs. Hill amassed many tangible objects from that field during her work with the Women's Board of the United Presbyterian Church of North America from 1896 to 1943. Hill was first stationed in Sialkot (present-day Pakistan but known at that time as India) and worked in the area as an evangelist and administrator. From 1927 until her retirement, she superintended mission hospitals in Sargodha and Sialkot.[74] Her collection presented Islamic material alongside images and objects of Hindus and Buddhists in South Asia.

On her first furlough of 1904 to 1906, Hill returned to her home church, the United Presbyterian Church in Newtown, Iowa. There, she set up a display across the front of the sanctuary featuring embroidered fabrics, items of clothing and jewelry, images of plant and animal life, a porcelain tea set, and other objects of interest, some of which were arranged within glass cases. A banner she stretched across the front of the sanctuary read: "India hath no sorrow Christ's message cannot heal" (Figure 6.1).[75] Local newspaper clippings attested to the large number of churches Hill visited on her fundraising tour through Iowa, Kansas, Nebraska, and Missouri, where she

Figure 6.1 United Presbyterian Church sanctuary, Newtown, Iowa (1905)
Source: Kate Alexander Hill Papers (Record Group 53, box 2, folder 12), Presbyterian Historical Society, Philadelphia.

gave nearly one hundred addresses and showed what the papers marketed variously as an exhibit of "India Curios" or a "rare collection of interesting relics from the heathen lands." A free-will offering for missions was collected at each location. In Newtown, events at the church catered to different segments of the population, with a morning meeting for children, an afternoon of "India Tea served—especially for ladies," and an evening address by Hill and another returned missionary, Laurella Dickson, during which several "young people of the church were dressed in native costume and seated on the stage."[76]

Newspaper coverage of these events explained that the "curios and relics exhibited by Miss Hill from India" were intended to "make the people of India, more of a reality, to those of her native country ... and through them to show the needs of this people of the land, to which she expects soon to return."[77] A report on Hill's visit to another church disclosed that the effect was not merely educational or inspirational but that her address "on the wonderful work God is doing in heathen India" was given "in such a clear and vivid way so as to make you almost feel you were in India." Hill invited her audience to come with her on her journey "from her home in Newton, Iowa, to New York, to Glasgow, Liverpool, down through the Mediterranean Sea and the Suez Canal, through the Indian Ocean to India."[78] Thus, Hill's lectures, when added to the material objects arrayed in the church and the young people dressed in local clothing brought specimens of Indian life to view, as in a museum, and endeavored to transport the audience to the mission field itself, like the immersive facades erected at the great international exhibitions.

Hill's collection expanded during her decades of service, and by her retirement in the 1940s it had become a true cabinet of curiosities that suggested her understanding of South Asian culture and religious traditions. It featured, among other items, photos of Buddhist statues in the Ajanta Caves of central India, a doll representing a Punjabi woman with a long scarf wound around her head, jars displaying "Herbs of the Punjab," figurines of oxen and elephants, and a small collection of Muslim rosaries (less grand than Zwemer's), accompanied by a note explaining that the beads were "99 in number for each of the 99 names of God" (Figure 6.2).[79] Also on display was a historical record of British colonialism, a "pass to the fort at Agra," India, issued to missionary Robert Fullerton (1821–1865) during what the caption called "the Sepoy Rebellion, 1857," a reference to the historic Indian uprising that Britain suppressed, thereafter consolidating its rule of India. Hill's

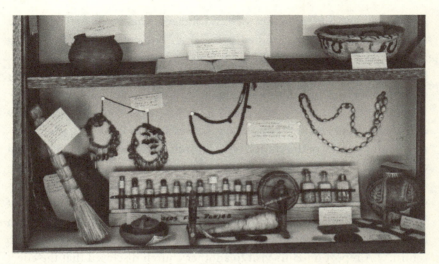

Figure 6.2 Islamic prayer beads on display (circa 1943–1944)
Source: Kate Alexander Hill Papers (Record Group 53, box 1, folder 26), Presbyterian Historical Society, Philadelphia.

exhibit explained that this pass "meant safety to him and other missionaries of Agra and Mainpuri stations, together with 300 Indian Christians."[80] The story of the revolt told on another shelf of the display represented the violence as not only anti-British but also anti-Christian and particularly incited by Muslims—similar to the way other missionaries of the late nineteenth century portrayed these events in religious terms. We might recall that when recounting this uprising another American missionary woman, Emily Humphrey, blamed Muslims for provoking Hindus to participate.[81] The large cross, a clear focal point in the center of the display, may have reinforced in the audience's minds a view of Christian supremacy over other religions, similar to the messages conveyed in Princeton Theological Seminary's museum.

Although Hill worked among Punjabi Muslims and Samuel Zwemer focused exclusively on Islam as a missionary in Arabia and Egypt, Islamic material culture did not feature prominently in either collection. Instead, like the museums of the LMS and ABCFM, Zwemer and Hill's collections were an amalgamation of religions and cultures in which the most exotic objects were the idols and strange gods desacralized within the Protestants' glass boxes. The materiality of Islam in missionary exhibits—represented through devotional items like rosaries and the prayer manuals that Constance Padwick (1886–1968), an English missionary of the CMS in Egypt, amassed to study Muslim practices[82]—actually shone light on the similarities between Christianity and Islam in contrast to the polytheistic traditions on display.

Through such exhibitions, missionaries used material objects to teach about other faiths and to demonstrate visually their differences from Christianity. The display of Islamic culture in missionary museums classified Islam as one of the world's religions, which irenic missionary thinkers like Padwick and her CMS colleague Temple Gairdner believed were moving toward but had not yet attained the ultimate truth of Christianity.[83] Other missionaries' virulent critiques of Muslim culture and gender norms were muted in the museum context, although Hill's reference to the Sepoy Rebellion suggested typical tropes about gender and violence.

I turn now to missionaries' performative use of Islamic costumes, which conveyed messages about Islam not through museum displays but on their own bodies.

Missionaries' Costumed Performances

In the photographs attached to mission reports or disseminated on missionary postcards, clothing was often a marker of "East–West" distinctions and of the drastic difference missionaries saw between non-Christian "natives" and converted Christians.[84] Missionaries' relationships to nonwestern clothing varied between mission societies and across regions of the world. In some colonial contexts, they imposed western dress norms on converts, while local Christians sometimes embraced and sometimes resisted such norms.[85] In other contexts, missionaries dressed themselves in the clothing of their host society as a sort of "spiritual passport" to move freely among the local people,[86] or they did so to express appreciation for the cultures within which they worked.[87] To educate their constituents, missionaries also donned "native" garb for photos, like the one that the aforementioned Kate Hill sent home around 1941 of herself in a sari given to her by the Indian nurses with whom she worked.[88] And missionaries dressed up during presentations for their supporters, appropriating the type of clothing that might be worn by those in their mission field, as occurred at The World in Boston and other missionary expositions.

Protestant missionaries in the nineteenth- and early twentieth-century Middle East rarely adopted local clothing styles for everyday wear, however. Rather, by wearing western attire they emphasized their difference from the peoples among whom they worked. Photos of missionaries and Middle

Easterners side by side reified such distinctions.[89] In Islamic societies where elite women commonly wore veils, missionaries described these women as encumbered by unnecessary garments and critiqued what they saw as Islamic cultural traditions that led Arab Christian women to cover their heads too.[90] Yet despite such critiques and their preference for western attire, many missionaries in the Middle East appeared in photographs wearing "native" costume.

In this section, I examine such staged portraits of Protestant missionaries in Islamic garb and snapshots of their live costumed performances. I then take a closer look at one such missionary in the Reformed Church of America's Arabian Mission, Dr. Eleanor Calverley, who dressed up for photographs in the attire of Kuwaiti Muslim women.

From Staged Portraits to Costumed Performances

As missionaries in Islamic contexts decided what their constituents at home should see and understand about Islam, for those who shared photographs of themselves in Islamic garb the use of visual images became intimately performative. One such photograph pictured the Dutch Reformed minister Cornelius Van Alen Van Dyck (1818–1895), a medical missionary and Bible translator for the American Syria Mission, in Syrian attire. Van Dyck sits behind a desk wearing a dark robe and tight-fitting embroidered hat, with pen, paper, and a microscope indicating his role as a doctor and scientist (Figure 6.3). In a second photo, Van Dyck wears similar Syrian attire while lounging on a garden terrace and smoking a water pipe.[91] Although these two photographs were used to eulogize Van Dyck after his death, their original purpose is unclear. Did the photos suggest the same type of orientalization and gendered pageantry of upper-class Americans in the nineteenth century who posed for portraits in "Oriental" costume? According to Timothy Marr, those Americans appropriated such garb as "a fresh cultural resource for the promotion of their own cosmopolitan power."[92]

The portraits of Van Dyck resemble somewhat the staged photos of British Anglican missionaries in "Eastern" garments that the London Jews Society (LJS) distributed on postcards during the same late nineteenth-century period. Samuel Schor (1859–1933), a missionary in Palestine, appeared on one postcard wearing a robe and turban and holding pen and paper. The caption read: "Rev. S. Schor as Eastern Scribe." A similar LJS photograph showed Rev. F. B. Mellor "in Costume of an Eastern Scribe" (Figures 6.4 and 6.5).

Figure 6.3 Dr. Cornelius Van Dyck (1818–1895)
Source: Henry Harris Jessup Papers (Record Group 117, box 10, folder 50), Special Collections, Yale Divinity School Library.

Figure 6.4 "Rev. S. Schor as Eastern Scribe"
Source: Missionary Postcard Collection (RG 101, box 87, item 102), Special Collections, Yale Divinity School Library.

216 RE-INVENTING ISLAM

REV. F. B. MELLOR IN COSTUME OF AN EASTERN SCRIBE.

Figure 6.5 "Rev. F. B. Mellor in Costume of Eastern Scribe"
Source: Missionary Postcard Collection (RG 101, box 87, item 95), Special Collections, Yale Divinity School Library.

The photo of Van Dyck at his desk may have functioned similarly to bolster the missionary's masculine and intellectual authority through a romantic appropriation of eastern wisdom. Schor used his portrait to raise funds for the LJS through the society's traveling "Palestine Exhibition" that he oversaw in Britain, which featured missionaries and mission supporters in attire from the region. Schor's photo and other staged pictures of Britons in what the LJS presented as Middle Eastern dress were among the hundreds of millions of picture postcards Europeans collected annually.[93] The Palestine Exhibition postcards also featured Schor's wife dressed as an Arab woman, another woman in front of a Bedouin tent, and a "group of natives" seated on a stage next to a tent. The biblical Orientalism of the LJS was also portrayed in postcard scenes showing individuals dressed in the same purportedly Palestinian garb reenacting the women disciples' visit to Jesus' tomb on Easter Sunday.[94]

Countless other missionaries similarly played "dress up" for American and European audiences, as Protestant archives attest. For instance, *The Oakland Post Enquirer* in 1927 featured photos of six American Congregationalist missionaries who were, as the newspaper put it, "All dressed up!" (Figure 6.6). On furlough from Turkey, these missionary women and men wore generic Middle Eastern attire during their public lectures intending to introduce the mission context. They put on a performance for American audiences that signaled stark differences between American Protestant dress norms and those for Turkish Muslims (and, considering the prevalent critique of Muslim women's head coverings, implied differing norms for male and female behavior). While the women displayed a variety of scarves and hats, some of them similar to images of Turkish women during the period, the two men in the photos wore long robes and headdresses, not typically worn by Turkish men in the 1920s.[95] The men adopted the more recognizable headdress of Bedouin Arabs rather than the fez that had been standard fare since the late nineteenth century for many men in Turkey, who typically wore turbans before that time.[96] Samuel Zwemer, for instance, wore comparable Bedouin attire in a photo representing his own mission field in the Arabian Gulf (Figure 6.7). American missionaries William and Elizabeth Freidinger, who began working in Lebanon in the early twentieth century, gave a similarly misleading missionary performance when they spoke to mission supporters clothed in garments they purchased not in Lebanon but hundreds of miles away and in a different cultural context in Mardin, Turkey (Figure 6.8).

Figure 6.6 Congregationalist missionaries in Middle Eastern attire (1927)
Source: "All Dressed Up," *Oakland Post Enquirer* (October 10, 1927): 1, in the Blake and Goodsell Family Papers (MS 4922, box 12), Congregational Library & Archives, Boston, MA. Pictured left to right: Dr. R. C. Waddell, Mrs. Ralph T. Fisher, Dr. Robert Brown, Mrs. E. C. Blake, Mrs. F. T. Watson and Mrs. Louis Bar.

Figure 6.7 Samuel M. Zwemer in Bedouin headdress (circa 1890s)
Source: Samuel M. Zwemer papers (W88-0128, box 1), Western Theological Seminary Collection at the Joint Archives of Holland. Photo used by permission.

Figure 6.8 William and Elizabeth Freidinger in Turkish attire
Source: Margaret Freidinger Kraushaar, *The Mulberry Juice Dress* (Santa Barbara: Fithian Press, 1996), 115.

In this case, William wore the traditional turban one might have expected one of the aforementioned Congregationalist missionaries to wear.

Such gendered pageantry also appeared in a travel scrapbook of two single Congregationalist missionary women working in Turkey in 1931, Gladys Perry and Dorothy Blatter, the children's book author. In several scrapbook photos documenting their vacation through Turkey, both young women wore black veils and robes. The handwritten subtitles on each photo described their changing appearances (Figures 6.9, 6.10, and 6.11): "A Turkish Haneem" (Blatter with head covered and bare face), "Almost lost the vision" (both women with veils up to their eyes), and "Submerged" (both with faces fully veiled).[97] The Turkish term *hanim* is an elite title for a woman of royal or aristocratic birth, the kind of women whom Perry and Blatter knew might be likely to cover their heads and faces entirely in public, as opposed to lower-class and rural Muslim women who often did physical labor outside the home and for whom face veils and gendered seclusion were impractical and less common. Similarly, a young missionary woman of the Algiers Mission Band who worked along with Lilias Trotter was photographed dressed up like an elite Algerian during a vacation in 1928 with family in the region. The caption next to the photo in her scrapbook read: "Interior of

Figure 6.9 Dorothy Blatter as "A Turkish Haneem" (1931)
Source: Gladys Perry album, 1931, Iain Campbell Papers (Record Group 0043, subgroup 2, series 2, A-27), Congregational Library & Archives, Boston, MA.

220 RE-INVENTING ISLAM

Figure 6.10 Dorothy Blatter and Gladys Perry, "Almost Lost the View" (1931)
Source: Gladys Perry album, 1931, Iain Campbell Papers (Record Group 0043, subgroup 2, series 2, A-27), Congregational Library & Archives, Boston, MA.

Figure 6.11 Dorothy Blatter and Gladys Perry, "Submerged" (1931)
Source: Gladys Perry album, 1931, Iain Campbell Papers (Record Group 0043, subgroup 2, series 2, A-27), Congregational Library & Archives, Boston, MA.

Figure 6.12 Eva Marshall in Bedouin costume (1927)
Source: Khalil A. Totah and Eva Marshall Totah Papers (MC 1210, box 4, folder 11), Quaker & Special Collections, Haverford College, Haverford, PA.

wealthy Arab's house."[98] Around that same time, in Palestine, Eva Marshall posed for several photographs dressed in Arab women's garb. In one she appeared as a Bedouin woman wearing black, and another showed her as a woman from Ramallah, the town where she worked, with a basket on her head and carrying a water jug (Figures 6.12 and 6.13).[99] Eva's photo album a decade later, after her marriage to Khalil Totah, showed images of two of her children similarly dressed in Palestinian garb during the Totahs' furlough in the United States during 1937–1938. Sibyl Totah wore the distinctive Ramallah dress, the same embroidery as Eva wore in 1927, while her brother Nabil wore the robes of the fellahin (peasants).[100]

These snapshots of missionaries literally putting themselves (or their children) into the shoes of Muslim men and women could possibly be interpreted as a move toward deeper understanding. Certainly, missionaries developed meaningful mutual relationships with Muslims, and they had insights to share that other Americans and Europeans would not otherwise have encountered. These insights were often based on the relationships and

222 RE-INVENTING ISLAM

Figure 6.13 Eva Marshall in Ramallah costume (1927)
Source: Khalil A. Totah and Eva Marshall Totah Papers (MC 1210, box 4, folder 11), Quaker & Special Collections, Haverford College, Haverford, PA.

trust they had built with local residents over decades. Yet the scrapbook photos and captions also conveyed that Muslim women's lives were mysterious, exotic, and encumbered—opposite from the ways missionary women presented their own lives, as independent religious workers who were free to don western or Middle Eastern clothing as they saw fit.

Of these various costumed missionaries, only Cornelius Van Dyck was known to wear Middle Eastern attire on a regular basis, and not only for the benefit of a viewing audience. Mission records signal that his reasons for dressing this way differed from those of other missionaries who did so for fundraising purposes, to bolster their own authority, to teach supporters about Middle Eastern customs, or to play the tourist on vacation. Van Dyck's American and Syrian contemporaries alike noted that the missionary doctor felt more fully at home in Syria than some other missionaries did.[101]

Van Dyck was the most accomplished member of the American mission when it came to the Arabic language. He formed lifelong friendships with Syrians and was known to support independent Arab educational and literary endeavors, even when it put him at odds with his missionary colleagues.[102] The two photos of Van Dyck, circulated for both American and Syrian audiences after his death, reflected his appreciative adoption of Syrian attire and his decision to remain part of Syrian society after retirement instead of returning to the United States.[103] Van Dyck gave no indication that he adopted indigenous garb as a strategy to introduce the gospel to Syrians. Rather, he felt an affinity with the people of Syria, and his attire reflected his sense of personal transformation after decades of life there. Yet other missionaries who did not adopt local clothing for daily wear likewise left the mission field profoundly changed by the experience, and often deeply appreciative of it.

Didactic Dress-Up

When she moved to Kuwait in 1911, at a time when few western women lived in the region, the missionary doctor Eleanor Taylor Calverley (1887–1968) faced the decision of what to wear in public. Eleanor, a Methodist who married the Presbyterian minister Edwin Calverley and joined him in working for the Arabian Mission, determined neither to veil her face nor to dress in the typical robes of Kuwaiti women. She explained that such an outfit would encumber her medical work in the clinic, and she preferred not to wear it in the street either. Calverley noted that her uncovered face and style of dress (including a white cork helmet for outdoor excursions) seemed strange to the local women at first. Nevertheless, she believed it would be "better to help the people of Kuwait become acquainted with customs associated with the freedom of women."[104] Thus, Calverley conveyed the view, still held by many Americans today, that western clothing signals the freedom of women while Islamic dress signals oppression.

In light of Calverley's decision to wear clothing that marked her as different, I consider here the photo shoots that she undertook wearing Kuwaiti attire. She posed for these photos while on furlough in 1914–1915 and in 1922. These professional shots of Calverley alone and others of the doctor with her daughters were preserved in family albums, reproduced in pamphlets for mission supporters, and printed in American newspapers. One photograph taken during the first furlough shows Calverley and her oldest daughter, Grace, then only a toddler (b. 1912; Figure 6.14). In a second photo,

224 RE-INVENTING ISLAM

Figure 6.14 Dr. Eleanor Taylor Calverley and Grace Calverley in Kuwaiti dress (circa 1914–1915)
Source: Edwin E. Calverley Papers (box 373), Hartford International University Archives, Hartford, CT.

from 1922, Calverley appears next to Grace and her two younger daughters, Elizabeth and Eleanor, in a photography studio. In each photo, the mother and daughters wear billowing robes and long head coverings (with faces unveiled). In a third photograph taken outdoors during the 1922 furlough,

PERFORMATIVE RE-INVENTIONS 225

Figure 6.15 Dr. Eleanor Taylor Calverley, Rev. Edwin Calverley, and daughters Grace, Elizabeth, and Eleanor (1922)
Source: Edwin E. Calverley Papers (box 373), Hartford International University Archives, Hartford, CT.

Edwin Calverley stands in a suit and tie next to his wife and daughters, who wear the same Kuwaiti attire as in the studio photograph (Figure 6.15).[105]

The intention to impersonate Muslims is unclear in the photos of Van Dyck or Totah, who lived among Arab Christians in Lebanon and Palestine, even though the images likely reinforced viewers' Orientalist notions about Middle Easterners. There can be no doubt, however, that the Congregationalist missionaries intended to portray Turkish Muslims or that the Calverleys' clothing was meant to convey the attire of Muslim women and girls in the Arabian Gulf. In Turkey the Christian community was largely Armenian and Greek, not Turkish; and in Arabia, unlike in Syria and Palestine, an indigenous Middle Eastern Christian community did not exist when American missionaries arrived, and it grew very slowly thereafter. American Christians had long understood that Muslim women and girls in these regions especially needed saving, physically and spiritually. The photo with Edwin in his usual western attire put these gendered notions in stark perspective, while the appearance of young girls laden with thick fabrics and head coverings emphasized how different the lives of Kuwaiti Muslims must be. The figure of Eleanor, a pioneering American woman doctor in the early twentieth century, covered head to toe, reinforced the need for the very work she endeavored to do in the region.

Indeed, this was the interpretation that one 1915 newspaper announcement offered alongside the first photo of Eleanor and Grace. The photo caption read, "Dr. Eleanor Calverley and Daughter in Arab Costumes," and the accompanying article announced Calverley's plans to speak at a Methodist church in Harrisburg, Pennsylvania. The article related that Calverley would address "how Muslims treat their women," explaining:

> She will tell her audience to-night that the Mohammedan religion teaches that a woman has no soul. A Moslem may have four wives and as many concubines as he desires and can afford. He may buy, capture or steal them, and the desires and wishes of the women themselves do not enter into the bargain. A Moslem woman must never show her face to anyone but her husband and they are kept in homes which have no windows facing the street. The jealousies and contentions among the women are a matter of course. The women are not taught to read, as it would make them still more troublesome. Girl babies are never welcomed. Dr. Calverley will tell of the curiosity of the Arabian women to see her daughter, Grace, a girl baby, who was welcome to both father and mother.[106]

The announcement's tone matched the sort of information which Calverley provided to her supporters in a newspaper article she wrote four years later, titled "An Arabian Harem." She concluded with the following pronouncement: "Mentally, physically, spiritually, the Arab woman has never had a chance."[107]

Statements like this aimed to move American readers with sympathy and to encourage their financial support for mission work among Muslim women, while marking the latter as religious—and often racial—others. Calverley's article and the 1915 church announcement both contributed to the sort of missionary discourse that rendered Muslim women as passive victims who needed western Christians to save them. As Lila Abu-Lughod indicated, this discourse persists in a modified, secularized form today.[108] Nevertheless, a closer examination of Calverley's writings about Muslim women and their attire reveals lessons that could counter contemporary American Christian fear and disparagement of Muslims.

Eleanor Calverley's 1958 autobiography *My Arabian Days and Nights* helps to contextualize the photos she took during her furloughs and to complexify her own reasons for donning Muslim garb then, even though she decided not to wear it publicly in Kuwait. Calverley's memoir reveals, first, that she was pictured in the attire of the well-to-do Kuwaiti women whom she came to know while visiting their homes and treating them in her clinic. The photographs thus legitimated her authority and expertise as one of very few westerners who had spent considerable time among Gulf women. Second, when Calverley dressed up for the photos, she reenacted her experience of dressing up in the homes of Kuwaiti friends, who themselves invited her to try on their clothing and jewelry when she visited.[109] Perhaps this was the Kuwaiti women's way of teaching Calverley what they felt was appropriate feminine attire in their society, similar to the way that the missionary doctor hoped her western clothing would expose them to ideas about freedom, as she perceived it.

Third, on at least one occasion, the missionary doctor appeared in public in Kuwait in Muslim garments and a full-face veil when a friend lent her clothing to wear to wedding festivities. That way, her companion suggested, Calverley would be appropriately dressed in "Arab clothes" and could "be inconspicuous among the veiled women waiting in the courtyard."[110] Calverley accepted this invitation without objections, showing her willingness to be guided by her Arab Muslim companions—a willingness that was not clear in her early news articles.

Fourth, rather than picturing herself fully veiled in street attire, through her photo shoot Calverley enabled her American supporters to experience what it was like to treat patients in the women's clinic or to enter the harem, parallel to the ways both male and female visitors at great exhibitions gained unrestricted access to Muslim women's spaces. In the clinic and homes of Kuwait, away from the watching eyes of men, the women removed the veils from their faces and took off their dark over-garments (or *abayas*), revealing what Calverley described as "gaily colored silken *thobes*." These were ankle-length robes worn with head coverings that framed their faces and, she said, "fell gracefully from the crown of the head to henna-stained bare feet."[111] Although Calverley lamented seeing Muslim women on the streets "shrouded in black" and hoped that Kuwaiti women would one day have the "freedom to walk on the streets unveiled,"[112] she found beauty in Arab women's harem attire. Therefore, for American viewers, she humanized Kuwaiti women by dressing in their indoor garments with her face unveiled even as she also insisted that Arab society needed changing.

This points to the didactic function of Calverley's photos and lectures, which informed Americans about the lives and societies of Muslims whom they would never meet. Calverley's intention to teach readers about Arab Muslim culture is also apparent throughout the autobiography, which offers basic information about Islamic beliefs and practices without issuing religious judgments. Readers of *My Arabian Days and Nights* encountered a more nuanced and appreciative understanding of Arab culture, Islam, and Muslim women's experiences than was offered in Calverley's photos alone or in her 1919 article. This shift in Calverley's public presentations of information about Islam mirrored a change in her personal understanding of Muslim life gained over the decades she lived in Kuwait. Her writings for mission supporters in the early twentieth century remained within the bounds of her audience's cultural expectations—like Fletcher explained performances typically do[113]—as she mimicked other Protestant missionaries' critiques of Islam from that time. Yet her wearing of Kuwaiti attire also helped viewers see the woman beneath the veil just as Calverley encountered individual Muslim women in her clinic. After the end of her missionary career, without the need to fundraise or justify her work in Kuwait, Calverley's memoir went even further to promote her readers' understanding of Islam and Kuwaiti culture, a shift toward cultural appreciation and even solidarity that other missionaries in the Middle East also upheld in the mid-twentieth century.

Conclusion

Katheryn Gin Lum has argued that "the heathen world has been constitutive, not incidental, to White Protestant Americans' sense of history and collective identity."[114] Although Muslims were not usually classified among "the heathen" in Protestant discourse, Lum's argument holds true for Muslim contexts as well, demonstrating how conceptions of racial and religious difference were formative for White American Protestant identity. A 1905 statement in an American periodical, *The Baptist Missionary Magazine*, that missionaries' work of the kingdom of God is the "triumph of Christ over heathenism, and fetishism and Islam" reflected the view across most Protestant missionary societies that lumped Islam, despite its distinct monotheism, together with "heathenism" in the group over which Christianity must eventually triumph.[115] If polytheistic religions and indigenous spirituality were objects of both fascination and repugnance for missionaries and their supporters because of their vast differences from Protestantism—as seen in the above discussion of museum displays—then due to its similarities with Christianity, Islam was equally an object of vitriol and voyeuristic fantasy. For these commonalities were understood as dangerous, making Islam a formidable force in competition for the souls of Asia and Africa.[116]

Similar to Lum's findings, missionary re-inventions of Islam tell us much about Protestant thought and identity formation. Like anthropological museums and great exhibitions, missionaries studied, collected specimens from, and taught others about Islamic contexts. They sought to impress upon their audiences the urgency of missions to Muslims and influence them to support this work through prayer, financial contributions, and auxiliary work or as missionaries themselves.[117] Thus, as Hasinoff claimed about Protestant expositions, missionary displays of Islam in museums and performances in Islamic costume became religious affairs.[118] Missionaries believed that a proper orientation toward Islam would demonstrate the superiority of Protestant faith and the compelling duty to bring the gospel to those they considered to be living in darkness. These efforts to understand the "other" therefore influenced Protestants' religious behavior and self-image. This resembled the way Lum described White American Protestants constructing their identity in opposition to the "heathen" world. The Protestant conception of other religions as arenas for evangelization, in turn, marked the evangelists as givers who were altruistically oriented toward the less fortunate.[119]

When re-inventing Islam for nineteenth- and twentieth-century American audiences, missionaries constructed a verbal and visual narrative about Islam, but they also embodied what it meant to be Protestant—and in particular what it meant to be a missionary. Missionaries were collectors and performers. They displayed Islam for supporters at home in ways that often conformed to their audiences' expectations, as shaped by Protestant theological pronouncements and broader western cultural discourses. They presented Islam not as a tradition of polytheistic idolatry whose claims could be debunked and whose deities could be desacralized by relocating them to glass boxes. Instead, missionaries saw in Islam a skewed or undeveloped version of truth—containing dangerous commonalities with Christianity. Some, like Zwemer, argued that the very foundations of Islam had to be destroyed to make way for Christian truth, while more open theologies, like that of Temple Gairdner, envisioned Christianity as the fulfillment of Islam.[120]

There was no single Protestant narrative about Islam; rather, missionaries chose from a variety of familiar critiques. Their re-inventions of Islam might stress the violent and licentious nature of Muslim men and emphasize the passive victimhood of Muslim women, as sexually exploited and physically repressed. Or alternatively, like the guidebook for The World in Boston, Protestant discourses might portray Muslim women as laborers serving their husbands' or children's needs, while characterizing Muslim men as lazy, effeminate, or otherwise falling short of western standards of masculinity. Yet missionary performances could also subvert such assumptions, either by emphasizing the positive (Zwemer's appreciation of Muslim devotional practices and Calverley's recognition of beauty in Muslim women's dress) or by avoiding tropes about violence (as did missionary men who appropriated eastern wisdom when dressing in Islamic costume, engaging in a romantic rather than a domineering form of Orientalism). In all of these cases, however, Protestant missionaries re-invented Islam, mediating it through the appropriation of Muslim objects and clothing. They used Islamic material culture for Protestant purposes, and in so doing they aimed to shape their Christian audiences' own sense of religious identity. While re-inventing Islam in ways that homogenized and obscured actual Muslims' lives, missionaries ultimately influenced the formation of twentieth-century American Protestantism.

So, what do missionary performances and exhibitions of Islam tell us about American Protestantism? Through the appropriation and repurposing of Islamic material culture for religious objectives, American Protestant identity became invested in the re-invention of Islam and the rearticulation of Protestantism as Islam's counter-image. Because the anti-Muslim narratives that developed within nineteenth- and twentieth-century American Protestantism are embedded in material practices and notions of the self, not just in patterns of thinking about the other, these narratives remain difficult to alter at present—despite the tremendous progress of the interfaith movement in recent years.

I conclude this chapter by considering four ways in which observations, comparisons, and judgments of Islamic material "specimens" added to the ideas that spread through missionary writings and photographs and transformed American Protestants' sense of identity and normative cultural-religious practice. First, Protestant obsessions with Muslim women's attire and practices of seclusion were entangled with age-old gender constructs and more recent religio-racial thought patterns. Recall that the Protestant Reformers had long before critiqued Muslim men for sexual immorality and for violating marriage through polygyny and concubinage. They described Muslim women as victims—treated like possessions or livestock—in contrast to what they presented as the elevated status of European Christian women. The earliest Protestants gave little attention to Muslim women's actual experiences, however, and did not focus on the veil or seclusion. This more recent fixation arose with the changing norms for western women after the eighteenth century, as the perceived oppression of Muslim and other non-western women helped to justify new public roles and freedoms for women in Europe or to uphold arguments that western norms of domesticity were superior.[121] Protestant women's involvement in missions in the nineteenth century also elevated this focus and added to the existing understanding of Muslim women as sex objects by making Muslim women's embodiment— either behind a face veil or behind the walls of the harem—a physical sign of victimhood. The need to save such presumably helpless women, spiritually and physically, in turn justified missionary women's leadership roles that transgressed the late nineteenth-century norms of womanhood and domesticity in the United States and Britain and made the independence of single women in the mission field more acceptable by the early twentieth century. It also represented a challenge to Protestant patriarchy and, for many denominations, was a precursor to women's ordination.

Second, racial undertones made more plausible the views of Muslim men as violent and Muslim women as needing to be saved. While the racial differences between western Protestant women and the Muslim women of Asia or Africa were typically implied in the activities of White women to save their less fortunate sisters, gender became performatively intertwined with race when missionaries wore Islamic garb. The White woman in Islamic attire did not need saving, for she could remove the restrictive veil at any time.

For her it did not symbolize submission to what she perceived as a patriarchal religion catering to men's desires. Likewise, Protestant men wearing Middle Eastern garb presented themselves not as violent warriors but as scholars, modeling a more appropriate form of masculinity for their viewers that enhanced their status as experts on Islam. Thus, comparable to museum curators' practices of placing idols within glass cases, missionary dress-up drained Islamic material culture of its power and informed audiences about Islamic practices while also reinforcing Protestant distinction. Missionary actors were free to adopt, appropriate, re-invent, or take off Muslim attire at will because of their own superior religious status, symbolized visually in their perceived racial and cultural difference from the societies that produced such garb.

Third, racialization of Islam helped White missionaries to distinguish it from Christianity, enabling their Anglo-Protestant constituents to internalize the narrative of difference and superiority. The idea of Christianity as White and as western was implied in missionary critiques of Islam, as seen in the previous chapters, and was explicit in the religio-racial taxonomies of museums and great exhibitions. Racial hierarchies were mapped onto religious hierarchies so that White American Protestants could believe that their race was superior to all others and that Christianity was the only fully developed and true religion. Such thinking came into play in Protestant encounters with multiple religious traditions, and not just Islam, as Lum signaled.[122] Yet its similarities with Christianity placed Islam higher on the imagined scale of spiritual development, and thus Protestants cited racial traits to reinforce their own theological claims and ultimately to re-invent Islam as Protestantism's uncivilized opposite.

Fourth and finally, this examination of material objects also reveals the nuances within missionary understandings of Islam and the ways in which personal relationships affected missionaries' views of Muslims. Indeed, even the embodied encounters that American audiences experienced with material things from Muslim societies could have a similar, though perhaps less profound, effect. Without negating the prevailing gender and race constructs, we must recognize that missionaries' close contact with Muslims led, by the mid-twentieth century, to deeper understanding and more humanizing approaches to Christian–Muslim relations and personal transformations, as seen in the writings of Calverley and Blatter. This, too, began to shape American Protestant identity, particularly as those mainline denominations involved in the earliest missions to Muslims began rethinking their approaches after World War I and became more open to interfaith dialogue after World War II.

Notes

1. Linda K. Jacobs, "'Playing East': Arabs Play Arabs in Nineteenth Century America," *Mashriq & Mahjar* 2, no. 2 (2014): 79–110.
2. Erin L. Hasinoff, *Faith in Objects: American Missionary Expositions in the Early Twentieth Century* (New York: Palgrave Macmillan, 2011), 5.
3. Manuel A. Vásquez, *More Than Belief: A Materialist Theory of Religion* (Oxford: Oxford University Press, 2011), 321. After arguing against approaches to religion that give more weight to belief and text than to ritual and practice, Vásquez explained, "Only when we see these discourses, beliefs, symbols, and texts as mobile yet relatively stable artifacts operating among and interacting with other material objects within the times and spaces constructed by the practices of situated individuals and groups can we avoid the threat of textualism, the temptation to make semiotic systems purely self-referential."
4. John Fletcher, *Preaching to Convert: Evangelical Outreach and Performance Activism in a Secular Age* (Ann Arbor: University of Michigan Press, 2013), 18.
5. Ibid. Fletcher also noted the unpredictability of the audiences' response.
6. On the policing of performative behavior, see Joy Palacios, "Introduction: Performing Religion," *Performance Matters* 3, no. 1 (2017): 1–6.
7. Although Vásquez critiqued approaches to religion that are purely textual or focused on doctrinal belief, he warned against making Protestantism out to be the villain despite its "logocentric orthodoxy." Rather, he challenged researchers to shift their gaze to see the material side of Protestantism. Vásquez, *More Than Belief*, 31–33.
8. This follows a broader pattern in Christian–Muslim studies, focusing primarily on textual comparisons and theological debates or dialogue.
9. Joseph Ho's study of missionary photography in China deeply engages the former. Joseph Ho, *Developing Mission: Photography, Filmmaking and American Missionaries in Modern China* (Ithaca, NY: Cornell University Press, 2021). Additionally, the Yale–Edinburgh Conference in 2006 focused on "Sight, Sound, and Touch: Visual, Musical, and Material Aspects of Christian Mission."
10. Charles D. Orzech, *Museums of World Religions: Displaying the Divine, Shaping Cultures* (London: Bloomsbury, 2020), 4.
11. Kathryn Gin Lum, *Heathen: Religion and Race in American History* (Cambridge, MA: Harvard University Press, 2022), 18, 48.
12. For examples, see Chapter 5 and "If You Were a Heathen Woman!," *Missionary Review of The World* 40, no. 11 (November 1917): 855.
13. On the ways in which such hierarchies became ingrained in the American legal system, see Sahar Aziz, *The Racial Muslim: When Racism Quashes Religious Freedom* (Oakland: University of California Press, 2022).
14. Willie James Jennings, *After Whiteness: An Education in Belonging* (Grand Rapids, MI: Eerdmans, 2020), 6. On missions and scientific racism, see Deanna Ferree Womack, "American Muslims, Arab Christians, and Religio-Racial Misrecognition," in *Alterity and the Evasion of Justice: Explorations of the "Other" in World Christianity*, ed. Deanna Ferree Womack and Raimundo C. Barreto. (Minneapolis: Fortress Press, 2023), 27–48.
15. See examples in David Lindenfeld, *World Christianity and Indigenous Experience: A Global History, 1500–2000* (Cambridge: Cambridge University Press, 2021), 32. Lindenfeld refers to missionaries who were "determined to understand as much as they could about the people they sought to convert," and thus they learned local languages and collaborated closely with "native speakers."
16. Orzech, *Museums of World Religions*, 26.
17. Michael M. Ames, *Cannibal Tours in Glass Boxes: The Anthropology of Museums* (Vancouver and Toronto: UBC Press, 1992), 16, 22.
18. Ibid., 50.

19. Ibid., 18–19.
20. Comparative religion was birthed in the "museum age." Orzech, *Museums of World Religions*, 19. See also Ames, *Cannibal Tours*, 51.
21. Ames, *Cannibal Tours*, 51.
22. Ibid., 17.
23. Ibid., 23.
24. Orzech, *Museums of World Religions*, 4. Orzech argued that theological assumptions were embedded in the comparative study of religion, developed in part through missionaries' involvement in the field's evolution.
25. Ibid., 25.
26. Ibid.
27. Ibid., 19.
28. Ibid., x, 6.
29. Ibid., 19.
30. Ibid., 20.
31. Ibid.
32. Walter Putnam, "'Please Don't Feed the Natives': Human Zoos, Colonial Desire, and Bodies on Display," *French Literature Series* 39 (2012): 56.
33. Orzech, *Museums of World Religions*, 21. See also Putnam, "'Please Don't Feed the Natives'"; Rikke Andreassen, *Human Exhibitions: Race, Gender and Sexuality in Ethnic Displays* (London and New York: Routledge, 2016); Dagnoslaw Demski and Dominika Czarnecka, *Staged Otherness: Ethnic Shows in Central and Eastern Europe, 1850–1939* (Budapest: Central European University Press, 2021); Sadiah Qureshi, *Peoples on Parade: Exhibitions, Empire, and Anthropology in Nineteenth-Century Britain* (Chicago: University of Chicago Press, 2011). Twenty-seven million people attended the Chicago World's Fair between May and October 1893. While "human zoo" is an apt description of these exhibitions from today's perspective, it is important to note that such activities were contemporary with the development of the first zoos and thus the result of similar emphasis on categorization and display of living beings rather than a variation on the zoo itself. See Isobel Charman, *The Zoo: The Wild and Wonderful Tale of the Founding of London Zoo: 1826–1851* (New York and London: Pegasus Books, 2017).
34. Ames, *Cannibal Tours*, 51.
35. Putnam, "'Please Don't Feed the Natives,'" 56.
36. Ibid.
37. Ibid., 57.
38. Ibid. Putnam documented the ticket sales for the three Paris exhibitions in this "hey-day" of the human zoo, from the 1870s to the early 1930s when cinema took over: 32 million in 1889, 48 million in 1900, and 33.5 million in 1931 (pp. 60–61).
39. Jennings, *After Whiteness*, 6.
40. Putnam, "'Please Don't Feed the Natives,'" 66–67.
41. Vendors and performers were not always employed in their own nations' exhibits.
42. Jacobs, "'Playing East.'"
43. Chris Wingfield, "Missionary Museums," in *Religion in Museums: Global and Multidisciplinary Perspectives*, ed. Gretchen Buggeln, Crispin Paine, and S. Brent Plate (London: Bloomsbury, 2017), 232; Felicity Jensz, "Collecting Cultures: Institutional Motivations for Nineteenth-Century Ethnographical Collections Formed by Moravian Missionaries," *Journal of the History of Collections* 24, no. 1 (2012): 67–70.
44. Wingfield, "Missionary Museums," 232.
45. Hasinoff, *Faith in Objects*, 11, 14, 136. The World in Boston was modeled on previous British missionary expositions, The Orient in London (1908) and Africa and the East (1909) (p. 14). The Boston exposition was largely organized by Congregationalists of the ABCFM.
46. *Handbook and Guide of The World in Boston: The First Great Exposition in America of Home and Foreign Missions, Held in Mechanics Building April 22–May 20, 1911* (Boston: The World in Boston, 1911), 32.
47. Ibid., 36.
48. Hasinoff, *Faith in Objects*, 155–57. Hasinoff noted that some missionary exhibitions involved "native helpers," a term usually indicating local converts to Protestantism who were employed by the mission.

49. *Handbook and Guide*, 32–33. These tents were also compared to the tents of the Israelites in the desert, and as Hasinoff noted, parts of the Palestine exhibit resembled other Holy Land immersion experiences like the Palestine Park. Hasinoff, *Faith in Objects*, 39.
50. *Handbook and Guide*, 35. Notably, these missionary expositions gave Protestant audiences, including men, full access to Muslim women's lives, whereas in the mission fields it was often only missionary women who could enter secluded women's spaces. See Hasinoff, *Faith in Objects*, 37–38.
51. For some of these overlooked Muslim perspectives, see Douglas Scott Brookes, *The Concubine, the Princess, and the Teacher: Voices from the Ottoman Harem* (Austin: University of Texas Press, 2008).
52. *Handbook and Guide*, 34.
53. A growing body of literature examines this historical phenomenon of missionary collecting, with particular attention to collections from the Pacific Islands. See Joachim G. Piepke, "The Kirschbaum Collection of the Missionary Ethnological Museum in the Vatican," *Anthropos* 107, no. 2 (2012): 560–64; Barbara A. Lawson, "Collecting Cultures: Canadian Missionaries, Pacific Islanders, and Museums," in *Canadian Missionaries, Indigenous Peoples: Representing Religion at Home and Abroad*, ed. Alvyn Austin and Jamie S. Scott (Toronto: University of Toronto Press, 2005), 235–61; Nicholas Thomas, *Entangled Objects: Exchange, Material Culture, and Colonialism in the Pacific* (Cambridge, MA: Harvard University Press, 1991), 151–61; Barbara Lawson, *Collected Curios: Missionary Tales from the South Seas* (Montreal: McGill University, 1994); Helen Gardner, "Gathering for God: George Brown and the Christian Economy in the Collection of Artifacts," in *Hunting the Gatherers: Ethnographic Collectors, Agents and Agency in Melanesia, 1870s–1930s*, ed. Michael O'Hanlon and Robert Welsch (New York: Berghahn Books, 2000), 35–54. On studies of missionary collections from other contexts, see Jean Cannizzo, "Gathering Souls and Objects: Missionary Collections," in *Colonialism and the Object: Empire, Material Culture and the Museum* (New York: Routledge, 1998), 153–66; Karen Jacobs, Chantal Knowles, and Christ Wingfield, *Trophies, Relics and Curios?: Missionary Heritage from Africa and the Pacific* (Leiden: Sidestone Press, 2015).
54. Rosemary Seton, "Reconstructing the Museum of the London Missionary Society," *Material Religion* 8, no. 1 (2012): 98. Seton quoted from the announcement of the museum's opening in *Evangelical Magazine and Missionary Chronicle* (October 1814): 405. On the LMS museum sending items on tour, see Wingfield, "Missionary Museums," 231.
55. Seton, "Reconstructing," 101.
56. Wingfield, "Missionary Museums," 231.
57. Seton, "Reconstructing," 98; David Morgan, "Museum Collection and the History of Interpretation," in *Religion in Museums: Global and Multidisciplinary Perspectives*, ed. Gretchen Buggeln, Crispin Paine, and S. Brent Plate (London: Bloomsbury, 2017), 121.
58. Seton, "Reconstructing," 99.
59. Ibid., 99–100. The museum catalogue related the zebra shown in the collection to the "wild ass" of Job 39:5 and the rhino to the unicorn referenced in Job 39:9–10.
60. Orzech, *Museums of World Religions*, 25; Seton, "Reconstructing," 101.
61. Lawson, "Collecting Cultures," 256.
62. Seton, "Reconstructing," 232.
63. *Annual Register of the Hartford Theological Seminary for the Sixty-Third Year, 1896–1897* (Hartford, CT: Hartford Seminary Press, 1897), 38; W. Henry Grant, "Foreign Missions Library," *Woman's Work for Woman* 10, no. 3 (March 1895): 81. The Presbyterian Board of Foreign Missions library in New York City held a collection of curios, photographs, and costumes from Asia and Africa.
64. Smalley described one such museum in China, eventually known as the Wainwright Institute, named after its British Baptist missionary founder, J. S. Wainwright. Martha Lund Smalley, "Missionary Museums in China," *Material Religion* 8, no. 1 (2012): 105–7. On similar museums established in missionary training colleges, see Wingfield, "Missionary Museums," 233.
65. Sally M. Promey, "Foreword," in *Religion in Museums: Global and Multidisciplinary Perspectives*, ed. Gretchen Buggeln, Crispin Paine, and S. Brent Plate (London: Bloomsbury, 2017), xx. On missionaries encasing idols for display, see David Morgan, *The Thing About Religion: An Introduction to the Material Study of Religions* (Chapel Hill: University of North Carolina Press, 2021), 170–78.
66. Iain Chambers et al., eds., *The Postcolonial Museum: The Arts of Memory and the Pressures of History* (Burlington, VT: Ashgate, 2014), 65.

67. *The Sedalia Capital* (August 29, 1931), 5; *Piqua Daily* (August 29, 1931), 5; *Alton Evening Telegraph* (August 29, 1931), 7; *Somerset Daily Herald Call* (August 29, 1931), 5; *Circleville Herald* (August 29, 1931), 3; *Corona Daily Independent* (August 29, 1931), 3; *New Philadelphia Daily Times* (August 29, 1931), 4.
68. Richard Fox Young, "Princeton Theological Seminary's Museum of Religion and Missions," *Material Religion* 8, no. 1 (2012): 108. See also Richard Fox Young, "Obliged by Grace: Edward Jurji's Legacy in the History of Religions at Princeton Theological Seminary, 1939–77," *Theology Today* 69, no. 3 (2012): 334–36; Edward J. Jurji, "Museum of Religion and Missions at Princeton Theological Seminary," *The Moslem World* 31, no. 3 (1941): 295–98.
69. Young, "Princeton Theological Seminary's Museum," 109. For a study on a discernable, if slight, change in Zwemer's approach to Islam over time, see John Hubers, "Samuel Zwemer and the Challenge of Islam: From Polemic to a Hint of Dialogue," *International Bulletin of Missionary Research* 28, no. 3 (July 2004): 117–21. Hubers noted that by the 1940s, Zwemer had recognized that Christians and Muslims worship the same God, even if he believed Muslim portrayals of God were inadequate (pp. 120–21).
70. Richard Fox Young email to author, July 3, 2022. Young also noted the collection contained a camel scapula inscribed with Qur'anic text and posters created by Chinese Muslims that contained Qur'anic passages in Arabic and Chinese. The Princeton Theological Seminary library sent the shoes to the Bata Shoe Museum in Toronto in the early 2000s.
71. *Annual Register of the Hartford Theological Seminary*, 38. Union Seminary in New York also established a similar museum of missionary objects. See http://tiny.cc/aohvyz. Accessed January 7, 2024.
72. Hasinoff, *Faith in Objects*, 7.
73. Eva Marshall to Family, November 13, 1927, Khalil A. Totah and Eva Marshall Totah Papers (MC 1210, box 4, folder 1) (hereafter *Totah Papers*), Quaker & Special Collections, Haverford College, Haverford, PA; "Foreign Mission Notes," *The Friend* 45, no. 6 (London, February 10, 1905): 91. The notice described preparations for a missionary exhibition at the Friends yearly meeting in Leeds that would include the sale of needlework, handicrafts, and sketches.
74. In addition to Sialkot and Sargodha, Hill worked in the Lyallpur (now known as Faisalabad) and Sangla Hill districts. Hill also served as Women's Board secretary while back in the United States in between her years working in India.
75. Photo of United Presbyterian Church sanctuary, 1905, Kate Alexander Hill Papers (Record Group 53, box 1, folder 25), Presbyterian Historical Society, Philadelphia (hereafter *PHS*). Another photograph of the sanctuary, with a caption describing this as an "Exhibit of Indian Things" in Newtown, Iowa, in 1905, appears in PHS 53-1-12.
76. Scrapbook of "Programs during First Furlough, 1904–1906," Kate Hill Papers, PHS 53-2. The names and dates of the newspaper clippings were not documented in the scrapbook. The clippings included an untitled full-page announcement of Hill's talk in Newtown and articles titled "Exhibition of India Curios" and "Curios Galore, an Interesting Collection."
77. "Interesting Exhibit: And Much Information in Talks by Misses Hill and Dickson last Friday and Saturday" in scrapbook of "Programs during First Furlough, 1904–1906," Kate Hill Papers, PHS 53-2.
78. "Church News Notes," in scrapbook of "Programs during First Furlough, 1904–1906," Kate Hill Papers, PHS 53-2.
79. Photo of Kate Hill's Islamic prayer bead collection, circa 1943–1944, Kate Hill Papers, PHS 53-1-26. The display also included photographs of Hill's most recent hospital work in Sialkot, newspaper announcements of the "India Curios" exhibit from her first furlough, and, on the bottom shelves, stacks of the albums and scrapbooks from her time in India. The photos of Ajanta Caves are found in PHS 53-1-25.
80. Agra Fort pass of Robert Fullerton (1857) and explanatory card, Kate Hill Papers, PHS 53-1-24.
81. See Chapter 3.
82. Catriona Laing, "A Provocation to Mission: Constance Padwick's Study of Muslim Devotion," *Islam and Christian–Muslim Relations* 24, no. 1 (January 2023): 27–42.
83. On Gairdner and Padwick, see Richard Sudworth, *Encountering Islam: Christian–Muslim Relations in the Public Square* (London: SCM Press, 2017), 101, 138–39, 145. Gairdner advocated an early inclusivist theology of religion that saw Christianity as fulfilling, rather than destroying, Islam. William H. T. Gairdner, *The Reproach of Islam* (London: Student Volunteer Movement, 1909).

84. Saloni Mathur, *India by Design: Colonial History and Cultural Display* (Berkeley and Los Angeles: University of California Press, 2007), 127–28. A portion of the material in this section was first published in Deanna Ferree Womack, "Lost in Translation: Missionaries in Islamic Garb," *Journal of Presbyterian History* 99, no. 1 (Spring/Summer 2021): 9–22.

85. Edward P. Antonio, "The Hermeneutics of Inculturation," in *Inculturation and Postcolonial Discourse in African Theology*, ed. Edward P. Antonio (New York: Peter Lang, 2006), 46. See also Claire Cooke, "Capping Power? Clothing and the Female Body in African Methodist Episcopal Mission Photographs," *Mission Studies* 31 (2014): 418–42; Kirsten Ruether, "Heated Debates over Crinolines: European Clothing on Nineteenth-Century Lutheran Mission Stations in the Transvaal," *Journal of Southern African Studies* 28, no. 2 (June 2002): 359–78; Victoria L. Rovine, "Colonialism's Clothing: Africa, France, and the Deployment of Fashion," *Design Issues* 25, no. 3 (Summer 2009): 44–61; Eliza F. Kent, *Converting Women: Gender and Protestant Christianity in Colonial South India* (Oxford: Oxford University Press, 2004), 199–233.

86. Gregory Adam Scott, "Timothy Richard, World Religion, and Reading Christianity in Buddhist Garb," *Social Sciences and Missions* 25 (2012): 60. See also Francis X. Clooney, "Roberto de Nobili, Adaptation and the Reasonable Interpretation of Religion," *Missiology: An International Review* 18, no. 1 (January 1990): 31.

87. Susan Fleming McAllister, "Cross-Cultural Dress in Victorian British Missionary Narratives: Dressing for Eternity," in *Historicizing Christian Encounters with the Other*, ed. John C. Hawley (London: Macmillan, 1998), 127–28.

88. Kate Alexander Hill in a sari, circa 1941, Kate Hill Papers, PHS 53-1-26. See http://tiny.cc/jqy8yz. Accessed January 7, 2024.

89. Mathur, *India by Design*, 127–28.

90. Henry Harris Jessup, *The Women of the Arabs* (New York: Dodd & Mead, 1873), 15, 19.

91. This photo appeared in Lutfi Sa'd, "Al-Hakim Cornelius Van Alen Van Dyck (1818–1895)," *Isis* 27, no. 1 (May 1937): 20.

92. Timothy Marr, *The Cultural Roots of American Islamicism* (Cambridge: Cambridge University Press, 2006), 266.

93. Mathur, *India by Design*, 114.

94. Postcards of "A Bedouin Tent," "A Group of Natives," "Mrs. Schor," and "Rock-Hewn Tomb," Missionary Postcard Collection, YDS 101-87.

95. Even before the modern Republic of Turkey undertook a westernizing agenda, in the nineteenth century the Ottoman Sultan Abdul Hamid wore a fez and western-style jacket and encouraged the empire's men to do the same. Deanna Ferree Womack, *Protestants, Gender and the Arab Renaissance in Late Ottoman Syria* (Edinburgh: Edinburgh University Press, 2019), 256. On Ottoman women's clothing patterns, see Anastasia Falierou, "From the Ottoman Empire to the Turkish Republic: Ottoman Turkish Women's Clothing Between Tradition and Modernity," in *From Traditional Attire to Modern Dress: Modes of Identification, Modes of Recognition in the Balkans (XVIth–XXth Centuries)*, ed. Constanta Vintila-Ghitulescu (Newcastle upon Tyne, UK: Cambridge Scholars Publishing, 2011), 175–94.

96. In fact, Ottoman rulers began to adapt and adopt western clothing styles for the military in the early nineteenth century—the reason why, perhaps, Turkish men's modern attire if worn by missionary men would not be distinct enough to attract the audience's attention. Onur Inal, "Women's Fashions in Transition: Ottoman Borderlands and the Anglo–Ottoman Exchange of Costumes," *Journal of World History* 22, no. 2 (June 2011): 262; Patricia L. Baker, "The Fez in Turkey," *Costume* 20 (1986): 73.

97. Gladys Perry album, 1931, Iain Campbell Papers (RG 0043-2-2, A-27), Congregational Library & Archives, Boston, MA. In the same scrapbook, the two also appear pictured as "Bedoins [sic.] selling brass" wearing striped Bedouin-style headdresses and carrying brass cookware.

98. "A Holiday in Algeria," July 1928, Arab World Ministries/Algiers Mission Band Papers (box 25, album 1), SOAS Special Collections, University of London.

99. Two photographs of Eva Marshall, December 1927, Totah Papers MC 1210-4-11. Both images were printed as a postcard, on the back of which was written "Eva Marshall Totah in Bedouin costume" and "This is the native Ram Allah costume."

100. Photographs of Sibyl and Nabil Totah, circa 1937–1938, Totah Papers MC 1210-4-14. This attire was distinctively Palestinian and not specifically Muslim or Christian. For the Totah children it signaled their Arab heritage.

101. Uta Zeuge-Buberl, *The Mission of the American Board in Syria: Implications of a transcultural Dialogue*, trans. Elizabeth Janik (Stuttgart: Franz Steiner, 2017), 152, 231; Sa'd, "Al-Hakim Cornelius Van Alen Van Dyck," 26.
102. Zeuge-Buberl, *Mission of the American Board in Syria*, 17, 52, 55, 89.
103. Ibid., 17, 91, 96.
104. Eleanor Jane Taylor Calverley, *My Arabian Days and Nights* (New York: Thomas Y. Crowell, 1958), 60.
105. Calverley family photographs, circa 1914–1915 and 1922, Edwin E. Calverley Papers (box 373), Hartford International University Library Archives, Hartford, CT.
106. "Missionary to Arabia Will Tell How Moslems Treat Their Women," *Harrisburg Telegraph*, September 30, 1915, 4. Another announcement featured the same photo: *Monmouth Democrat* (Freehold, NJ), September 16, 1915, 1.
107. Eleanor Jane Taylor Calverley, "An Arabian Harem: Impressions of an American Girl on a Visit to the Home of the Woman of the Near East," *The Buffalo Commercial*, April 24, 1919, 6.
108. Lila Abu-Lughod, *Do Muslim Women Need Saving?* (Cambridge, MA: Harvard University Press, 2013).
109. Calverley, *My Arabian Days and Nights*, 80.
110. Ibid., 83.
111. Ibid., 34. Italics in original.
112. Ibid., 173. By *unveiled* she meant without a face covering.
113. Fletcher, *Preaching to Convert*, 18.
114. Lum, *Heathen*, 16.
115. "Thousands Uniting in Study," *The Baptist Missionary Magazine* 85, no. 9 (September 1905): 358.
116. Zwemer warned of Islam's "widespread and aggressive power as a missionary religion." Samuel M. Zwemer, *Islam: A Challenge to Faith* (New York: Student Volunteer Movement, 1907), vii.
117. See Hasinoff, *Faith in Objects*, 23. Michael Ames similarly argued that the purpose of anthropology is "to study others in order to understand ourselves." Ames, *Cannibal Tours*, 14.
118. Hasinoff, *Faith in Objects*, 7.
119. Lum, *Heathen*, 18.
120. Gairdner, *Reproach of Islam*; James A. Tebbe, "Kenneth Cragg in Perspective: A Comparison with Temple Gairdner and Wilfred Cantwell Smith," *International Bulletin of Missionary Research* (January 2002): 16–18.
121. See Chapter 2.
122. Lum, *Heathen*.

7
The Ongoing Effects of Missions
American Islamophobia and Openings for Christian–Muslim Dialogue

The first six chapters of this book charted how gender constructs informed historical Protestant perceptions of Islam, especially in the far-reaching textual, visual, and material influences of the American and British movement for missions to Muslims. In those chapters, I also diagnosed a problem: Anglo-Protestants re-invented and perpetuated malevolent stereotypes about Muslim women and men to achieve particular Protestant purposes. Specifically, missionaries in the nineteenth and early twentieth centuries used negative representations of gender in Islam to advance:

- Protestant theological teachings
- evangelistic outreach
- humanitarian concerns
- Eurocentric views of civilization
- White supremacy
- the cultural, economic, and military expansion of Protestant empire
- the desires of Anglo-Protestant women to participate more fully in missions and ministry, given the patriarchal structures of western church and society

In this final chapter, I address some shifts in American engagements with Muslims since the mid-twentieth century, and I consider the needs of contemporary Christian–Muslim relations. The anti-Muslim rhetoric that has affected American geopolitical involvements and local Christian–Muslim relations in the United States since the early twentieth century was, at least in part, a consequence of missionary aims to justify and raise support for their work. The resulting stereotypes, fear, and discrimination reflect neither the principles of mainline Protestant theology today nor even the complete views

Re-inventing Islam. Deanna Ferree Womack, Oxford University Press. © Oxford University Press 2025.
DOI: 10.1093/9780197699195.003.0007

of Protestant missionaries who intentionally or inadvertently transmitted these tropes.

The building of deeper Christian–Muslim understanding and cooperation in the United States is not a task that can be accomplished only through occasional gatherings of well-intentioned individuals for conversation or shared meals—the kind of activities often associated with interfaith dialogue. Because of the residual anti-Muslim sentiment that has too often led to deadly actions against Muslims, this urgent task will also require the more grueling work of breaking down the prejudices entrenched in American Protestant culture and wider American social and political structures.[1] To do so, we need to understand how these prejudices spread in the first place.

Considering the devastating consequences that anti-Muslim incidents continue to have in the United States in the early twenty-first century, in what follows I seek to help readers—Americans, Christians, Muslims, and others—understand why my historical diagnosis of this problem matters for American society today. Recognizing the ways in which missionaries drew on and re-invented centuries-old Protestant discourses about Muslims and gender, I return to the practical question I posed at the opening of this book: *What bearing does the history told in the preceding pages have on the birth of Islamophobia in the late twentieth century and on efforts for Christian–Muslim dialogue in the United States today?* I begin with contemporary anti-Muslim sentiment and, in subsequent sections, address the post–World War II geopolitical and demographic shifts that transformed American encounters with Muslims. I consider the rise of formal interfaith dialogue efforts amidst the mainline–evangelical divisions of the mid-twentieth century before returning to early twentieth-century missionary sources to identify openings for dialogue from which we can still learn today.

Protestant Missions and the Roots of Contemporary Islamophobia

As the twentieth century progressed, images of Islam proliferated in the United States. Some of them originated in the missionary enterprise. Others—whether snapshots by American tourists in the Middle East or Hollywood films featuring Muslim villains—built on the foundation that missionaries had laid but took on a life of their own outside of church circles. With the growing presence over time of American diplomats, businesspeople, tourists, and humanitarian workers in Muslim societies, Anglo-Protestant missionaries were not the only ones to transmit ideas about Islam to American audiences. Yet, due to their close, long-term contact with Muslims up through the interwar period—and with the aid of a highly developed publishing network—missionaries possessed the tools and authority to shape American Protestant and wider American cultural discourses about Islam quite significantly. They also informed the ideas of producers (journalists, filmmakers, news anchors, politicians) and consumers of the popular media representations that became more common by the mid-twentieth century. The missionary narratives and images I have examined in this book therefore had long aftereffects, and among the most devastating to American Christian–Muslim relations were the tropes about Islam and gender. We might recall that the seminal women's volume originating from the Cairo Conference of 1906 claimed that Muslim women's lives were the same everywhere. It equated spiritual darkness and physical abuse with the symbols of the veil and the harem, and it placed the blame on Islam, on Muslim men, and sometimes even on Muslim women themselves.[2] In using the metaphor of *darkness*, missionaries intended to provoke their supporters' pity and financial contributions, but such language also rendered a judgment about civilizational and racial difference upon which Americans drew in legal cases against Muslim immigrants' citizenship in the early twentieth century.[3] Such judgments also shaped the way in which American Protestants thought about the rising American Muslim population after mid-century.

In considering the bulleted list of missionary motivations articulated at the opening of this chapter, we must recognize that negative gender tropes unfortunately remained constant in most missionary discourses about Islam even though mainline missionaries' *theological teachings* and approaches to *evangelistic outreach* shifted significantly in the mid-twentieth century toward *humanitarian concerns*. The persistent gender critique—like the discourse of the veil in the background of Dorothy Blatter's *Cap and Candle* (1961)—exposes the troubling dimensions of Protestant missionary activities that I noted at the outset: Eurocentrism, White supremacy, and Protestant imperial expansion. These factors were not rooted in religious thought or practice but rather reflected Anglo-Protestant desires to impose western socio-cultural, political, and economic norms. Two other items on the list—*humanitarian concern* born out of religious conviction or human connection and *Anglo-Protestant women's aspirations* to change their own circumstances—remind us of Protestant missionaries' own humanity, although this does not negate the ways they used anti-Muslim polemic for their own benefit. As other scholars of mission have noted, altruistic concerns for Muslim lives often existed in tension with imperialist and ethnocentric impulses.[4]

Longstanding views of Muslim men as threatening violence and Muslim women as oppressed continue today, views that originated during the eighteenth-century rise of western imperial and Orientalist power. These views are transmitted just as easily through Protestant religious rhetoric as through secular discourses and popular media—another clue that these are not innately Protestant or religious ideas. Americans now use the same anti-Muslim tropes in secular contexts when they are not speaking as religious actors or when they do not themselves identify as religious. Such malleable tropes have been repeatedly recycled and re-invented to serve all sorts of religious and political purposes, including to justify legal actions against Muslims and to incite anti-Muslim hate crimes.[5] The gendered imagery of the Anglo-Protestant missionary movement predisposed Americans to view Muslim men as violent and to disparage Islam. Blended with American civil religion and ideas about White superiority,[6] this fed a culture of *Islamophobia*, as it would become known at the end of the twentieth century.

I have not used the term *Islamophobia* in the previous chapters to describe the negative sentiments toward Islam that historical Protestant missionaries displayed or shaped because this term, describing "a *social* anxiety toward Islamic traditions and Muslim-majority cultures,"[7] came into common usage in the United States only in the 1990s.[8] According to Stephen Sheehi, "Islamophobia, in its current form, is a new ideological formation that has taken full expression since the collapse of the Soviet Union" but that notably preceded the anti-Muslim backlash following the attacks of September 11, 2001.[9] A significant amount of scholarship on American Muslims and Islamophobia since 9/11 has debated whether the negative rhetoric and escalating hate incidents against American Muslims should be called *Islamophobic* or *anti-Muslim*, terms that some scholars use interchangeably while others posit a distinction.[10] For example, Peter Gottschalk and Gabriel Greenberg distinguished Islamophobia, as an anxiety "that mainstream American society has perpetuated in popular memory," from anti-Muslim sentiment, "the racist and ethnocentric attitudes and emotions that particularly have burgeoned among Americans in the past few decades." Differentiating between Islam as a religion and Muslims as people, they explained that Islamophobia manifests as fear of Islamic religious ideology and practice, while anti-Muslim prejudice fosters repugnance and "rejection of certain types of [Arab, Pakistani, and other Muslim] bodies."[11] In a related approach, Sahar Aziz defined *anti-Muslim racism* as a manifestation of *Islamophobia*, describing both together in the American context as

> an exaggerated fear of, hatred of, and hostility to Islam and Muslims by the state and the public as a result of imputed inferior biological and cultural traits based on religious identity *that produce* systemic bias, discrimination, marginalization, and exclusion of Muslims from social, political, and civic life.[12]

Both Aziz and Erik Love have identified racism as being at the core of contemporary Islamophobia, while Sherene Razack has focused on *anti-Muslim racism* because, in her view, the term *Islamophobia* fails to indicate how negative discourses on Islam contribute to White supremacy.[13] In other studies on the topic, Khaled Beydoun and Nazia Kazi have both pointed out Islamophobia's private dimensions (individual acts of discrimination and hate) as well as the structural/institutional and legal/political dimensions, all of which are often attached to race.[14] Finally, Todd Green, Caleb Iyer Elfenbein, and Nathan Lean have attended more closely to the way Islamophobic rhetoric harnesses fear and hatred.[15]

Despite the noted limitations, the term *Islamophobia* conveys the way in which anti-Muslim perceptions and actions spread today through rhetoric and imagery that prey on fears about Islam. Such fears, built on assumptions about Muslim men as terrorists, are unique to the late twentieth- and early twenty-first-century context and are also distinct from other forms of racism, xenophobia, and religious bigotry in US society. The existing anti-Muslim prejudices that American Protestant missionaries and others have passed down since the nineteenth century have bolstered contemporary Islamophobia, making it systemic, pervasive, and deeply embedded in the American psyche.

While these studies on Islamophobia and others too numerous to name have demonstrated that a myriad of factors emerging since the 1990s contributed to American Islamophobia,[16] my study of Protestant texts, images, and performances indicates that the missionary movement of the nineteenth and early twentieth centuries is one significant and much older root of the anti-Muslim discourses and actions that we see today. Both fearful and racist responses to Muslims take on a gendered dimension, which has been a less prominent focus in these studies on Islamophobia. Certainly, plentiful studies now exist about women, gender, and Islam, including those covering American and European views and other scholarship exploring such issues from an Islamic studies perspective.[17] Yet while noting the discriminatory treatment of women in hijabs (headscarves) and the fearful prejudices against Muslim men, studies on Islamophobia tend to focus on recent history or emphasize the roots of anti-Muslim racism,[18] without tracing the deeper historical origins of gender discourses that later became intertwined with such racism. Gendered ideas about Islam, like those that Protestant missionaries transmitted, were a primary mechanism through which racism against Muslims spread over the nineteenth and twentieth centuries, eventually manifesting in present-day Islamophobia.

Such sentiments are present in the often-undocumented ways in which non-Muslim Americans think about, speak about, and treat Muslim women in their communities. Americans also publicly voice assumptions about Muslim women's oppression or their attire in support of political action. This was the case in 2001 when some public figures promised that the US invasion of Afghanistan would liberate Afghani women from the burqa.[19] These internalized notions appear also in extreme acts of hostility and violence, particularly against Muslim women in the United States, who are often targeted for head coverings or dress styles that are not mainstream. For example, the American Civil Liberties Union found that between 2000 and 2006, the number of American Muslim women who reported being discriminated against rose 674% from 366 to 2467, with most of this unprecedented increase coming after 9/11. The same study also noted that sixty-nine percent of Muslim women who wear the hijab had reported at least one instance of discrimination in comparison to twenty-nine percent of those Muslim women who did not wear the hijab. Although almost half (forty-four percent) of these instances involved women who were prohibited from wearing a head covering, Muslim women have also been targeted by individuals attempting to remove their headgear with force.[20] The FBI does not track gender statistics for anti-Muslim hate crimes, but the following cases are telling:

- In September 2016, a woman in New York City, who was later arrested, physically and verbally attacked two Muslim women wearing hijabs and tried to rip the scarves off their heads while telling them that they did not belong in the United States.[21]

- In Dallas in late 2018, a woman yelled at American Muslim Jenan Ayesh, hit her, and pulled the scarf from her head, telling her to go back to her country.[22]
- In October 2022, a ninth-grade Muslim girl whose family had recently immigrated from Afghanistan was beaten and had her hijab pulled off while attending a Baltimore school.[23]
- In October 2023, a man in New York City attacked a sixteen-year-old Muslim teenager on a subway, pulling on her hijab after telling her "you're a terrorist, you don't belong here."[24]

The most recent incident listed above occurred in the wake of the Hamas attacks against Israelis on October 7, 2023, and the subsequent war in Gaza, the combination of which prompted an increase in both anti-Muslim and anti-Jewish incidents in the United States.[25] The subway attacker's language also appeared to demonstrate Shakira Hussein's argument that in the post-9/11 context, Muslim women have gone from being viewed as victims to being treated as suspects.[26] In all of these instances, however, the assailants both marked their targets as outsiders and attempted to remove their headscarves—recalling the longstanding discourse of the veil and Protestant missionaries' call for its removal as a sign of modernization or westernization. While the twentieth-century missionaries covered in this study advocated only for the removal of the face veil, Islamophobic attacks today often target Muslim women's entire head coverings, not in an attempt to save these women physically or spiritually but to force them to conform to perceived American dress norms. Gender discourses about Islam are therefore still being re-invented.

While Muslim men in the United States have similarly been targets of individual acts of discrimination, they have also been subjected to more systematic male-focused forms of Islamophobia, including police custody, interrogation, surveillance, and the No Fly List, often only because of their identities as Muslim and male.[27] At the same time, when Muslim men anywhere perpetrate horrific violence like the 9/11 attacks or the 2023 Hamas attacks, many Americans take this as proof of the prevalent tropes and, moreover, associate such acts with *all* Muslims. This, prosecutors claimed, was the case in the violent October 2023 murder of a six-year-old Palestinian Muslim boy, Wadea al-Fayoume, by his landlord in a Chicago suburb and the severe wounding of the boy's mother. The Department of Justice launched a hate crime investigation because the perpetrator screamed not only "You Muslims have to die" but also "You are killing our kids in Israel," equating his Palestinian Muslim neighbors with Hamas.[28] Although there are many factors shaping American reactions to the Israel–Hamas war in Gaza, Islamophobic sentiments and long-held anti-Muslim ideas are one background against which we can understand both the extremely violent responses against American Muslims and more veiled Islamophobic reactions. The post–World War II transformations of the ways in which Americans have transmitted and received anti-Muslim imagery complicate attempts to trace a direct line of causality between missionary rhetoric and such contemporary vitriol. Nevertheless, this backlash indicates that Americans have become conditioned to seeing Muslims as dangerous. Islamophobia, then, has become another way of re-inventing of Islam.

Post–World War II Transitions and Transformations

Missionary discourses were never the only driver of American views on Islam, and by the 1970s they were but one influence among the cacophony of ideas about Muslims circulating in response to world events and demographic changes in the United States. One pattern remained consistent, however: amidst the radical transformations of the post–World War II era, Americans' fixation on gender tropes about Islam continued. While missionary voices diminished as the century progressed, missionaries simultaneously found more room to speak publicly in humanistic terms about their experiences living alongside Muslims, and some began engaging in formal efforts of interreligious dialogue. What were the mid-twentieth-century changes that made missionaries only one of many American sources of information about Islam? Among the new developments external to Anglo-Protestantism were the expansion of US film and news media industries, the rising American political and economic presence in the Middle East, and the growing American Muslim population. With post–World War II shifts in American religion and society in mind, here I give a few illustrations showing how ideas about Islam were re-invented in gendered terms from the mid-twentieth century to the present.

Both Orientalism and anti-Muslim sentiments were operative in twentieth-century Hollywood films featuring Arab or Muslim characters, as demonstrated in Melani McAlister's book *Epic Encounters: Culture, Media, & US Interests in the Middle East Since 1945* and Jack G. Shaheen's

Reel Bad Arabs: How Hollywood Vilifies a People.[29] Shaheen examined over nine hundred films produced between 1896 and 2001 featuring Arab or Muslim characters and concluded that nearly all of them dehumanized these characters.[30] In addition to the 1928 silent film *Harem Scarem* and several adaptations on the same theme (addressed in Chapter 5), among the early twentieth-century examples was the wildly popular film *The Sheik* (1921). This desert drama starring Rudolph Valentino as Sheikh Ahmed Ben Hassan and based on Edith Hull's bestselling 1919 novel launched Valentino's career. In the film, Valentino is a barbaric but handsome Arab Muslim with whom a young English heroine falls in love, despite the fact that he abducts her. She only marries Ahmed, however, once he is revealed to be an Englishman in disguise. Valentino's Mediterranean heritage as an Italian American represented the similarly complex racial status of Arabs in the early twentieth-century American context. Furthermore, the film showed fierce saber-wielding desert Arabs and portrayed Arab women as exotic belly dancers and as property—captive, muted, and sold to harems. With the exception of Ahmed, who actually turns out to be European, the film portrayed all Arabs negatively.[31]

Among the growing number of post–World War II films depicting Muslims were several that Shaheen found repeatedly playing on TV from the mid-1980s onward, indicating their continued influence over generations of viewers long after their box office releases.[32] These included: *The Steel Lady* (1953), in which four Americans crash in the Sahara, find bellydancing maidens in an oasis, and shoot at marauding Arabs; *The Exodus* (1960), which introduces viewers to the Arab–Israeli conflict and portrays the Grand Mufti (chief Islamic authority) of Jerusalem and his associates as gangsters and other Arabs as vicious murderers; and *The Black Stallion* (1979), in which a young American boy in North Africa frees a wild stallion after turbaned Arabs abuse the horse in a scene that did not appear in the bestselling book.[33] With the foundation for interpreting such images of Muslims built by missionary discourses and Orientalist production, the film industry continued to play on American assumptions about the exotic Middle East or about dangerous Muslim men. By the 1990s that industry tended to portray Muslims as terrorists.[34]

In the background of such films were two concerns related to the Middle East in the second half of the twentieth century according to McAlister: 1) US military and political interests, especially in using strategic alliances with Middle Eastern nations to check the influence of the Soviet Union, and

2) American access to Middle Eastern oil as a major postwar policy goal. Because of such growing interests, more Americans began working in the region, often for oil companies, or were stationed there in military or diplomatic roles in large numbers by the 1970s.[35] Moving beyond views of the Middle East mainly as an area of religious interest (for missions and Holy Land tours), this expanding American involvement brought possibilities of economic, diplomatic, and cultural partnership, as well as situations of economic exploitation and political pressure. The latter included the CIA's role in overthrowing the democratically elected Iranian prime minister Mohammed Mossadegh (1882–1967) in 1953 after he attempted to nationalize his country's oil.[36]

Building on the longstanding American associations between Islam and the Middle East that missionary discourses supported, in the second half of the twentieth century Americans regularly conflated Middle Eastern political events with the actions of Muslims broadly. In this context, McAlister maintained, Islam "became highlighted as the dominant signifier of the region, rather than oil wealth, Arabs, or Christian Holy Lands."[37] This skewed the actual global Muslim diversity and politicized the Islamic tradition. Thus, political and social movements that included Muslims became closely associated with Islam at large.[38] Such presumptions were apparent in American political cartoons from the 1950s to 2000, which, according to Gottschalk and Greenberg, must be read with attention to gender. Similar to missionary images of an earlier period, the cartoons they studied used Muslim men "to depict the supposed oppressiveness of Islam toward women" or to symbolize Islam itself. As they explained, "In an odd reenactment of the very patriarchal focus on men that they so often criticize in Islamic traditions, most American cartoonists exclude women as symbols of the religion."[39] When Muslim women do appear in such cartoons, they are nearly always veiled. Gottschalk and Greenberg's study found that, like early twentieth-century missionary references to the veil, political cartoonists used the veil "to symbolize all Islamic traditions and their implied oppressiveness. In other words, it is the invisibility of a woman, seldom her presence, that symbolizes Islam."[40]

The authors also noted that specifically in response to the Iranian hostage crisis of 1979, when Iranian students seized the US embassy and took hostages, the political activities of people who happened to be Muslim became strongly associated with Islam itself. They explained, "Many Americans assumed Islamic ideologies to have been the motivating force behind all Iranian revolutionaries, when, in fact, they were not. . . . This portrayal indicted not only Iranian Muslims but all Islamic traditions."[41] Such ideas were remarkably widespread and influential because TV news broadcasters brought the hostage crisis into American homes each night for over a year as the United States worked for the captives' release. As McAlister explained, "militant Islam" became the focus of US media coverage of events in Iran, which also conflated Islam with terrorism.[42] For consumers of American mass media, such depictions were believable not because some Muslims in Iran violently attacked the embassy but because Americans were preconditioned—by missionary reports and images, among other influences—to see Muslim male violence as representative of Islam.

From 1979 onward, cartoonists continually recycled such portrayals to depict political events in the Middle East, and this approach shaped their responses to 9/11 and their illustrations of the US invasions of Afghanistan in 2001 and Iraq in 2003.[43] For example, a 2002 cartoon used imagery from *The Wizard of Oz* showing four turbaned men huddled together facing a large projected image of Osama bin Laden's head with flames surrounding it, which resembled the wizard's head in the classic film. The caption read: "Pay no attention to that man behind the curtain." The figure behind the curtain had devil's horns and a forked tail, and the word "ISLAM" appeared across the backs of the four men cowering beneath bin Laden's menacing face. Gottschalk and Greenberg noted the cartoon's implication that men alone define the Islamic tradition and the insidious "notion that terrorist organizations like bin Laden's can dupe and befoul an entire religion."[44] In this instance, because the actions of Muslim men are seen to represent the whole religion, all negative stereotypes that accrue to figures like bin Laden are also applied to Islam. Thus, similar to the way in which western Christians made the Ottoman sultan a symbol of tyranny and gender oppression in the eighteenth and nineteenth centuries, Muslim men and Islam itself became symbols of terrorism from the late twentieth century onward.[45]

At the same time, a key demographic transition was occurring in the United States, due in part to the 1965 Immigration and Nationality Act that repealed the nativist immigration quotas of 1924: Muslims began arriving in the United States as legal immigrants in higher numbers, some of them leaving the very areas of conflict and economic hardship that political cartoonists were depicting so egregiously. Since the late nineteenth and early twentieth centuries, Arab migrant communities, including small numbers of Muslims, had been present in the United States in places like New York City and Detroit.[46] Yet the 1960s brought many more Muslims of diverse backgrounds, and the African American Muslim community experienced significant growth both through the Nation of Islam and through conversion to Sunni Islam.[47] White Americans, including Protestants, often viewed their American Muslim neighbors through the lens of race first and then religion, and the US government (likewise largely White, Protestant, and male) marked African American Muslims as politically suspect, tying Islam to negative racializations in ways that foreshadowed contemporary anti-Muslim racism, as Razack, Love, and Aziz have described.[48]

From negative depictions of Middle Eastern Muslims to racist and xenophobic reactions to Muslims in the United States, these post–World War II developments can be tied to the production of knowledge about Muslims to which Anglo-Protestant missionaries contributed. According to McAlister, the spread of such ideas about the Middle East and Islam has occurred not through conspiracy or intentional collaboration (between missionaries and representatives of the film or news media industries, for instance) but rather through shared cultural practices that embed certain messages by repetition. She emphasized, as well, "the ways that different sets of texts, with their own interests and affiliations, come to overlap, to reinforce and revise one another toward an end that is neither entirely planned nor entirely coincidental."[49] In the United States, gendered views of Islam as oppressive and violent have become "naturalized by repetition," to adopt McAlister's terminology.[50] The images of Muslims that nineteenth- and twentieth-century Protestant missionaries had *re-invented* were yet again recycled, recast, and adapted to the political and social contexts of late twentieth- and early twenty-first-century America. Yet these enduring images are not the only resources available for American Protestant engagements with Islam today.

Openings for Dialogue Beneath the Missionary Veil

The changes occurring within Protestant theologies and religious practices after World War II were just as drastic as the political, economic, and demographic transformations of that period. Among these were growing divisions between mainline and evangelical Protestants.[51] The fundamentalist–modernist controversies of the 1920s pitted theological liberals, whose biblical hermeneutics incorporated modern science and historical-critical scholarship, against conservatives, who supported literal interpretations of scripture that, among other things, rejected Charles Darwin's theories of evolution. Liberal Protestants described doctrinal rigidity as stifling to Christianity and accused fundamentalists of ignoring social conditions, while conservatives saw these moves toward more dynamic theologies as bending to worldly influences and threatening the future of their faith.[52] The conflict came to a head in 1925 at the trial of John Thomas Scopes, who was prosecuted for teaching evolution in a Tennessee public school.[53] These theological and cultural clashes influenced American Protestant approaches to missions by solidifying divisions within the ecumenical missionary movement that had always included both members who emphasized evangelism for conversion and those who saw social work like education and medical care as an end in itself.[54] Supporters of the latter approach emphasized a "preference for an evangelism of service and personal example." They also challenged the missionary movement's tendency to impose western forms of Christianity and culture rather than indigenizing the gospel.[55]

Mainline Protestants in the United States, including Presbyterians, Congregationalists, Methodists, Lutherans, and Episcopalians, became more committed to efforts for social change rather than direct evangelism after World War II. One telling example of this shift in missions among Muslims appeared in reports from the Methodist Episcopal Mission in North Africa. After a 1967 trip to view the mission's work in Algeria, the Methodist magazine *Together* quoted J. Harry Haines of the Methodist Committee for Overseas Relief as saying, "Muslims have never really felt that we were interested in them for their own sake." The magazine continued, "Instead of viewing Muslims as potential converts, [Haines] added, 'Perhaps we should stop worrying... and just love them as people.'"[56] Such language contrasted with missionary discourses of the early twentieth century, instead echoing the processes of decolonization just then occurring in Asia and Africa. This developing approach also resulted from the long-term contact that missionaries like Eleanor Calverley and Cornelius Van Dyck had with Muslims, the relationships these individuals formed with Kuwaitis and Syrians, and their increased understanding of Islamic doctrines. Such views recognized and affirmed commonalities and showed admiration for Islamic devotion, even when still emphasizing the ways that Christianity and Islam differ.

Beginning in the interwar period, some missionaries and mission supporters also advocated for interreligious collaboration, as reflected in the 1932 Laymen's Report on the future of missions in Asia, which was authored by a group of American Protestant laymen under the leadership of Harvard professor William Ernest Hocking. Among the findings that some Protestants leaders embraced and others denounced as heresy, this controversial study, published as *Re-Thinking Missions: A Laymen's Inquiry After One Hundred Years*, did not advocate for the end of missions. Rather, it called for collaboration among people of different religions in response to the growing dangers of secularism, and it warned against western missionary paternalism.[57] Mission historian William R. Hutchison summed up Hocking's view as follows:

> A missionary agenda predicated on the superiority of Western and Christian institutions, and announcing the right of Christian soldiers to conquer and displace other systems, may have been inevitable, [Hocking] thought, at a certain stage of history. What was emerging, however, was a "permanent" stance that would recognize the right of all peoples to autonomy and respect, and would acknowledge the spiritual vitality and reforming zeal in other world religions. Christianity and Western culture must question, with respect to achievement if not to aspiration, their own convictions about a superior spirituality. At the least they must be content to cherish such convictions without parading them, or maintaining them as working assumptions, in their relationships with the East.[58]

With the debates it prompted in the missionary movement and beyond, the Laymen's Report represented a turning point for missionaries in their public discourses: it gave them license to preach about social justice or even interreligious collaboration.[59] Missionaries working among Muslims, therefore, found more openings to share their ideas about Christian–Muslim commonalities and their admiration for the spiritual riches of the Islamic tradition. British missionary Constance Padwick, for instance, did so through her long-term study and collection of Muslim prayer books in Egypt.[60]

Most American mainline mission organizations took a centrist position on the Laymen's Report. In the decade following this publication, moderate mainline mission boards outnumbered conservative boards ten to one, signaling the significant number of missionaries who no longer portrayed other religions as Christianity's (and Christ's) enemies.[61] Without embracing all of the commission's recommendations, missionaries working for these organizations began adopting more appreciative views of Islam and other faiths, opening a pathway toward theological inclusivism—or recognition of the possibility that God might be working within non-Christian traditions.[62]

Yet differences of opinion over the proper missionary approach to other religions continued, both within the ecumenical missionary movement and between ecumenical Protestants and members of new evangelical, non-denominational mission organizations.[63] In a stunning reversal of the 1930s mission environment, by the early 1980s missionaries of these conservative organizations had come to outnumber mainline missionaries ten to one.[64] The ecumenical–evangelical split is another twentieth-century landmark for missions and for Protestant approaches to interfaith dialogue.

Protestants built momentum toward interreligious collaboration through gatherings like the 1936 World Congress of Faiths in London, which revealed the close ties between British and American Protestant leaders; and they expanded into the realm of formal interreligious dialogue under the auspices of the World Council of Churches (WCC) after World War II. The monumental shifts toward interfaith appreciation during the Second Vatican Council (1962–1965), however, were also significant in the mid-twentieth century, not only for Catholics but also for the Protestants it influenced and for preceding the interfaith efforts of the WCC.[65] The first formal WCC dialogue event held in Lebanon in 1970 paved the way for the creation of a sub-unit for dialogue in 1971, and these activities built on more localized work of the WCC in the 1960s.[66] The World's Parliament of Religions in Chicago in 1893 had foreshadowed such Protestant ecumenical activities and was the first organized event of interreligious dialogue in the modern western world—one in which missionaries participated. Yet the Parliament was a largely American Protestant affair, both in the composition of its delegates and in its theological ethos.[67]

It was in part the formal Protestant movement for dialogue of the 1960s and 1970s, accompanied with theological openness to other faiths, that prompted a growing population of evangelicals to break from the WCC in 1974 and create the Lausanne Movement, which was centered around strategies for world evangelization.[68] Evangelical missionaries formally associated with the Lausanne Movement or embracing similar approaches to evangelism arrived in the Middle East and other Islamic contexts in increasing numbers after the 1970s, just as the presence of mainline missionaries in these regions was declining.[69] Inheriting the work of non-denominational faith missions like the Egypt General Mission and Algiers Mission Band, these missionaries often developed far more nuanced views of the people among whom they worked than did their evangelical constituents back home. Melani Trexler demonstrated, for example, how conservative Baptist missionaries in Lebanon in the mid- to late twentieth century differed considerably from Baptist leaders in the United States in their understandings of Middle Eastern politics and their approaches to missions, in part because the Lebanese Baptists had forced missionaries to hear their desires and critiques of mission practices.[70]

Thomas Kidd has shown that American evangelical missionaries' heightened focus on Muslims after the 1980s added to a rising eschatological fascination with Islam and expectations of violence in the Middle East leading to the end times.[71] Yet the skewed depictions of Islam permeating American culture today are just as much the result of the messages that mainline missionaries had begun seeding nearly two centuries prior. The denominational missionaries featured in this book, along with a smaller number of faith missions focusing on Muslims through the 1920s, established the Protestant theological discourse on Islam that continued among American Protestants who had rejected the inclusivist and pluralist theological notions about Islam that liberal missionaries and theologians like the influential Wilfred Cantwell Smith (1916–2000) were developing after mid-century.[72] Yet from the 1970s onward conservative missionaries too sought approaches to evangelism that respected and accommodated Muslims' cultural values and circumstances.[73]

It was the Protestant missionaries' cultural (rather than theological) discourses that had more long-lasting influence on American society, and among many evangelicals and mainline Protestants alike the negative gender discourse about Islam persisted. Liberal Protestants' turn toward theological openness therefore did not automatically translate into a shift in cultural presumptions. Recall the following reasons why missionaries employed these gendered tropes: Eurocentric views of civilization; White supremacy; and the cultural, economic, and military expansion of Protestant empire. Such motivations were not based on Protestant theological doctrines, although these western views, as well as negative characterizations of Muslim men and women, were easily woven into theological discourses. When the theologies changed—as we saw in Chapter 4 comparing missionary fiction of the 1920s to Margaret Hamm's and Dorothy Blatter's stories in the 1950s and 1960s—the cultural critique remained. For another example, we can turn to Calverley's 1958 autobiography, *My Arabian Days and Nights*, in which the retired missionary doctor described the beauty she saw in Arab women's harem attire, a beauty that her more critical writings of the early twentieth century had not recognized (see Chapter 6). Yet she still lamented seeing Kuwaiti women on the streets "shrouded in black" and hoped that they would one day have the "freedom to walk on the streets unveiled."[74] It is precisely because of the gendered lens that this book keeps coming up against the most negative rhetoric, whereas a study on missionary approaches to Islamic doctrine might find many more openings for dialogue over time.

Initially used by missionaries to cast doubt on Islamic theology, and later vigorously taken up and re-invented by missionary women, the persistent critique of veiling and seclusion has had an enduring effect on American views of Islam, shaping what today we know as Islamophobia. Yet missionaries' private views were also veiled, so to speak, from the eyes of their constituents. Their public performances, analyzed throughout this book in textual, visual, or material form, depicted Islam in ways that largely expressed the motivations of missions, drew on missionaries' own cultural biases, and conformed in large part to the expectations of their supporters, whose ideas reflected similar biases but were usually not informed by personal Christian–Muslim interactions. Therefore, this study has demonstrated, on the one hand, that gender tropes have become ingrained in American views of Islam, feeding present-day Islamophobia and posing a barrier to positive Christian–Muslim relations. On the other hand, it has shown that efforts at Christian–Muslim understanding were not completely absent in earlier periods, although they were rarely central to missionaries' fundraising campaigns. For example, missionaries humanized Muslims by making them familiar through personal accounts, fictional tales, images, and even costumed performances. These presentations drew on commonalities and helped audiences feel empathy, and not just pity, for Muslim women, men, and children. We saw this in the stories about young Muslim girls like Fatmeh, Noorah, Lindao, and Filiz, stories aimed at young Protestant readers whom the authors attempted to draw in with winsome, spunky protagonists whose hopes and fears were not so different from their own. For readers who viewed Islam as a strange, distant, monolithic religion, such stories made Muslims familiar—and more importantly made them human. Rather than treating Muslims as dangerous rivals or targets of conversion, these recognizable Muslim characters could help Protestant readers—in the words of the Methodist leader Harry Haines—to "just love them as people."[75]

Yet considering the persistent gender tropes, where can we look to find hopeful openings for dialogue beneath the missionary discourses of the veil? I conclude here with three points from my study of early twentieth-century missionary sources. *First, the discourse of the veil did not always dominate in missionary writings about Muslim women.* We can see this in the letters missionaries sent home—letters which were "private" or not written for dissemination beyond friends and family. Eva Marshall, for instance, wrote to her family from Palestine in 1927 about the Muslim girls in the Quaker mission school in Ramallah, saying:

> They are very sweet and devoted girls and I like them especially. They are careful about going out in public unless they are covered, and do not go to our Sunday service at the church, chiefly for that reason I think, but nearly every other part of our activities they take full part in.[76]

Marshall offered no criticism of the girls' practices and instead expressed affection for them. She later wrote with excitement about an upcoming visit to the home of a wealthy Muslim pupil, with whom she planned to stay for a week, saying, "I should learn much from them about Moslem life and customs, position of women, politics, religion etc. I have an excellent book on Islam I want to read before I go so that I can be more intelligent in conversation."[77] These expressions from behind the scenes reveal that gender critique was not always the central category through which missionaries themselves approached Muslims. Instead, we find Marshall describing fellow human beings with whom she had built a positive relationship and from whom she was eager to learn more about Islam.

Second, missionaries accommodated Islamic gender norms, exemplifying a posture that is important for interreligious understanding. While they critiqued practices of seclusion or veiling in their messages to mission supporters, missionaries in the field often adapted to indigenous ways of life and even enabled certain practices that matched their own western Protestant gender norms—like the concept of "woman's work for woman," which held that women missionaries were needed to work in the feminine sphere. Thus, female-only schools, like the one where Marshall taught in Palestine, gave missionary women a higher level of agency and authority, within the bounds of Protestant patriarchal norms. As we learn from other, non-missionary sources, women-led activities and female-only spaces could likewise give Muslim women a similar sense of agency and authority, within the limits of their own patriarchal societies.[78]

Third, educational or ethnographic-type material in missionary accounts promoted intercultural and interreligious awareness without engaging in gender critique. Such missionary writings (like Margaret Hamm's and

Dorothy Blatter's descriptions of Filipino and Turkish engagement practices and dress styles) showed missionary attention to learning other cultures and reflected their relationships with Muslims. This spread knowledge and understanding in a way that could lay the groundwork for Christian–Muslim dialogue. Sometimes missionaries' ethnographic depictions of Islamic *gender norms* also helped nuance or even directly challenge negative generalizations about Muslim women and men—such as accounts or photographs of the wide diversity in Muslim women's dress habits and family experiences.

Long-solidified views of other people (here Muslims) are particularly hard to soften, *unless* people either become more conscious of their own culturally conditioned behaviors or form friendships and actually get to know "others" in meaningful ways. I hope that awareness of the history told in these pages will prompt readers to do just that. Change is possible, whether through personal relationship-building, educational efforts, or scholarly contributions that continue uncovering and challenging the negative perceptions about Islam that contemporary Americans have inherited and absorbed. Indeed, significant transformations in Christian–Muslim relations have already occurred, even through the missionary encounters this book examined. We can learn, for example, from outliers like Mary Mills Patrick, who resisted the dominant discourse of the early twentieth century and spoke in humanizing ways about Turkish women and about Islam. We can also find openings for Christian–Muslim understanding in the positive portrayals of Muslims in children's missionary fiction, which emphasized what young Muslims had in common with young Christian readers. And in recognizing the ways that missionaries like Calverley softened their narratives over time, we can see the transformative power of personal interreligious relationships between Protestants and Muslims.

Today, Islamophobic ideas remain embedded in American culture, but they persist alongside countless organized interreligious efforts that have blossomed since the 1990s and alongside everyday friendships between Christians and Muslims at the local level. For American Christians of diverse Protestant, Catholic, and Orthodox denominations involved in such work, the aforementioned theological and demographic shifts since the mid-twentieth century were pivotal. Although I have identified anti-Muslim gender discourses as uniquely entrenched, my research shows that change has occurred in this arena too. Ideas about Muslim women's attire shifted in Protestant minds between the Reformation period and the early imperial era, for instance, from symbolizing modesty and devotion to symbolizing imprisonment and oppression. It is time for another paradigm shift, one not based on images that can be manipulated for self-interested political or religious gain but built upon interpersonal relationships and acceptance, deep understanding of differences, and affirmations of and openness to our common humanity.

Notes

1. This point relates to Khaled Beydoun's definition of Islamophobia as having private, structural, and dialectical dimensions, the latter aspect binding the first two forms together as state action legitimates private misconceptions, while popular tropes lead individuals to lobby for structural Islamophobic policies. Khaled A. Beydoun, *American Islamophobia: Understanding the Roots and Rise of Fear* (Oakland: University of California Press, 2018), 29, 40–44.
2. Annie Van Sommer and Samuel M. Zwemer, ed., *Our Moslem Sisters: A Cry of Need from Lands of Darkness Interpreted by Those Who Heard It* (New York: Fleming H. Revell Company, 1907).
3. See especially the second chapter in Sarah M. A. Gualtieri, *Between Arab and White: Race and Ethnicity in the Early Syrian American Diaspora* (Berkeley: University of California Press, 2009).
4. Eleanor H. Tejirian and Reeva S. Simon, eds. *Altruism and Imperialism: Western Religious and Cultural Missions to the Middle East* (New York: Middle East Institute of Columbia University, 2002).
5. See the list of hate incidents against Muslim women included later in this section.
6. Important studies linking Islamophobia and American racism include: Erik Love, *Islamophobia and Racism in America* (New York: New York University Press, 2017); Sahar Aziz, *The Racial Muslim: When Racism Quashes Religious Freedom* (Oakland: University of California Press, 2022); Sherene H. Razack, *Nothing Has to Make Sense: Upholding White Supremacy Through Anti-Muslim Racism* (Minnesota: University of Minnesota Press, 2022).
7. Peter Gottschalk and Gabriel Greenberg, *Islamophobia and Anti-Muslim Sentiment: Picturing the Enemy*, 2nd ed. (Lanham: Rowman & Littlefield, 2019), 4. Italics in original. This book's first edition was Gottschalk and Greenberg, *Islamophobia: Making Muslims the Enemy* (Lanham, MD: Rowman and Littlefield, 2007).
8. The term's origins in French date to the early twentieth century. One key English-language publication introducing this term in a report on Muslims in Britain was Runnymede Trust, *Islamophobia: A Challenge for Us All* (London: Runnymede Trust, 1997), accessed January 7, 2024, https://www.runnymedetrust.org/publications/islamophobia-a-challenge-for-us-all.
9. Stephen Sheehi, *Islamophobia: The Ideological Campaign Against Muslims* (Atlanta: Clarity Press, 2011), 31, 34. Sheehi distinguished this post-1990s form of Islamophobia from previous iterations of anti-Arab racism and Orientalism (p. 37).
10. Aziz, *Racial Muslim*, 21.
11. Gottschalk and Greenberg, *Islamophobia*, 4.
12. Aziz, *Racial Muslim*, 21. Italics in original.
13. Love, *Islamophobia and Racism*, 2; Razack, *Nothing Has to Make Sense*, 15.
14. Locating the study of Islamophobia within race studies, Kazi identified Islamophobia as not simply individual acts of anti-Muslim prejudice but "as a cornerstone of an overarching system of white supremacy." Nazia Kazi, *Islamophobia, Race, and Global Politics* (Lanham, MD: Rowman & Littlefield, 2019), 8; Beydoun, *American Islamophobia*, 29, 40–44.
15. Nathan Lean, *The Islamophobia Industry: How the Far Right Manufactures Fear of Muslims*, 2nd ed. (London: Pluto Books, 2017); Todd H. Green, *The Fear of Islam: An Introduction to Islamophobia in the West* (Minneapolis: Fortress Press, 2015); Caleb Iyer Elfenbein, *Fear in Our Hearts: What Islamophobia Tells Us About America* (New York: New York University Press, 2021).
16. For other important research on Islamophobia, see the *Journal of Islamophobia Studies*, founded in 2012.

17. Leila Ahmed, *Women and Gender in Islam: Historical Roots of a Modern Debate* (New Haven, CT: Yale University Press, 1992); Ziba Mir-Hosseini, *Islam and Gender: The Religious Debate in Contemporary Iran* (Princeton, NJ: Princeton University Press, 1999); Kecia Ali, *Sexual Ethics and Islam: Feminist Reflections on Qur'an, Hadith, and Jurisprudence* (Oxford: Oneword Publications, 2006); Leila Ahmed, *A Quiet Revolution: The Veil's Resurgence from the Middle East to America* (New Haven, CT: Yale University Press, 2012); Lila Abu-Lughod, *Do Muslim Women Need Saving?* (Cambridge, MA: Harvard University Press, 2013); Maryam Khalid, *Gender, Orientalism, and the "War on Terror": Representation, Discourse, and Intervention in Global Politics* (London and New York: Routledge, 2017); Celene Ibrahim, *Women and Gender in the Qur'an* (Oxford: Oxford University Press, 2020); Hadia Mubarak, *Rebellious Wives, Neglectful Husbands: Controversies in Modern Qur'anic Commentaries* (Oxford: Oxford University Press, 2022); Roshan Iqbal, *Marital and Sexual Ethics in Islamic Law: Rethinking Temporary Marriage* (Lanham, MD: Lexington Books, 2023).
18. Aziz showed that it is possible and important to study Islamophobia through the lens of race. Aziz, *Racial Muslim*.
19. Lila Abu-Lughod, "Do Muslim Women Really Need Saving? Anthropological Reflections on Cultural Relativism and Its Others," *American Anthropologist* 104, no. 3 (September 2002): 784–86.
20. American Civil Liberties Union, "Discrimination Against Muslim Women," ACLU Foundation Women's Rights Project, November 2008, accessed January 7, 2024, https://www.aclu.org/documents/discrimination-against-muslim-women-fact-sheet.
21. Katie Reilly, "Muslim Women and Children Attacked in Hate Crime, New York City Officials Say," *Time* (September 10, 2016), accessed January 7, 2024, http://tiny.cc/gtjvyz.
22. Patrina Adger, "Muslim Woman Living in Oklahoma Attacked in Dallas for Wearing Hijab," KOCO News 5, January 5, 2019, accessed January 7, 2024, http://tiny.cc/jtjvyz.
23. Annie Rose Ramos, "Staff Member Fired for Involvement in Attack on Muslim Student at Baltimore School," WJZ News, October 12, 2022, accessed January 7, 2024, http://tiny.cc/uvjvyz.
24. Marc Santia, "Muslim Teen Girl Called 'Terrorist,' Attacked While Riding Subway to School: Police," NBC New York, October 23, 2023, accessed January 7, 2024, http://tiny.cc/zvjvyz.
25. Chelsea Bailey, "Reports of Antisemitism, Anti-Arab and Anti-Muslim Bias Continue to Surge Across the US, New Data Shows," *CNN*, December 11, 2023, accessed January 7, 2024, http://tiny.cc/0wjvyz.
26. Shakira Hussein, *From Victims to Suspects: Muslim Women Since 9/11* (Sydney: University of New South Wales, 2016).
27. Beydoun, *American Islamophobia*, 103–5; Love, *Islamophobia and Racism*, 101–2.
28. Marlene Lenthang, Kailani Koenig, Samira Puskar, and Corky Seimaszko, "Suspect in Death of 6-Year-Old Palestinian American Boy Was Obsessed with Israel–Hamas War, Prosecutors Say," NBC News, October 16, 2023, accessed January 7, 2024, http://tiny.cc/5wjvyz.
29. McAlister explained the limits of the lens of Orientalism and ways that the post–World War II United States built new frameworks for understanding the Middle East. Melani McAlister, *Epic Encounters: Culture, Media, & U.S. Interest in the Middle East Since 1945*, updated ed. (Berkeley: University of California Press, 2005), 10–11. See also Jack Shaheen, *Reel Bad Arabs: How Hollywood Vilifies a People* (New York: Olive Branch Press, 2001), and the 2006 documentary film of the same title, based on the book.
30. Shaheen, *Reel Bad Arabs*, 233.
31. McAlister, *Epic Encounters*, 24–25; Shaheen, *Reel Bad Arabs*, 422–23, 425. Ahmed has an English father and a Spanish mother. Valentino also starred in *The Son of the Sheik* (1926) and *She's a Sheik* (1927).
32. Shaheen lists the following as the most often replayed films vilifying Arabs: *The Sheikh* (1921), *The Mummy* (1932), *Cairo* (1942), *The Steel Lady* (1953), *Exodus* (1960), *The Black Stallion* (1979), *Protocol* (1984), *The Delta Force* (1986), *Ernest in the Army* (1997), and *Rules of Engagement* (2000). Shaheen, *Reel Bad Arabs*, 5.
33. Ibid., 102–3, 189–91, 457–58. Shaheen noted that in the book *The Black Stallion*, in contrast, "a benevolent Arab Sheikh befriends an American boy, giving the youth the Arabian's first foal" (pp. 102–3).
34. Gottschalk and Greenberg, *Islamophobia*, 195–229.

35. McAlister, *Epic Encounters*, 32–34; Toby Craig Jones, "America, Oil, and War in the Middle East," *American History* 99, no. 1 (June 2012): 210–12.
36. McAlister, *Epic Encounters*, 32–33.
37. Ibid., 200.
38. Gottschalk and Greenberg, *Islamophobia*, 131. Missionaries commonly made religious identity the primary lens through which they understood Muslims, regardless of national or cultural background or level of religious commitment, so this politicization of Muslim identity had earlier precedents.
39. Ibid., 65.
40. Ibid., 67.
41. Ibid., 144.
42. McAlister, *Epic Encounters*, 200, 211.
43. Gottschalk and Greenberg, *Islamophobia*, 150–62.
44. Ibid., 67.
45. Ibid., 71.
46. Most Arab Americans then were Christian, and the same is still true today.
47. Robert Dannin, *Black Pilgrimage to Islam* (Oxford: Oxford University Press, 2005).
48. On American Muslim experiences in the twentieth century, see Edward E. Curtis IV, *Muslims of the Heartland: How Syrian Immigrants Made a Home in the American Midwest* (New York: New York University Press, 2022); Thomas Kidd, *American Christians and Islam: Evangelical Culture and Muslims from the Colonial Period to the Age of Terrorism* (Princeton, NJ: Princeton University Press, 2009), 96–119. African American Protestants also engaged ideas about Islam. McAlister, *Epic Encounters*, 84–124; Kidd, *American Christians*, 102–4, 110–12.
49. McAlister, *Epic Encounters*, 8.
50. Ibid.
51. Martin E. Marty, *Modern American Religion*, vol. 2, *The Noise of Conflict, 1919–1941* (Chicago: University of Chicago Press, 1991), 3.
52. William Hutchison, *Errand to the World: American Protestant Thought and Foreign Missions* (Chicago: University of Chicago Press, 1987), 148–50.
53. Bradley J. Longfield, *The Presbyterian Controversy: Fundamentalists, Modernists, and Moderates* (Oxford: Oxford University Press, 1993), 154–56.
54. Some within the latter group were affiliated with the Social Gospel Movement, which saw missions as not only spiritually focused but concerned with justice and the social transformation of the world.
55. Hutchison, *Errand to the World*, 151.
56. Emil Paul John, "Through the Valley of the Shadow," *Together* (January 1968): 68.
57. William Ernest Hocking, *Re-Thinking Missions: A Laymen's Inquiry After One Hundred Years* (New York and London: Harper & Brothers, 1932). The report, also known as the *Laymen's Inquiry*, which the US Federal Council of Churches commissioned, began with a 1930 meeting of Baptist laymen that John D. Rockefeller, Jr., organized. Hutchison, *Errand to the World*, 159–75; on the call for interreligious collaboration, see especially 161–62. See also "Missions Report Scored as Heresy: Findings of Laymen's Inquiry Assailed by RE-emphasis Group at Mass Meeting," *The New York Times* (March 21, 1933), 19.
58. Hutchison, *Errand to the World*, 162.
59. Ibid.
60. Catriona Laing, "A Provocation to Mission: Constance Padwick's Study of Muslim Devotion," *Islam and Christian–Muslim Relations* 24, no. 1 (January 2023): 27–42.
61. Hutchison, *Errand to the World*, 175. Hutchison noted that the Congregationalists of the ABCFM were most favorable to the report; Methodists and Episcopalians showed some uneasiness; and Northern Baptists, Presbyterians, and Dutch Reformed raised more objections, while all admired certain parts of the report (pp. 165–66).
62. On inclusivism and other theologies of religion, see Thomas Albert Howard, *The Faiths of Others: A History of Interreligious Dialogue* (New Haven, CT: Yale University Press, 2021), 23–27.
63. One such debate arose in reaction to Dutch Reformed missiologist Hendrik Kraemer's message about missions to the non-Christian world at the 1938 International Missionary Council conference in Tambaram, India. S. Mark Heim, "Mission and Dialogue: 50 Years After Tambaram," *Christian Century* (April 6, 1988): 340.

64. Hutchison, *Errand to the World*, 175–77.
65. Howard, *Faiths of Others*, 136–234.
66. The conference papers were published in S. J. Samartha, *Dialogue Between Men of Living Faiths: Papers Presented at a Consultation Held at Ajaltoun, Lebanon, March 1970* (Geneva: World Council of Churches, 1971). On prior WCC efforts at Christian–Muslim dialogue, see John B. Taylor and Muzammil H. Siddiqui, "Understanding and Experience of Christian–Muslim Dialogue," in *Dialogue Between Men of Living Faiths*, 59–74.
67. On the World's Parliament, see Howard, *Faiths of Others*, 79–135.
68. The movement originated from the International Congress on World Evangelization in Lausanne, Switzerland, in 1974 under the leadership of John Stott and Billy Graham. The incorporation of the International Missionary Council into the WCC in 1961 also influenced the Lausanne Movement's formation. Tormod Engelsviken, "The Role of the Lausanne Movement in Modern Christian Mission," in *The Lausanne Movement: A Range of Perspectives* (Minneapolis: Fortress Press, 2014), 26–44. Hutchison noted that evangelicals' disappointments about their lack of influence during WCC deliberations at Uppsala (1968) and Bangkok (1973) ensured that they would continue their own gatherings. Hutchison, *Errand to the World*, 192.
69. Kidd, *American Christians*, 75–95, 120–43.
70. Melani E. Trexler, *Evangelizing Lebanon: Baptists, Missions, and the Question of Cultures* (Waco, TX: Baylor University Press, 2016), 99–106, 186, 191.
71. Kidd, *American Christians*, 121.
72. Smith was a missionary in South Asia and taught Islamic history at Forman Christian College in Lahore and the Henry Martyn School of Islamic Studies in Hyderabad before founding the Institute of Islamic Studies at McGill University and later joining the faculty of Harvard Divinity School. His appreciation of the Islamic faith is clear in his publications, including *Islam in Modern History* (Princeton, NJ: Princeton University Press, 1977). On the differences of Smith's approach from that of two other Prominent missionaries in Islamic contexts, Kenneth Cragg and Temple Gairdner, see James A. Tebbe, "Kenneth Cragg in Perspective: A Comparison with Temple Gairdner and Wilfred Cantwell Smith," *International Bulletin of Missionary Research* (January 2002): 16–21.
73. For example, missionary discussions in 1978 at the North American Conference on Muslim Evangelization, associated with the Lausanne Movement, focused serious attention on cultural relevance and the problem of imperialism. Kidd, *American Christians*, 123–24.
74. Eleanor Taylor Calverley, *My Arabian Days and Nights* (New York: Thomas Y. Crowell, 1958), 173.
75. John, "Through the Valley of the Shadow," 68.
76. Eva Marshall to Family, December 10, 1927, Khalil A. Totah and Eva Marshall Totah Papers (MC 1210, box 4, folder 1) (hereafter *Totah Papers*), Quaker & Special Collections, Haverford College, Haverford, PA.
77. Eva Marshall to Family, June 30, 1928, Totah Papers MC 1210-4-2.
78. Saba Mahmood, *Politics of Piety: Islamic Revival and the Feminist Subject* (Princeton, NJ: Princeton University Press, 2012).

Bibliography

Archives

Angus Library and Archive, University of Oxford, Oxford, England
The Archives of the Reformed Church in America, New Brunswick, NJ
The British Library, London, England
The Burke Library Archives at Union Theological Seminary, New York, NY
Centre for Muslim–Christian Studies, Oxford, England
Congregational Library & Archives, Boston, MA
Evangelical Lutheran Church of America Archives, Chicago, IL
Hartford International University Archives and Special Collections, Hartford, CT
International Missionary Photography Archive, University of Southern California Libraries, Los Angeles, CA
National Library of Scotland, Edinburgh, Scotland
Presbyterian Historical Society, Philadelphia, PA
Quaker & Special Collections, Haverford College, Haverford, PA
Special Collections, School of Oriental and African Studies, University of London, London, England
Special Collections, Yale Divinity School Library, New Haven, CT
Special Collections and Archives, Pitts Library, Candler School of Theology, Atlanta, GA
United Methodist Church Archives, Madison, NJ
Western Theological Seminary Collection at the Joint Archives of Holland, Holland, MI

Mission and Church Periodicals

Algiers Mission Band
Arabian Mission: Quarterly Letters from the Field
Baptist Children's Magazine and Juvenile Missionary Record
The Baptist Missionary Magazine
Baptist Missionary Society Report
Blessed Be Egypt
The Bookman
The Bookseller: A Newspaper of British and Foreign Literature
The Children's Missionary and Sabbath School Record
Children's Work for Children
Daughters of Syria
The Friend
Friends Missionary Advocate
The Friends' Review
Heathen Woman's Friend
The Indian Interpreter: A Religious and Ethical Quarterly
The International Review of Missions
The Kurdistan Missionary
Life and Light for Heathen Women

Life and Light for Women
London Friend
The Missing Link
Mission Studies: Woman's Work in Foreign Lands
Mission Tidings
The Missionary Calendar of the Augustana Foreign Missionary Society
The Missionary Helper
The Missionary Herald Missionary Review of the World
Missionary Survey: The Presbyterian Church in the U.S. at Home and Abroad
The Moslem World
Neglected Arabia: Missionary Letters and News
Outlook of Missions
Over Sea and Land: A Missionary Magazine for the Young
A Quarterly Token for Juvenile Subscribers
The Record of the Home Foreign Mission Work of the United Free Church of Scotland
Wesleyan Juvenile Offering: A Miscellany of Missionary Information for Young Persons
Woman's Missionary Friend
The Women's Missionary Magazine
Woman's Work for Woman
World Comrades

Primary Sources

Adams, Hannah. *A Dictionary of Religions and Religious Denominations, Jewish, Heathen, Mahometan, and Christian, Ancient and Modern*. 4th ed. Boston: James Eastburn and Co., 1817.

"All Dressed Up." *Oakland Post Enquirer*, October 10, 1927.

Amin, Qasim. "The Liberation of Women." In *The Liberation of Women and the New Woman: Two Documents in the History of Egyptian Feminism*. Translated by Samiha Sidhon Peterson, 1–106. Cairo: The American University of Cairo Press, 2022.

Annual Register of the Hartford Theological Seminary for the Sixty-Third Year, 1896–1897. Hartford, CT: Hartford Seminary Press, 1897.

Balph, James McKinnis. *Fifty Years of Mission Work in Syria: A Brief Compend of the Mission Work of the Reformed Presbyterian Church in Northern Syria, Asia Minor and Cyprus*. Pittsburgh: Murdoch, Kerr, & Co., 1913.

Blatter, Dorothy. *Cap and Candle*. Philadelphia: Westminster Press, 1961.

Buchanan, Claudius. *Christian Researches in Asia: With Notices of the Translation of the Scriptures into Oriental Language*. Boston: Samuel T. Armstrong, Cornhill, 1811.

Calverley, Eleanor Jane Taylor. "An Arabian Harem: Impressions of an American Girl on a Visit to the Home of the Woman of the Near East." *The Buffalo Commercial*, April 24, 1919.

Calverley, Eleanor Jane Taylor. *My Arabian Days and Nights*. New York: Thomas Y. Crowell, 1958.

Calvin, John. *The Institutes of the Christian Religion*. Translated by Henry Beveridge. London: James Clarke & Co, 1953.

Carus-Wilson, Mary Louisa, and Georgina Petrie. *Irene Petrie: Missionary to Kashmir*. London: Hodder and Stoughton, 1901.

Central Committee on the United Study of Foreign Missions (CCUSFM). *The Story of the Jubilee: An Account of the Celebration of the Fiftieth Anniversary of the Beginnings in the United States of Woman's Organized Work for Foreign Missions, 1860–1910*. West Medford, MA: CCUSFM, 1911.

The Christian Occupation of Africa: The Proceedings of a Conference of Mission Boards Engaged in Work in the Continent of Africa. New York: Committee of Reference and Counsel of the Foreign Missions Conference of North America, 1917.

Cooper, A. A. "Syria and Palestine: Beyrout." In *The Ninety-Sixth Report of the British and Foreign Bible Society*. London: Gresham Press, 1900.
The Customs and Manners of Bedouin Arabs. Philadelphia: American Sunday-School Union, 1838.
Daubendiek, Letha Idell. "The Christian Approach to Muslim Women in India." MA thesis, Hartford Seminary Foundation, 1930.
Dennis, James S. *World Atlas of Christian Missions: Containing a Directory of Missionary Societies, a Classified Summary of Statistics, an Index of Mission Stations, and Maps Showing the Location of Mission Stations Throughout the World*. New York: Student Volunteer Movement, 1911.
Edib, Halide. *Memoirs of Halidé Edib*. London: John Murray, 1923.
Entwistle, Mary. *The Bible Guide Book: A Companion to Bible Study for Young People and Their Teachers*. London: Student Christian Movement Press, 1936.
Entwistle, Mary. *Habeeb: A Boy of Palestine*. London: Church Missionary Society, 1927.
Entwistle, Mary. *Little Children of Mission Lands*. New York: G. H. Doran, 1925.
Entwistle, Mary. *Musa: Son of Egypt*. London: Edinburgh House Press, 1927.
Entwistle, Mary, and Elizabeth Harris, *The Call Drum: African Stories and Studies for Primary Children*. New York: Friendship Press, 1928.
Gairdner, William H. T. *The Reproach of Islam*. London: Student Volunteer Movement, 1909.
Gibbon, Edward. *The History of the Decline and Fall of the Roman Empire*. Vol. 3. New York: J. J. Harper, 1831.
Handbook and Guide of The World in Boston: The First Great Exposition in America of Home and Foreign Missions, Held in Mechanics Building April 22–May 20, 1911. Boston: The World in Boston, 1911.
al-Haqq, Zahur. *Autobiography of Rev. Zahur-al-Haqq: First Convert in the Mission of the Methodist Episcopal Church in India*. Translated by E. J. Humphrey. New York: The Missionary Society, 1885.
Hayward, John. *The Book of Religions: Comprising the Views, Creeds, Sentiments, or Opinions of All the Religious Sects in the World, Particularly All Christian Denominations in Europe and America, to Which Are Added Church and Missionary Statistics, Together with Biographical Sketches*. 2nd ed. Boston: John Hayward, 1842.
Henrich, Sarah, and James L. Boyce. "Martin Luther—Translations of Two Prefaces on Islam: Preface to the *Libellus de ritu et moribus Turcorum* (1530), and Preface to Bibliander's Edition of the Qur'an (1543)." *Word & World* 16, no. 2 (Spring 1996): 250–66.
Hocking, William Ernest. *Re-thinking Missions: A Layman's Inquiry After One Hundred Years*. New York and London: Harper & Brothers, 1932.
Holliday, G. Y. "Awakening Womanhood." In *Daylight in the Harem: A New Era for Moslem Women*, edited by Annie Van Sommer and Samuel M. Zwemer, 117–29. New York: Fleming H. Revel, 1911.
Hooker, Edward William. *Memoir of Mrs. Sarah L. Huntington Smith: Late of the American Mission in Syria*. New York: American Tract Society, 1845.
Hume-Griffith, M. E. *Behind the Veil in Persia and Turkish Arabia*. Philadelphia: J. B. Lippincott, 1909.
Humphrey, E. J. *Gems of India: Or, Sketches of Distinguished Hindoo and Mahomedan Women*. New York: Nelson & Phillips, 1875.
Humphrey, E. J. *Six Years in India: Or, Sketches of India and Its People as Seen by a Lady Missionary*. New York: Carlton & Porter, 1866.
Humphrey, J. L. "Our First Convert in India a Mohammedan." *The Epworth Herald* 19, no. 15 (September 5, 1908): 35–36.
Hutcheon, Edith J. *The Pearl of the East*. London: British Syrian Mission, 1920.
Jenkins, Hester Donaldson. *Behind Turkish Lattices: The Story of a Turkish Woman's Life*. London: Chatto & Windus, 1911.
Jenkins, Hester Donaldson. *An Educational Ambassador to the Near East: The Story of Mary Mills Patrick and an American College in the Orient*. New York: Revell, 1925.

Jessup, Henry Harris. *Fifty-Three Years in Syria.* Vol. 1. New York: Fleming H. Revell, 1910.
Jessup, Henry Harris. *The Mohammedan Missionary Problem.* Philadelphia: Presbyterian Board of Publication, 1879.
Jessup, Henry Harris. *The Setting of the Crescent and the Rising of the Cross, or Kamil Abdul Messiah: A Syrian Convert from Islam to Christianity.* Philadelphia: Westminster Press, 1898.
Jessup, Henry Harris. *The Women of the Arabs.* New York: Dodd & Mead, 1873.
John, Emil Paul. "Through the Valley of the Shadow." *Together* (January 1968): 67–71.
Jowett, William. *Christian Researches in Syria and the Holy Land in 1823 and 1824 in Furtherance of the Objects of the Church Missionary Society.* Boston: Crocker & Brewster, 1826.
Jowett, William. *Christian Researches in the Mediterranean, from 1815 to 1820, in Furtherance of the Object of the Church Missionary Society.* 2nd ed. London: L. B. Seeley and J. Hatchard & Son, 1822.
Jurji, Edward J. "Museum of Religion and Missions at Princeton Theological Seminary." *Moslem World* 31, no. 3 (1941): 295–98.
Knox, John. "A Treatise on Prayer." In *Writings of the Rev. John Knox, Minister of God's Word in Scotland*, edited by The Religious Tract Society. London: William Clowes, 1831.
Kraushaar, Margaret Freidinger. *The Mulberry Juice Dress.* Santa Barbara: Fithian Press, 1996.
Labaree, Mary Schauffler. *The Child in the Midst: A Comparative Study of Child Welfare in Christian and Non-Christian Lands.* West Medford, MA: Central Committee on the United Study of Foreign Missions, 1914.
Luther, Martin. *Luther's Works.* Vols. 1–30, edited by Jaroslav Pelikan. St. Louis: Concordia Publishing House, 1955–1976. Vols. 31–55, edited by Helmut Lehmann. Philadelphia: Fortress Press, 1957–1986.
Malcolm, Urania Latham. *Children of Persia.* New York: F. H. Revell, 1911.
Martyn, Henry. *Controversial Tracts on Christianity and Mohammedanism. By the Late Rev. Henry Martyn, B.D., of St. John's College, Cambridge, and Some of the Most Eminent Writers of Persia.* Translated by S. Lee. Cambridge: J. Sith, 1824.
Maurice, Frederick Dennison. *The Religions of the World and Their Relations to Christianity.* Boston: Gould and Lincoln, 1854.
Meinhoff, Carl. "The Moslem Advance in Africa." In *Islam and Missions: Being Papers Read at the Second Missionary Conference on Behalf of the Mohammedan World at Lucknow, January 23–28, 1911*, edited by E. M. Wherry, S. M. Zwemer, and C. G. Mylrea, 76–86. New York: Fleming H. Revell, 1911.
"Missionary to Arabia Will Tell How Moslems Treat Their Women." *Harrisburg Telegraph*, September 30, 1915.
Montgomery, Helen Barrett. *Western Women in Eastern Lands: An Outline Study of Fifty Years of Woman's Work in Foreign Missions.* New York: Macmillan, 1910.
Mott, John R. *Conferences of Christian Workers Among Moslems, 1924: A Brief Account of the Conferences Together with Their Findings and Lists of Members.* New York: International Missionary Council, 1924.
Muir, William, trans. *The Apology of Al Kindy, Written at the Court of al Mamun in Defense of Christianity Against Islam.* 2nd ed. London: Society for Promoting Christian Knowledge, 1887.
Münster, Sebastian. *Cosmographiae Universalis.* Basel: Petri, 1550.
One Hundred Most Popular Missionary Books. New York: Missionary Education Movement of the United States and Canada, 1912.
One Hundred Syrian Pictures: Illustrating the Work of the British Syrian Mission. London: S. W. Partridge, 1903.
Padwick, Constance E. "Lilias Trotter of Algiers." *International Review of Mission* 21, no. 1 (January 1932): 119–28.
Patrick, M. M. "Among the Educated Women of Turkey." In *Daylight in the Harem: A New Era for Moslem Women*, edited by Annie Van Sommer and Samuel M. Zwemer, 71–90. New York: Fleming H. Revel, 1911.

Pfander, C. G. *The Mizan Ul Haqq; Or, Balance of Truth.* Translated by R. H. Weakley. London: Church Missionary House, 1866.
Pitman, Emma R. *Missionary Heroines in Eastern Lands: Woman's Work in Mission Fields.* London: S. W. Partridge, 1884.
Presbyterian Church of the United States of America. *The Thirty-Sixth Annual Report of the Board of Foreign Missions of the Presbyterian Church of the United States of America.* New York: Mission House, 1873.
Rouse, G. H. *Tracts for Muhammadans.* 2nd ed. London and Madras: The Christian Literature Society for India, 1897.
Sa'd, Lutfi. "Al-Hakim Cornelius Van Alen Van Dyck, 1818–1895." *Isis* 27, no. 1 (1937): 20–45.
Sanders, E. "The Nile Mission Press." *Moslem World* 34, no. 3 (July 1944): 209–13.
Sarasvati, Pundita Ramabai. *The High-Caste Hindu Woman.* Philadelphia: J. B. Rodgers, 1887.
Smith, D. T. *Faith Working by Love: As Exemplified in the Life of Fidelia Fiske.* Boston: Congregational Publication Society, 1868.
Smith, Susette. "Notes from a Hareem Visitor at Beyrout." *The Missing Link* (August 1, 1876): 243–44.
Smith, Wilfred Cantwell. *Islam in Modern History.* Princeton, NJ: Princeton University Press, 1977.
Stobart, J. W. H. *Islam and Its Founder.* New York and London: Society for Promoting Christian Knowledge and E. S. Gorham, 1911.
Stuart, Emmeline. "The Ministry of Healing." In *Daylight in the Harem: A New Era for Moslem Women,* edited by Annie Van Sommer and Samuel M. Zwemer, 131–46. New York: Fleming H. Revel, 1911.
Stuart, Helen I. Moody. *Fatmeh: A Common Story of Mission Schools for Moslem Girls.* London: British Syrian Mission, circa 1920.
Stuart, I. R. Govan. *The Love That Was Stronger.* London: Lutterworth Press, 1958.
Swain, Clara A. *A Glimpse of India: Being a Collection of Extracts from the Letters of Dr. Clara A. Swain, First Medical Missionary to India of the Woman's Foreign Missionary Society of the Methodist Episcopal Church in America.* New York: J. Pott, 1909.
Swan, George. *"Lacked Ye Anything?": A Brief Story of the Egypt General Mission.* London: EGM, 1932.
Swan, George. "Miss Annie Van Sommer." *Blessed Be Egypt* 37, no. 151 (April 1937): 22–24.
Thomson, William M. *The Land and the Book: Or Biblical Illustrations Drawn from the Manners and Customs, the Scenes and Scenery of the Holy Land.* Exp. ed. New York: Harper & Brothers, 1886.
Trotter, Lilias I. *The Debt of Ali Ben Omar.* Cairo: Nile Mission Press, 1928.
Trotter, Lilias I. *Lilias Trotter's 1889 Sketchbook: Scenes from North Africa, Italy & Switzerland.* Lilias Trotter Legacy, 2020.
United Presbyterian Church of North America. *Thirty-First Annual Report of the Board of Foreign Missions of the United Presbyterian Church of North America.* Philadelphia: Edward Patterson, 1890.
Van Sommer, Annie. "A New Era for Moslem Womanhood." In *Daylight in the Harem: A New Era for Moslem Women,* edited by Annie Van Sommer and Samuel M. Zwemer, 21–51. New York: Fleming H. Revel, 1911.
Van Sommer, Annie, and Samuel M. Zwemer, eds. *Daylight in Harlem: A New Era for Moslem Women.* New York: Fleming H. Revel, 1911.
Van Sommer, Annie, and Samuel M. Zwemer, eds. *Our Moslem Sisters: A Cry of Need from Lands of Darkness Interpreted by Those Who Heard It.* New York: Fleming H. Revell, 1907.
Warne, Frank W. "Methodists and Mohammedanism." *The Epworth Herald* 19, no. 15 (September 5, 1908): 36.
Watson, Charles R. "The American Christian Literature Society for Moslems." *The Moslem World* 8, no. 2 (April 1918): 178–82.

Wherry, Clara M. "Training of Converts." In *Daylight in the Harem: A New Era for Moslem Women*, edited by Annie Van Sommer and Samuel M. Zwemer, 167–82. New York: Fleming H. Revel, 1911.
Wherry, E. M. *Islam and Christianity in India and the Far East*. New York: Fleming H. Revell, 1907.
Wherry, E. M., ed. *Methods of Mission Work Among Moslems*. New York: Revell, 1906.
Wherry, E. M. *Zeinab, the Panjabi: A Story Founded on Facts*. New York: American Tract Society, 1895.
Wherry, E. M., S. M. Zwemer, and C. G. Mylrea, eds. *Islam and Missions: Being Papers Read at the Second Missionary Conference on Behalf of the Mohammedan World at Lucknow, January 23–28, 1911*. New York: Fleming H. Revell, 1911.
Woman's Foreign Missionary Society of the Methodist Episcopal Church (WFMSMEC). *Year Book: Being the Sixtieth Annual Report of the Society*. Boston: WFMSMEC, 1929.
Zwemer, Amy E. Wilkes. *Two Young Arabs and the Travels of Noorah and Jameel*. West Medford, MA: Central Committee on the United Study of Foreign Missions, 1926.
Zwemer, Samuel M. *Arabia, the Cradle of Islam*. New York: Fleming H. Revell, 1900.
Zwemer, Samuel M. "Introduction." In *Our Moslem Sisters: A Cry of Need from Lands of Darkness Interpreted by Those Who Heard It*, edited by Annie Van Sommer and Samuel M. Zwemer, 5–10. New York: Fleming H. Revell, 1907.
Zwemer, Samuel M. *Islam: A Challenge to Faith*. New York: Student Volunteer Movement, 1907.
Zwemer, Samuel M. "A Sketch of the Conference at Lucknow." In *Daylight in the Harem: A New Era for Moslem Women*, edited by Annie Van Sommer and Samuel M. Zwemer, 11–20. New York: Fleming H. Revel, 1911.
Zwemer, Samuel M., and Arthur Judson Brown. *The Nearer and Farther East: Outline Studies of Moslem Lands and of Siam, Burma, and Korea*. New York: Macmillan; West Medford, MA: Central Committee on the United Study of Foreign Missions, 1908.
Zwemer, Samuel M., E. M. Wherry, and James L. Barton, eds. *The Mohammedan World of To-Day: Being Papers Read at the First Missionary Conference on Behalf of the Mohammedan World Held at Cairo April 4th–9th, 1906*. New York: Fleming H. Revell, 1906.
Zwemer, Samuel M., and Amy E. Zwemer. *Moslem Women*. West Medford, MA: Central Committee on the United Study of Foreign Missions, 1926.
Zwemer, Samuel M., and Amy E. Zwemer. *Topsy-Turvy Land: Arabia Pictured for Children*. New York: Fleming H. Revell, 1902.

Secondary Sources

Abu-Lughod, Lila. *Do Muslim Women Need Saving?* Cambridge, MA: Harvard University Press, 2013.
Abu-Lughod, Lila. "Do Muslim Women Really Need Saving? Anthropological Reflections on Cultural Relativism and Its Others." *American Anthropologist* 104, no. 3 (September 2002): 783–90.
Ackerman, Gerald M. *The Life and Work of Jean-Léon Gérôme*. New York: Sotheby's, 1986.
Afsarrudin, Asma. *The First Muslims: History and Memory*. London: Oneworld, 2008.
Ahmed, Leila. *A Quiet Revolution: The Veil's Resurgence from the Middle East to America*. New Haven, CT: Yale University Press, 2012.
Ahmed, Leila. *Women and Gender in Islam: Historical Roots of a Modern Debate*. New Haven, CT: Yale University Press, 1992.
Ali, Kecia. "Progressive Muslims and Islamic Jurisprudence: The Necessity for Critical Engagement with Marriage and Divorce Law." In *Progressive Muslims: On Justice, Gender and Pluralism*, edited by Omid Safi, 176–77. London: Oneworld, 2003.
Ali, Kecia. *Sexual Ethics and Islam: Feminist Reflections on Qur'an, Hadith, and Jurisprudence*. Oxford: Oneworld Publications, 2006.

Alloula, Malek. *The Colonial Harem*. Translated by Myrna Godzich and Wlad Godzich. Minneapolis: University of Minnesota Press, 1986.
American Civil Liberties Union. "Discrimination Against Muslim Women." ACLU Foundation Women's Rights Project. November 2008. Accessed January 7, 2024 https://www.aclu.org/documents/discrimination-against-muslim-women-fact-sheet.
Ames, Michael M. *Cannibal Tours in Glass Boxes: The Anthropology of Museums*. Vancouver and Toronto: UBC Press, 1992.
Andreassen, Rikke. *Human Exhibitions: Race, Gender and Sexuality in Ethnic Displays*. London and New York: Routledge, 2016.
Antonio, Edward P. "The Hermeneutics of Inculturation." In *Inculturation and Postcolonial Discourse in African Theology*, edited by Edward P. Antonio, 29–59. New York: Peter Lang, 2006.
Arjana, Sophia Rose. *Muslims in the Western Imagination*. Oxford: Oxford University Press, 2015.
Atkins, Gareth. "William Jowett's *Christian Researches*: British Protestants and Religious Plurality in the Mediterranean, Syria and the Holy Land, 1815–30." *Studies in Church History* 51 (2015): 216–31.
Aziz, Sahar. *The Racial Muslim: When Racism Quashes Religious Freedom*. Oakland: University of California Press, 2022.
Baker, Patricia L. "The Fez in Turkey." *Costume* 20 (1986): 72–85.
Balserak, Jon. "Philip Melanchthon." In *Christian–Muslim Relations: A Bibliographical History*. Vol. 7, *Central and Eastern Europe, Asia, Africa and South America (1500–1600)*, edited by David Thomas and John A. Chesworth, 246–52. Leiden: Brill, 2015.
Baron, Beth. *The Orphan Scandal: Christian Missionaries and the Rise of the Muslim Brotherhood*. Stanford, CA: Stanford University Press, 2014.
Baumgartner, Kabria. *In Pursuit of Knowledge: Black Women and Educational Activism in Antebellum America*. New York: New York University Press, 2019.
Behdad, Ali. *Camera Orientalis: Reflections on Photography of the Middle East*. Chicago: University of Chicago Press, 2016.
Bennett, Clinton. "The Legacy of Henry Martyn." *International Bulletin of Missionary Research* 16, no. 1 (January 1992): 10–15.
Bennett, Clinton. "The Legacy of Karl Gottlieb Pfander." *International Bulletin of Missionary Research* 20, no. 2 (April 1996): 76–81.
Berman, Jacob Rama. *American Arabesque: Arab, Islam, and the 19th Century*. New York: New York University Press, 2012.
Beydoun, Khaled A. *American Islamophobia: Understanding the Roots and Rise of Fear*. Oakland: University of California Press, 2018.
Bishin, Benjamin G., and Feryal M. Cherif. "Women, Property Rights, and Islam." *Comparative Politics* 49, no. 4 (July 2017): 501–20.
Bonnington, Stuart. "Calvin and Islam." *Reformed Theological Review* 68, no. 2 (August 2009): 77–87.
Boone, Joseph A. "Vacation Cruises; Or, the Homoerotics of Orientalism." *PMLA* 110, no. 1 (January 1995): 89–107.
Booth, Marilyn. *The Career and Communities of Zaynab Fawwaz: Feminist Thinking in Fin-de-siècle Egypt*. New York: Oxford University Press, 2022.
Boulos, Samir. *European Evangelicals in Egypt (1900–1956): Cultural Entanglements and Missionary Spaces*. Leiden: Brill, 2016.
Braude, Ann. *Radical Spirits: Spiritualism and Women's Rights in Nineteenth-Century America*. 2nd ed. Bloomington: Indiana University Press, 2001.
Brookes, Douglas Scott. *The Concubine, the Princess, and the Teacher: Voices from the Ottoman Harem*. Austin: University of Texas Press, 2008.
Brotton, Jerry. *The Sultan and the Queen: The Untold Story of Elizabeth and Islam*. New York: Viking, 2016.

Brown, Mark. "Ethnology and Colonial Administration in Nineteenth-Century British India: The Question of Native Crime and Criminality." *British Journal for the History of Science* 36, no. 2 (June 2003): 201–19.

Brush, Stanley E. "Presbyterians and Islam in India." *Journal of Presbyterian History* 62, no. 3 (Fall 1984): 215–22.

Butler, Judith. *Gender Trouble: Feminism and the Subversion of Identity*. New York: Routledge, 1990.

Cannizzo, Jean. "Gathering Souls and Objects: Missionary Collections." In *Colonialism and the Object: Empire, Material Culture and the Museum*, 153–66. New York: Routledge, 1998.

Chambers, Iain, Alessandra De Angelis, Celeste Ianniciello, Mariangela Orabona, and Michaela Quadraro, eds. *The Postcolonial Museum: The Arts of Memory and the Pressures of History*. Burlington, VT: Ashgate, 2014.

Charman, Isobel. *The Zoo: The Wild and Wonderful Tale of the Founding of London Zoo: 1826–1851*. New York and London: Pegasus Books, 2017.

Choi, David. "Martin Luther's Response to the Turkish Threat: Continuity and Contrast with the Medieval Commentators Riccoldo da Monte Croce and Nicolas of Cusa." PhD diss., Princeton Theological Seminary, 2003.

Choi, Hyaeweol. *Gender and Mission Encounters in Korea: New Women, Old Ways*. Berkeley: University of California Press, 2009.

Christian, William A., Jr., and Amira Mittermaier. "Muslim Prayer on Picture Postcards of French Algeria, 1900–1960." *Material Religion: The Journal of Objects, Art, and Belief* 13, no. 1 (2017): 25–51.

Clooney, Francis X. "Roberto de Nobili, Adaption and the Reasonable Interpretation of Religion." *Missiology: An International Review* 18, no. 1 (January 1990): 25–36.

Colpe, Carsten. "The Science of Religion, the History of Religion, the Phenomenology of Religion." *Historical Reflections* 20, no. 3 (Fall 1994): 403–11.

Cook, Miriam. "Islamic Feminism Before and After September 11th." *Duke Journal of Gender Law & Policy* 9, no. 2 (2002): 227–35.

Cooke, Claire. "Capping Power? Clothing and the Female Body in African Methodist Episcopal Mission Photographs." *Mission Studies* 31 (2014): 418–42.

Curtis, Benjamin. *The Habsburgs: The History of a Dynasty*. London: Bloomsbury, 2013.

Curtis, Edward E., IV. *Muslims of the Heartland: How Syrian Immigrants Made a Home in the American Midwest*. New York: New York University Press, 2022.

Curtis, Heather D. *Holy Humanitarians: American Evangelicals and Global Aid*. Cambridge, MA: Harvard University Press, 2018.

Dannin, Robert. *Black Pilgrimage to Islam*. Oxford: Oxford University Press, 2005.

Davis, John. *The Landscape of Belief: Encountering the Holy Land in Nineteenth-Century American Art and Culture*. Princeton, NJ: Princeton University Press, 1996.

Demski, Dagnoslaw, and Dominika Czarnecka. *Staged Otherness: Ethnic Shows in Central and Eastern Europe, 1850–1939*. Budapest: Central European University Press, 2021.

Dimmock, Matthew. *New Turkes: Dramatizing Islam and the Ottomans in Early Modern England*. Aldershot, UK: Ashgate, 2005.

Dobie, Madeleine. *Foreign Bodies: Gender, Language, and Culture in French Orientalism*. Stanford, CA: Stanford University Press, 2002.

Elbirlik, Leyla Kayhan. "Negotiating Matrimony: Marriage, Divorce, and Property Allocation Practices in Istanbul, 1755–1840." PhD diss., Harvard University, 2013.

Elfenbein, Caleb Iyer. *Fear in Our Hearts: What Islamophobia Tells Us About America*. New York: New York University Press, 2021.

Engelsviken, Tormod. "The Role of the Lausanne Movement in Modern Christian Mission." In *The Lausanne Movement: A Range of Perspectives*, 26–44. Minneapolis: Fortress Press, 2014.

Falierou, Anastasia. "From the Ottoman Empire to the Turkish Republic: Ottoman Turkish Women's Clothing Between Tradition and Modernity." In *From Traditional Attire to Modern*

Dress: Modes of Identification, Modes of Recognition in the Balkans (XVIth–XXth Centuries), edited by Constanta Vințilă-Ghițulescu, 175–94. Newcastle upon Tyne, UK: Cambridge Scholars Publishing, 2011.

Fehrenbach, Heide, and Davide Rodogno, eds. *Humanitarian Photography: A History.* Cambridge: Cambridge University Press, 2014.

Fischer-Galati, Stephen. *Ottoman Imperialism and German Protestantism, 1521–1555.* Cambridge, MA: Harvard University Press, 1959.

Fleischmann, Ellen L. "The Impact of American Protestant Missionaries in Lebanon on the Construction of Female Identity, c. 1860–1950." *Islam and Christian–Muslim Relations* 13, no. 4 (2002): 411–26.

Fletcher, John. *Preaching to Convert: Evangelical Outreach and Performance Activism in a Secular Age.* Ann Arbor: University of Michigan Press, 2013.

Francisco, Adam S. *Martin Luther and Islam: A Study in Sixteenth-Century Polemics and Apologetics.* Leiden: Brill, 2007.

Gabry-Thienpont, Séverine, and Norig Neveu. "Missions and the Construction of Gender in the Middle East." *Social Sciences and Missions* 34, no. 1–2 (2021): 1–27.

Garcia, Humberto. *Islam and the English Enlightenment, 1670–1840.* Baltimore: John Hopkins University Press, 2011.

Gardner, Helen. "Gathering for God: George Brown and the Christian Economy in the Collection of Artifacts." In *Hunting the Gatherers: Ethnographic Collectors, Agents and Agency in Melanesia, 1870s–1930s,* edited by Michael O'Hanlon and Robert Welsch, 35–54. New York: Berghahn Books, 2000.

Gaskell, Ivan, and Sarah Anne Carter. "Introduction: Why History and Material Culture?" In *The Oxford Handbook of History and Material Culture,* 1–13. Oxford: Oxford University Press, 2020.

Genell, Aimee M. "Empire by Law: Ottoman Sovereignty and the British Occupation of Egypt, 1882–1923." PhD diss., Columbia University, 2013.

Glick, Peter, and Susan T. Fisk. "The Ambivalent Sexism Inventory: Differentiating Hostile and Benevolent Sexism." *Journal of Personality and Social Psychology* 70, no. 3 (March 1996): 491–512.

Goffman, Carolyn McCue. *Mary Mills Patrick's Cosmopolitan Mission and the Constantinople Women's College.* Lanham, MD: Lexington Books, 2020.

Goldhill, Simon. "Photography and the Real: The Biblical Gaze and the Professional Album in the Holy Land." In *Travel Writing, Visual Culture, and Form, 1760–1900,* edited by Mary Henes and Brian H. Murray, 87–111. New York: Palgrave, 2015.

Goody, Jack. *Islam in Europe.* Cambridge: Polity Press, 2004.

Gordon, Bruce. "Heinrich Bullinger." In *Christian–Muslim Relations: A Biographical History 1500–1900.* Vol. 6, *Western Europe (1500–1600),* edited by David Thomas and John A. Chesworth, 716–19. Leiden: Brill, 2014.

Gordon, Bruce. "Theodor Bibliander." In *Christian–Muslim Relations: A Biographical History 1500–1900.* Vol. 6, *Western Europe (1500–1600),* edited by David Thomas and John A. Chesworth, 680–85. Leiden: Brill, 2014.

Gottschalk, Peter, and Gabriel Greenberg. *Islamophobia and Anti-Muslim Sentiment: Picturing the Enemy.* 2nd ed. Lanham, MD: Rowman & Littlefield, 2019.

Grafton, David D. *An American Biblical Orientalism: The Construction of Jews, Christians, and Muslims in Nineteenth Century American Evangelical Piety.* Lanham, MD: Lexington Books, 2019.

Grafton, David D. "The Legacy of Ion Keith-Falconer." *International Bulletin of Missionary Research* 31, no. 3 (July 2007): 148–52.

Grafton, David D. "Martin Luther's Sources on the Turk and Islam in the Midst of the Fear of Ottoman Imperialism." *Muslim World* 107 (October 2017): 665–83.

Grafton, David D. *Muhammad in the Seminary: Protestant Teaching About Islam in the Nineteenth Century.* New York: New York University Press, 2024.

Grafton, David D. *Piety, Politics, and Power: Lutherans Encountering Islam in the Middle East.* Eugene, OR: Wipf & Stock, 2009.
Green, Todd H. *The Fear of Islam: An Introduction to Islamophobia in the West.* Minneapolis: Fortress Press, 2015.
Gregory, Jeremy. "Homo Religiosus: Masculinity and Religion in the Long Eighteenth Century." In *English Masculinities, 1660–1800,* edited by Tim Hitchcock and Michelle Cohen, 85–110. London: Routledge, 1999.
Gualtieri, Sarah M. A. *Between Arab and White: Race and Ethnicity in the Early Syrian American Diaspora.* Berkeley: University of California Press, 2009.
Hale, S. "Edward Said—Accidental Feminist: Orientalism and Middle East Women's Studies." *Amerasia Journal* 31, no. 1 (2005): 1–5.
Hartmann, Denise Alexandra. "The Apocalypse and Religious Propaganda: Illustrations by Albrecht Dürer and Lucas Cranach the Elder." *Marginalia* 11 (October 2010): 1–10.
Hasinoff, Erin L. *Faith in Objects: American Missionary Expositions in the Early Twentieth Century.* New York: Palgrave Macmillan, 2011.
Hassan, Riffat. "Islamic Hagar and Her Family." In *Hagar, Sarah, and Their Children: Jewish, Christian, and Muslim Perspectives,* edited by Phyllis Trible and Letty M. Russell, 149–70. Louisville, KY: Westminster John Knox, 2006.
Heim, Mark S. "Mission and Dialogue: 50 Years After Tambaram." *Christian Century* (April 6, 1988): 340–43.
Herbert, Christopher. *Culture and Anomie: Ethnographic Imagination in the Nineteenth Century.* Chicago: University of Chicago Press, 1991.
Heyrman, Christine Leigh. *American Apostles: When Evangelicals Entered the World of Islam.* New York: Hill and Wang, 2015.
Hill, P. *The World Their Household: The American Woman's Foreign Movement and Cultural Transformation, 1870–1920.* Ann Arbor: University of Michigan Press, 1985.
Ho, Joseph. *Developing Mission: Photography, Filmmaking and American Missionaries in Modern China.* Ithaca, NY: Cornell University Press, 2021.
Hourani, Albert. *Arabic Thought in the Liberal Age, 1798–1939.* Cambridge: Cambridge University Press, 1983.
Howard, Thomas Albert. *The Faiths of Others: A History of Interreligious Dialogue.* New Haven, CT: Yale University Press, 2021.
Hubers, John. "Samuel Zwemer and the Challenge of Islam: From Polemic to a Hint of Dialogue." *International Bulletin of Missionary Research* 28, no. 3 (July 2004): 117–21.
Hunter, Shireen T., ed. *Reformist Voices of Islam: Mediating Islam and Modernity.* New York: Routledge, 2009.
Hunter, Tera W. *Bound in Wedlock: Slave and Free Black Marriage in the Nineteenth Century.* Cambridge, MA: Belknap Press of Harvard University Press, 2017.
Hussein, Shakira. *From Victims to Suspects: Muslim Women Since 9/11.* Sydney: University of New South Wales Press, 2016.
Hutchison, William R. *Errand to the World: American Protestant Thought and Foreign Missions.* Chicago: University of Chicago Press, 1987.
Ibrahim, Celene. *Women and Gender in the Qur'an.* Oxford: Oxford University Press, 2020.
Inal, Onur. "Women's Fashions in Transition: Ottoman Borderlands and the Anglo-Ottoman Exchange of Costumes." *Journal of World History* 22, no. 2 (June 2011): 243–72.
Ingram, Anders. "'The Glorious Empire of the Turkes, the Present Terrour of the World': Richard Knolles' *Generall Historie of the Turkes* (1603) and the Background to an Early Modern Commonplace." In *Explorations in Cultural History,* edited by D. Smith and H. Philsooph, 197–216. Aberdeen, UK: BPR Publishers, 2010.
Ingram, Anders. "The Ottoman Siege of Vienna, English Ballads, and the Exclusion Crisis." *The Historical Journal* 57, no. 1 (2014): 53–80.
Iqbal, Roshan. *Marital and Sexual Ethics in Islamic Law: Rethinking Temporary Marriage.* Lanham, MD: Lexington Books, 2023.

Jacobs, Karen, Chantal Knowles, and Chris Wingfield. *Trophies, Relics and Curios?: Missionary Heritage from Africa and the Pacific.* Leiden: Sidestone Press, 2015.

Jacobs, Linda K. "'Playing East': Arabs Play Arabs in Nineteenth Century America." *Mashriq & Mahjar* 2, no. 2 (2014): 79–110.

Jenkins, Paul. "The Earliest Generation of Missionary Photographers in West Africa and the Portrayal of Indigenous People and Culture." *History in Africa* 20 (1993): 89–118.

Jennings, Willie James. *After Whiteness: An Education in Belonging.* Grand Rapids, MI: Eerdmans, 2020.

Jensz, Felicity. "Collecting Cultures: Institutional Motivations for Nineteenth-Century Ethnographical Collections Formed by Moravian Missionaries." *Journal of the History of Collections* 24, no. 1 (2012): 67–70.

Johnston, Anna. *Missionary Writing and Empire, 1800–1860.* Cambridge: Cambridge University Press, 2003.

Jones, Arun W. *Missionary Christianity and Local Religion: American Evangelicalism in North India, 1836–1870.* Waco, TX: Baylor University Press, 2017.

Jones, Arun W. "Reshaping the American Evangelical Conversion Narrative in Nineteenth-Century North India." In *Godroads: Modalities of Conversion in India*, edited by Peter Berger and Sarbeswar Sahoo, 179–98. New Delhi: Cambridge University Press, 2020.

Jones, Toby Craig. "America, Oil, and War in the Middle East." *American History* 99, no. 1 (June 2012): 208–18.

Junior, Nyasha. *Reimagining Hagar: Blackness and the Bible.* Oxford: Oxford University Press, 2019.

Kabbani, Rana. *Europe's Myths of Orient.* Bloomington: Indiana University Press, 1986.

Kahf, Mohja. *Western Representations of the Muslim Woman: From Termagant to Odalisque.* Austin: University of Texas Press, 1999.

Kannan, Divya. "'Children's Work for Children': Caste, Childhood, and Missionary Philanthropy in Colonia India." *The Journal of the History of Childhood and Youth* 14, no. 2 (Spring 2021): 234–53.

Kazi, Nazia. *Islamophobia, Race, and Global Politics.* Lanham, MD: Rowman & Littlefield, 2019.

Keane, Webb. *Christian Moderns: Freedom and Fetish in the Mission Encounter.* Berkeley: University of California Press, 2007.

Keddie, Nikki R. *Women in the Middle East: Past and Present.* Princeton, NJ: Princeton University Press, 2007.

Kent, Eliza F. *Converting Women: Gender and Protestant Christianity in Colonial South India.* Oxford: Oxford University Press, 2004.

Khalid, Maryam. *Gender, Orientalism, and the "War on Terror": Representation, Discourse, and Intervention in Global Politics.* London and New York: Routledge, 2017.

Kidd, Thomas. *American Christians and Islam: Evangelical Culture and Muslims from the Colonial Period to the Age of Terrorism.* Princeton, NJ: Princeton University Press, 2009.

Kieser, Hans-Lukas. *Nearest East: American Millennialism and Mission to the Middle East.* Philadelphia: Temple University Press, 2010.

Kim, Il. "Reading Cusanus' Cribratio Alkorani (1461) in the Light of Christian Antiquarianism at the Papal Court in the 1450s." In *Nicolas of Cusa and Times of Transition: Essays in Honor of Gerald Christianson*, edited by Thomas M. Izbicki, Jason Aleksander, and Donald Duclow, 113–27. Leiden: Brill, 2018.

King, Richard. *Orientalism and Religion: Postcolonial Theory, India and "The Mystic East".* London and New York: Routledge, 1999.

Knipp, C. "The 'Arabian Nights' in England: Galland's Translation and Its Successors." *Journal of Arabic Literature* 5 (1974): 44–54.

Kritzeck, James Aloysius. *Peter the Venerable and Islam.* Princeton, NJ: Princeton University Press, 2016.

Laing, Catriona. "A Provocation to Mission: Constance Padwick's Study of Muslim Devotion." *Islam and Christian–Muslim Relations* 24, no. 1 (2013): 27–42.

Lambert-Hurley, Siobhan. "An Embassy of Equality? Quaker Missionaries in Bhopal State, 1890–1930." In *Rhetoric and Reality: Gender and the Colonial Experience in South Asia*, edited by Avril Powell and Siobhan Lambert-Hurley, 247–81. Oxford: Oxford University Press, 2006.

Lambert-Hurley, Siobhan, ed. *A Princess's Pilgrimage: Nawab Sikandar Begum's A Pilgrimage to Mecca*. Bloomington and Indianapolis: Indiana University Press, 2008.

Lambert-Hurley, Siobhan, and Sunhil Sharma, eds. *Atiya's Journeys: A Muslim Woman from Colonial Bombay to Edwardian Britain*. Oxford: Oxford University Press, 2020.

Lawson, Barbara. *Collected Curios: Missionary Tales from the South Seas*. Montreal: McGill University Libraries, 1994.

Lawson, Barbara. "Collecting Cultures: Canadian Missionaries, Pacific Islanders, and Museums." In *Canadian Missionaries, Indigenous Peoples: Representing Religion at Home and Abroad*, edited by Alvyn Austin and Jamie S. Scott, 235–61. Toronto: University of Toronto Press, 2005.

Lean, Nathan. *The Islamophobia Industry: How the Far Right Manufactures Fear of Muslims*. 2nd ed. London: Pluto Books, 2017.

Lewis, Reina. *Gendering Orientalism: Race, Femininity and Representation*. London and New York: Routledge, 1996.

Lindenfeld, David. *World Christianity and Indigenous Experience: A Global History, 1500–2000*. Cambridge: Cambridge University Press, 2021.

Lindner, Christine B. "'Long, Long Will She Be Affectionately Remembered': Gender and the Memorialization of an American Female Missionary." *Social Sciences and Missions* 23, no. 1 (2010): 7–31.

Lindsey, Peggy Bowler. "Around the World in 238 Days: Traveling with the Laymen's Foreign Missions Inquiry Commission of Appraisal." *International Bulletin of Mission Research* 46, no. 4 (2022): 492–503.

Longfield, Bradley J. *The Presbyterian Controversy: Fundamentalists, Modernists, and Moderates*. Oxford: Oxford University Press, 1993.

Louis, Wm. Roger. *The British Empire in the Middle East, 1945–1951: Arab Nationalism, the United States, and Postwar Imperialism*. Oxford: Oxford University Press, 1984.

Love, Erik. *Islamophobia and Racism in America*. New York: New York University Press, 2017.

Lum, Kathryn Gin. *Heathen: Religion and Race in American History*. Cambridge, MA: Harvard University Press, 2022.

Mahmood, Saba. *Politics of Piety: Islamic Revival and the Feminist Subject*. Princeton, NJ: Princeton University Press, 2012.

Makdisi, Ussama. *Artillery of Heaven: American Missionaries and the Failed Conversion of the Middle East*. Ithaca, NY: Cornell University Press, 2008.

Marcos, Ramy Nair. *The Emergence of Evangelical Egyptians: A Historical Study of the Evangelical–Coptic Encounter and Conversion in Late Ottoman Egypt, 1854–1878*. Lanham, MD: Lexington Books, 2024.

Marr, Timothy. *The Cultural Roots of American Islamicism*. Cambridge: Cambridge University Press, 2006.

Marten, Michael. *Attempting to Bring the Gospel Home: Scottish Missions to Palestine, 1839–1917*. London: I. B. Tauris, 2005.

Marten, Michael. "The Free Church of Scotland in 19th-Century Lebanon." *CHRONOS: Revue d'Histoire de l'Université de Balamand* 5 (2002): 51–106.

Marty, Martin E. *Modern American Religion*. Vol. 2, *The Noise of Conflict, 1919–1941*. Chicago: University of Chicago Press, 1991.

Masuzawa, Tomoko. *The Invention of World Religions*. Chicago: University of Chicago Press, 2005.

Matar, Nabil. *Islam in Britain, 1558–1685*. Cambridge: Cambridge University Press, 1998.

Mathur, Saloni. *India by Design: Colonial History and Cultural Display*. Berkeley and Los Angeles: University of California Press, 2017.

McAlister, Melani. *Epic Encounters: Culture, Media, & U.S. Interest in the Middle East Since 1945*, updated ed. Berkeley: University of California Press, 2005.
McAllister, Susan Fleming. "Cross-Cultural Dress in Victorian British Missionary Narratives: Dressing for Eternity." In *Historicizing Christian Encounters with the Other*, edited by John C. Hawley, 122–34. London: Macmillan, 1998.
Meggitt, Justin J. *Early Quakers and Islam: Slavery, Apocalyptic and Christian–Muslim Encounters in the Seventeenth Century*. Eugene, OR: Wipf & Stock, 2013.
Melman, Billie. *Women's Orients: English Women and the Middle East, 1718–1918: Sexuality, Religion and Work*. Ann Arbor: University of Michigan Press, 1992.
Miller, Gregory J. "Theodor Bibliander's Machumetis saracenorum principis eiusque successorum vitae, doctrina ac ipse alcoran (1543) as the Sixteenth-Century 'Encyclopedia' of Islam." *Islam and Christian–Muslim Relations* 24, no. 2 (2013): 241–54.
Miller, Gregory J. *The Turks and Islam in Reformation Germany*. New York: Routledge, 2018.
Miller, Karen Li. "The White Child's Burden: Managing the Self and Money in Nineteenth-Century Children's Missionary Periodicals." *American Periodicals* 22, no. 2 (2012): 139–57.
Mir-Hosseini, Ziba. *Islam and Gender: The Religious Debate in Contemporary Iran*. Princeton, NJ: Princeton University Press, 1999.
Morgan, David. "Museum Collection and the History of Interpretation." In *Religion in Museums: Global and Multidisciplinary Perspectives*, edited by Gretchen Buggeln, Crispin Paine, and S. Brent Plate, 117–27. London: Bloomsbury, 2017.
Morgan, David. *Protestants and Pictures: Religion, Visual Culture, and the Age of American Mass Production*. Oxford: Oxford University Press, 1999.
Morgan, David, ed. *Religion and Material Culture: The Matter of Belief*. New York and London: Routledge, 2010.
Morgan, David. *The Thing About Religion: An Introduction to the Material Study of Religions*. Chapel Hill: University of North Carolina Press, 2021.
Morrison, Hugh. *Protestant Children, Missions and Education in the British World*. Leiden: Brill, 2021.
Mubarak, Hadia. *Rebellious Wives, Neglectful Husbands: Controversies in Modern Qur'anic Commentaries*. Oxford: Oxford University Press, 2022.
Murre-van den Berg, Heleen. "'Dear Mother of My Soul': Fidelia Fiske and the Role of Women Missionaries in Mid-Nineteenth Century Iran." *Exchange* 30, no. 1 (January 2001): 34–48.
Okkenhaug, Inger Marie. *The Quality of Heroic Living, of High Endeavor and Adventure: Anglican Mission, Women, and Education in Palestine, 1888–1948*. Leiden: Brill, 2002.
Okkenhaug, Inger Marie, and Karène Sanchez Summerer, eds. *Christian Missions and Humanitarianism in the Middle East: Ideologies, Rhetoric, and Practices*. Leiden: Brill, 2020.
Orzech, Charles D. *Museums of World Religions: Displaying the Divine, Shaping Cultures*. London: Bloomsbury, 2020.
Palacios, Joy. "Introduction: Performing Religion." *Performance Matters* 3, no. 1 (2017): 1–6.
Peirce, Leslie. *The Imperial Harem: Women and Sovereignty in the Ottoman Empire*. Oxford: Oxford University Press, 1993.
Pennington, Brian K. *Was Hinduism Invented?: Britons, Indians, and the Colonial Construction of Religion*. New York: Oxford University Press, 2005.
Pestana, Carla Gardina. *Protestant Empire: Religion and the Making of the British World*. Philadelphia: University of Pennsylvania Press, 2009.
Piepke, Joachim G. "The Kirschbaum Collection of the Missionary Ethnological Museum in the Vatican." *Anthropos* 107, no. 2 (2012): 560–64.
Powell, Avril A. "The Legacy of Henry Martyn to the Study of India's Muslims and Islam in the Nineteenth Century." Unpublished presentation at Cambridge Center for Christianity Worldwide, July 2017. https://www.cccw.cam.ac.uk/wp-content/uploads/2017/07/Powell-Dr-Avril.pdf.
Powell, Avril A. *Muslims and Missionaries in Pre-Mutiny India*. Richmond, UK: Curzon Press, 1993.

Promey, Sally M. "Foreword." In *Religion in Museums: Global and Multidisciplinary Perspectives*, edited by Gretchen Buggeln, Crispin Paine, and S. Brent Plate, xix–xxv. London: Bloomsbury, 2017.

Pruitt, Lisa Joy. *A Looking-Glass for Ladies: American Protestant Women and the Orient in the Nineteenth Century.* Macon, GA: Mercer University Press, 2005.

Putnam, Walter. "'Please Don't Feed the Natives': Human Zoos, Colonial Desire, and Bodies on Display." *French Literature Series* 39 (2012): 55–68.

Quinn, Frederick. *The Sum of All Heresies: The Image of Islam in Western Thought.* Oxford: Oxford University Press, 2008.

Qureshi, Sadiah. *Peoples on Parade: Exhibitions, Empire, and Anthropology in Nineteenth-Century Britain.* Chicago: University of Chicago Press, 2011.

Ralston, Joshua. *Law and the Rule of God: A Christian Engagement with Shari'a.* Cambridge: Cambridge University Press, 2020.

Razack, Sherene H. *Nothing Has to Make Sense: Upholding White Supremacy Through Anti-Muslim Racism.* Minneapolis: University of Minnesota Press, 2022.

Reeves-Ellington, Barbara. *Domestic Frontiers: Gender, Reform, and American Interventions in the Ottoman Balkans and the Near East.* Amherst: University of Massachusetts Press, 2013.

Richter, Amy G. *At Home in Nineteenth-Century America: A Documentary History.* New York: New York University Press, 2015.

Robert, Dana L. *American Women in Mission: A Social History of Their Thought and Practice.* Macon, GA: Mercer University Press, 1997.

Robert, Dana L. *Christian Mission: How Christianity Became a World Religion.* Chichester: UK, Wiley-Blackwell, 2009.

Robert, Dana L. "Revisioning the Women's Missionary Movement." In *The Good News of the Kingdom: Mission Theology for the Third Millennium*, edited by Charles E. Van Engren, Dean S. Gilliland, and Paul Pierson, 109–18. Eugene, OR: Wipf & Stock, 1993.

Rockness, Miriam Huffman. *A Passion for the Impossible: The Life of Lilias Trotter.* Grand Rapids, MI: Discovery House, 1999.

Rogers, Stephanie Stidham. *Inventing the Holy Land: American Protestant Pilgrimage to Palestine, 1865–1941.* Lanham, MD: Lexington Books, 2011.

Rovine, Victoria L. "Colonialism's Clothing: Africa, France, and the Deployment of Fashion." *Design Issues* 25, no. 3 (Summer 2009): 44–61.

Ruether, Kirsten. "Heated Debates over Crinolines: European Clothing on Nineteenth-Century Lutheran Mission Stations in the Transvaal." *Journal for Southern African Studies* 28, no. 2 (June 2002): 359–78.

Said, Edward W. *Culture and Imperialism.* New York: Vintage Books, 1993.

Said, Edward W. *Orientalism.* New York: Vintage Books, 1978.

Samartha, S. J. *Dialogue Between Men of Living Faiths: Papers Presented at a Consultation Held at Ajaltoun, Lebanon, March 1970.* Geneva: World Council of Churches, 1971.

Semple, Rhonda Anne. *Missionary Women: Gender, Professionalism and the Victorian Idea of Christian Mission.* Woodbridge, UK: Boydell Press, 2003.

Seton, Rosemary. "Reconstructing the Museum of the London Missionary Society." *Material Religion* 8, no. 1 (2012): 98–102.

Schueller, Malini Johar. *U.S. Orientalisms: Race, Nation, and Gender in Literature, 1790–1890.* Ann Arbor: University of Michigan Press, 1998.

Scott, David W. *Mission as Globalization: Methodists in Southeast Asia at the Turn of the Twentieth Century.* Lanham, MD: Lexington Books, 2016.

Scott, Joan. "Gender: A Useful Category of Historical Analysis." *American Historical Review* 91, no. 5 (December 1986): 1053–75.

Scott, Gregory Adam. "Timothy Richard, World Religion, and Reading Christianity in Buddhist Garb." *Social Sciences and Missions* 25 (2012): 53–75.

Sha'ban, Fuad. *Islam and Arabs in Early American Thought: The Roots of Orientalism in America.* Durham, NC: Acorn Press, 1991.

Shaheen, Jack. *Reel Bad Arabs: How Hollywood Vilifies a People*. New York: Olive Branch Press, 2001.
Sharkey, Heather J. *American Evangelicals in Egypt: Missionary Encounters in an Age of Empire*. Princeton, NJ: Princeton University Press, 2008.
Shattuck, Gardiner H., Jr. *Christian Homeland: Episcopalians and the Middle East, 1820–1958*. Oxford: Oxford University Press, 2023.
Sheehi, Stephen. *The Arab Imago: A Social History of Portrait Photography, 1860–1910*. Princeton, NJ: Princeton University Press, 2016.
Sheehi, Stephen. *Islamophobia: The Ideological Campaign Against Muslims*. Atlanta: Clarity Press, 2011.
Sinclair, Lisa M. "The Legacy of Isabella Lilias Trotter." *International Bulletin of Missionary Research* 26, no. 1 (January 2002): 32–35.
Slomp, Jan. "Calvin and the Turks." *Studies in Interreligious Dialogue* 19, no. 1 (2009): 50–65.
Smalley, Martha Lund. "Missionary Museums in China." *Material Religion* 8, no. 1 (2012): 105–7.
Smith, Charlotte Colding. *Images of Islam, 1453–1600*. New York: Routledge, 2018.
Smith, Ian. *Black Shakespeare: Reading and Misreading Race*. Cambridge: Cambridge University Press, 2022.
Smith, Jane I. "Christian Missionary Views of Islam in the Nineteenth and Twentieth Centuries." *Islam and Christian–Muslim Relations* 9, no. 3 (2007): 357–73.
Smith, Jane Idelman, and Yvonne Yazbeck Haddad. *The Islamic Understanding of Death and Resurrection*. New York: Oxford University Press, 2002.
Smith, Sarah Frances. "'She Moves the Hands That Move the World': Antebellum Childrearing: Images of Mother and Child in Nineteenth-Century Periodicals for Mothers." PhD diss., University of Minnesota, 2006.
Sonbol, Amira el-Azhary. *Beyond the Exotic: Women's Histories in Islamic Societies*. Syracuse, NY: Syracuse University Press, 2005.
Spivak, Gayatri Chakravorty. "Can the Subaltern Speak?" In *Marxism and the Interpretation of Culture*, edited by Cary Nelson and Lawrence Grossberg, 271–313. Urbana: University of Illinois Press, 1988.
Stanley, Brian. *The World Missionary Conference, Edinburgh 1910*. Grand Rapids, MI: Eerdmans, 2009.
Stebbins, H. Lyman. *British Imperialism in Qajar Iran: Consuls, Agents, and Influence in the Middle East*. London: Bloomsbury/I. B. Taurus, 2016.
Stephens, W. P. "Understanding Islam—In the Light of Bullinger and Wesley." *Evangelical Quarterly* 81, no. 1 (2009): 23–37.
Strong, Rowan. *Anglicanism and British Empire, c. 1700–1850*. Oxford: Oxford University Press, 2007.
Sudworth, Richard. *Encountering Islam: Christian–Muslim Relations in the Public Square*. London: SCM Press, 2017.
Tan, Alexis, and Anastasia Vishnevskaya. *Stereotypes of Muslim Women in the United States: Media Primes and Consequences*. Lanham, MD: Lexington Books, 2022.
Taylor, John B., and Muzammil H. Siddiqui. "Understanding and Experience of Christian–Muslim Dialogue." In *Dialogue Between Men of Living Faiths: Papers Presented at a Consultation Held at Ajaltoun, Lebanon, March 1970*, edited by S. J. Samartha, 59–72. Geneva: World Council of Churches, 1971.
Tebbe, James A. "Kenneth Cragg in Perspective: A Comparison with Temple Gairdner and Wilfred Cantwell Smith." *International Bulletin of Missionary Research* (January 2002): 16–21.
Tejirian, Eleanor H., and Reeva S. Simon, eds. *Altruism and Imperialism: Western Religious and Cultural Missions to the Middle East*. New York: Middle East Institute of Columbia University, 2002.
Tejirian, Eleanor H., and Reeva S. Simon. *Conflict, Conquest, and Conversion: Two Thousand Years of Christian Missions in the Middle East*. New York: Columbia University Press, 2012.

Thomas, Nicholas. *Entangled Objects: Exchange, Material Culture, and Colonialism in the Pacific.* Cambridge, MA: Harvard University Press, 1991.

Toenjes, Christopher. *Islam, the Turks and the Making of the English Reformation: The History of the Ottoman Empire in John Foxe's Acts and Monuments.* Frankfurt: Peter Lang, 2016.

Tong, Benson. *Unsubmissive Women: Chinese Prostitutes in Nineteenth-Century San Francisco.* Norman: University of Oklahoma Press, 2000.

Trexler, Melanie E. *Evangelizing Lebanon: Baptists, Missions, and the Question of Cultures.* Waco, TX: Baylor University Press, 2016.

Tweed, Thomas A. "An American Pioneer in the Study of Religion: Hannah Adams (1755–1831) and Her 'Dictionary of All Religions.'" *Journal of the American Academy of Religion* 60, no. 3 (Autumn 1992): 437–64.

Vásquez, Manuel A. *More Than Belief: A Materialist Theory of Religion.* Oxford: Oxford University Press, 2011.

Vehlow, Katya. "The Swiss Reformers Zwingli, Bullinger and Bibliander and Their Attitude to Islam (1520–1560)." *Islam and Christian–Muslim Relations* 6, no. 2 (1995): 229–54.

Vitkus, Daniel J. "Introduction." In *Three Turk Plays from Early Modern England: Selimus, A Christian Turned Turk, and The Renegado*, edited by Daniel J. Vitkus, 1–53. New York: Columbia University Press, 2000.

Vitkus, Daniel J. *Turning Turk: English Theater and the Multicultural Mediterranean, 1570–1630.* New York: Palgrave Macmillan, 2003.

Weber, Charlotte E. "Making Common Cause?: Western and Middle Eastern Feminists in the International Women's Movement, 1911–1948." PhD diss., Ohio State University, 2003.

Weir, Christine. "'Deeply Interested in These Children Whom You Have Not Seen': The Protestant Sunday School View of the Pacific, 1900–1940." *Journal of Pacific History* 8, no. 1 (2013): 43–62.

Welter, Barbara. "The Cult of True Womanhood: 1820–1860." *American Quarterly* 18, no. 2, part 1 (Summer 1966): 152–74.

West, James Ryan. "Evangelizing Bengali Muslims, 1793–1813: William Carey, William Ward, and Islam." PhD diss., Southern Baptist Theological Seminary, 2014.

Wilson, J. Christy, Jr. "The Legacy of Samuel M. Zwemer." *International Bulletin of Missionary Research* (July 1986): 117–18.

Wingfield, Chris. "Missionary Museums." In *Religion in Museums: Global and Multidisciplinary Perspectives*, edited by Gretchen Buggeln, Crispin Paine, and S. Brent Plate, 231–39. London: Bloomsbury, 2017.

Womack, Deanna Ferree. "American Muslims, Arab Christians, and Religio-Racial Misrecognition." In *Alterity and the Evasion of Justice: Explorations of the "Other" in World Christianity*, edited by Deanna Ferree Womack and Raimundo C. Barreto, 27–48. Minneapolis: Fortress Press, 2023.

Womack, Deanna Ferree. "Edward Said and the Orientalized Body: A Call for Missiological Engagement." *Swedish Missiological Themes/Svensk Missionstidskrift* 99, no. 4 (2011): 441–61.

Womack, Deanna Ferree. "Imperial Politics and Theological Practices: Comparative Transformations in Anglo-American and Russian Orthodox Missions to Syria–Palestine." *ARAM Periodical* 25, no. 1–2 (2013): 1–12.

Womack, Deanna Ferree. "Lost in Translation: Missionaries in Islamic Garb." *Journal of Presbyterian History* 99, no. 1 (Spring/Summer 2021): 9–22.

Womack, Deanna Ferree. "Protestant Portrayals of Islam: From the Reformation to Modern Missions." *Interpretation: A Journal of Bible and Theology* 76, no. 2 (2022): 140–55.

Womack, Deanna Ferree. *Protestants, Gender and the Arab Renaissance in Late Ottoman Syria.* Edinburgh: Edinburgh University Press, 2019.

Womack, Deanna Ferree. "A View from the Muslim Arabic Press, 1928: The International Missionary Conference in Jerusalem." *Exchange: Journal of Contemporary Christianities in Context* 46, no. 2 (2017): 180–205.

Yeğenoğlu, Meyda. *Colonial Fantasies: Towards a Feminist Reading of Orientalism.* Cambridge: Cambridge University Press, 1998.
Young, Richard Fox. "Obliged by Grace: Edward Jurji's Legacy in the History of Religions at Princeton Theological Seminary, 1939–77." *Theology Today* 69, no. 3 (2012): 333–43.
Young, Richard Fox. "Princeton Theological Seminary's Museum of Religion and Missions." *Material Religion* 8, no. 1 (2012): 108–9.
Zeuge-Buberl, Uta. *The Mission of the American Board in Syria: Implications of a Transcultural Dialogue.* Translated by Elizabeth Janik. Stuttgart: Franz Steiner, 2017.

Index

For the benefit of digital users, indexed terms that span two pages (e.g., 52–53) may, on occasion, appear on only one of those pages.

Figures are indicated by an italic *f* following the page number.

1965 Immigration and Nationality Act, 249–50
9/11, 242–43, 244, 245, 249
1001 Arabian Nights, 112–13, 119–20, 147n.1

abd al-Masih, Kamil, 14, 19–20, 115
Actes and Monuments (1563), 44–45
    influence of, 44–45
    See also Foxe
Adams, Hannah, 60, 66n.133
    Dictionary of All Religions and Religious Denominations (1817), 60
Adivar, Halide Edib, 152n.127
agency
    of Hagar, 101, 111n.180
    negative, 140
    of Protestant children, 112–13
    of Protestant women through missions, 71
    of Muslim women, 66n.116, 69–70, 85, 91–92, 97–98, 105n.58, 111n.180, 130–31, 146–47, 256
    through girls' schools, 256
    world's fairs and, 203
alcohol
    prohibitions against, 52, 61, 64n.55
Algeria, 15–16, 31n.73, 31–32n.79, 82–83, 89, 91–92, 127–28, 169–70, 188–89, 251
Algiers Mission Band (AMB), 15, 170, 219–21, 253–54. *See also* Trotter
alterity, 208–9, 233n.14
    museums and, 208–9
    radical, 202, 203, 208–9
    See also "others"
ambivalent sex theory, 63n.27
American Board of Commissions for Foreign Missions (1810) (ABCFM), 12–13, 30n.57, 68–69, 97–98, 109n.145, 135–37, 148n.6, 148n.11, 151n.99, 152n.127, 193n.79, 234n.45
    curiosity collections of, 207–8, 209, 212–13
    Missionary Herald, 97–98, 148n.6
    Missionary success and, 148n.6
    See also Blatter; Fiske; Hamlin; Hamm; Patrick; World in Boston

American Christian Literature Society for Moslems (1911), 83–84. *See also* Nile Mission Press
American Lutheran Orient Mission to Kurdistan (1910), 10, 15–16
Anglo-American captivity writing, 59
anthropology, 73–74, 195, 200, 202
    classification and interpretation of, 200
    great exhibitions and, 202
    museums and, 199–200
    purpose of, 238n.117
    See also travel writing
antichrist, 8, 9, 38–39
anti-Muslim sentiment, 230–31, 239–43, 245–46
    gendered dimension of, 243–44
    and hate crimes, 242, 244–45, 255, 258n.5
    and Islamophobia, 242–43, 245–46
    and racism, 242–44, 249–50
apocalypticism, 38–39, 254
apologetics, Islam in, 16–19
appropriation, 196, 214–16, 230–31
Arabian Mission (1889), 15, 82–83, 106n.79
authority
    British imperial, 53–54
    dress and, 222, 227
    of male Protestant missionaries, 71, 84–85, 214–16
    through images, 214–16
    through personal contact, 67–68, 240–41
    of female Protestant missionaries, 71, 84–85, 99–100, 256
    western, 53, 197

ballads, 51–52
barbarism, 72, 246–47
barbary
    coast, 66n.128
    pirates, 59
    See also captivity writing
Barrow, Isaac, 51
Barton, James, 84–85
Basel Mission, 12, 192n.77

Begum, Shahjahan, 80, 106n.68, 106n.70
Begum, Sikander, 76–77, 80, 106n.68, 106n.70
Bey, Muhammad Sadiq, 190n.28
Biblewomen, 14–15, 125
Bibliander, Theodor, 6–7, 8, 9, 10, 28n.19, 28–29n.26, 37
Blatter, Dorothy, 136–40, 141–43, 146–47, 151nn.99–100
  Cap and Candle (1961) (*see Cap and Candle*)
  scrapbook costumes, 219–21, 219–20f
  See also ABCFM
Blessed Be Egypt, 107n.85. *See also* Trotter
Boas, Franz, 202
Bonfils, Félix, 166–69, 177
British East India Company, 12
British Empire, 11–12, 53–54
Brown, Arthur Judson
  The Nearer and Farther East (1908), 98
Buchanan, Claudius, 104n.30. *See also* British East India Company
Bullinger, Heinrich, 6–7, 10, 44–45
  antichrist and, 38–39
  Christian laxity and, 38–39
  marriage and, 37
  on the Qur'an, 37
  violence and, 38
  women and, 37
Bunyan, John, 50–51
burqa, 92, 244. *See also* veil/veiling

Cairo, missionary achievements at, 31n.78, 82, 83–84, 86–87, 90–91
Cairo Conference (1906), 85
  Our Moslem Sisters and, 86–87, 96–97
  See also missionary conferences
captivity writing, 59
Calverley, Edwin, 223, 225f
Calverley, Eleanor (child), 200, 223–25
Calverley, Eleanor (Dr.), 15, 177, 223, 224f, 251
  attire of, 223, 224–25f, 226, 227–28
  contextualizing women's attire, 227–28
  My Arabian Days and Nights (1958), 227, 228, 254–55
  personal transformation and, 232–33
  shifting understanding of Muslim life of, 228
Calverley, Elizabeth, 223–25, 225f
Calverley, Grace, 223–25, 224–25f
Calvin, John, 6–7, 9, 10, 29n.43, 37, 38–39, 62n.19
  antichrist and, 38–39
  papacy and Islam and, 38–39
Cantine, James, 15, 68–69
Cap and Candle (1961), 136–41, 139f, 142–43, 241–42, 254–55

gender customs in, 137–38
veil in, 241–42
See also Blatter
Carey, William, 12, 30n.53, 32n.94
cartoons, American political, 248
  gender tropes in, 248–49
  response to 9/11, 249
Central Committee on the United Study of Foreign Missions (CCUSFM), 98, 110n.162
children
  American and British missionary publications for, 112–52
  books on Islam and, 24–25, 102, 112–52 (*see also* Entwistle)
  as "Christ's Crusaders," 128
  development of, 122
  dress of, 122, 138–40, 175–77, 176f
  education of, 112–13, 129, 136–37
  fiction for, 112–52, 257
  giving, to missionary work, 113
  as little missionaries, 113
  magazines for, 112–52, 148n.10 (*see also* CWC, Quarterly Token)
  missionaries as role models for, 114
  missionary appeals to, 113
  missionary responsibility of, 102
  non-fiction for, 113 (*see also Children of Persia*)
Children of Persia (1911), 119–20, 121–23, 144–45
  British distribution of, 119
  See also Revell
Children's Work for Children (CWC), 112–13, 114–17
  content of, 144
  Over Sea and Land (renamed), 114–15
  prayer postures in, 178
  subscribers, 114–15
Christian Literature Society of India, The, 78
Christian-Muslim dialogue, 1, 3–4, 61, 239–61
Christian Researches in Syria and the Holy Land (1826), 74. *See also* Jowett
Christian Researches in the Mediterranean (1812), 74. *See also* Jowett
Church of England, 12. *See also* Zenana Missionary Society
Church of Prussia, 12
Church of Scotland, 12
Church Missionary Juvenile Instructor, 112–13
Church Missionary Society (CMS), 12, 112–13, 125–26, 147n.4, 207–8
circumcision
  conversion and, 48–49, 64n.65
  of heart, 64n.65

classification
  comparative religion and, 200–1
  museums and, 200, 207–8
  of Muslims, 74
  of humans, 72, 74, 200
  postcards and, 160
Clive, Lady Charlotte Florentia, 73–74
clothing. *See* costumes; dress
collections. *See* great exhibitions; missionaries' personal collections; museums
comparative (study of) religion, 5, 195–238, 234n.20
  museum age and, 234n.20
complementarity (gender roles), 69–70
concubinage, 60, 85, 231
Congregational Woman's Board of Missions of the Interior, 95–96
Constantinople Woman's College, 92–93
Controversial Tracts on Christianity and Mohammedanism (1824), 77–78. *See also* Martyn
conversion, 46, 47–48, 60, 81
  classification and, 74
  from Islam, 13
  in literature, 66n.126, 126, 127–28, 146–47
  of Muslims, 81, 96
  as rescue, 66n.126
  as salvation, 72
  violence and, 81
costumes, 195–238
  alternative identities through, 203
  men's, 198
  missionary, 195–238, 210–25f (*see also* Blatter; Eleanor Calverley; Freidinger; Marshall; Van Dyck; Samuel Zwemer)
  performing in, 255
  theater, 201–2
  women's, 132, 182, 183f
  World in Boston, 205
  world's fairs performers and, 203
  See also dress
Cragg, Kenneth, 23, 261n.72
Cranach the Elder, Lucas, 40
curiosities, 25, 73–74, 206–9, 210–11
  cabinets of, 173–74, 195, 199–203, 211–12
  collections of, 198 (*see also* great exhibitions; world's fairs)
  tours of, 210–11

darkness
  daylight versus, 91

  physical, 87
  spiritual, 72, 87
  veil as symbol of, 87, 88
Daylight in the Harem (1911), 90–95, 97–98, 99–100, 101–2, 108n.132, 110n.169
de Boulainvillier, Henri, 55–56
  La Vie de Mahomet, 55–56
decolonization, 251
de Nicolay, Nicolas, 41–42, 55–56. *See also* costumes; dress
dialogue
  Christian-Muslim, 1, 3–4, 26, 61, 255–57 (*see also* World Council of Churches; World's Parliament of Religions)
Dickson, Laurella, 210–11
Dictionary of All Religions and Religious Denominations (1817), 60
difference, 197
  and comparison, 197
  legal judgments and, 240–41
  and organization, 197
  racial, 240–41
divorce, 35–36, 78–79, 85, 86, 88, 89, 94, 96–97, 105n.42
  Muslim men initiating, 35–36, 105n.58
  Muslim women's debates on, 105n.42
domesticity, 70, 88, 145, 231
  as idealized Christian woman's space, 21–22, 70, 88
  gender roles and, 145–46, 151n.82
dowry, 66n.123, 94, 135–38
dress, 40–42, 92, 109n.141, 122
  of Arab Bedouins, 74–75, 205–6, 216–19
  as educative, 213
  impersonating Muslim, 225–28
  missionary, 213–23 (*see also* Blatter; Eleanor Calverley; Marshall; Van Dyck)
  of Muslims, 225–26
  of Muslim men, 41f, 42–43, 43f
  of Muslim women, 63n.27, 73–74, 75–76, 130, 132, 138–40, 141–42, 152n.106, 182–84, 228 (*see also* veil/veiling)
  "native" costume, 214
  norms, 144–45, 185, 216–19
  salvation of Muslims and, 226
  shifting styles, in Egypt, 108n.134
  as "spiritual passport," 213
  transformation of through mission work, 177
  See also burqa; dress-up; veil
"dress-up," 198, 216–21, 217–25f
  didactic, 223–28
  as exoticizing Muslims, 221–22

"dress-up" (*cont.*)
  reasons for, 222
  as understanding, 221–22
  See also costumes
Dutch Reformed Church, 15, 214, 260n.63

ecumenical
  missionary movement, 112–13, 119, 250–51, 252–53
  enthusiasm, 99
  women's movement, 90–95
ecumenical-evangelical split, 252–53
Eddy, Mary Pierson, 14–15
Eddy, William K., 107n.95
Edwards, Jonathan, 59–60
Egypt General Mission (EGM), 15–16, 83, 253–54
  See also Van Sommer
Egypt Mission Band, 15–16, 17–18. *See also* Egypt General Mission
empire
  agents of, 200–1
  commercial, 53–54
  extent of, 202
  and missionaries, 199
  Protestant, 239, 254–55
  theory of, 53–54
enslavement
  of Christians and Muslims, 45–46, 63n.45
  domestic, 118, 120–21
Entwistle, Mary, 102
  children's books by, 102, 112–52
  Habeeb: A Boy of Palestine (1924), 125–27
  Lifestyles of Muslims in books by, 144, 146
  Musa: Son of Egypt (1927), 125–27
ethnographic accounts. *See* travel writing

Fatmeh: A Common Story of Mission Schools for Moslem Girls (circa 1920), 124–25, 129–34, 137–38, 140, 142, 146–47
  violence of Muslim men in, 134, 134f
  See also Helen Stuart
Fawwaz, Zaynab, 103n.7, 145–46
  depictions of Muslim women by, 145–46
  gender separation and, 103n.7
  women's professions and, 103n.7
Federation of Women's Boards of Foreign Missions, The, 98
femininity (as symbol), 61
feminization of missions, 84–85
fez (hat), 216–19
fiction
  attraction of, 106n.72, 124
  fundraising through, 124, 126, 141–42, 147n.4, 148n.6
  for improving Muslims' lives, 124
  by men (*see* Elwood Wherry)
  by women, 124
film, 129, 154
  American industry, 188–89
  Black Stallion, The (1979), 247, 259n.33
  Exodus, The (1960), 247
  Harem Scarem (1932), 188–89, 194n.99, 246–47
  Harum Scarum (1965), 189
  Mickey in Arabia (1932), 188–89
  Sheik, The (1921), 246–47, 259n.32
  Steel Lady, The (1953), 247, 259n.32
  Muslim racial stereotypes and orientalization in, 188–89, 246–50
  violence in, 188–89 (*see also* violence)
Fiske, Fidelia, 32n.98, 114, 148n.11
Foxe, John, 9–10, 44–46
  Actes and Monuments (1563), 9, 45
  Islam and, 50
  slavery and, 45–46
Free Baptist Woman's Missionary Society, The, 98
  The Missionary Helper and, 98
freedom
  Christian women's alleged, 73, 202–3, 223, 227
  Daylight in the Harem and, 90–91 (*see also* Lucknow Conference)
  Muslim men's, 138
  Muslim women's, 71, 89, 93–94
  Muslim women's property rights, 93 (*see also* Patrick)
  sexual, 57, 58
  as sign of Christian/Protestant superiority, 56, 58–59, 69–70
  veil and, 109n.135, 132
  western women's, 231
  women's, 69–70, 85–86 (*see also* seclusion; veil/veiling)
Freidinger, Elizabeth and William, 216–19, 218f
Friends Missionary Advocate, 98, 111n.173
fundraising, 3–4, 102, 186–87, 255
  in America, 21, 22
  children and, 112–13, 116
  cultural critiques, 16–17
  dress-up and, 222
  theological claims about, 72
  Christian/western superiority and, 72

INDEX 285

exhibitions and displays for, 197, 209–10
missionary task of, 186–87
mission museums for, 204, 206–7
Muslim women as tool for, 101–2
performance activism and, 196
photography for, 175 (*see also* photography)
and women, 21, 22, 71
Fyzee, Atiya, 76–77, 85–86

Gairdner, Temple, 213, 229–30
Cairo Study Center and, 32n.81
gaze
biblical, 160–61, 186–87
great exhibitions and, 201–3
on inferiors, 186–87
material, 233n.7
missionary, 186–87
Orientalist, 57
on "others," 186
photography as cultivating Protestant, 166
Protestant, 153–94
racialized, 174–75
voyeuristic, 202–3
gender
and Butler, Judith, 33n.104
definition of, 21
gender constructs/norms/tropes, 2, 3–4, 21–22, 68–70, 120–23, 145, 240–42
accommodating, 92, 256
American views of, 22–23, 102, 145, 231
in children's fiction, 128–34, 137–38, 143
contesting universalizing claims about, 89–90
critiques of, 102, 137, 143
ethnographic depictions of, 256–57
European, 72, 231
film and, 188–89
images reinforcing, 184, 231
inequality, 184
of Middle Eastern women, 76
missionaries', 68–70, 73, 76, 84–85, 142–43
in missionary literature, 83–86, 241–42
Muslim, 120, 145, 184–85
ordination (women's) and, 231
patriarchy and, 69–70, 71, 72, 130–31, 206, 231
power differentials and, 85–86, 202–3
purposes of, 239
racist, 198
roles (Protestant), 71
roles (Islamic), 71
salvation and, 231–32
Victorian, 14–15, 69–70, 88

in writing, 20–21, 73–80, 83–86, 143
See also dowry; marriage; prayer; seclusion; veil/veiling
gendered discourses (of missionaries), 1–2, 73–82, 135
George of Hungary, 8, 36, 39–40
Georgievic, Bartholomaeus, 8
Gibbon, Edward, 55–56
on Muhammad, 55–56
Giovio, Paolo, 40
Grant, Elihu
archaeology and, 161–63
photographer, 161–63, 162–63*f*
Great Awakenings, 10–11
Great Commission, The, 10–11
great exhibitions, 199–203
agency at, 203
Chicago World's Fair (Columbian Exposition), 1893, 201–2, 204, 234n.33
as colonial theater, 201–2
empire and, 201–2
England's Great Exhibition (Crystal Palace Exhibition), 1851, 201–2
Exposition Universelle, Paris, 1867, 202, 204
exoticism and, 202–3
as "human zoos," 202–3, 234n.33, 234n.38
as "living museums," 201–3
Paris World's Fair, 1867, 1889, 201–2
Philadelphia World's Fair, 1876, 201–2
polytheistic religious artifacts, traditions and, 203, 212–13, 229
South Kensington World's Fair, England, 1886, 201–2
as voyeuristic, 202–3
World's Parliament of Religions, 1893, 82, 201–2, 252–53
See also missionary society expositions

Habeeb: A Boy of Palestine, 125–27, 129, 131*f*, 146. *See also* Entwistle
Hagar, 9–10, 89, 100
in African American tradition, 111n.180
as agent, 101, 111n.180
as archetypal Muslim woman, 67–68, 87, 88, 100
character traits of, 100
condemnation of polygyny and, 89
as Egyptian foremother of Arab Muslims, 100–1
as enslaved African, 100–1
ethnic background of, 100–1, 111nn.180–183
as faithful and trusting victor, 101
Hadith and, 111n.181

Hagar (*cont.*)
  hajj and, 111n.183
  as helpless, passive, powerless, 100–1
  and Ishmael (*see* Hagar and Ishmael story)
  in Islamic tradition, 101
  Mecca and, 101
  missionary magazines and, 98
  missionary use of, 99
  as (Muslim) lost sheep, 89
  as proactive, 101
  Qur'an and, 111n.181
  relevance for all needing to escape misery, 100–1
  representing oppressed women, 91–92, 100–1, 111n.180
  symbolic of need for Christian conversion, 67–111
  "When Hagar returns to Christ, Ishmael shall live," 67–111
  See also The Land and the Book
Hagar and Ishmael story
  as archetype for Christian missionary work, 99–100
  conversion and, 70
  as negative archetype for Muslims, 10
  to reinforce religio-racial hierarchies, 100–1
Haines, J. Harry, 251, 255
Hamlin, Cyrus, 193n.79
Hamm, Margaret, 135–36, 142–43, 254–55, 256–57
  "Lindao's Dowry" and, 135–40, 141–43, 254–55
  in the Philippines, 135–36
al-Haqq, Zahur, 13, 14
harem (or *seraglio*)
  abuse and, 240–41
  attire, beauty of, 227–28, 254–55
  Biblewomen as visitors, 14–15
  "daylight" in the, 90–95
  definition of, 56–57, 66n.115, 205–6
  demystification of, 58–59
  depiction of, 79, 194n.99, 205–6, 240–41
  home and, 21–22, 70–71, 79
  injustice of treatment of western women and, 59
  missionary women visiting, 14–15, 71
  Muhammad and, 78
  oppression and, 46, 57, 226
  Orientalism and, 57
  Othello and, 47
  pornographic photography in, 156, 158, 169–70

  as prison, 56–57, 58–59, 81, 188–89, 226, 231, 240–41
  as sanctuary, 81, 206
  veil and, 57, 240–41 (*see also* veil/veiling)
  victimhood and, 231
  western woman and home and, 57–58, 59, 70–71
  See also film
Harris, Ara Elsie (Dr.), 14–15, 31n.71
hate crimes. *See* anti-Muslim sentiment; violence
Haworth, Blanch, 15
Hayward, John, 60
head covering
  women's, 121, 130, 138, 216–21, 217*f*, 219–25*f*, 224*f*, 225–26, 227–28, 244, 245 (*see also* chador; headdress; hijab; veil/veiling)
  men's, 169*f*, 216*f*, 216–19, 217–18*f* (*see also* fez)
headdress (men's), 166–69, 169*f*, 216–19, 218*f*
headdress (women's), 237n.97
headgear, 138–40, 152n.106, 169*f*, 223 (cork helmet) 218*f*, 244. *See also* fez; headdress; headscarf; hijab; turban; veil
headscarf, 130, 131*f*, 164, 211–12, 243–44, 245. *See also* hijab; veil/veiling
heathen, 115
  curio collections and, 210–11
  definition of, 197–98
  idols, 208
  as polytheists, 197–98
  racial inferiority and, 197–98
  religious inferiority and, 197–98
  role in shaping White American Protestant identity, 197–98, 228–29
heathenism, 228–29
Heathen Woman's Friend, 72, 110n.163. *See also Woman's Missionary Friend*
heaven, 50–51
  gender and, 66n.133
  Islamic notions of (by Christians), 59–60, 66n.133
  sensual vision of, 59–60
  "Women in Heaven," 37, 59–60, 66n.133
Hill, Kate, 166–69, 209–12, 213, 236n.74
  fundraising tour of, 210–11, 210*f*
  material object displays by, 209–13, 210–12*f*
  missionary photo album of, 166–69
  photos of clothing, 213
hijab, 243–45
  hate crimes and, 244–45
Hinchcliffe, William, 55–56

history of religions, 5, 200, 208. *See also* comparative religion
Hocking, William Ernest, 251–52
Holliday, Grettie Y., 86, 91–92
Holy Land, 41–42
  appearance of people in, 41–42
  conditions of, 74, 76
  photo albums of, 186–87. *See also* photography albums
  pristine, 160–70
  See also Thomson
home (Muslim), 8, 205–6
  Christian v., 70–71, 118, 133–34, 143
  at great exhibitions, 227–28
  as prison, 21–22, 56–58, 70–71, 75–76, 81, 85, 96, 103n.15, 118, 120–21, 130–31, 226 (*see also* seclusion; "separate spheres" ideology; sequestration; veil/veiling)
  as sanctuary, 14–15, 70, 81, 99–100 (*see also* harem; zenana)
  visiting, 14–15, 227, 256
  women's role in, 70–71, 88, 143 (*see also* domesticity)
  See also harem; zenana
homosexuality, 39–40
humanitarian services of missionaries, 2, 135, 142–43, 173–74, 239, 241–42
  image sharing and, 173–74, 185, 188, 193n.96
  Laymen's Foreign Missions Inquiry (1932) recommendations for, 135
  shift to, from evangelistic outreach, 142–43, 241–42
  See also medical services/missions
Humphrey, Emily Jane (1833–1894), 13, 77–80, 101, 105n.53
  depicting Muslim women, 80, 82
  disrupting discourse of the veil/seclusion, 101
  Gems of India (1875), 13, 79–80
  on Muslim women leaders in India, 79–80, 101
  on Muslim violence, 77–78, 211–12
  on similarities between Christianity and Islam, 13
  Six Years in India (1866), 13
Huntington Smith, Sarah L., 32n.98
Hutcheon, J. Edith, 124–25, 182–84
  Pearl of the East (1920), 124–25, 182–84

idolatry
  Calvin on, 29n.43
  Islam as, 122
  Islam as polytheistic, 229–30
  prohibitions against, 61
  rejection of Christ as, 9
idols
  in missionary exhibits, 212–13
  in museums, 206–9, 231–32, 235n.65
  See also Pantheon of Strange Gods
ignorance
  books and, 130
  in Muslim lands, 74
  salvation of females from, 3–4, 67–68, 85, 88, 117–18, 122–23, 129–30 (*see also Our Moslem Sisters*)
images
  to advance Protestantism and Catholicism, 193n.89
  capturing, 108n.123, 157–60, 161, 182, 185, 186–87
  collecting, 160, 186–88, 192n.53 (*see also* photographs; postcards; scrapbooks)
  devotional use of, 187–88
  dissemination of, 40, 184–85, 186–88
  fundraising through, 186–87, 188, 209–10, 214–16
  impact of, 40
  interpretive method for, 155–57
  missionary recruitment through, 186–87, 188
  photographs, 25, 157–60
  Protestant superiority through, 187–88
  Protestant faith practices and, 186–87
  purpose of, 164, 170–71, 185, 186–88
  See also photographs/y; postcards
imperialism
  British, 65n.104
  cultural, 11, 72
  European, 10–11, 34, 159–60
  language of, 54
  missionary, 157–58, 241–42
  Protestant, 11–12, 21
  western, 25
inclusivism, theological, 252–53, 260n.62
India
  Muslims in, 87, 91–92, 96, 101, 109n.139, 118, 127–28, 148–49n.25, 150n.53, 175–76, 176f, 177, 184, 209–11, 236n.74 (*see also* Hill; Humphrey; Lucknow Conference; Swain; *Two Young Arabs*; Elwood Wherry; *Zeinab, the Punjabi*)
Indian Muslim reformists, 85–86. *See also* Fyzee
interfaith dialogue/understanding, 3–4, 23, 69, 82, 101, 135, 143–47, 232–33, 240, 251–53
  through children's literature, 143–47

Iranian hostage crisis (1979), 248–49
Ishmael, 10, 67–111, 111n.178
   Arabs as descendants of, 68, 76, 105n.44, 111n.178, 192n.57
   as archetype of Islam, 100, 192n.57
   as lost sheep, 89
   Muhammad and, 77–78
   and Muslim converts, 70
   description of, 10, 75, 76, 77–78
   Protestant role toward, 88, 100, 111n.178, 146
   See also Hagar; Jowett; Thomson; Van Sommer
Islam
   academic study of, 55–58
   Arab identity conflation with, 192n.74
   carnal desires and, 46, 60–61, 77, 132–33 (*see also* Muslim men)
   commentaries on, 38
   conflation with terrorism, 248–49
   as creed, 55, 60, 74
   defense of, by Christian missionaries, 94
   expansion of, 6–7, 34–36, 38–39, 42, 43, 60, 62n.1
   humanizing, 3–4, 182–84
   images of, 240–41 (*see also* paintings; photographs)
   literature on (sixteenth century), 8–10
   militant, 248–49
   as military and spiritual threat, 6–7, 11, 22, 81, 164
   propagation of, 59–61, 77–78
   Protestant critiques of, 60–61, 115–16, 117–18, 181–82, 186, 229–30
   racialization of, 122–23, 184, 232, 249–50
   rules and rituals of, 127, 177–84 (*see also* rituals; rules)
   similarities with Christianity, 10, 13, 87–88, 212–13, 228–29, 232
   truth and, 18–19
   and violence, 77–78, 135, 181, 182–84
Islamic world (term), 26n.1
Islamophobia (American), 1, 24, 239–61
   since 9/11, 242–46
   American racism and, 258n.6, 258n.14
   in contemporary American culture, 1, 3–4, 257
   definitions of, 3–4, 242–44, 258n.1, 258n.8, 258n.9
   forms of (toward men), 245–46
   historical reasons for, 240, 255
   identity and, 260n.38
   origins of, 26
   private dimensions of, 243

   Protestant missionary origins of, 23–24, 69, 243–44 (*see also* gender constructs)
   race and, 259n.18
   race studies and, 258n.14
   reasons for (since 1990), 243–44
   research on, 258n.16
   rhetoric of, 243
   roots of, 23–24
   veil and, 35 (*see also* veil/veiling)
   White superiority and, 242
   See also anti-Muslim sentiment

Jessup, Henry Harris (1832–1910), 2, 14, 77–80, 112–13, 142–43
   Bedouin portrayal and, 83, 118, 191n.47
   British Empire and, 30n.51
   gendered seclusion and, 79
   Islamic violence and, 77–78
   Muslim marriage and divorce, 78–79
   Muslim men and, 118
   Muslim women and, 79–80, 85, 112–13, 118
   zenana and, 79
Jesus, 121, 126, 132
   identity of, 19, 29n.43, 125–27, 188
   Islam's portrayal of, 9, 32n.95
   mission and, 113
   Muhammad and, 116, 149n.40
   Muslims and, 6, 9, 121, 129, 186–87
   salvation of Muslims through, 121
   spiritual conquest of Islam through, 114–15
Jowett, William, 74, 76
   difficulty of conversion of Muslims, 74
   Muslims as Ishmael's heirs, 74, 76
   travel writing of, 74
juvenile mission bands (juniors), 148n.6

Kamil, abd al-Masih, 14–15, 19–20. *See also* Jessup
   conversion of, 14–15, 19–20, 31n.77
Kayble Mission, 15. *See also* North Africa Mission
Keith-Falconer, Ion, 14, 19–20
Ketton, Robert, 7, 28–29n.26
Knolles, Richard, 50
Knox, John, 9

Lausanne Movement, 253–54, 261n.68, 261n.73
Laymen's Foreign Missions Inquiry (1932), 251–53, 260n.57
leadership
   limits of, on Protestant women, 14–15
   of Muslim women in India, 79–80
Leland, John, 59–60

letters (missionary), 58–59, 187–88, 191n.40, 193n.97, 255–56
Lewis, Lucy, 15
literacy
  biblical, 175–76
  Europeans', 40
  of Muslim women and girls, 129, 132
  of Muslim women in India, 79–80
literature
  devotional, 102
  dissemination, 2, 96–97, 102, 255–56
  fundraising through, 102, 148n.6, 227
  humanizing/de-humanizing impulses in, 7, 26, 45, 69, 82, 114, 143–44, 154
  production, 20, 21, 96–97, 197
  and promotion, 96–98
  about Muslim children, 146 (see also Fatmeh; Habeeb; Musa; Topsy-Turvy Land; Two Young Arabs)
  recruitment through, 25–26, 102
  women writing, 33n.117, 58, 150n.53
London Jews Society (LJS), 214–16
London Missionary Society (LMS), 12, 206
  museum, 206–8
Lucknow Conference (1911), 82, 83, 90–91, 92–93, 95, 96–97
  Daylight in the Harem (1911) and, 90–95, 97–98
Luther, Martin, 6–7, 10, 27n.10, 28–29n.26, 36–37, 38–40, 41–42
  characterizations of Islam by, 6–7
  characterizations of Muhammad by, 36–37
  Crusades and, 62n.19
  dress and, 39–40, 41–42
  marriage and polygyny, 36–37, 78–79
  polygyny and, 78–79
  veiling and, 39–40
  violence and, 38

Mahmood, Saba, 69–70
Malcolm, Urania Latham (Dr.), 119, 121–23, 149n.38. See also Children of Persia
Marlowe, Christopher, 46, 47
marriage, 35–38, 50–51, 94, 105n.42
  arranged, 88, 136–37, 141, 142, 143
  child, 85, 88, 118, 121, 132–33, 135–38, 151n.89
  in children's books, 128, 129, 132–34, 135–38
  description of, 141
  dowry and, 94, 108n.123, 135–38, 151n.98 (see also "Lindao's Dowry")
  education and/or, 105n.42, 116–18, 129, 132, 133–40, 141–42

love, 141
  practices (Muslim), 35–36, 50–51, 85, 88, 132–33, 141–42
  property and, 94
  as symbol of darkness, 87, 88
  See also polygyny
Marshall, Eva, 176–77, 191n.40, 199, 209–10, 219–21, 221f, 255–56. See also Eva Totah
Martyn, Henry, 9, 12, 14, 17–18, 19–20, 77–78
  Controversial Tracts on Christianity and Mohammedanism (1824), 77–78
  on Muhammad, 77–78
masculinity, 66n.120
  Protestant Christian, 61, 66n.120
  Muslim, 39, 61 (see also Muslim men)
  virtues of, 66n.120
mass media, 154, 189, 239–61
  distribution networks, 5, 99
material culture, 25, 153–94, 195–238
  consumption and, 204
  control of Muslims and, 196
  documentation of Muslims and, 196
  missionary collections of, 1–2, 208
  at mission society expositions, 204
  missionaries' use of, 195–238
  in performances, 196
  of Protestantism (see Protestantism)
  religious identity and, 230–31
  role in perpetuating stereotypes, 231
material culture (Islamic), 153–94, 212–13
  collectors of, 200–1
  costumes, 195–238
  critiques of Islam through, 195
  definitions of, 189n.3
  diaries, 156
  as entertainment, 195–96
  exhibitions of, 195–238, 236n.73 (see also great exhibitions)
  images as, 153–94
  museums and, 196 (see also museums)
  as oppressive, 185
  objects, 189, 195–238
  paintings, 153–94
  as performative practice, 156, 195–238, 233n.6
  photographs, 153–54, 156, 157–60
  postcards, 153–54, 160
  religious identity and, 153–94
  shoes, 208–9
  sketches, 153–54
  voyeurism through, 195–96
  See also paintings; photographs

material culture (Protestant), 153–94, 197
　dissemination of, 186
　embroidery, 210–11, 214, 219–21, 236n.73
　images in, 197 (*see also* photographs; postcards)
　photographs, 186
　religious identity and, 186
　sketches, 236n.73
material religion, 153–94, 196–97
"material turn," 156–57, 193n.92
Maurice, Frederick Dennison, 60–61
medical services/missions, 15, 84–85, 125–26
　missionary women's medical roles in, 104n.17, 121, 129
　See also Eleanor Calverley; Malcolm; Emmeline Stuart; Van Dyck; Watson; Zenana Bible and Medical Mission (ZBMM)
Mellor, F.B., 214–16, 216*f*
menstruation, 37–38, 130–31
Methodist Episcopal Church, 19
Methodist Episcopal Mission of India, 175–76
Methods of Mission Work Among Moslems (1906), 84–85
Middle East
　Americans and, 145–46, 189, 195–96, 197, 213–14, 228, 240–41, 246–50, 253–54, 259n.29
missions
　beginning of, 15
　forms of, 186–87
　shifting purposes of, 142–43
missionaries' personal collections, 209–13
missionary
　personal contact with Muslims, 4, 10–11, 34–35, 43–44, 67–68, 232–33, 233n.15, 257–58
missionary conferences, 82
　in Cairo (1906), 82, 83–84
　in Edinburgh (1910), 82
　First Missionary Conference on behalf of the Mohammedan World (1906), 83–84
　International Missionary Council, Tambaram, India (1938), 260n.63
　in Jerusalem (1928), 82, 106n.77
　in Lucknow (1911), 82, 83, 90–91, 92–93, 95, 96–98, 109n.137
　in Middle Eastern locations (1924), 82
Missionary Herald, 97–98, 148n.6
missionary magazines, 33n.117, 96–98
　women and girls in, 73–75
　survey of, 96–98, 109n.150

missionary museums, 206–13. *See also* museums
mission(ary) societies, 10–11, 195–238
　Algiers Mission Band, 170, 219–21, 253–54 (*see also* Trotter)
　American Baptists, 12–13
　American Board of Commissioners for Foreign Missions (ABCFM), 12–13, 30n.57, 84–85, 97–98, 135–37, 142–43, 148n.6, 148n.11, 151n.99, 152n.127, 193n.79, 207–8, 209, 212–13, 234n.45
　American Episcopalians, 12–13, 31–32n.79
　American Lutherans, 12–13
　American Lutheran Orient Mission to Kurdistan (1910), 15–16 (*see also* Kurdistan Missionary Society)
　American Methodist Episcopal Mission, 12–13, 31–32n.79, 251
　American Quakers, 12–13
　American Syria Mission, 14 (*see also* Jessup; Thomson)
　Arabian Mission, 15, 95–96, 125–26, 176–77, 214, 223
　Baptist Missionary Society, 12, 18–19, 29n.48
　Board of Foreign Missions of the Presbyterian Church, 12–13, 207–8
　Board of Foreign Missions of the United Presbyterian Church in North America (UPCNA), 12–13
　British Methodists, 12–13, 207–8
　British Quakers, 11–13
　British Syrian Mission (BSM), 14–15, 104n.20, 124–25, 182
　Church Missionary Society (CMS), 12, 112–13, 181
　Church of Scotland, 12
　as communication systems, 159
　Egypt General Mission (EGM), 15–16, 253–54
　Free Church of Scotland, 12, 31n.66
　Kurdistan Missionary Society, 32n.80
　London Missionary Society (LMS), 12, 206
　Methodist Episcopal Mission in North Africa, 251
　Methodist Episcopal Mission of India, 176–77, 232–33, 233n.15, 257–58
　North Africa Mission, 15, 31n.74, 31n.78
　Presbyterian Board of Foreign Missions, 12–13, 207–8, 235n.63
　Reformed Presbyterian Church of America, 12–13
　South Arabia Mission, 14
　United Free Church of Scotland, 96–97

INDEX

Zenana Bible and Medical Mission (ZBMM), 14–15, 31n.72
See also non-denominational missions
missionary society expositions, 166–70, 204–6
  Britain (1908), 204
  descriptions of, 204–6
  Exposition Universelle, Paris, 1867, 204
  The World in Boston, 1911, 204–6, 213, 230, 234n.45
missionary women, 6, 14–15, 21, 69–73, 83, 95–96
  access to Muslim women's spaces, 71, 216–19
  agency and authority of, 256
  as evangelists, 14–15, 19–20
  exclusion of, 19–20
  influence of, 126
  leadership roles of, 231
  performance and, 216–21 (*see also* Blatter; dress-up; Perry)
  perpetuating stereotypes, 21
  as publishers, 15–16
  as nurses/doctors for Muslim women, 14–15, 71, 104n.17
  on seclusion, 71, 92, 95–96, 216–19
  shifting stereotypes about Islam, 99–102
  teachers, 71, 256
  on veiling, 95–96, 221–22*f*, 255
  as writers and lecturers, 20–21, 58, 68, 69–73, 91–92, 99
  See also Algiers Mission Band; Eleanor Calverley; Fiske; Haworth; Huntington Smith; Lewis; Padwick; Trotter; Van Sommer; "woman's work for woman"
missionary work, 166
  gendered norms of, 71
  gendered power differentials in, 84–85
  objects of, 158
  photographs as reporting on, 159, 160, 166
  shifting focus from evangelism, 2, 142–43, 144, 241–42
  as women's work, 103n.6
"Mohammedan World," 1–2, 25–26, 83–84
Mohammedan World of To-Day (1906), 84–85, 181
money
  missionaries soliciting from children, 72–73, 148n.9
  Muslim women and, 58, 66n.123, 93 (*see also* dowry)
Montagu, Lady Mary Wortley, 58, 93
  comparing English/Turkish/Islamic women, 58–59
  harem demystification and, 58

Orientalist writing of, 58–59
veil and, 58
Montgomery, Helen Barrett, 110n.162
Western Women in Eastern Lands (1910), 110n.162
monogamy
  Qur'anic laws and, 94, 109n.148
mosque
  Jama Masjid, 184, 193n.80
  as men's space, 130–31, 178–80
  painting of (*Prière dans la Mosque*), 178
  school, 129
  teacher, 125–26, 129, 146
  Umayyad (Great Mosque), 178–80, 182–84, 193n.80
  women and, 94, 130–31, 184
Mughal Empire, 11–12, 79–80, 184
Muhammad, Prophet, 2, 8, 18, 19, 36–37, 98
  caricatures of, 77–78
  character of, 4–5, 35, 78
  early career of, 78
  as good, unexceptional man, 55–56
  as great lawgiver, 50–51
  as immoral (alleged), 18–19
  Jesus and, 116, 149n.40, 149n.46
  as licentious (alleged), 37
  polygyny and, 37
  as preacher, 18–19
  Protestant views of as false prophet, 111n.185, 115–16, 122, 147n.1, 148n.18
  religious charisma of, 61–62
  as respecter of women, 93
  sexual deviance of (alleged), 78
  sword and, 45–46
  and violence, 56, 78, 115–16, 166–69
  See also Luther
Muir, William, 78
  English translation of *Apology of al-Kindi* (1882), 78
Münster, Sebastian, 42–43
Musa: Son of Egypt (1927), 125–27. *See also* Entwistle
museum(s)
  anthropological, 207–8
  Ashmolean, 200, 206
  British, 200, 206
  classification in, 200
  control and, 200, 207–8
  constructing alterity, 208–9
  curio cabinets
    and, 200 (*see also* curiosities)
  empire and, 207–8
  fundraising through, 206–7

museum(s) (*cont.*)
  gender norms and, 202–3, 205–6, 213, 246–50
  goals of, 207–9
  Hartford Seminary library, 209
  hierarchy and, 202–3
  humanism and, 206–7
  idols in, 206–8
  "living," 201–3 (*see also* human zoos)
  missionaries' roles in, 200–1
  missionary, 206–9
  missions and, 198
  Pitt Rivers, 206
  Princeton Theological Seminary, 207–9
  private collections to public, 200
  purposes of, 197, 208
  racial hierarchies in, 209
  religio-racial taxonomies of, 232
  role of, 197
  study purpose of, 208–9
  systemization of, 200, 207–8
  theological framing of, 207–8
"museumify," 200
Muslim (term), 35, 42–43
Muslim men (and boys), 128
  as abusive, controlling, 81, 118, 146
  aggression of, 54–55
  behavior of, 128, 205–6, 247
  as central to Islam, 60–61
  character of, 46, 56
  depictions of, 8, 46, 54–55, 57–58, 61–62, 81, 84–85, 134*f*, 140, 146–47, 154–56, 166–69, 169*f*, 173, 173*f*, 205–6
  dress of, 8, 40–43, 166–69 (*see also* dress)
  divorce initiation by, 105n.58
  education of, 140, 148n.21
  evangelizing, 19–20
  excesses of, 61–62
  images of reform-minded, 101
  immorality, 17
  laziness of, 205–6
  lust of, 47–48, 77
  military might of, 8, 47–48
  hypermasculinity of, 35
  hypersexualized, 22, 39–40
  licentiousness of, 57–58
  marriage and, 226
  Muhammad and, 61–62
  parenting of, 91–92, 118, 125–28, 129, 133–41, 146–47
  positive qualities of, 56
  religion and, 130–31
  sexual behaviors of, 35–36, 54–55, 57, 78 (*see also* polygyny; polygamy)
  social norms of, 8
  as specimens, 173, 173–74*f*, 202
  as terrorists, 243, 247, 249 (*see also* 9/11)
  treatment of women, 133–34
  violence of, 39, 42–43, 57–58, 69, 75, 77–78, 88, 91–92, 115, 133–34, 134*f*, 140, 146, 166–69, 242, 243 (*see also* violence)
  as wild animals, 173, 174*f*
Muslims
  as dangerous, 245–46
  education of, 63n.38, 91–92, 105n.42, 142–43, 148n.21
  as inferior to White Christians, 60–61
  See also Muslim men; Muslim women
Muslim tyranny, 2, 59–60
  American Revolution and, 56, 59–60
Muslim women (and girls), 57–58
  absence of in public worship, 130–31
  access to, 227–28, 235n.50 (*see also* seclusion)
  agency and, 85, 91–92, 97–98
  baptism of, 92, 109n.141
  condition of, 68, 77, 78–81, 85, 86–88, 89, 91, 93, 96, 110n.164
  character, reflecting nation's character, 88
  degradation of, 3–4, 67–68, 69, 86, 88, 96–97, 174–75, 202–3 (*see also* veil/veiling)
  depictions of, 57, 72, 77–78, 79, 81, 88, 117–19, 126, 132–34, 146–47, 152n.127, 154, 167*f*, 170–77, 172*f*, 172*f*, 202–3 (*see also* film; postcards; photographs)
  devotional meetings for, 111n.176
  domestic virtues of, 57–58
  dress of, 34, 40, 58–59, 75–76, 81, 92, 120–21, 130, 138–40, 141–42, 144–45, 170, 171, 171*f*, 172*f*, 182, 183*f*, 185, 231–32, 237n.96, 245, 257–58 (*see also* dress)
  education of, 85–86, 92, 105n.42, 117–18, 121, 129, 135–37, 148n.21
  financial independence of, 58, 93 (*see also* Montagu)
  helpless, 2, 81, 99–100, 231
  Hagar as representing, 87, 88, 99, 100–1
  images of, 54–55, 56–58, 100, 101, 130
  lived experience of, 99
  marriage and, 101, 135–37
  missionary neglect of, 87
  missionary responsibility toward, 87
  modesty of, 36, 39–40, 57–58
  negative agency of, 140
  obedience of, to males, 39–40, 57–58

oppression of, 46, 54–55, 59, 60–61, 69, 90, 92–93, 99–100, 101, 117–18, 121, 135, 145, 182, 198, 223, 231, 242, 244
   as passive, 54–55, 100–1, 198, 205–6, 227, 230
   polygyny debates and, 105n.42, 148n.21 (*see also* polygyny)
   professional lives of, 94
   property rights of, 92–93, 94, 101–2, 105n.42
   as reformists, 107n.98
   rights of, 94, 105n.42
   as sex objects, 231
   on stage, 47–48
   as suspects, 245
   treatment of, by Muslim men, 35–36
   as terrorists, 245
   as trophies, 47–48
   veil/veiling of (*see* headscarf; hijab; veil/veiling)
   as victims, 46, 57, 58–59, 80, 99–101, 227, 230, 231, 245
   wedding dress, 141
   See also gender constructs; veil/veiling
Muslim world. *See* Islamic world

Neglected Arabia: Missionary Letters and News, 82–83, 106n.79
Nile Mission Press (1905), 15–16, 31n.78, 32n.81, 83–84, 107n.85, 107n.86
   Van Sommer and, 15–16, 83
Nile Mission Press Auxiliary (American Christian Literature Society for Moslems, 1911), 83–84
non-denominational Missions, 83, 252–54
   Algiers Mission Band (AMB), 15, 82–83, 170, 219–21, 253–54 (*see also* Trotter)
North Africa Mission (or Kayble Mission) (1861), 15, 31n.74, 31n.78

Ockley, Simon, 55–56
   History of the Saracens (1718) and, 55–56, 65n.108
One Hundred Syrian Pictures (1903), 182
oppression. *See* Muslim women
Orient, the, 53, 57, 73–74
   invention of, 27n.4
   Occident and, 2, 22, 65n.94
   Said on, 27n.4, 65n.94 (*see also* Orientalism; Said)
   women of, 95–96
Oriental
   customs, 76
   type, 159

Orientalism (Said, 1978), 21–22, 23, 27n.4, 53, 65n.94
Orientalism, 2, 11, 72
   "American Biblical," 160–63
   biblical, 74–75, 100, 214–16
   in Britain, 55
   control and, 200
   critique of, 155
   definition of, 2, 4, 21–22, 53
   as Enlightenment activity, 53
   films and, 246–47
   gender and, 21–22
   indifference to Muslims, 55–56
   influence on theology and religion, 22–23
   pictorial, 169–70
   results of, 4
   romantic, 16–17, 230
   Said on, 11, 53, 57, 65n.94
   in scholarship, 11, 53–54, 55–56, 58
   subordination and, 200–1
   world religions and, 4
   writing and, 55–56, 58–61
Orientalists, 55–56
Othello (play), 46–47
Othello (character), 46, 47, 49. *See also* Tamerlane
"others," 73–74, 197, 202–3, 257
   cultural superiority and, 73–74, 197–98, 202–3, 207–8, 213
   differentiation through material objects, 195, 197
   humanization of, 173–74, 186, 255, 257
   Protestant gaze on, 186
   Protestantism v., 229
   racial and religious, 166, 186, 187–88, 196–98, 227
   reinforcement of difference in, 61, 187–88
   See also alterity; heathen; heathenism
Our Moslem Sisters, 86–90, 95, 96–97, 98, 174–75. *See also* Van Sommer; Samuel Zwemer

Padwick, Constance, 15–16, 212–13, 252
paintings, French, 177–78
Palestine Park, 161, 235n.49
Pantheon of Strange Gods exhibit, 208–9
patriarchy
   Muslim, 206 (*see also* gender constructs; Muslim men)
   Protestant, 70, 72, 130–31, 231–32
Patrick, Mary Mills, 91–93, 101–2, 105n.42, 257. *See also* Constantinople Women's College

Pearl of the East (1920), 124–25, 128–29. See also Hutcheon
performance
  definition of, 190n.9
performance/performers, 25–26, 196
  missionaries as, 1–2
  messages of, 196
performance activism, 196
performance analysis, 190n.9
performative practice, 195–238
  as display of religious and cultural objects, 196
  through missionary Muslim costumes, 196, 213–23
  Perry, Gladys, 219–21
  scrapbook dress-up, 219–21, 220f, 237n.97
photograph(er)
  professional, 158, 160–61, 166, 182, 189n.2, 223–25 (see also Bonfils)
photograph album, 25, 166–69, 177, 186–87, 189n.2, 219–22, 223–25
photography/s
  anonymous, 166, 173–74
  Arab, 190n.28
  arranged scenes in, 161–63 (see also photographs (staged))
  boys and men in, 161–63, 168–69f
  captions of, 157, 166–69, 174–75, 178–80, 182, 184, 214–16, 219–22, 226
  child sponsorships through, 173–74
  colonial, 159, 169–70, 177–78, 185, 190n.17, 191n.29, 191n.36
  of costumes, 155–56, 187–88, 195–238, 235n.63
  curating, 1–2, 188, 213
  of dress, 166–69, 185, 195
  eliciting mission support through, 175, 177
  erotic and exotic, 158–59, 169–70, 247
  ethnological, 159, 177–78
  fundraising through, 157–58, 175–76, 214–16
  gender shaping through, 154, 185, 187–88, 195
  generic labeling of, 166, 176–77
  humanitarian, 193n.96
  intentions of, 156, 157–58
  landscape, 161–63, 166
  mass-produced, 159–60, 166, 186
  by missionaries, 153–94, 233n.6
  in missionary reports, 175, 188
  of missions, 175, 182
  people as symbols in, 164
  as portraiture, 160, 166–77
  of prayer/praying, 154, 177–78, 185
  Protestant identity in, 175–76, 231–33

  racialized, 154, 174–75, 184–85
  of religious practices (see rituals; rules)
  resistance to, 176–77, 213
  scale in, 157–58, 161–63
  scientific classification and, 160
  "scenes and types," 160, 177–78
  "specimens" in, 173–75, 173–74f, 176–77
  staged, 158, 160–64, 166–77, 185, 193n.80, 214–23 (see also tableau vivant)
  stereoscope, 160, 161
  stock photos, 158, 166, 170, 173–75, 182
  studio, 153–54, 159, 160, 166–70, 185, 190n.28, 191n.29, 223–25
  subjects of, 158
  tableau vivant, 160, 191n.41
  types in, 154–55, 158–59, 160, 170, 173–75
  See also images, portraits, "vacant" landscapes
Pfander, Karl Gottlieb, 12, 14, 17, 18–19
  approach to evangelizing Muslims, 19–20
  Balance of Truth, The (1866), 18, 77–78
  Muhammad and, 18
  Qur'an and, 18
pietism, 10–11, 29n.46
piety
  American evangelical, 160–61
  Muslim, 17–18
  Muslim women's, in India, 80
  women's, 70
piracy, 43–44
  barbary, 59
  British, 43–44, 52, 59, 65n.102
  Islam and, 56–57
Pococke, Edward, 50–51, 55
polygamy, 37–38, 60, 78–79
  Adams on, 60
  Bibliander on, 37
  destructive nature of, 46, 96–97
  European fascination with, 37–38
  Jessup on, 46
  Our Moslem Sisters and, 96–97
  Patrick on, 93
  purpose of, 60
  Qur'anic laws about, 109n.148
polygyny, 36–38, 39–40, 46, 60–61, 62n.10, 62n.12, 78–79, 85, 88, 118, 132–33, 205–6, 231
  Bibliander on, 37
  biblical, 50–51
  Calvin on, 37
  condemnation of, 89
  decline of, 89
  German pamphleteers and, 39–40
  European fascination with, 37–38, 44

in fiction, 81
legal prohibition of, 62n.12
Luther on, 36–37
Muhammad and, 37
Qur'ānic laws about, 50–51, 62n.12, 109n.148
rates of, 78–79
religious laws on, 37
term, 62n.10
women debating, 105n.42
See also Two Young Arabs
portraits, 166–77, 214–23, 215–22f
as didactic, 187–88
fundraising through, 214–16
Protestant gaze and, 166
staged, 166–77, 214–23, 215–22f
postcard(s), 25, 153–94
biblical gaze through, 160–61
biblical themes on, 160–64, 191n.43
booklets of, 178
captions, 154, 163–64, 166, 171–73, 174–75
children on, 171, 172–74f
clothing on, 213, 215–16f (*see also* dress)
collecting/collections, 154–55, 157, 160, 170, 178
colonial, 169–70
conversion and, 164, 170
curating, 188–89
didactic purpose of, 178, 187–88
as disseminating knowledge, 160, 192n.53
empire and, 159, 160
French, 178–80
as hobby, 160
humans as types in, 161–64, 169–71
industry, 159
mission-produced, 191n.37
mission support through, 158
prayer, 177–78, 179f, 182 (*see also* prayer)
production of, 159–60
proliferation of, 189n.2, 190n.25, 191n.29
racializing and exoticizing images on, 174–76
reinventing persons and scenes, 164, 166, 192n.74
and religious judgment, 170
repetition, relabeling, and conflating of images on, 166–70, 178–82, 193n.83
staged, 163–64
as transnational, 159–60
types of, 161–63
See also dress; images
prayer
admiration and judgment of Muslims at prayer, 178, 181–82
beads, 208–9, 212f

books/manuals of (Muslim), 212–13, 252
children's (Christian), 113, 116, 122–23, 125, 126–27, 149n.32, 154
clothing and washing before, 121, 130–31, 149n.46, 214–16
CMS Prayer Cycle, 102
daily, 177–80, 179f
desert, 177–78
great, 177–78, 184
Hagar's, 101
images of, 178–80, 179–83f, 182–84 (*see also* postcards; photographs)
location of, 177–78, 182, 184
materiality of, 185
men at, 178, 179–83f, 182–84
menstruation and, 130–31
about Muslims, 9–10
Muslim religious practices, 36
Muslim women's, 130–31, 150n.79, 184
paintings of, 178
postcards of, 177–78, 182, 193n.83 (*see also* postcards)
posture in, 13, 159–60, 177–82, 192n.77, 193n.86
Prayer Union of Egypt, 107n.85
as support, 1–2, 197
and theater, 203
women and, 130–31
preaching
Biblewomen, 14–15
conversion and, 80–81
English Protestant, 43–44
gospel, 60
Laymen's Report and, 252–53
photos of, 175
Reformers (Protestant), 34–35
reinvention through, 40
rhetoric of, 51
textualism and, 196–97
toleration in, 50–51 (*see also* Bunyan)
vernacular, 17–18 (*see also* Martyn)
by women, 94, 103n.6
See also pulpit; sermons
Prideaux, Humphrey, 51, 65n.82
The True Nature of Imposture Fully Displayed in the Life of Mahomet (1697), 51
programming
devotional, 21
educational, 21
gendered, 124
proselytization
Muslims as objects of, 182–84
publishing restrictions and, 19

Protestant
　Holy Land mania, 161
　superiority, 7, 11, 17–18, 69, 160–61, 187–88, 197–98, 200, 202–3, 207–8, 209, 229, 232, 242, 252
　supremacy, 16–17
　textualism, 1–2, 26, 61, 67, 68, 99, 155–56, 196–97
　transformation, 154, 231–33, 246, 250–51, 257
Protestantism
　as counter-image of Islam, 113, 117–18, 119–23, 133–34, 222, 230–33, 233n.4
　doctrinal beliefs of, 156–57, 197, 233n.3, 258n.7
　embodying, 229–30
　logocentric orthodoxy of, 233n.7
　materialism of (*see* material objects)
providence
　geopolitical shifts and, 11–12
publishing, 20–21, 67–111, 107nn.85–86, 124, 186–87, 240–41
　fundraising through, 25–26 (*see also* fundraising)
　gendered nature of, 124
　men and, 24–25, 84–85, 155–56
　missionary vocation and, 186–87
　network, 240–41
　restrictions on proselytizing, 19
　women and, 68, 84–85, 124
　women's organizations and, 112–13
　See also fiction
pulpit, 46–49. *See also* sermons
purdah, 92, 104n.18. *See also* seclusion
purity laws, 37–38

Quarterly Token, 112–13, 114–15, 117–18, 144, 147n.4
Qur'an, 2, 7
　character of, 50, 55–56
　congruencies between Bible and, 10, 18
　divine inspiration and, 17–18 (*see also* Martyn)
　English translation of, 55–56 (*see also* Sale)
　Islamic law and, 7
　Jesus and, 9
　Luther and, 10, 28n.20, 36–37
　male readers of, 148n.21
　missionary work and, 10
　as Muhammad's creation, 18
　property rights, women's rights and, 94
　Reformers (Protestant) and, 10, 37–38
　sex and, 37–38
　Tamburlaine and, 64n.54
　translation of, 7

racial characteristics, 39, 73–74
racial hierarchy, 122, 157
　basis of, 72, 100
　biblical basis of, 100
　colonial photography reinforcing, 159
　in American legal system, 233n.13
　images and, 157
　museums supporting, 197
　religious hierarchies and, 232
　scientific basis of, 72
　and supremacy, 123, 157
racism, 55–56, 72, 122–23, 250
　anti-Muslim, 242–44, 249–50, 258n.6
　biological, 122, 173–74
　cultural superiority and, 197–98
　Islamophobia and, 242–44
　Orientalism and, 39, 60
　rhetoric of, 73
　scientific, 198, 202–3, 233n.14
　of White Christians, 39, 100–2, 197–98, 250
　re-inventions of Islam, reasons for, 1–33, 197, 229
religion (Protestant)
　iconoclastic leanings of, 186
　materiality of, 186–87, 189 (*see also* world's fairs)
　superiority of, 7, 11, 16–17, 55–56, 69, 72, 77, 116, 126–27, 154, 186, 197, 198, 200, 202–3, 207–9, 229, 232, 242, 252
religious history, 5–6, 127–28
repetition
　of information about Islam, 2–3, 7, 85–86, 250
representation, 42–43, 72
　cultural, 59
　cultural superiority and, 77
　ethnocentric, 72
　favorable, of Muslims/Islam by Christians, 16–17, 77, 83 (*see also* Orientalism, romantic; missionary, personal contact)
　material, of Muslims, 153–54, 155–56, 158
research (missionary), 3, 74, 83, 104n.30, 145, 196–97
Revell, Fleming H. (publisher), 86–87, 90–91, 103n.10
　Daylight in the Harem, 90–95
revolutions
　American, 59–60
　constitutional (Middle East), 83, 90–91
　evangelism and, 83 (*see also* Trotter; Van Sommer; Elwood Wherry)

INDEX 297

women's increasing freedom and, 90–92
rhetoric
  anti-Muslim, 239–40
  of cultural and religious superiority, 77
  dehumanizing, 188
  gendered, 36
  media, 240–41
  of Muslims/Islam (by Christians), 2, 21, 24, 34, 51, 60–61, 72, 155, 164, 182, 184–89, 239
    about Muslim violence, 77–78, 242
    of Muslim women, 56–57, 61–62, 72, 83, 164, 206 (*see also* Humphrey)
    racist, 72, 73 (*see also* cartoons; films)
    of veiling, 24, 34, 61, 75–76, 167f, 170 (*see also* veil/veiling)
Riccoldo of Monte Croce, 7, 36–37
Riggs, James Stevenson, 166–69
rituals (Islamic), 177–84
Ross, Alexander, 50
Rouse, George, 17, 18–19, 32n.94, 78
  conversion through debate and, 19–20
  Muhammad and, 18–19, 78
  Tracts for Muhammedans (1897), 18–19
rules (Islamic), 149n.46, 177–84
Ruskin, John, 173–74

Said, Edward, 11, 16–17, 21–22, 23, 27n.4, 53, 54–56, 57, 159
Sale, George, 50, 55–56
salvation
  civilization and, 164
  as freedom, 81
  Hagar and, 67–68
  from Islam, 174–75
  Muslim understanding of, 74
  Orientalism and, 72
  photographs and, 164
  through conversion to Christianity, 72, 81
Samaritan woman at well, 164
savior
  Orientalism and savior mentality, 72
  White women as, 72, 99
schools
  evangelism through, 118, 125, 126–27, 128–30
  girls', 14–15, 71, 89–90, 91–93, 99–100, 118, 255–56
  girls and, 117–18, 128
  and marriage, 133, 134, 135–36, 137–38, 140 (*see also* Cap and Candle; "Lindao's Dowry")
  material objects in, 195

mission, 12–13, 14, 121, 122–23, 124–25, 126, 128–29, 135–36, 158, 161–63 (*see also* Whatley; Taylor)
Mount Zion School in Jerusalem, 125–26
Muslim, 148n.24
  in Persia, 122–23
  photographs of, 158, 175–76, 176f, 178–80, 181f (*see also* "Hope of India")
  Sabbath (*see* Sunday)
Saint Paul's School in Damascus, 14–15, 130, 150n.57
seclusion in, 101–2, 124–25
single female missionaries and, 103n.6
Sunday, 1–2, 111n.173, 112–13, 114–15, 118–19, 124
veiling and dress norms at, 130
Schor, Samuel, 214–16, 215f
science of religion, 5, 200, 201–2
Scopes, John Thomas, 250–51
  trial of (1925), 250–51
scrapbooks, 25, 177, 219–21
Second Vatican Council (1962–1965), 253
seclusion, 137, 235n.50
  contesting assumptions of, 92–93
  Hindu practices of, 104n.18
  missionary accommodations of, 101–2
  of women, 56–57, 85, 89, 99–100, 138–41, 226, 231
  The World in Boston and, 205–6
  of women in India, 79–80, 96
  of women in Indonesia, 85–86
  of women in Persia, 109n.135
  empowerment of women through, 76
  gender, 76, 81, 92, 103n.7, 130–31, 132
  of missionaries, 14–15
  protection of women through, 76
  See also harem; segregation; sequestration; veil; segregation
"separate spheres" ideology, 14–15, 71, 145–46
sequestration (of women), 70–71
sermons, 43–44, 48–49, 51, 59–60
  Luther's, 6–7
  women's, 94
  See also Barrow; preaching; Tennent
Servetus, Michael, 29n.43
sexual practice(s), 35
Shakespeare, William, 46, 47
Siege of Vienna (1683), 6–7, 51, 53, 65n.92
slavery. *See* enslavement
Smith, Wilfred Cantwell, 23, 254, 261n.72
Social Gospel Movement, 260n.54
sodomy, 37–38
Spivak, Gayatri, 72, 104n.26

stereoscope, 160, 161. *See also* photographs
Stobart, James
   Islam and Its Founder (1877), 78–79
   polygyny and, 78–79
Stuart, Helen Moody, 124–25
   character depictions by, 146
   Fatmeh (circa 1920), 124–25
Stuart, Emmeline M. (Dr.), 109n.135
Stubbe, Henry, 50–51
Student Volunteer Movement (SVM), 82, 98, 106n.77
Sunni Islam, 37, 101, 249–50
superiority
   White Christian, 118, 161, 197, 207–8
   White Supremacy, 243, 254–55, 258n.14
Swain, Clara (Dr.), 14–15
sword, 55–61, 77–78
   of Islam, 111n.185, 133–34
   Muslims and, 38
   propagation of Islam through, 115–16
   of spirit, 116, 133–34
   See also violence

Tamerlane (or Timur), 32n.80, 46, 52
Tamburlaine, 46, 47–48
   religious identity of, 64n.54
Taylor, Jessie, 13–14
Tennent, Gilbert, 59–60
text v. material religion, 196–97, 233n.3
The Arabian Mission: Quarterly Letters from the Field, 106n.79. *See also* Neglected Arabia
theater
   English, 46–49
   stereotypes in, 46–49
   See also stage
The General Historie of the Turkes (1603), 50
The Nearer and Farther East (1908), 98
   See also Brown; Samuel Zwemer
The Land and the Book (1858/1860), 74–76
   biblical Orientalism of, 100
   popularity of, 76, 161
   prayer depictions in, 178
   See also Thomson
The Turkes Storye (1603), 9, 44–45, 46
The Wesleyan Juvenile Offering, 112–13, 148n.5
Thomson, William McClure, 74–76
   The Land and the Book, 74–76, 100, 161, 178
Toledo Collection, 7
topsy-turvy, 119–20, 146, 149n.39
Topsy-Turvy Land: Arabia Pictured for Children (1902), 119–20, 178
   Arab hospitality in, 152n.118
   conversion to Christianity in, 146

   depicting Islam and of Muslim life in, 123
   educating through, 144, 145
   humanizing Muslims in, 144, 146–47
   prayer and agency of females in, 114, 150n.79
   See also Amy Zwemer; Samuel Zwemer
Totah, Eva (Marshall), 187–88, 191n.40, 219–21, 221*f*, 223–25, 237n.99
   costumed photos of, 219–21, 221–22*f*
   photography and, 185
   photograph dissemination and, 187–88
   publicizing missionary work, 188
   needlework and, 209–10, 236n.73
   schools for girls and, 255–56
Totah, Khalil, 161–63, 219–21
Totah, Nabil, 219–21, 237n.100
Totah, Sibyl, 219–21, 237n.100
trade, 8–9, 52
   agreements and alliances, 8–9, 10–11, 43–44, 49–50, 52, 63n.43
   British missionary-Muslim contact through trade, 52
   coffee, 44, 52, 61
   collaborations, 49–50
   goods, 43–44
   increased cultural understanding through, 10–11, 44, 49–50, 52, 61
   of sugar, 65n.90
travel writing, 73–77, 256–57
   Muslim women's, 76–77
Trotter, Isabella Lilias, 14–15, 19–20, 82–83, 90, 108n.133, 109n.137, 170–75, 185, 192n.53, 192n.61, 192n.64
   Algiers Mission Band (founder), 170
   "Christless future" and, 170, 186–87
   in Evangelical circles, 107n.85
   paintings of, 173–74, 192n.61
   postcards and, 170–75
   racism of, 173–74
   staged photographs, 170, 177–78
turban, 216–19, 218*f*
"turn Turke," 45–46, 48–49, 51
Two Young Arabs: The Travels of Noorah and Jameel (1926), 123, 127–28, 149–50n.51, 166–69
   polygyny in, 132–33
   violence v. peace in, 133–34
   See also Amy Zwemer
types, 166
   human, 173–74
   Muslim, 173–74
   physical, 120–21
   racial, 166

of women, 169–70
See also ethnology

United States
  Christian-Muslim relations in, 239–41 (*see also* cartoons; Iranian hostage crisis; Islamophobia)
  immigration to, 249–50
  material culture access in, 153, 188
  missionary exhibitions in, 204 (*see also* museums)
  missionary images and performances in, 155, 195–96
  missionary literature promotion in, 96–97, 99, 125–26, 175–76, 192n.53
  as New World promised land, 161
  Nile Mission Press Auxiliary in, 83–84
  social change and, 239
  women's domesticity, 70, 231–32
  women's missionary movement in, 95
  See also 9/11; film; World in Boston; world's fairs
Upson, Arthur, 83–84, 106n.78

"vacant" landscapes, 160–64, 166
  paintings of, 160–61
  photographs of, and spirituality, 166
Van Dyck, Cornelius Van Alen (Dr.), 214, 251
  attire of, 214–16, 215f, 222–25
  linguistic ability of, 222–23
  long-term contact with Muslims, 251
  personal transformation of, 222–23
Van Sommer, Annie, 15–16, 67–68, 83
  Daylight in the Harem (1911) co-editor, 90–95, 110n.169
  Egypt General Mission (EGM) and, 83
  Egypt Mission Band and, 15–16, 83
  Fellowship of Faith for Muslim and, 107n.85
  Hagar and Ishmael and, 67–68, 70, 87, 99, 100
  Nile Mission Press and, 15–16, 83
  Our Moslem Sisters (1907) co-editor, 86–88, 89
  Prayer Union for Egypt and, 107n.85
Vásquez, Manuel, 156–57
  materiality of religion and, 156–57, 195–96, 233n.3, 233n.7
  threat of textualism and, 233n.3, 233n.7
veil/veiling, 2, 26, 54–57, 58, 72, 85, 103n.7, 120–21, 152n.120, 182, 231–32
  cartoons and, 248
  children's fiction and, 128, 131–32, 144–45, 241–42
  contesting assumptions of, 92–93
  discourse of, 255–56
  dwindling power of, 91
  as encumbering, 213–14, 227–28
  freedom and, 254–55
  as harem symbol, 57, 81
  in India, 79–80, 96
  in Indonesia, 85–86
  as legitimating missionary work, 99–100, 143
  in Persia, 109n.135
  in photographs, 167f, 170, 219–21, 219–20f
  seclusion and, 71, 72, 99–100, 101, 128, 130–32, 144–45, 182, 255 (*see also* seclusion)
  salvation and, 231–32
  in schools, 130
  spiritual darkness and, 258n.12
  submission and, 231–32
  sword and, 55–61
  as symbol of women's oppression, 61, 88, 111n.185, 143, 182–84, 198, 231
  as symbol promoting women's freedom, 231
  in Syria, 109n.141
  in Persia, 91
  in Turkey, 91
  in *Two Young Arabs*, 131–32
  types of, 41–42, 91, 132, 151n.87
  worship and, 109n.135
Vienna. *See* Siege of Vienna.
violence, 35–43
  American, 244–46
  anti-Christian, 45–46, 211–12
  anti-Muslim, 245
  apocalypticism and, 39, 254
  children's books and, 115, 116
  Christian, 72–73
  conversion through, 77–78
  films and, 188–89 (*see also* film)
  images of, 42
  Islam and, 38, 42–43, 181
  marital norms and, 60 (*see also* gender constructs)
  masculinity and, 44, 61–62, 69, 77, 115, 135, 182–84, 188–89 (*see also* Muslim men)
  military, 35–36, 42–44, 46, 77–78
  sex and, 39, 46
  tropes of violence, 36, 213, 230, 248–49
visual culture, 86–87
  inspiring spiritual calling, 159–60
  inspiring humanitarianism, 186
  See also paintings; photographs; postcards
Von Breydenbach, Bernard, 41–42

Walton, John, 59–60
Warne, Frank W. (Bishop), 19

Watson, Anna, 84–85
Western Women in Eastern Lands (1910), 110n.162
Whatley, Mary Louisa, 14
Wherry, Clara
    Daylight in the Harem chapter, 92
    training Indian women converts from Islam and, 92
    veils and, 109n.141
Wherry, Elwood, 80–81, 82–83
    as fiction writer, 124
    as missionary conference organizer, 83
    on Muslim women, 85
    Mohammedan World of To-Day (1906) co-editor, 84–85
Whipple, William Levi, 115–16
White, Joseph, 56, 65n.111
widowhood
    high-caste in India, 106n.74
    of Muslims, 80–81
Wollstonecraft, Mary, 59
    class and gender oppression, 66n.127
    captivity of western women and, 59
Woman's Foreign Missionary Society (Methodist Episcopal Church), 72, 82, 96–97, 105n.51
    and *Woman's Missionary Friend*, 96–97
Women, European ideal, 47–48, 57–58, 231
    contrast with Muslim, 39–40, 58–59, 61–62, 75–76, 159, 231, 243–44. *See also* Gender constructs
Woman's Missionary Friend, 96–97, 110n.163
"woman's work for woman" (catchphrase), 14–15, 19–21, 71, 88, 91–92, 95, 96, 107n.92, 256
Woman's Work for Woman, 91–92, 95–97
Women's Missionary Magazine, 96–97
World Congress of Faiths, London, 1936, 253
World Council of Churches (WCC), 253–54, 261n.66, 261n.68, 261n.73
world's fairs, 73–74
    Chicago, 82, 161, 202, 234n.33

colonial materiality of, 196
costumes at, 203
Muslims featured at, 203
World in Boston, The. *See* missionary society expositions
World's Parliament of Religions, 1893, 82, 201–2, 204, 253
World War II (WWII), 1, 3–4, 25–26, 135, 142–43, 184, 188–89
    transformations after, 3–4, 26, 245–51, 253

Zeinab, the Punjabi: A Story Founded on Facts (1895), 80–81, 104n.25. *See also* Elwood Wherry
zenanas, 14–15, 96, 104n.18
    definition of, 78–79
    See also purdah
Zenana Bible and Medical Mission (ZBMM) (1880), 14–15, 31n.72
Zenana Missionary Society, 31n.72
Zwemer, Amy, 119–20, 127–28, 142, 144
    Muslim women and, 123
    See also Topsy-Turvy Land; Two Young Arabs
Zwemer, Peter, 1–2
Zwemer, Samuel M., 14, 15, 19–20, 31n.78, 82–83, 123, 142–43, 174–75, 178, 212–13
    Cairo Study Center and, 32n.81
    critique of men and Islam, 85
    Daylight in the Harem (1911) co-editor, 90–95
    dress-up and, 216–19, 218f
    as missionary conference organizer, 83
    missionary museums and, 208
    Mohammedan World of To-Day (1906) co-editor, 84–85
    On Muslim women, 85
    Our Moslem Sisters (1907) co-editor, 86
    The Moslem World, founder, editor, 107n.84
    The Nearer and Farther East (1908), 98
    Topsy-Turvy Land (1902), 119–23
    See also Neglected Arabia
Zwingli, Huldrych, 6–7, 10, 38–39